Marketing & Selling the Travel Product

SECOND EDITION

Marketing & Selling the Travel Product

SECOND EDITION

James F. Burke, Ph.D.

Dean, The Collins School of Hospitality Management
California State Polytechnic University, Pomona

Barry P. Resnick, Ed.D.

Professor of Travel and Tourism
West Los Angeles College

Africa • Australia • Canada • Denmark • Japan • Mexico • New Zealand • Philippines
Puerto Rico • Singapore • Spain • United Kingdom • United States

NOTICE TO THE READER

Publisher does not warrant or guarantee any of the products described herein or perform any independent analysis in connection with any of the product information contained herein. Publisher does not assume, and expressly disclaims, any obligation to obtain and include information other than that provided to it by the manufacturer.

The reader is expressly warned to consider and adopt all safety precautions that might be indicated by the activities herein and to avoid all potential hazards. By following the instructions contained herein, the reader willingly assumes all risks in connections with such instructions.

The publisher makes no representation or warranties of any kind, including but not limited to, the warranties of fitness for particular purpose or merchantability, nor are any such representations implied with respect to the material set forth herein, and the publisher takes no responsibility with respect to such material. The publisher shall not be liable for any special, consequential, or exemplary damages resulting, in whole or in part, from the readers' use of, or reliance upon, the material.

Delmar Staff:
Business Unit Director: Susan L. Simpfenderfer
Executive Editor: Marlene McHugh Pratt
Editorial Assistant: Judy Roberts
Executive Marketing Manager: Donna Lewis
Executive Production Manager: Wendy A. Troeger
Production Editor: Elaine Scull
Cover Illustration: Edwin Lacy
Cover Design: Elaine Scull

Printed in Canada
1 2 3 4 5 6 7 8 9 10 XXX 04 03 02 01 00 99

For more information, contact Delmar, 3 Columbia Circle, P.O. Box 15015, Albany, NY 12212-0515; or find us on the World Wide Web at http://www.delmar.com

Library of Congress Cataloging-in-Publication Data

Burke, James F.
Marketing & selling the travel product / James F. Burke, Barry P. Resnick.—2nd ed.
p. cm.
Includes bibliographical references.
ISBN 0-8273-7648-0
1. Tourism—Marketing. 2. Travel agents—Vocational guidance. I. Resnick, Barry Paul.
II. Title. III. Title: Marketing and selling the travel product.
G155.A1B88 1999
338.4'791—dc21 99-43258
CIP

Dedication

To my parents, John and Monica, who made sure that I started in the right direction; to my wife Susan, whose love keeps me going; and to my children, J.T. and Kim, who make it all worthwhile.

Dr. James F. Burke

To my parents, Max and Sylvia, for their years of support in all my endeavors. To my wife Adrienne for her love and devotion; to my children, Scott and Bryan, who are the source of my inspiration; and to the memory of Abraham Green whose love for learning will always be an inspiration to me.

Dr. Barry P. Resnick

CONTENTS

Preface xvii

About the Authors xix

Part One Marketing the Travel Product 1

Chapter 1 Understanding Marketing and Sales 3

Objectives 3
What is Marketing? 4
Marketing and Sales 4
Marketing and Sales in Travel and Tourism 4
Introducing the Marketing of the Travel Product 4
Marketing Theory 5
The Marketing Plan 5
The Marketing Cycle 6
Factors Affecting Marketing 9
A Brief History of Travel Marketing and Sales 9
Ancient Times 9
Middle Ages 10
Seventeenth and Eighteenth Centuries 10
Nineteenth Century 10
Twentieth Century 10
A Sampling of Careers in Travel Marketing and Sales 12
Travel Agent 12
Destination Marketer 13
Tour Operator 14
Marketing Director 14
Sales Manager 14
Sales Representative 15
Chapter Summary 15
Key Terms 16
Discussion Questions 16
Study Guide 17
Worksheet 21

Chapter 2 Analyzing the Travel Product 25

Objectives 25
What is the Travel Product? 25
Characteristics of the Travel Product 26
Intangibility 26
Simultaneous Production and Consumption 27
Perishability 28

Seasonality 28
Parity 29
Uniqueness 29
Complementarity 30
The Service Aspect 30
Relationship of Travel Products and Services 32
Service Quality and the Travel Product 32
Chapter Summary 33
Key Terms 33
Discussion Questions 34
Study Guide 35
Worksheet 37

Chapter 3 Selecting Target Markets 39

Objectives 39
Why Travel Markets Need to Be Segmented 39
Characteristics of a Market Segment 40
Methods of Segmenting Travel Markets 41
Demographic Segmenting 41
Geographic Segmenting 45
Psychographic Segmenting 45
Behavioristic Segmenting 46
Why Companies Do Market Research 48
Expanding into New Geographic Areas 48
Recognizing Growing Markets 49
Identifying Lifestyle Trends 50
Attracting More Visitors 50
Market Research as a Tool 51
Database Target Marketing 51
How People Do Market Research 52
Defining the Marketing Research Problem 52
Developing and Executing the Research Plan 52
Producing Useful Results 53
Drawing Conclusions and Making Recommendations 53
Using Market Research 53
Chapter Summary 54
Key Terms 54
Discussion Questions 54
Study Guide 55
Worksheet 59

Chapter 4 Positioning the Product 65

Objectives 65
The Principles of Product Positioning 66
Establishing a Position 68
Analyzing Your Product 68
Identifying Your Current Position and Image 69
Comparing Your Current Position with Your Marketing Objectives 70

Creating the Positioning Statement ... **72**
Examples of Positioning Statements and Strategies ... **73**
Positioning Relative to a Target Market ... 73
Positioning by Product Benefits ... 74
Positioning by Price and Quality ... 74
Positioning Relative to a Product Class ... 74
Positioning Relative to a Competitor ... 75
The Role of Image in Buying Decisions ... **77**
Chapter Summary ... **77**
Key Terms ... **78**
Discussion Questions ... **78**
Study Guide ... **79**
Worksheet ... **83**

Chapter 5 Creating Marketing Strategies ... **87**

Objectives ... **87**
Marketing Objectives ... **87**
Examples of Marketing Strategies ... **88**
Market Leader ... 88
Market Challenger ... 89
Market Follower ... 90
Market Niche Player ... 90
Marketing Mix ... **91**
Product ... 91
Place/Process of Delivery ... 92
Price ... 92
Promotion ... 92
Physical Environment ... 93
Purchasing Process ... 93
Packaging ... 93
Participation ... 94
Managing the Marketing Mix ... **94**
The Product/Service Combination ... 95
The Presentation Mix ... 95
Marketing Communications ... 97
A Marketing Strategy in Practice ... **103**
Chapter Summary ... **104**
Key Terms ... **104**
Discussion Questions ... **104**
Study Guide ... **105**
Worksheet ... **109**

Chapter 6 Implementing the Marketing Plan ... **113**

Objectives ... **113**
The Marketing Plan ... **113**
Introduction ... 114
Rationale ... 114
Implementation ... 115

Setting the Marketing Budget 116
Characteristics of a Good Marketing Budget 116
Budget-Setting Methods 116
Controlling the Marketing Process 119
Gathering Information and Keeping Records 119
Monitoring Spending 122
Progress Reports 122
Monitoring Employee Performance 122
Evaluating the Marketing Plan 123
Performance Standards 123
Measurement Techniques 123
Marketing Evaluation Case Study 124
Evaluation Follow-Up 126
Chapter Summary 127
Key Terms 127
Discussion Questions 128
Study Guide 129
Worksheet 131

Part Two Selling the Travel Product 133

Chapter 7 Understanding the Traveler's Needs 135

Objectives 135
The Steps of the Buying Process 137
Feeling and Recognizing a Need or Desire 137
Seeking Information 137
Understanding the Value of Products 138
Deciding Whether to Buy 138
Experiencing and Evaluating the Purchase 138
The Needs of the Leisure Traveler 138
The Need to Travel 139
The Wheres and Hows of Travel 140
Barriers to Travel 142
The Needs of the Business Traveler 142
The Need for Efficiency 142
The Special Needs of Women Travelers 145
Chapter Summary 146
Key Terms 146
Discussion Questions 147
Study Guide 149
Worksheet 153

Chapter 8 Identifying the Seller 155

Objectives 155
Special Characteristics of the Travel Product 155
Intangibility 155
Perishability 156
Complementarity 156

Types of Sellers **156**
Suppliers 156
Intermediaries 156
Direct Distribution **158**
Supplier Advantages of Direct Distribution 158
Customer Advantages of Direct Distribution 161
Indirect Distribution **161**
Travel Agents 161
Corporate Travel Departments 162
Tour Operators 162
Specialized Travel Distributors 163
Supplier Advantages of Indirect Distribution 165
Customer Advantages of Indirect Distribution 165
Distribution Models **166**
One-Stage Direct Distribution 166
Two-Stage Indirect Distribution 167
Three-Stage Indirect Distribution 168
Automation and Travel Sales Distribution **168**
Computer Reservations Systems 168
Current Trends in Automation 170
Chapter Summary **171**
Key Terms **171**
Discussion Questions **171**
Study Guide **173**
Worksheet **177**

Chapter 9 Evaluating the Travel Product **179**

Objectives **179**
Gathering the Information **180**
Computer Reservations Systems 180
Print Sources 182
Firsthand Experience 186
Assessing the Value of Travel **187**
Quality and Quantity 187
Price and Value 188
How to Compare Prices 189
Perceived Benefits and Value 191
Chapter Summary **192**
Key Terms **192**
Discussion Questions **192**
Study Guide **193**
Worksheet **197**

Chapter 10 Setting Up the Sale **201**

Objectives **201**
Advertising **201**
Steps of the Advertising Process 203
Selecting and Scheduling Media 205

Public Relations **207**
Newsworthy Information 209
Media Contacts 210
Public Relations Techniques 210
Sales Promotion **211**
Customer-Oriented Sales Promotion 211
Trade-Oriented Sales Promotion 213
Chapter Summary **214**
Key Terms **215**
Discussion Questions **215**
Study Guide **217**
Worksheet **221**

Chapter 11 Using Personal Selling Techniques **225**

Objectives **225**
Personal Selling Defined **226**
Basic Steps of Personal Selling **227**
Gathering Information from the Customer 227
Making Recommendations 229
Closing the Sale 234
Additional Aspects of Group and Corporate Selling **235**
Prospecting 236
Writing a Sales Proposal 237
Making Sales Presentations 238
Chapter Summary **238**
Key Terms **239**
Discussion Questions **239**
Study Guide **241**
Worksheet **245**

Chapter 12 Satisfying the Customer **249**

Objectives **249**
Principles of Customer Service **249**
Actions 250
Appearance 250
Communication Skills 250
Providing Superior Service **250**
Providing Service with the Sale 250
Providing Service with the Product 252
Following Up the Sale **253**
Communicating 253
Providing Incentives 255
Servicing a Business Account 255
Maintaining a Professional Level of Service **256**
Continuing Education 256
Legal Responsibilities 256
Ethical Behavior 257

High-Tech Service **257**
In the Office 259
Outside the Office 260
Marketing Information and Market Trends **260**
Recognizing Market Trends 260
The Ongoing Value of Marketing **262**
Chapter Summary **262**
Key Terms **263**
Discussion Questions **263**
Study Guide **265**
Worksheet **269**

Appendix A: Commonly Used Abbreviations **273**

Appendix B: Travel Associations and Organizations **275**

Glossary of Key Terms **281**

PREFACE

THE IMPORTANCE OF TRAVEL AND TOURISM

The travel and tourism industry has become one of the world's largest and fastest growing industries. By some estimates, it is already *the* largest; other determinations suggest that it will become the world's largest early in the twenty-first century. Spurred by a convergence of social, economic, and technological developments, the travel business continues to quicken its pace worldwide. As a result, more people travel for leisure, and more people travel as a part of their employment than ever before. Today, travelers have a myriad of choices in terms of transportation, accommodation, activity, and destination.

Because of this growth in demand for travel services, the travel industry offers exciting career opportunities. Many of these careers fall into the category of marketing and sales. With the travel industry growing ever more competitive, the role of marketing and sales becomes increasingly vital to every type of travel organization. Destination marketer, travel agent, public relations professional, marketing research director, and group sales representative are just a few of the marketing and sales positions available with travel and tourism organizations.

Marketing and Selling the Travel Product introduces you to marketing and sales principles and procedures. Selling travel products is the goal of a series of marketing steps designed to identify customers and to inform and persuade them of the benefits associated with experiencing travel products. Anyone considering a career in travel marketing and sales needs to understand how travel organizations use marketing techniques and strategies to enhance their ability to sell their products. In today's competitive travel marketplace, marketing is the key to success.

The Content and Organization

Marketing and Selling the Travel Product is divided into two parts of six chapters each. Part One focuses on marketing principles and procedures as they apply to the travel industry and its products and services. Chapter 1 provides an introduction to basic marketing theory, a brief historical overview of travel marketing and sales, and a sampling of careers in the field. The second chapter details the special and unique characteristics of travel products, emphasizing why service is a critical element of marketing travel products. In Chapter 3, you will learn about target markets and the basic market segmentation techniques used to identify and isolate those targets. Chapter 3 also describes market research—techniques and outcomes—emphasizing their value throughout the steps of the marketing cycle. Chapter 4 explains the basic principles of positioning travel products and the importance of product image to the positioning process and the success of the product sales. The fifth chapter focuses on the development and implementation of marketing strategies designed to achieve specific marketing objectives, including the eight *P*s—the variables comprising the marketing mix. Ending Part One, Chapter 6 looks at how marketing plans are implemented and evaluated on an ongoing basis. This last step is critical to making the refinements and adjustments necessary for continuing marketing efforts to be successful.

Part Two focuses exclusively on ways of achieving the goal of all travel-related marketing—selling travel products. Chapter 7 begins by examining what salespeople need to understand about the motivations for travel. Chapter 8 explains who sells travel products and through what channels. Chapter 9 describes the various methods and sources used by travel salespeople to gather information about travel products and to evaluate them. Chapter 10 focuses on how advertising, public relations, and sales promotion are used to support the sales effort by generating demand for the travel product. The actual process of personal selling is delineated step-by-step in Chapter 11, including the special methods required for selling travel products to major corporate clients. Chapter 12 is concerned with gaining repeat business from customers, with a primary emphasis on the importance of consistently excellent service. Market research and evaluation techniques are reemphasized in this context as an ongoing means of staying in touch with and anticipating customers' travel needs.

The Learning Features

To help you understand what you are reading, this text incorporates several learning aids.

Objectives. Each chapter begins with a list of its main objectives. These focus on the chapter's main points and help you to see in advance the sequence in which they will be covered.

Chapter Summaries. Each chapter concludes with a summary listing its main points. These summaries make it easy to review the central ideas presented in each chapter.

Key Terms. This text introduces you to many terms which are part of the language of the travel industry and/or marketing and sales. To help you learn these terms easily, the text features them in bold type at their first use and defines the terms in context. These key terms are also reviewed in a list appearing at the end of each chapter. In addition, an alphabetical glossary of terms is included at the end of this book, listing and defining all of the key terms that have appeared in the twelve chapters of the text.

The travel industry also has many of its own abbreviations and acronyms. These are described in their full form the first time they are used; thereafter, they are abbreviated in most cases. A list of frequently used abbreviations and acronyms is included in the appendix.

Discussion Questions. A list of discussion questions appears at the end of each chapter to help you think critically about what you have read. These questions challenge you to think about the real world implications and applications of the chapter content.

Study Guides. At the end of each chapter, you will find study guides, consisting of review questions requiring short answers. Your instructor will assign these or suggest how you can make the best use of them.

Worksheets. Also at the end of each chapter are worksheet exercises. These are designed to reinforce what you have already learned. Some require research on your part; others challenge you to consider hypothetical situations and to make decisions about how you would handle them.

Marketing Impressions. In addition to the learning aids, a special feature—Marketing Impressions—has been created for each chapter to enhance your understanding of how travel products are developed, marketed, and sold. These one-page features focus on how travel professionals and their organizations use the marketing and sales principles and procedures introduced in the text.

Instructor's Manual and Key. An instructor's manual and key is available to accompany this text. This manual restates each chapter's objectives and contains answers to end-of-chapter discussion questions, study guides, and worksheet exercises.

ACKNOWLEDGMENTS

The authors would like to acknowledge Hans Resnick, Robert J. Gandolfo, and Jeffrey R. Miller, Esq., as well as thank the following reviewers:

Linda Cropper
El Paso Community College
El Paso, TX

Scott Feinerman
West Los Angeles College
Culver City, CA

Jill Gerlinger
Conlin-Hallisey Travel School
Ann Arbor, MI

Donna Morn
Art Institute of Fort Lauderdale
Fort Lauderdale, FL

Russell Nauta
Woodland Park, CO

David Schoenberg
LaGuardia Community College
Long Island City, NY

Rex Yentes
Webber College
Winterhaven, FL

ABOUT THE AUTHORS

DR. JAMES F. BURKE

James Burke is the dean of the Collins School of Hospitality Management at California State Polytechnic University, Pomona. He has also served as the president of the International Travel and Tourism Research Association, and a trustee of the National Tourism Foundation, as well as the chairman of its Education Advisory Council. During the past few years, he has also been a member of the Issues Task Force and the Research Committee for the White House Conference on Travel and Tourism, a member of the U.S. Department of Commerce Task Force on Accountability Research, and the chairman of the Tourism Educators Council of the New York State Hospitality and Tourism Association. In addition, he has been the president and chairman of the board of the International Society of Travel and Tourism Educators, and received the Society's Lifetime Achievement Award in 1997.

Dr. Burke has also been the director for both the Tourism Destination Management Program and the Accelerated Masters of Tourism Administration in the Department of Tourism and Hospitality Management at George Washington University and the director of the School of Hospitality and Tourism Management at Ryerson Polytechnic University. He has also served as an associate professor at the Rochester Institute of Technology, the director of the Hospitality and Tourism Graduate Program at the University of Wisconsin-Stout, and a tourism development specialist for the University of Minnesota Extension Service. After graduating from Dartmouth College, he began his career in tourism as a media researcher/time-buyer for Leo Brunett Advertising, where he worked on travel accounts.

Dr. Burke has addressed regional, state, provincial, and national tourism conferences throughout the world on evaluating tourism marketing and measuring service quality, and has written a number of articles on the same topics. He has served as a consultant to states, provinces, corporations, and universities. He earned his Ph.D. at the University of Minnesota, as well as master's degrees at Temple University and Utah State University.

DR. BARRY P. RESNICK

Barry Resnick possesses a diverse background in the tourism and higher education fields with over two decades of experience. Since 1977, he has been a professor of travel and tourism at West Los Angeles College. Additionally he has served as department chairman of the Travel and Tourism Department at Rancho Santiago College and as a lecturer for the Recreation and Leisure Studies Department at California State University, Long Beach.

Prior to his experience in the higher education field, Dr. Resnick held positions in travel sales, marketing, and tour management for major multinational corporations. In 1984 he was instrumental in bringing one of the first installations of the American Airlines SABRE system to a higher education institution. Subsequently, he coauthored the first and second edition of *SABRE Reservations: Basic and Advanced Training.*

Dr. Resnick is active in a number of industry organizations. He has served as chairman and president of the International Society of Travel and Tourism Educators, and in 1995 was the recipient of the Society's Lifetime Achievement Award. He also served two years as a member of the American Society of Travel Agents' Education Committee. Dr. Resnick is frequently called upon to speak on tourism marketing and has served as a consultant on marketing and training issues for a number of organizations, including Continental Airlines and the System One Learning Center.

A graduate of the University of Southern California, Dr. Resnick holds master's degrees from California State University, Long Beach, and National University. Research for his doctorate, which was earned at Brigham Young University, centered upon the training programs of major U.S. airlines in the post-deregulation era.

PART ONE

Marketing the Travel Product

CHAPTER 1 Understanding Marketing and Sales

CHAPTER 2 Analyzing the Travel Product

CHAPTER 3 Selecting Target Markets

CHAPTER 4 Positioning the Product

CHAPTER 5 Creating Marketing Strategies

CHAPTER 6 Implementing the Marketing Plan

Understanding Marketing and Sales

OBJECTIVES

When you have completed this chapter, you should be able to:

- Describe the difference between marketing and sales.
- Describe the roles of sellers, buyers, and intermediaries.
- Differentiate among product-oriented, sales-oriented, and customer-oriented marketing.
- Explain why a marketing plan is important for the modern travel industry.
- Identify the major components of the marketing cycle.
- Identify some major historical developments affecting travel products and the ways they are sold.
- Explain examples of careers in travel marketing and sales.

In the early 1950s, Walt Disney saw the need for a new kind of outdoor family entertainment. At that time, America's amusement parks, which had been a traditional setting for family outings, were becoming dreary places. Disney envisioned a clean, wholesome environment with attractions and rides the entire family could enjoy. He dreamed of a park built around themes from his movies and inhabited by his cartoon characters. The product of Disney's imagination was Disneyland, the first major theme park in the United States.

Disney's perception of what people wanted was correct. Since its opening in July 1955, Disneyland has been an outstanding success. By its fortieth anniversary in 1995, more than 375 million people had passed through its gate, and attendance has continued to soar. Inspired by the success of Disneyland in Anaheim, California, Disney began the much larger Walt Disney World in Orlando, Florida. Disney World has grown further to include three major additions in the form of EPCOT Center, the Disney/MGM Studios Theme Park, and Pleasure Island. It is now both the world's largest theme park and its number one tourist attraction. A Disneyland has also been constructed in Tokyo, and another, called Euro Disney, is outside of Paris. In addition, the success of Disneyland has spawned the development of more than thirty other theme parks around the United States. In 1998 alone, the theme park industry generated $60 billion in revenue.

The growing Disney empire is an example of successful marketing; Disney identified a need and then developed a product to satisfy that need. Marketing is important to all businesses, and the travel and tourism industry is no exception. This chapter and those that follow examine travel and tourism marketing activities and strategies in depth.

WHAT IS MARKETING?

Like most people, you are affected by marketing almost every day. You are probably most familiar with the sales part of marketing. For example, you may have been overwhelmed by the number of walking and running shoes available for sale in a sporting goods store, and a salesperson helped you select a comfortable pair. Perhaps you have been persuaded to buy a life insurance policy while you were buying a policy for your automobile. Or shopping at a self-service drugstore, you may have been uncertain as to which brand of shampoo to buy. Then you spotted a label you had seen advertised on TV or on a Web site. When you made each purchase, you probably did not realize all of the things that had to happen to make these products available to you.

Marketing and Sales

The terms "marketing" and "sales" are often used interchangeably. They are not, in fact, the same thing. ***Marketing*** is the sum of all the decisions and activities that sellers undertake to convince buyers to commit to a particular product or service instead of to the many other products and services available. Marketing includes finding out what customers want, offering a product to meet their needs, identifying the best place in which to market the product, informing high-potential prospective customers of the product's availability, making the sale, and finally, evaluating the entire marketing process. ***Sales*** are made when customers exchange money for a product or a promise to deliver a product or service. The sales transaction is only one aspect of the marketing process. Salespersons focus on selling products and services.

Marketing and Sales in Travel and Tourism

How does the marketing process apply specifically to the travel and tourism industry? This chapter provides an overview and Chapters 2 through 6 describe steps in the marketing process in detail, including:

* Analyzing the Travel Product.
* Selecting Target Markets.
* Positioning the Product.
* Creating Marketing Strategies.
* Implementing the Marketing Plan.

Advertising and selling the product are also important components of the marketing process. These aspects are emphasized in the second half of the book, in Chapters 7 through 12:

* Understanding the Traveler's Needs.
* Identifying the Seller.
* Evaluating the Travel Product.
* Setting Up the Sale.
* Using Personal Selling Techniques.
* Satisfying the Customer.

Introducing the Marketing of the Travel Product

An important aspect of learning about marketing in the travel and tourism industry is understanding the roles of its important human participants. This will help you better understand what constitutes a market for travel products and who supplies and purchases them.

The Sellers. The sellers are the producers—the ones who have something for sale. They include large corporations, small businesses, and individuals. In the travel and tourism industry, the sellers include providers of transportation (airlines, car rental agencies, cruise lines, railroads, motor coach companies), lodging (hotels, motels, inns, hostels, etc.), restaurants, tourist attractions (festivals, theme parks, museums, etc.), and related services such as tour guides. Tourism promotion agencies (both government and private) also participate in selling travel products directly to buyers.

The Buyers. The buyers are, of course, the people who purchase travel products and services. The industry rec-

A travel agency is one marketplace where buyers and sellers of travel meet. (Photograph by Michael Dzamen)

ognizes three groups of customers, based on their reasons for traveling. Business travelers travel as part of their jobs. They must travel to get their work done. Most pleasure or leisure travelers, on the other hand, do not have to travel. They take leisure trips to have fun, relax, or see new places. Travelers visiting friends and relatives constitute the largest group within the leisure category.

A third group comprises those who have to travel for special purposes, such as going to or from college, attending a religious ceremony, or because there is an illness or death in the family. Since marketing has little influence on this third group, this text focuses on business and leisure travel marketing.

The Intermediary. An intermediary is a seller of travel products who acts as a link between a seller (supplier) and a buyer (customer). The travel industry includes three general groups of intermediaries: travel agents, tour operators, and specialized distributors (such as meeting planners). Although all three sell travel products to customers on behalf of the suppliers who produce the travel product, each intermediary group operates in a different way.

The Market. This concept refers to a group of people with similar needs or desires and the money to satisfy those needs or desires. The total market for travel products consists primarily of the two large segments mentioned previously: business travelers and leisure travelers. Often, certain groups are distinguished from the total market by characteristics such as their age, gender, geographic location, income, purchase behavior, preferences, and lifestyles or attitudes. Using these factors individually or together, marketing professionals attempt to target their marketing efforts toward a specific portion of the total market. The market for traveling on the Concorde, for example, consists primarily of wealthy, sophisticated travelers; whereas the market for discounted flights might include budget-conscious younger students.

MARKETING THEORY

Marketing concepts are a relatively recent development. Before 1900, travel products and services, like those of other industries, were sold in straightforward, traditional ways. Not much thought was given to the process, especially since there were only a limited number of destinations, routes, or facilities from which to choose. Only in the twentieth century have theories of marketing evolved and been applied extensively within the travel industry.

Traditionally, companies simply developed a product and then hoped that customers would buy it. Even as improvements in transportation, communication, and industrial machinery helped start a period of mass production, little attention was paid to the customer at first, as long as the product was profitable. The principle of this approach, known as ***product-oriented marketing***, is that if you create the best product, customers will flock to your door. The success of the airlines at the expense of long haul passenger railroads is an example of product-oriented marketing.

As production capacity increased further in the United States in the late 1920s, business leaders began to realize that they would have to persuade people to buy all the products they could make. To do this, they expanded marketing activities to include improving sales staffs through training, incentives, and sales management. The theory behind these actions is called ***sales-oriented marketing***. This approach equates marketing effort with sales, as when a downtown hotel, designed for business travelers, actively sells its services (usually at a discount) to leisure travelers and convention attendees even if their rooms don't truly meet the needs of these longer-stay travelers. In addition, the rapid growth of radio and television enabled sales messages to go to millions of people at one time, providing potent advertising for sellers.

Since the 1950s, companies have recognized the fact that people will not buy or continue to buy a product if it does not meet their needs. The market for travel products and services has become extremely competitive, and marketing techniques have become more sophisticated and professional as a result. Companies have placed more emphasis on conducting research to determine what consumers really need and want. Marketing theory has expanded to include market research as well as product design and development. Thus, modern ***customer-oriented marketing*** is conducted from the consumer's point of view. An example of customer-oriented marketing is a resort that changes its emphasis from rest, relaxation, and rich food to sports, fitness, and low-calorie meals in reaction to changing preferences among customers and potential customers.

The Marketing Plan

Marketing has become an important academic discipline. People attend colleges and universities to learn marketing concepts and techniques. Companies have marketing departments and marketing directors who prepare formal, written plans and oversee marketing programs. Successful organizations do not wander haphazardly into the market. They know in advance exactly where they are headed and what they intend to accomplish, because they have prepared ***marketing plans*** which identify opportunities, match products and consumers, and provide tactics and strategies for accomplishing marketing goals.

Systematic planning is particularly important to the travel and tourism industry because considerable competition exists. This competition was made even more intense with the deregulation of the domestic airlines in 1978. Before that time, the federal government had regulated many competitive elements of airline travel such as routes, pricing, and classes of service. Since deregulation, airlines have competed with each other for passengers, resulting in expanded routes, multiple fares, and in some cases, reduced airfares.

Two other situations have dramatically increased competition in the travel and tourism industry in the last decade. First, more and more destinations (towns, cities, states, provinces, countries, etc.) have recognized the economic value of tourism and are actively attracting tourists through expensive promotional programs. This is particularly true for emerging countries and those communities in developed countries that have lost other important industries like manufacturing, mining, forestry, or fishing.

Secondly, lodging chains have developed a series of products in many different price categories, in order to attract different market segments, and/or to develop customer loyalty so that travelers will choose their lodging products whenever the need for an overnight stay arises. Marriott, which offers a full range of accommodation products, from luxury hotels, resorts, and midpriced hotels (Marriott Marquis, Renaissance Hotels, Residence Inn, Courtyard, Fairfield Inn), is an example of this strategy. In addition to competition, the growth of technology has created a situation in which the ability to provide travel products has surpassed the capacity to sell them. Unsold airline seats and hotel rooms are examples of this increased excess capacity.

The Marketing Cycle

The steps in the marketing process form a cycle, with the last step leading back into the first step (see Figure 1-1). Travel and tourism organizations that engage in customer-oriented marketing are constantly moving through this cycle.

The Nature of the Product. The marketing cycle begins when a company conceives an idea for a product or service or determines a way to improve an existing product. Market research then establishes whether a demand exists for the product or whether improving the product will increase sales. This procedure can also be reversed, too. By doing market research, a company can identify unfilled needs and come up with an idea for a new product or service or a way of improving an existing one.

To remain competitive and increase sales, companies are constantly working to develop and refine products. New and revitalized products are essential to company growth. For instance, having developed the market for business traveler bookings to a great degree, car rental agencies are now seeking to expand their leisure rental volume. In response to the surge in demand for short pleasure trips, hotels have developed suite concepts and a variety of weekend vacation packages. One relatively new rental car company, Enterprise, will even pick you up at your home or workplace, free of charge. They provide this service to make it easier to rent a car and to encourage you to choose them rather than their competitors.

The Nature of the Market and the Product. In the late 1980s, a travel agent in the Eastern United States had an idea for a new travel product. Called Grandtravel, it is based on a recognition of a need in contemporary society. Many of today's working parents do not have time to take their children on long vacations. Many grandparents, on the other hand, do have the time, energy, money, and desire to travel. Capitalizing on these trends, Grandtravel arranges special tours for grandparents and grandchildren vacationing together. Recently, these tours have become immensely successful.

Through market research, companies find out who prospective customers are and what they want to buy. Questionnaires, personal interviews, and client records are some tools used to gather this information. U.S. Census Bureau studies and news articles on social and economic trends also help to identify potential markets. Once the information has been gathered, it must be carefully analyzed and interpreted. Companies need an efficient and effective information-gathering system so that they are always up-to-date with what is happening in the marketplace.

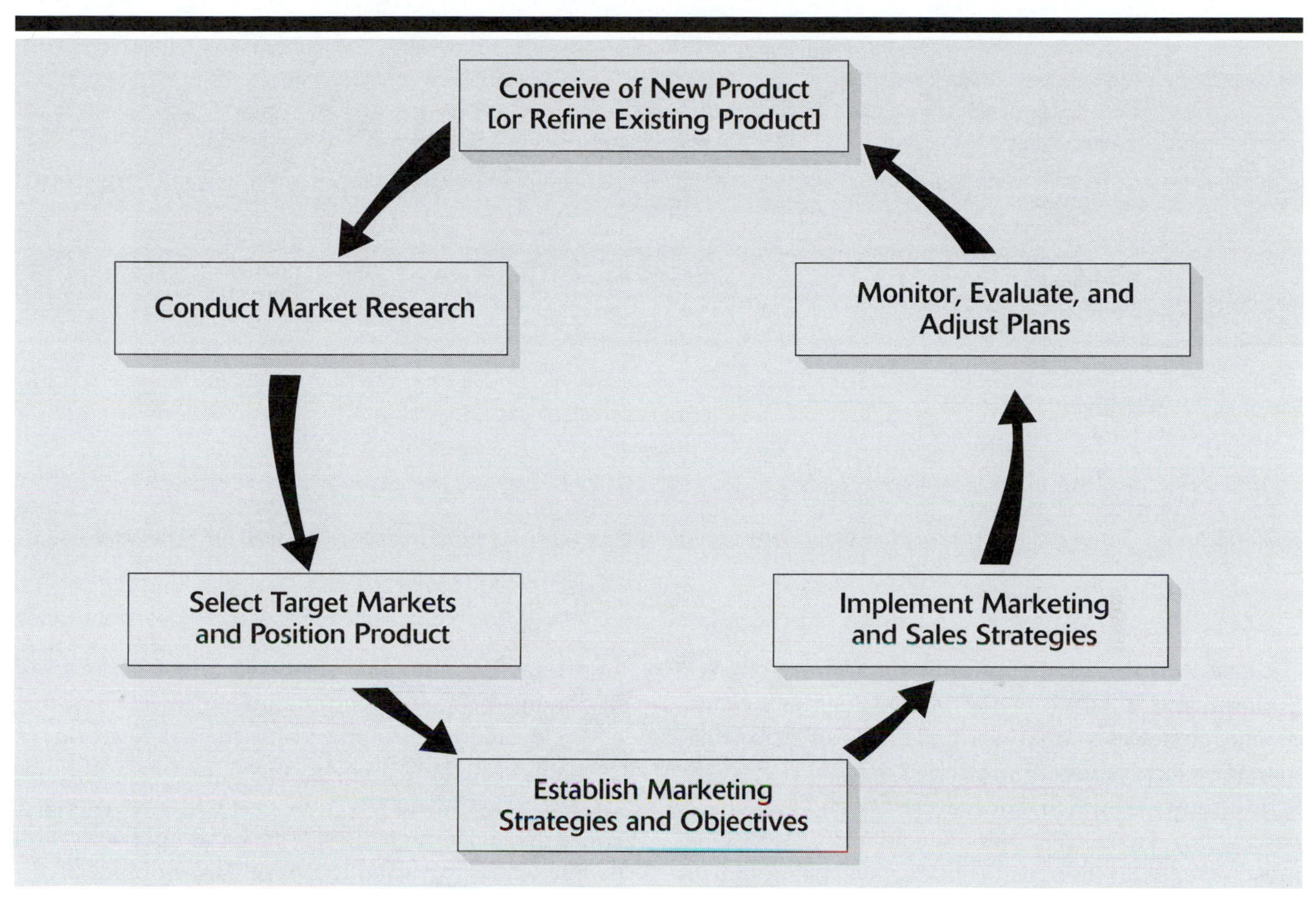

FIGURE 1–1 The steps of the marketing process form a continuous cycle.

Rather than try to meet the needs of all travelers, companies generally choose to direct their products or services to a segment (portion) of the market, called a ***target market***. A target market contains a sizable, yet manageable, group of people who might be expected to purchase the same products and services. Target markets are based on a variety of factors such as purpose for travel (business, vacation, visiting friends and relatives), age and marital status (young singles, senior citizens, parents with young children), economic status (upscale, middle-income, low-income), or interests (adventure, art and music, health). Target marketing involves developing products and promotional strategies to appeal to specific market segments, as illustrated in Figure 1-2.

An important marketing concept is ***product positioning***. At one time in the history of horse racing, jockeys attempted to maneuver their horses into a favorable starting position, a practice known as "jockeying for position." Likewise, to increase their chances for success in the market, companies must establish a position for their products and communicate this clearly to consumers. Some resorts, for example, position themselves as luxury hotels for the wealthy, while others are positioned as family vacation resorts or as convention sites for corporations and associations.

Marketing Strategies and Objectives. Basic to every marketing plan are ***marketing objectives***. These are the goals the travel company hopes to achieve over a certain time frame. Establishing marketing objectives helps a company focus its efforts and measure its success. The goals might be long term—perhaps five or ten years, or they might be short term—perhaps three months to a year. A long-term objective for a travel agency might be to increase car rental sales from 3 percent to 10 percent of the total annual sales volume within three years. A short-term objective might be to sell fifty luxury cabins at a special fare on a particular cruise line between July 8 and December 23 of this year.

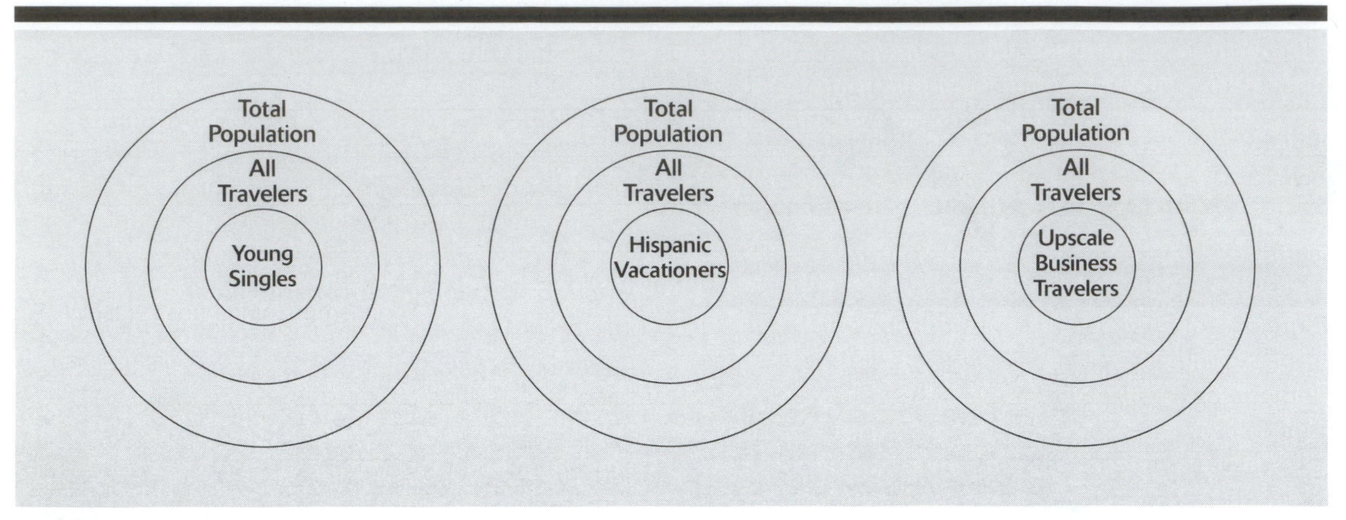

FIGURE 1–2 Travel and tourism products should target specific groups within the travel market, rather than the population as a whole.

After establishing objectives based on a market position and a target market, companies next must develop strategies to capture a larger share of an existing market or to penetrate an untapped market. Their marketing strategies will include decisions about product design and image, distribution, and price. Decisions must be made about how the product will be promoted so the marketing objectives will be met. All these decisions must be made in relation to the company's resources. In other words, does the company have the finances and personnel to implement the strategy? If it does, and if the sales strategies and methods are well conceived and executed, strong sales are the likely result.

Monitor, Evaluate, and Adjust Plans. Successful companies and organizations monitor the market's response to their products and services from the moment they are available for sale. This allows them to immediately gauge whether their market research and objectives were realistic and to adjust product price, concept, or distribution channels quickly to meet market behavior. Nor does the marketing process end once the sale has been made. Instead, successful companies evaluate how effective their marketing strategies have been. They use market research to measure the consumer's perspective of the product or service. Hotels, for instance, frequently ask guests to fill out questionnaires indicating their impressions of the hotel's service quality. On the basis of customer and employee evaluations and changes in demand in their target market, organizations begin the marketing cycle again by adjusting or modifying their products and services and improving their marketing strategies.

Consider the situation of Walt Disney World. In the late 1980s, after having been in business since 1971, Disney World was still evaluating its products and services. Through guest letters and interviews with people who had visited the park, Disney officials discovered gaps in the park's entertainment menu. The Magic Kingdom, which was targeted for five- to ten-year-olds, bored adolescents. In response, the company decided to add Typhoon Lagoon, the world's largest water park. The company also found that young children were leaving the park in tears because they hadn't seen Mickey Mouse. The company then created Mickey's Birthdayland, a place where Mickey could always be found. Also, adults were driving to nightclubs in Orlando because the Disney complex had no nighttime entertainment. To remedy this situation, Pleasure Island, a complex of nightclubs, theaters, restaurants, and shops, was developed.

Another aspect of this part of the marketing cycle is maintaining a relationship with existing customers. A common mistake of travel companies is to spend so much of their effort on developing new customers that little attention is paid to keeping the customers they already have. Without marketing after the sale, a great deal of business may be lost. To ensure repeat business, successful travel and tourism companies reward existing customers with price discounts or membership in special clubs. Many companies maintain client profiles so that they can customize sales or notify customers when appropriate products and services become available. This type of marketing, which maintains consistent communication with existing customers, is referred to as ***relationship marketing***.

Factors Affecting Marketing

No matter how diligently a company attempts to plan and implement its marketing process, uncontrollable factors outside the company will influence, and even disrupt, the course of events. When this happens, the company must be flexible enough to adapt to the situation. Market research can also forecast some of these situations and prepare a company to handle them.

Many external factors can affect marketing, particularly economic and political conditions. Political unrest in a foreign country will discourage travel to that country. Economic conditions such as inflation, currency exchange rates, and the cost of credit influence how effective marketing budgets will be, as well as how much travelers will be willing and/or able to spend. As a result of changes in these factors, travel to countries throughout the world fluctuates over time (see Figure 1-3). Thus, ongoing marketing is required to inform and persuade potential and experienced visitors.

The growing consumer movement, which is manifested in the expectation that tourist attractions will not overpromise and underdeliver, as well as the demand for an airline passenger's bill of rights and other reforms, is influencing marketing strategies. In addition, technological and social changes have affected both the nature of travel itself and the way travel products are marketed and sold.

A BRIEF HISTORY OF TRAVEL MARKETING AND SALES

Throughout history people have traveled from one destination to another for a variety of reasons. In doing so, they have made purchases from suppliers of transportation, accommodations, food services, and attractions. Over the centuries the quantity and kinds of travel purchases have increased as a result of social change, economic development, telecommunications, and technological advances.

Ancient Times

In ancient times, wealthy people often traveled for pleasure. Wealthy Romans, for instance, enjoyed

WORLD'S TOP DESTINATIONS 2020

Rank in 2020	Rank in 1997	Country	Tourist Arrivals (Million)	Market Share (%)	% Growth rate p.a. 1995-2020
1	6	China	137.1	8.6	8.0
2	2	US	102.4	6.4	3.5
3	1	France	93.3	5.8	1.8
4	3	Spain	71.0	4.4	2.4
5		Hong Kong	59.3	3.7	7.3
6	4	Italy	52.9	3.3	2.2
7	5	UK	52.8	3.3	3.0
8	7	Mexico	48.9	3.1	3.6
9		Russian Fed.	47.1	2.9	6.7
10		Czech Rep.	44.0	2.7	4.0
		TOTAL	708.8		

FIGURE 1-3 Many factors influence the changing popularity of a destination. *Source:* World Tourism Organization Vision 2020.

trips to attractions such as the Baths of Caracalla. Each destination had different costs, appeal, and status, and those who hosted the Roman guests emphasized the differences. The universal coinage of the Roman Empire made travel easier—travelers could use the same form of money throughout the empire to pay for their travel expenses. Artwork and written accounts from ancient times show that wealthy Phoenicians, Chinese, and Egyptians also enjoyed leisure travel.

Middle Ages

Business travel may seem like a modern concept, but it is not new to the twentieth century. Merchants and traders have always traveled to places where they could buy and sell goods. In his diaries, the famous traveler Marco Polo described commercial travel to Beijing in the thirteenth century. Traders paid to stay in the hostels that were established for them in the suburbs around the Chinese imperial city. A special hostel was established for each nationality—Lombards, Germans, French, and others—and, for reasons relating to security, the emperor required the hostels to register the names of the guests and the date of their arrival and departure. (These practices might be considered early forms of market research.)

For most of history, poor people generally have not been able to afford leisure travel. Religious pilgrimages to far-off shrines were a notable exception. In the fourteenth century, for instance, English peasants journeyed to Rome, Jerusalem, and other holy places to fulfill a vow, do penance for their sins, or pay homage to a saint. They had to purchase a permit from the King before they could leave England. They then had to pay sixpence to be ferried across the English Channel (two shillings if they had a horse). Once on the continent, the pilgrims rested in the inns that sprang up along their route. Therefore, innkeepers and other enterprising merchants had a convenient market (the pilgrims) for selling religious relics or souvenirs.

Seventeenth and Eighteenth Centuries

In the 1600s and 1700s, aristocratic English families spent three or four thousand pounds a year to send their sons on a trip through Europe. The "grand tour," as these travels were called, usually lasted three years and conferred considerable status upon the wealthy young travelers. The purpose was to complete the education of the young man and turn him into a gentleman. The young man, along with his tutor, traveled to the centers of culture in Europe, especially cities in France and Italy. He studied works of art, visited places of antiquity such as the Roman Colosseum, attended the opera, and learned the manners of high society. The grand tour was the forerunner of today's cultural tours of Europe, which are a mainstay of business for the travel industry.

Nineteenth Century

In the nineteenth century, leisure travel began to open up for Europe's growing middle class. More people had the time and money to travel. Furthermore, they had a desire to travel. Living in the bleak cities of the Industrial Revolution, they looked forward to escaping to the countryside or seashore for their holidays. The invention of the steam locomotive and the laying of the first railroad tracks in the 1830s made it easier for them to travel.

In 1841, Thomas Cook, a Baptist missionary in England, conceived the idea for a new kind of travel product—the package tour. He decided to organize a group of people opposed to the consumption of alcohol to attend a rally. With the promise of a sizable number of passengers, Cook persuaded a local railway company to run a special train from Leicester to Loughborough, eleven miles to the north. Then he persuaded 570 customers to purchase his travel package. For one shilling, each traveler received a train ride (twenty-two miles round-trip), entertainment (a band played hymns), a picnic lunch, afternoon tea, and the services of a tour escort (Cook himself). Cook, who became the world's first travel agent, eventually expanded his tours to the European continent, to the Holy Land, and to the United States.

Twentieth Century

New forms of transportation also increased travel between the United States and Europe. In the 1860s, trans-Atlantic steamships made the trip in two weeks. Later, screw-propeller luxury liners crossed the Atlantic in six days. Encouraged that it took less time to reach their destination, more Americans bought package tours of Europe. On the eve of World War I, tours of Europe cost between $178 and $400 for five weeks and $1,000 for an eight-country, all-summer luxury tour.

Still, travel to far-off destinations was largely the privilege of the wealthy, who could afford the time and expense. It wasn't until the development of the automobile and the airplane following World War II that travel became accessible to the majority of people.

Marketing Impressions

MANAGER OF PROMOTIONS AND PROGRAMS
COLONIAL WILLIAMSBURG FOUNDATION

Advertising copy and layout to be approved, a radio air-check to be reviewed, a proposal for a promotional partnership, airline tickets to be sent to a sweepstakes winner . . . on most days any or all of these things may be found in the in-box of Tracy Mastaler, manager of promotions and programs for the marketing department at the Colonial Williamsburg Foundation.

Colonial Williamsburg is an authentically restored eighteenth-century town and living history museum. "Colonial Williamsburg is a challenge to market in the age of high-tech amusements and glitzy theme parks," says Mastaler. "Positioning history as interesting and fun is the key to successful promotional programs. Stressing Colonial Williamsburg's role as the site of the birth of America, a free nation, is another message vital to marketing efforts."

The Colonial Williamsburg Foundation is a nonprofit organization. This status increases the marketing challenge because successful marketing initiatives must be compelling, yet implemented utilizing limited funding.

"Developing strategic partnerships in key markets is paramount to the success of many programs," says Mastaler. Her responsibilities include identification of potential promotional partners, creation of a mutually beneficial partnership proposal, negotiating the terms of the agreement, and fulfilling the obligations of the partnership on behalf of Colonial Williamsburg. Business relationships are formed with a variety of partners and include radio, television and print media, purveyors of travel-related services, retail stores, consumer product manufacturers, and other partners who may not seem likely candidates. For example, Colonial Williamsburg has partnered with a manufacturer of popular historically based dolls, accessories, and books. Together the two have created a program which appeals to young girls. The girls' interest in history is sparked by the dolls, whose stories are set in the eighteenth century, just prior to the American Revolution. The partnership has energized product sales for the doll company and created a niche market for Colonial Williamsburg to pursue. Mastaler administers the program, including preparation of marketing plans, production and dissemination of advertising materials, customer service training regarding the program, and frequent communication with the partner. Mastaler says, "It is exciting to have a relationship that enables both partners to teach children the importance of history by making it educational as well as entertaining. The idea that, as a tourist destination, Colonial Williamsburg brings history to life for children appeals to the entire family. This partnership has inspired many little girls to influence their family vacation decision."

Many promotions involve production and distribution of discount coupons and point-of-sale collateral, direct mail, and the creation of radio, television and print advertising. Promotions usually feature some or all of these awareness-building tactics coupled with a sweepstakes offer. "Many of the partnerships take the form of sweepstakes promotions," Mastaler says. "When revenue is limited, it is effective to use the appeal of Colonial Williamsburg, an attractive tourist destination, as a leveraging asset. Often, partners will accept complimentary trips to the area—complete with air transportation, rental car, accommodations, meals, admission tickets and more—in addition to or in lieu of a cash investment in a partnership." When a promotion features a sweepstakes, Mastaler is responsible for all communication with winners, including legal documentation, travel arrangements, and familiarizing winners with Colonial Williamsburg and other attractions in the area. Mastaler says the winners are usually very excited, but sometimes people are skeptical and think that there must be a "catch" to their being offered such a great prize with no obligation. Her job is to raise anticipation for a wonderful travel experience, and deliver just that.

"The success of a promotion can be measured in many ways: coupon redemptions, reservations generated, revenue realized. Another vital form of measurement is the satisfaction of a guest whose positive word-of-mouth advertising can create interest and excitement in other potential visitors." When Mastaler receives positive guest comments she says, "I gain a real sense of accomplishment knowing I have contributed to the quality of a guest's vacation experience."

Mastaler enjoys the challenge of it all. "My projects, although conceptually similar, are very diverse. Each demands its own special kind of attention. I may be immersed in one partnership project when a situation arises with another that requires immediate action or a crucial decision," says Mastaler. She has become accustomed to the fast-paced environment of tourism promotions. Even so, Mastaler points out that it is important to take time from a busy, detail-laden schedule to develop strategic plans. "Marketing a tourism attraction in today's economic climate requires forward thinking and a solid plan for the future. Competition for tourism revenue is so fierce that it is imperative to be on the 'cutting edge,' taking advantage of as many profitable opportunities as possible." This fact will keep Mastaler busy indefinitely, bringing the eighteenth century into the next millennium.

First, the airliner reduced travel time between America and Europe from five days to one day. Then, the flight of the first passenger jet in 1958 cut travel time from twenty-four hours to eight hours. Today, the travel time is about six hours; three hours on the Concorde.

Faster transportation meant that ordinary people with just two weeks of vacation could travel to distant places. Middle-class citizens of industrial nations were also finding that they had more money to spend on travel.

Improvements in transportation and increases in leisure time and income have created a tremendous market for travel. As a result, tourist arrivals at countries throughout the world have increased steadily (see Figure 1–4). New airlines, hotels, cruise lines, travel agencies, and attractions have sprung up everywhere. Marketing efforts and budgets have increased dramatically to capture this expanding travel market. Sales figures have soared, as has spending by tourists in the destinations they visit (see Figure 1–5), making travel and tourism the number one industry in many parts of the world.

A SAMPLING OF CAREERS IN TRAVEL MARKETING AND SALES

As the travel industry and the role of marketing within it have grown, travel sales and marketing have expanded as well (see Figure 1–5). Today a wide array of jobs is associated with the marketing and sales of travel products. Before moving on to learn more about the principles of travel marketing and sales, it's worth taking some time to examine a few careers in this increasingly important field.

Travel Agent

To the public, the most visible career in travel marketing and sales is often that of the retail ***travel agent***. Approximately thirty thousand agencies currently are operating in the United States alone.

A travel agent is essentially a counselor who sells the products and services of the travel businesses represented by their agencies. The kinds of products depend on the size and purpose of the agency. Many agents handle general travel arrangements and sell a wide variety of products, such as tour packages; transportation on airlines, railroads, motor coaches, and cruise lines; attraction tickets; and hotel and resort accommodations. Travel agents can also be independent entrepreneurs, or may work for a department within a large agency or for a specialty agency selling a more limited range of products.

Travel agents help customers make travel plans and reservations. Through careful interviewing, agents find out what customers want—the type of destination,

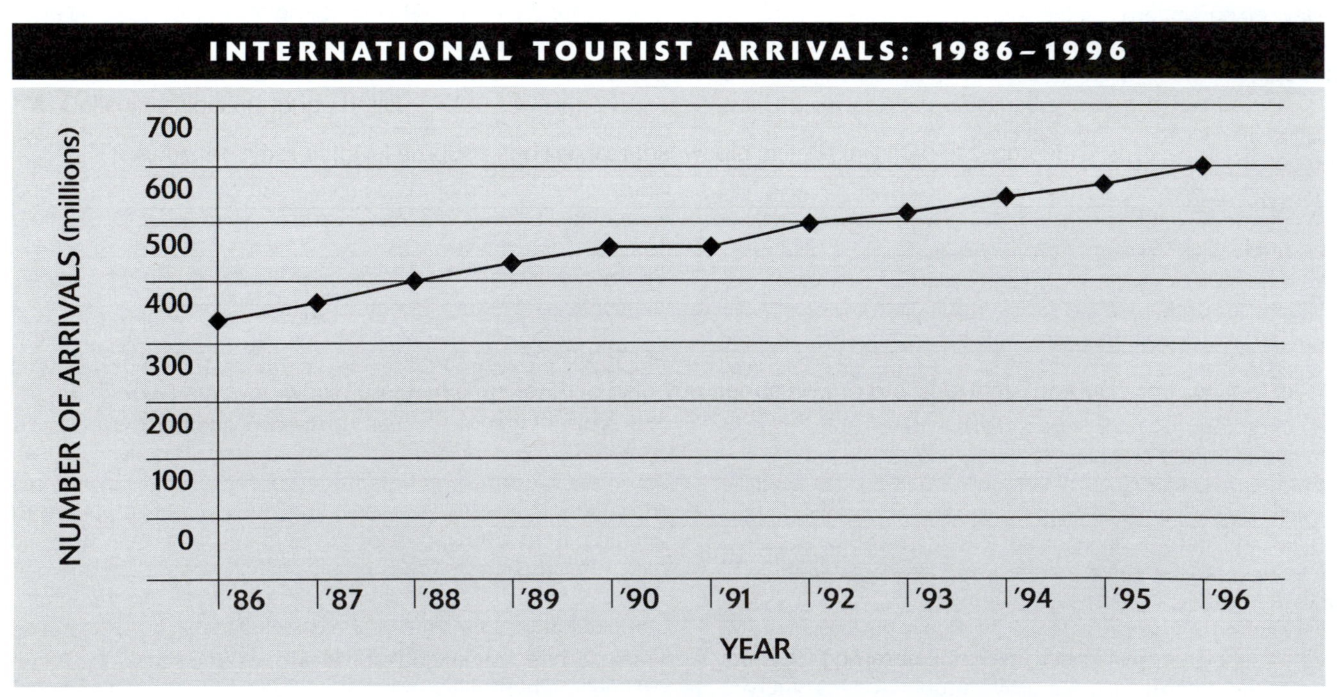

FIGURE 1–4 The number of international travelers continues to climb steadily. *Source:* World Tourism Organization, Tourism Market Trends, 1997.

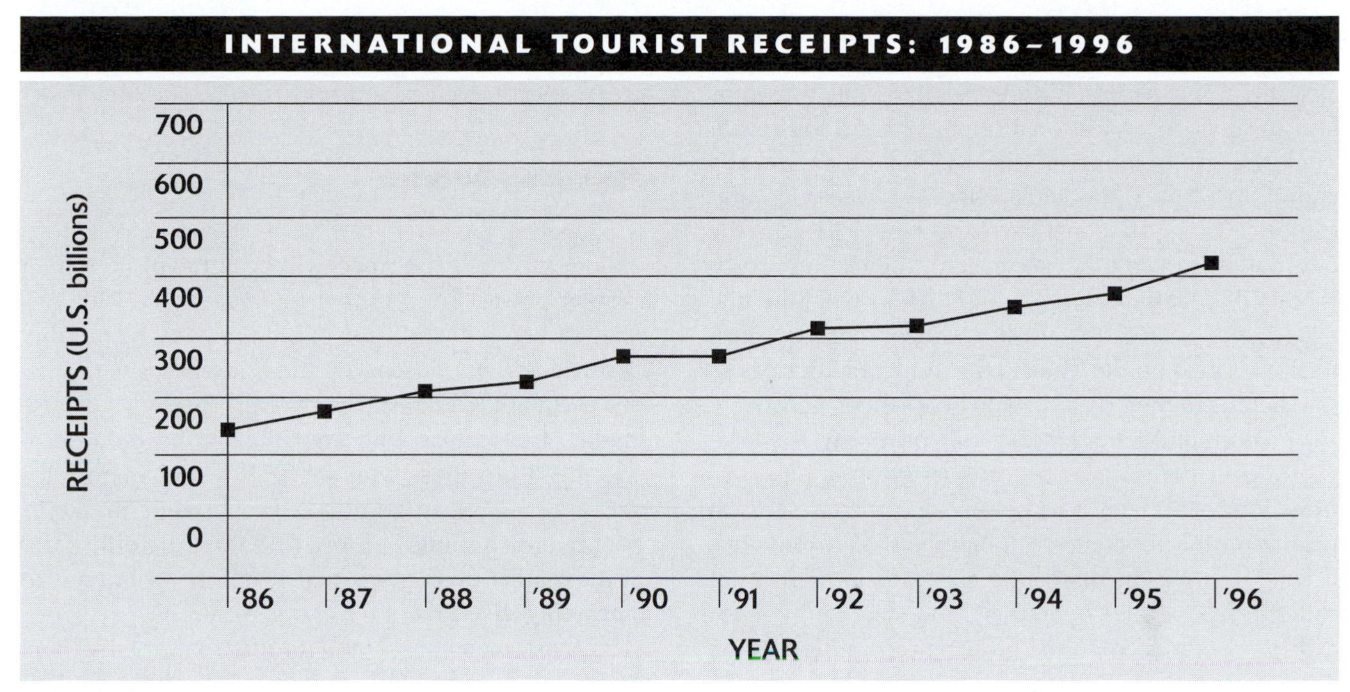

FIGURE 1–5 International tourists spending increased to over $400 billion in 1996. *Source:* World Tourism Organization, Tourism Market Trends, 1997.

mode of transportation, travel dates, price range, accommodations required—and then try to match these needs with the appropriate travel products. When customers have decided on certain products, travel agents complete the sales transaction by making reservations, providing vouchers, or writing tickets.

Travel agents use intelligence, perseverance, and an understanding of human psychology to turn an inquiry from an interested customer into a solid booking. In addition to being enthusiastic about the products they sell, travel agents must be able to locate a variety of information quickly and accurately. They must be able to give their customers up-to-date information on schedules, fares, rates, special discounts, regulations, and travel conditions. A top-notch travel agent is aware of information not available in a travel brochure, such as what the driving conditions in a foreign country are like or what a traveler should expect to pay for a meal in a restaurant.

As travel products become more complex and competitive, college-level learning is becoming more important for travel agents. Courses in business and foreign language are useful, as are courses in travel agency operation. Broad traveling experience is extremely helpful, and a good knowledge of geography is essential. Travel agents hoping for advancement can specialize in a certain area of travel, become agency managers, move to larger agencies, or open their own agencies.

In addition to working for retail travel agencies, travel agents can work for airlines, cruise lines, railroads, automobile clubs, tour operators, and government tourist offices. Some travel agents work for organizations that plan incentive trips, which are used as prizes in contests or as rewards for employee performance. Others work for corporations that have their own travel departments.

Destination Marketer

New York City attracts more than thirty-three million visitors every year. These visitors spend about $18 billion, which makes tourism one of the city's largest industries. This success is due in part to the superb marketing efforts of the New York Convention and Visitors Bureau. The ***destination marketers*** who work for the Bureau focus on New York's glamorous attractions such as Broadway theaters, department stores, Central Park, Times Square, Wall Street, the Statue of Liberty, and the Empire State Building.

Destination marketers also work for destination marketing companies (private) or destination marketing organizations (public). They attempt to stimulate interest in their town, city, state, province, or region so that individual travelers, meeting and convention planners, tour operators, and travel agents will recommend it to their organizations and clients. Rather than representing a certain company, the marketer tries to sell all aspects of a destination—its hotels and restaurants, its museums and theaters, its recreational opportunities, and so on. They sell the destination with the aid of multimedia shows, brochures, special promotions, Web sites, and exhibits. Often, these marketers will bring clients to the destination so that they can see it for themselves, which is called a familiarization trip. After whetting the appetites of prospective customers, these marketing professionals pass on the leads to the individual businesses that belong to their organization or are their clients.

Destination marketers work primarily for local visitor and convention bureaus (nonprofit organizations funded in large part by private businesses), local tourist promotion agencies (chambers of commerce), private destination marketing companies (sometimes called receptive tour operators), and state and provincial travel offices. With the growing recognition of the economic importance of tourism, almost every city in North America has established some form of tourism promotion agency. This, in turn, creates a need for destination marketers, making it one of the hottest careers in tourism sales and marketing. Advancement comes by working up through the organization as a manager to reach the level of vice president or president/Chief Executive Officer (CEO), or by moving to another office in a larger, more popular destination.

Tour Operator

Tour operators design and sell tours and travel packages for independent travelers or escorted clients. They plan itineraries—what routes to take, where to stay, and what to see—and make all arrangements for the tour or package in advance. They purchase or reserve all the necessary components such as airline transportation, hotel accommodations, and admission to attractions. They may also recruit and train tour escorts or purchase these services from other sources. Tour operators then sell these packages to consumers, either through retail travel agencies or directly.

Tour operators may be small family-run companies or large corporations such as American Express, with tours going all over the world. In the corporate case, many levels of marketing employees would be required. For example, the sales representative of the tour operator would have responsibility for promoting the company's tour products and services. Tour operators that are small companies, or even individuals, often specialize in specific geographic regions or types of travel. For example, Mush Alaska, a successful Alaskan tour operator, packages winter dogsled excursions to Denali National Park.

Marketing Director

During the early years of the twenty-first century, middle-aged baby boomers will be at the peak of their earning power. The number of households with two wage earners will continue to grow, as will the number of single-parent households and households with only one occupant. Older Americans will represent a diverse market, from those who are homebound because of poor health to those who are healthy and anxious for new experiences. In addition, the Hispanic market is expected to continue to grow. And these are only a few of the market predictions that would be of interest to ***marketing directors*** of travel organizations.

Most large travel and tourism companies and organizations have marketing directors, although their duties may vary considerably. In some companies, the marketing director supervises the entire marketing process—including sales. In companies where marketing and sales are separate departments, the marketing director usually oversees market planning and the sales manager assumes responsibility for sales transactions.

Whatever their duties, all marketing directors are concerned with analyzing the market potential for a particular product or service. They study sales figures, supervise research, anticipate market demand, and create strategies and tactics. Marketing directors are responsible for the final interpretation of data and recommend a course of action that meets objectives and is within the budget, resources, and capabilities of the company.

Many years of experience are needed to become a marketing director. Many marketing directors have earned a master's degree. Starting out in sales, advertising, or product development is a way of pursuing this career opportunity.

Sales Manager

A ***sales manager*** has responsibility for the sales department of a company or organization. Sales managers train, direct, and evaluate the sales staff of cruise lines, hotel chains, tour operators, attractions, and other travel companies. They coordinate the operation of the sales department by establishing client lists, goals, and quotas for sales representatives. They represent their products and services at trade association conventions and meetings. Some sales managers also become involved in market research and product development. The company's size determines a sales manager's exact responsibilities. Small companies and organizations may have only one sales manager. Large corporations, on the other hand, may have sales managers to direct each level of marketing and sales or each product category.

Like marketing directors, sales managers must have years of experience in sales and marketing. A bachelor's or master's degree is usually required. The customary career path is to start as a sales representative or associate.

Sales Representative

All major destination marketing organizations, airlines, hotels, cruise lines, motor coach companies, car rental agencies, and tourist attractions employ ***sales representatives***. Sales representatives must know their products and services extremely well and be able to explain how they meet customers' needs. Although advertising and other promotional efforts may encourage customers to buy travel products, the efforts of salespeople are needed to close the sale. As with other sales careers, knowledge, enthusiasm, and a positive attitude are essential.

Hotel Sales Representative. Hotel sales representatives contact government, business, and professional associations and societies, to capture their corporate accounts and solicit their convention business for the hotel. The representative analyzes the group's requirements, such as amount of space, audiovisual needs, food service, and events, and then quotes prices. He or she may be on hand during the convention to take care of last-minute details or to resolve problems.

Rental Car Sales Representative. During the 1990s, the rental car industry enjoyed a huge upswing in business. Much of this growth can be attributed to the efforts of car rental sales representatives, who call on business accounts to promote car rentals to business travelers or use telemarketing to generate sales. They also work with travel agents, airlines, tour operators, and hotels in setting up package deals for corporate customers who rent cars in large volume.

Cruise Line Sales. Cruise line sales representatives work closely with tour operators and travel agents. They try to persuade them to represent the products of the cruise line. Sales representatives instruct these operators and agents about the products so that they are better informed when dealing with the public. Sales representatives also help travel agencies and tour operators with promotions.

Tour Company Representative. For decades, European and Asian markets have favored traveling in groups for vacations (holidays). In recent years, North Americans have begun to appreciate the value of independent and preformed (clubs, social groups, athletic teams, etc.) group travel. Representatives of tour companies contact group leaders (responsible for planning trips) of scholastic athletic departments, alumni groups, travel agents, travel clubs, and other organizations that travel in groups, to encourage them to purchase travel products and services. They offer packaged trips, optional tours, and exceptional rates to an increasingly diverse clientele.

Destination Marketing Company Representative. As demand and corresponding supply for a destination expand, the role of destination marketing companies (receptive tour operators) has increased in importance. In popular destinations they purchase accommodations, meals, transfers, and admissions to attractions in large volume, and at discounted prices. Their marketing representatives then sell these products and services to corporations, tour operators, and large travel agencies that send customers to that destination. The destination marketing company then "receives" the visitors once they reach their destination, handling local transportation, transfers, attractions admissions, hotel registrations and meals, on behalf of the tour operator, travel agent, or organization that sold the travel products and services directly to the individual visitor (or group).

Travel marketing and sales is an exciting field offering a variety of challenging careers. Marketing and sales professionals identify customer needs and devise and implement the strategies and methods that persuade customers to buy their travel products. They work creatively to stimulate demand for their products in order to stay ahead of their competition in the dynamic travel marketplace.

CHAPTER SUMMARY

- The terms "marketing" and "sales" are not interchangeable. The process of marketing includes finding out what consumers want, offering a product to meet consumer needs, identifying the market, informing consumers of the product's availability, making the sale, and evaluating the entire process. The sale is an exchange of money for a product or a promise to deliver a product, often facilitated by a salesperson.

* To be successful in today's marketplace, companies must pay attention to marketing. This is especially true for the travel and tourism industry, which is characterized by intense competition.
* Market research attempts to discover potential markets by understanding consumers' needs and wants. It also tries to determine consumers' reactions to products and services that they have purchased.
* Customer-oriented companies develop their products and services to meet the needs of a segment of the market. At the same time, the ways in which companies respond to the marketplace must make business sense for the organization.
* A marketing plan is used to determine and implement the steps of the marketing cycle.
* Evaluation and follow-up are important components of the marketing process.
* Social, economic, and technological change have historically influenced the way travel products have been marketed and sold.
* Many exciting career opportunities are available in travel marketing and sales.

KEY TERMS

marketing
sales
product-oriented marketing
sales-oriented marketing
customer-oriented marketing
marketing plans
target market
product positioning
marketing objectives
relationship marketing
travel agent
destination marketers
tour operators
marketing directors
sales manager
sales representatives

DISCUSSION QUESTIONS

1. What aspect of marketing do you think has changed the most in the past ten years? Explain your answer.
2. Do you think the market for travel and tourism will continue to grow? Why or why not?
3. What are the components of the marketing cycle? Why is the marketing process described as a cycle?
4. Why is a marketing plan important for the modern travel and tourism industry?
5. Why do you think intelligence, perseverance, and an understanding of psychology are important for travel sales representatives?
6. Do you think the demand for products and services offered by tour operators is likely to increase or decrease in the near future? Why?

STUDY GUIDE

Understanding Marketing and Sales

Name: ______________________________ Date: ______________

Directions: Answer these questions as you read the chapter. You will be able to use these answers to help you review the chapter.

1. What is the difference between marketing and sales?

____

____

____

____

2. Who are the sellers of the travel industry?

____

____

____

____

3. What are the three main categories of buyers in the travel industry?

____

____

____

____

4. What are the three categories of intermediaries?

____

____

____

____

5. What is a market?

____

____

____

____

6. Briefly describe each type of marketing.

Product-oriented: ______________________________

Sales-oriented: ______________________________

Customer-oriented: ______________________________

7. Which of the types of marketing listed in Question 6 is used most often today? Why?

8. Name and briefly describe the basic steps of the marketing cycle.

9. What is a target market?

10. What does it mean to position a product?

11. Define a marketing objective and give an example.

12. Why doesn't the marketing cycle end when a sale is made?

13. How can relationship marketing enhance a business?

14. What nineteenth-century advances in transportation opened the travel market to Europe's middle classes?

15. How did twentieth-century advances in transportation further expand the travel market?

16. What is the difference between a travel agent and a destination marketer?

17. Briefly describe the job duties of each occupation.

Tour operator:

Marketing director:

Sales manager:

18. Name three types of sales representatives.

WORKSHEET

Understanding Marketing and Sales

CHAPTER

Name: ______________________________ Date: ______________

TRAVEL AND TOURISM CAREER SEARCH

You have just completed your third year as a travel agent in a large, diversified company located in a major city. You have gained experience handling all types of tour arrangements. During the past year you have also attended classes in travel marketing in order to advance to a higher-paying job with more (and different) responsibilities than those you have had as a travel agent. You are considering applying for one or more of the following types of positions. Answer the questions related to each of the following jobs:

1. Travel Agency Director

A. What are the basic responsibilities?

____

____

____

____

____

B. What background and training are needed?

____

____

____

____

____

C. How are marketing skills used in this position?

____

____

____

____

____

2. Destination Marketer

A. What are the basic responsibilities?

____

____

____

____

____

B. What background and training are needed?

C. How are marketing skills used in this position?

3. Tour Operator

A. What are the basic responsibilities?

B. What background and training are needed?

C. How are marketing skills used in this position?

4. Marketing Director

A. What are the basic responsibilities?

B. What background and training are needed?

C. How are marketing skills used in this position?

5. Sales Manager

A. What are the basic responsibilities?

B. What background and training are needed?

C. How are marketing skills used in this position?

6. Sales Representative (hotel, car rental company, or cruise line)

A. What are the basic responsibilities?

B. What background and training are needed?

C. How are marketing skills used in this position?

7. Tour Company Representative

A. What are the basic responsibilities?

B. What background and training are needed?

C. How are marketing skills used in this position?

Analyzing the Travel Product

OBJECTIVES

When you have completed this chapter, you should be able to:

- Give examples of ways in which the travel and tourism industry markets and sells its intangible products and services.
- Explain how simultaneous production and consumption makes each travel product unique.
- Explain the concept of perishability and its effect on marketing travel products.
- Define seasonality, parity, uniqueness, and complementarity, and tell how these characteristics influence the marketing of travel products.
- Discuss the relationship between travel products and service quality.

Janet and Richard Hawkins, a retired couple from Iowa, are customers of the travel and tourism industry. Their most recent trip was a cruise along the southeastern Alaskan coast. They paid Jackson Tours $6,000 for this package tour. For their money, they received air transportation to Vancouver, British Columbia to start the tour, accommodations on a cruise ship and a hotel (for a total of ten nights), a white-water rafting trip, and a trip on a float plane over Misty Fjords. All tips for bellmen (porters) and local guides were included in the price of the tour. Additionally, Janet and Richard purchased their meals on land as well as admission to attractions such as the Alaska Indian Arts Center and St. Michael's Cathedral (Russian Orthodox), which is now a cultural center.

WHAT IS THE TRAVEL PRODUCT?

As you know, an industry is a group of businesses or corporations and the people who work for them. The automobile industry, the insurance industry, and the computer industry are a few examples of better-known industries in the United States. Industries produce a product, a service, or a mix of products and services. A product is something that is developed, manufactured, grown, or extracted. It is meant to be consumed or used by the buyer. An automobile, a bushel of wheat, and iron ore are examples of products. A service, on the other hand, is an activity or a deed that benefits someone. If you hire an accountant to figure out your income taxes or consult a physician about your chest cold, you are purchasing a service.

Janet and Richard received many services when they purchased their cruise from Jackson Tours. (Courtesy of Crystal Cruise Lines)

Most industries produce either products or services. But the travel and tourism industry is unusual in that it simultaneously produces both products and services. When Janet and Richard purchased their cruise—a product—they were also purchasing many services. Someone else planned the itinerary for them, made their hotel and ship arrangements, assisted them en route and made meal reservations for them. In fact, Janet and Richard decided to purchase a cruise—rather than travel on their own—so that they would get these services.

CHARACTERISTICS OF THE TRAVEL PRODUCT

Travel products have several characteristics that distinguish them from the products of most other industries. These include intangibility, simultaneous production and consumption, perishability, seasonality, parity, uniqueness, and complementarity. Each of these characteristics influences how travel products are marketed and sold.

Intangibility

By the time Janet and Richard returned home, they had acquired an Alaskan smoked salmon, a small collection of brochures they had picked up along the way, and some Inuit painted scarves. They also had a receipt from the cruise company, a copy of their itinerary, and a map showing their route along the coast. Considering that they had spent over $6,000, Janet and Richard didn't seem to have much to show for their trip. Even so, they felt that the money had been well spent. They returned home relaxed and refreshed. They had learned about a part of the country they had never seen before, and they had made many new friends.

Janet and Richard's trip illustrates a major characteristic of travel and tourism products. The products of most industries are ***tangible***. They can be seen, touched, and sometimes even smelled and tasted. They have weight and take up space. An automobile, a pair of shoes, and a washing machine are tangible products.

Travel products, on the other hand, have certain ***intangible*** aspects. The latter cannot be seen or touched. Travel products include experiencing a flight on an airplane, a cruise on an ocean liner, a night's rest in a hotel, a visit to an art museum, a view of the mountains, a good time in a nightclub, and much more. These products are experiences. Once they have taken place, they exist only as memories that can be recalled and relished. Tangible objects such as a seat on an airplane, a bed in a hotel room, and food in a restaurant are used to help create the experiences, but these are not what the customer is seeking. Rather, the customer wants the intangible benefits—pleasure, relaxation, convenience, excitement—that the experiences can yield. The tangible products that are purchased provide access to the intangibles that are sought.

Marketing and Selling Tangible Products. A tangible product can be sold on the basis of how it looks and performs. A guarantee of satisfaction usually accompanies a tangible product—if the product is defective, the customer can return or exchange it. For example, a salesperson in an automobile showroom can interest a prospective buyer in a car's observable features—aerodynamic design, all-leather upholstery, front-wheel drive, and so on. The customer can take the car for a test drive to see how it handles on the road. To clinch the sale, the salesperson can point out the thirty-six-month bumper-to-bumper warranty.

Marketing and Selling Intangible Products. Because of the intangible nature of travel products, they are more difficult to market and sell than tangible products. A travel agent, for example, can't place a trip in front of prospective customers and tell them to look at it from all angles. Customers can't try the trip out before paying for it. If the customers go on the trip and have a bad experience they can't return it. Customers have to trust that destinations and travel companies will deliver on their promises.

The travel and tourism industry must, therefore, rely on other methods to sell its products. One method is to strengthen the customer/supplier relationship. Travel suppliers seek to gain the confidence of customers through their record of performance or through personalized service. Customers then come to trust what companies say about their products and services.

Another method is to emphasize the benefits to be gained from buying travel products. Wherever possible, the industry seeks to make these benefits seem tangible by representing travel products visually. An example would be colorful photographs in glossy brochures and magazines. Janet and Richard originally became interested in taking a trip to Alaska after attending a travel party sponsored by Jackson Tours. At the party they viewed a videotape of happy, healthy people sunning themselves on the ship's deck; enjoying a barbecue ashore; posing beside colorful Indian totem poles; photographing otters, bald eagles, and seals; and taking in the spectacular scenery. The videotape suggested that if Janet and Richard purchased this cruise, they, too, could enjoy such experiences.

When focusing on benefits, the travel industry recognizes that travel products mean different things to different people. For example, business travelers see an airline flight as a necessary part of getting their jobs done. The marketing focus is likely to be on timely arrival and speed. Vacation and leisure travelers see a flight as an experience representing an escape from their everyday world. Promotions for leisure travel feature images of excitement, glamour, romance, and relaxation. In contrast, an airline ticket is a stressful purchase for people traveling because of a family crisis, and they will need a higher level of understanding and efficiency.

Travel products do not come off an assembly line. Each product is unique—depending on the moment in time, the place, and the people involved.

Simultaneous Production and Consumption

Most travel products are produced and consumed in the same place and at the same time. To understand the significance of such interdependence, consider first how most tangible products are produced and consumed: they are produced in one location and consumed in another location. A factory in Michigan manufactures a line of washing machines with the model number KAWE900. The washing machines are shipped to retail stores all over the United States. A customer in Montana buys Model KAWE900 and takes it home. A customer in Kentucky also buys Model KAWE900. Because the procedure and machinery for manufacturing the washing machines were standardized at the factory and closely supervised, each customer's washing machine should be exactly the same—even though the machines may have been assembled on different days.

In contrast most *travel products are sold first, then simultaneously produced and consumed.* For example, when Janet and Richard bought their cruise package, they used it (experienced it) as the cruise progressed (was produced), mile after mile. In the same way, an airline passenger consumes a flight as it is being produced, and a hotel guest uses a hotel room as it is made available for a night's sleep. Thus, these travelers are participating in a situation of ***simultaneous production and consumption***.

The fact that travel products are produced and consumed simultaneously creates a certain level of ***interdependence*** between suppliers and customers. Because the production and consumption of travel products occur in the supplier's equipment or on the supplier's premises, customers and suppliers must interact, and their interaction shapes the travel experience. Janet and Richard, for example, could not take their cruise home with them. In fact, they had to leave their home in Fort Dodge, Iowa, and "pick up" the cruise in Vancouver. The tour took place on a ship belonging to a travel product supplier of Jackson Tours, in this case a cruise line.

The actions and attitude of the ship's staff—representatives of the supplier—and the actions and expectations of the travelers on the cruise did much to determine what kind of trip everyone had. Janet and

Richard's trip was made more pleasant because the ship's staff were friendly and helpful and their fellow passengers were cheerful and considerate. The interdependence of travelers with travel company employees is one of the reasons consistent, high-quality service is critical in the travel industry.

Perishability

Janet and Richard's cruise was supposed to reach Petersburg by the second night of their trip. The group had dinner reservations for a smorgasbord at the Sons of Norway Hall. Because they unexpectedly sighted and followed some humpback whales earlier that day, they were fifty miles away from Petersburg at dinnertime. The cruise director telephoned the Sons of Norway Hall and cancelled the group's dinner for that evening and then made other arrangements. Although the restaurant collected a cancellation fee from the tour company, the restaurant still lost money since it was not able to sell the dinners to other travelers that night. The dinners could not be sold as planned and therefore "perished."

Perishability is another characteristic of travel and tourism products. It is related to the fact that travel products are intended to be consumed as they are produced. An airline has a specific number of seats to sell on each of its flights. A hotel has a specific number of rooms available for each night of the week. If no one purchases a ticket for a particular airline seat by the time the flight departs or stays in a particular hotel room before the night is over, then the opportunity to sell that product is lost and gone forever. It can't be kept in the travel company's inventory.

By contrast, tangible products have a much longer shelf life, or period in which they can be sold. Consider again the example of the washing machines. After coming off the assembly line the washing machines can be stored in a warehouse until they are ready for distribution. Once in the retail stores, they can stay on the floor for months. If they aren't sold right away, they might be moved to another part of the store, shipped to another outlet, or put back in inventory for a while. Their price can be reduced to encourage a quick sale. Tangible products vary in the length of their shelf life, but even more perishable items such as fruits and vegetables can be sold beyond their freshness date. The same is not true of intangible travel products.

The travel industry, however, has developed several marketing strategies to protect itself against unsold products. One strategy is overbooking. An airline will sell more seats than are actually available on a flight, anticipating that a certain number of passengers will fail to show up for the flight. That way, the airline can fill seats that would otherwise remain empty.

Another strategy is multiple distribution. The washing machines can only be purchased through retail stores or wholesale dealers. A customer doesn't ordinarily go directly to the manufacturer to buy a washing machine. A travel product, on the other hand, can often be purchased directly from the supplier or from wholesale or retail outlets. A customer can buy an airline ticket directly from an airline, a tour operator, or from a travel agent. Providing more distribution outlets for travel products increases the chances that they will be sold and not "perish." More details about travel product distribution are provided in Chapter 8.

Seasonality

Many travel and tourism products are subject to seasonality. ***Seasonality*** is the fluctuation in demand for travel at different times of year. In the winter, people in northern North America flock to the sunny and warm climates of Florida, Arizona, Mexico, and the Caribbean to escape the cold weather. The demand for travel products such as rooms in hotels and resorts increases in those regions in the winter. The demand decreases in the summer when northerners stay home to enjoy their own cooler climate.

Although seasonality generally refers to travel products affected by weather conditions, it can also refer to fluctuations in demand according to the day of the week, or even the hour of the day. This is very apparent with the airlines. The demand for flights on Friday or Monday is often greater than for flights Tuesday through Thursday because most people—especially business travelers—want to be home on the weekends. The demand for day flights, particularly early morning and late afternoon, is greater than for late-night flights because most travelers would rather arrive at their destination during daylight hours. Holidays also influence the demand for travel products. Ski resorts, for instance, are more crowded than usual over the Christmas holiday.

For products affected by seasonality, the marketing challenge is to produce revenue during off-peak seasons. Travel suppliers try to even out the use of their products or to create demand for their products during down periods. The most notable way of doing this is to lower prices during the off-season. Airlines, for example, offer reduced fares to encourage travelers to take weekend or late-night flights. A stay at a Caribbean resort is usually less expensive in the summer than in the winter. This marketing technique appeals to travelers who are looking for a bargain or seeking to avoid crowds.

Another technique for overcoming seasonality is to create special activities for off-peak seasons. Rather than bemoaning the cold weather, several northern cities have turned it into a tourist attraction by creating winter carnivals. The St. Paul (Minnesota) Winter Carnival, for instance, attracts thousands of visitors with its ice sculptures, torchlight parade, dogsled races, ice fishing contests, and many other winter activities. Some tourism businesses change their focus altogether during the off-season. Instead of closing for the summer, some ski resorts offer their facilities as convention or cultural (concerts, theater, etc.) centers.

Finally, travel suppliers keep track of the seasonal rise and fall of their profits and adjust their production capacity accordingly. This might mean, for example, reducing the number of employees or closing a percentage of hotel rooms during the off-season. Travel businesses can also raise prices or require a minimum stay during high-demand periods to help cover losses incurred during slower seasons.

Parity

Some travel products—especially the products of transportation companies—are essentially comparable; that is, they possess ***parity***. Parity means that competing companies offer the same basic product. A flight on one airline is very much like a flight on another airline, since the airplanes may be manufactured by the same company and because government regulations require all pilots to meet the same training standards. Even the food served on airlines is similar, very often having been prepared in an airport kitchen that supplies more than one airline. If passengers were to close their eyes, they might not remember on which airline they were flying.

The fact that so many qualities are the same creates a marketing problem. How can one airline or hotel convince consumers to choose its product over an identical competing one? To be successful in the marketplace, a company must address the problem of parity. One way to do this is to make a product seem different from that of its competitors, even though no meaningful difference actually exists. Thus, a company will emphasize differences that are linked to benefits that will be provided, rather than the product itself.

Janet and Richard, for example, chose Jackson Tours largely because its cruise brochure included photographs of older travelers. Jackson's chief competitor, Blueline Tours, offered virtually the same itinerary at a lower price, but its brochure used photos with very young attractive models. Almost without realizing it, Janet and Richard found themselves feeling more comfortable with the prospect of the cruise with Jackson Tours rather than Blueline Tours.

More recently, companies that provide travel products and services have focused on the level and quality of their service to differentiate themselves from their competitors. Consistent, predictable service excellence is relished by all travelers, but is expected by business travelers. For example, when you fly American Airlines you are flying "something special in the air"; when you fly on Delta you will find that "we love to fly and it shows." Good service makes a travel experience more enjoyable, rewarding, and relaxing. Those companies and organizations that meet their customers' service expectations will earn their repeat business.

Another technique companies use to solve the problem of parity is frequent travel programs. A company will entice customers to keep using its product by offering various incentives including reduced prices and special services. Frequent-flier/guest programs are perhaps the most common example of an attempt to build ***brand loyalty***. For every mile flown (or night's stay), the customer accumulates points that can be applied to free travel/nights, upgrades in class, or discounted fares/rates.

Uniqueness

Of course, parity is not a problem when the travel product is unique. Many destinations and attractions, for instance, have built-in appeal because they are so different and remarkable. Places such as Hawaii, Washington, D.C., Yellowstone National Park, the Eiffel Tower, Buckingham Palace, and the Statue of Liberty offer experiences with ***uniqueness***, that cannot be duplicated anywhere else, and thus attract thousands of customers with relatively little promotion. Although it is true that standardization appeals to many travelers, others prefer the charm of nonstandardized products—perhaps a stay in a quaint bed-and-breakfast inn rather than in a chain hotel.

The *unique aspects of a travel product should be featured in all marketing efforts conducted on behalf of that product.* This helps potential customers to clearly differentiate it from similar products by identifying the appealing characteristics and the benefits that will be experienced.

Complementarity

A traveler rarely purchases just a single travel product. As mentioned, in addition to paying for a cruise package, Janet and Richard purchased some meals in restaurants and admission to several tourist attractions. Even business travelers, who are primarily interested in getting to their destinations quickly and efficiently, will purchase rental cars and hotel accommodations in addition to air transportation.

The purchase of one travel product sets up a chain reaction of travel purchases (see Figure 2–1). *As a result, what affects one product affects another—for better or for worse.* If an airline that flies skiers to a resort changes its frequency of flights or goes out of business, the ski resort's business will suffer. If fewer skiers are coming to the ski resort, there will be fewer customers for nearby restaurants and shops. The fortunes of all these businesses are linked even though they may be separately owned. This close relationship of travel products is referred to as ***complementarity***, and it is a characteristic of all travel products.

Travel suppliers are becoming increasingly aware of the complementarity of their products. As a result, more and more companies are participating in joint marketing ventures. Fly/cruise packages, whereby an airline and a cruise company cooperate in designing a travel package, are one example of joint marketing. Frequent traveler programs are also a source of cooperation among companies. By patronizing a particular hotel chain, for instance, a guest accumulates points that can be applied to discounts on car rentals or airline tickets, and vice versa.

Joint marketing ventures and other mutual efforts are especially necessary because of the competition for the discretionary dollar: the money people have left to spend after the necessities of life—food, clothing, and shelter—have been paid for. Spending money on vacations or leisure travel is only one way of using the discretionary dollar. New houses, VCRs, personal computers, and many other tangible products entice consumers in the market. Whereas most people tend to think of travel suppliers as competing with each other, competition from nontravel products is even more threatening. The various components of the travel industry need to work together to promote travel products and their destinations as the most desired activity for the discretionary dollar.

THE SERVICE ASPECT

As mentioned, a service is an activity or deed performed for the benefit of others. The service can be performed by a human being or by a machine. The banking industry provides a service by keeping people's money safe. If you want to withdraw money from

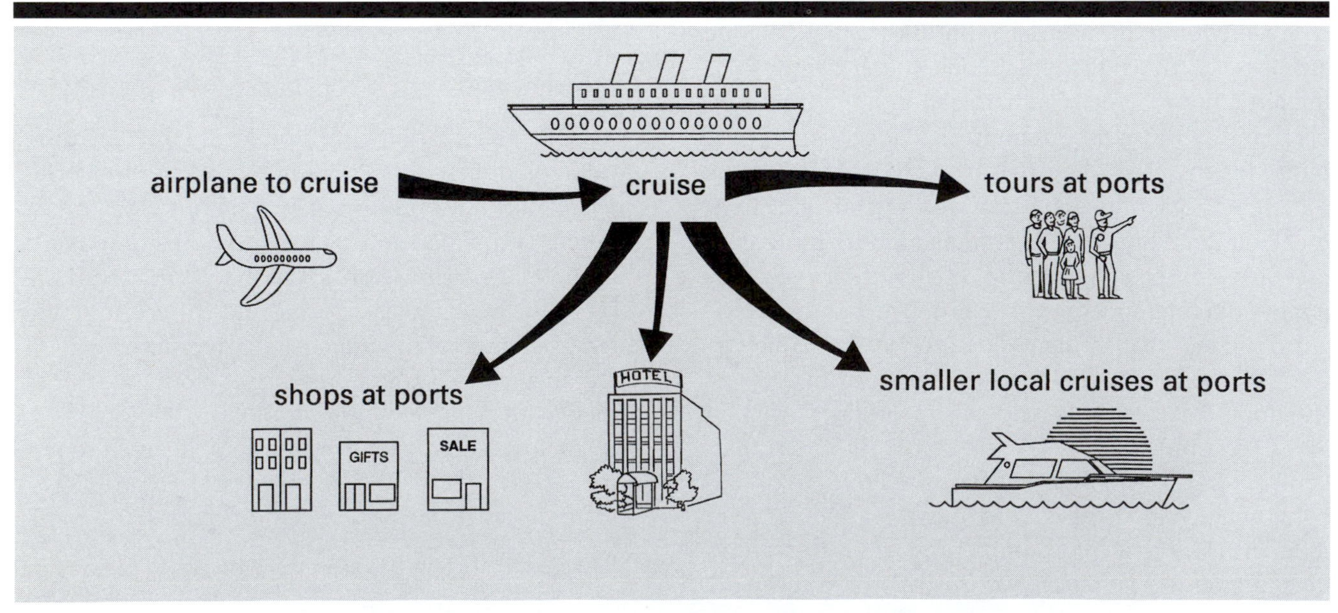

FIGURE 2–1 The purchase of one travel product causes a chain reaction, since consumers rarely buy just one travel product. Many products go hand in hand.

Marketing Impressions

"THE EVER-EVOLVING WORLD OF EVENT MANAGEMENT"
BY SUZANNE BRISTOW, CSEP

The new world of event management is both an art and a science. It requires not only extreme creativity, but meticulous attention to detail.

Dr. Joe Goldblatt, CSEP, in his book *Special Events: Best Practices in Modern Event Management,* writes "the most interesting finding of the International Special Events Society study was that only 50 percent of the event managers' work was invested in the management of events. This explains the *'multidisciplinary'* nature of this emerging discipline." So if only 50 percent of event management time is spent on management, what makes up the other 50 percent? The answer: (1) *research,* (2) *design,* (3) *planning,* (4) *coordination,* (5) *marketing,* and (6) *evaluation.*

The *research* phase of an event is extremely important and requires the most time of the six disciplines. If your research is complete, your event is a success.

Designing the event is the creative phase. The look and feel of the event is developed based on your research. Brainstorming techniques are used for the theme, the decor, the catering, and the entertainment.

Planning the event requires particular attention to detail and logistics for the event to succeed.

The challenge of the event *coordination* phase is to make sure that the event manager coordinates the event components properly. The event manager is responsible for the coordination of full-time staff and volunteers, training, orientation, and all the necessary disciplines within the event.

Marketing the event is key. You can have the best event in the world but if no one knows about it—it will not be a success.

The *evaluation* of the event is as important to the client as it is to the event manager. It serves as a measure of success, and provides invaluable records.

The industry definition of an event manager is: an individual who is responsible for the total delivery of an event. While they may participate in the event planning, their primary purpose is to coordinate and manage the various parties involved in the event, both internal and external, so that the end result is the *competent, safe delivery* of the event.

I am sure that many of you reading this have, at some time, managed an event. Were you aware of the areas of crisis and risk management, the importance of liability insurance, the absolute necessity to know local by-laws and permit requirements?

Associations such as ISES (International Special Events Society) and MPI (Meeting Professionals International) continue to raise the bar on professionalism and insist on an ever-increasing knowledge of the industry.

Courses in event management are offered at universities and colleges around the world. Degrees and certifications are available both from within the industry and at the universities. Event management is an industry hurtling toward a profession.

Individuals and corporations are investing millions of dollars in events. They deserve, and have the right to expect, a highly qualified individual to manage their investment.

If you are a student of philosophy or psychology you cannot talk to Plato or Freud, but as a student of event management you can talk to the experts.

Suzanne Bristow is a Certified Special Events Professional, one of three in Canada and fifty in the world. She is president and CEO of Crossroads Entertainment and Event Corporation in Toronto and a professor at Ryerson Polytechnic University, where she teaches the course, "Managing Festivals, Events, and Attractions."

your account, you can go to an automatic teller machine, or you can ask a bank teller to make the transaction for you.

Although it's possible to receive some travel services from machines (you can purchase an airline ticket from an automated ticketing machine, for instance), most services in the travel and tourism industry are performed by human beings. People performed many services for Janet and Richard throughout their Alaska trip. Restaurant servers, housekeepers, and tour guides all provided services essential to making their vacation enjoyable. Performers entertained them at a Russian dance festival, and salespeople assisted them in shops.

Of course, the main service coordinators were the ship's captain, its steward, and its on-board naturalist, all of whom combined to make their cruise safe, trouble-free, and educational.

Relationship of Travel Products and Services

Industries may or may not produce services along with their products. Industries that produce tangible products aren't likely to produce services as well. Customers don't need assistance in purchasing or using these products. A box of detergent or a jar of pickles, for instance, can be purchased in a self-service store. A pair of shoes or a set of bath towels can be ordered through a catalog. These products do not require major repair services to make them last longer.

Other industries that produce tangible products offer supporting services to enhance the value of their products. Supporting services might include installing the product or making repairs readily available. In the case of a more complicated product such as a computer, a company might offer to teach customers how to use it. Often, customers decide to purchase a product largely on the basis of these supporting services; for example, they choose to buy a car from a dealership that has a good service department or a washing machine from a store with its own repair staff.

With intangible products, service is not an addition to the product, but an integral part. Indeed, industries that produce intangible products must emphasize their service. Otherwise the product would not be appealing. A flight on an airplane wouldn't be possible without the efforts of pilots, mechanics, flight attendants, and many more people (see Figure 2–2). A night's stay in a hotel depends on the activities of a hotel manager, front desk associates, bellmen, and housekeeping personnel. While producing its products, the travel industry is also providing services. As you read about travel products throughout this book, keep in mind that the element of service is included and is critical to customer satisfaction.

Service Quality and the Travel Product

Earlier in this chapter you read about the differences in the way tangible and intangible products are produced and consumed. Consider again the example of the washing machines. Because tangible products are produced in one place and consumed in another, the workers who manufacture the washing machines are never in contact with the customers who eventually buy them. Since the customers never see them, it doesn't matter what the workers look like or how they behave.

In contrast, intangible products are consumed as they are produced (interdependence), bringing suppliers and customers in direct contact. This means that the actions and attitudes of all employees—from a front desk associate to a hotel manager—are important in selling and marketing travel products. The difficulty in standardizing performance presents another challenge for marketing travel products—it is more difficult to sell products when their quality is unpredictable. Guaranteeing satisfaction with an intangible product isn't as easy as with a tangible product. Thus, if employees of travel companies are rude, inattentive, or slovenly, they will create a bad impression of the travel product, and they may ruin a customer's experience. Customers may even decide not to buy the product again.

For travel products to be successful in the market, the level of service provided must be more than adequate. It must be outstanding. When Janet and Richard returned home, they agreed that they had been treated royally throughout all of their trip. The hotels along the way had given their tour group a special welcome. Restaurants both on-board and ashore were waiting for them with reserved tables and speedy service. The entire crew of the cruise ship had not just performed their jobs—they had gone out of their way to be friendly and helpful. For example, the naturalist made special arrangements so that Janet, who loves to fish, could go out on a charter fishing boat when the ship moored overnight near Sitka.

As mentioned earlier, many travel products are essentially similar, so ***service quality*** becomes even more important given the parity among travel prod-

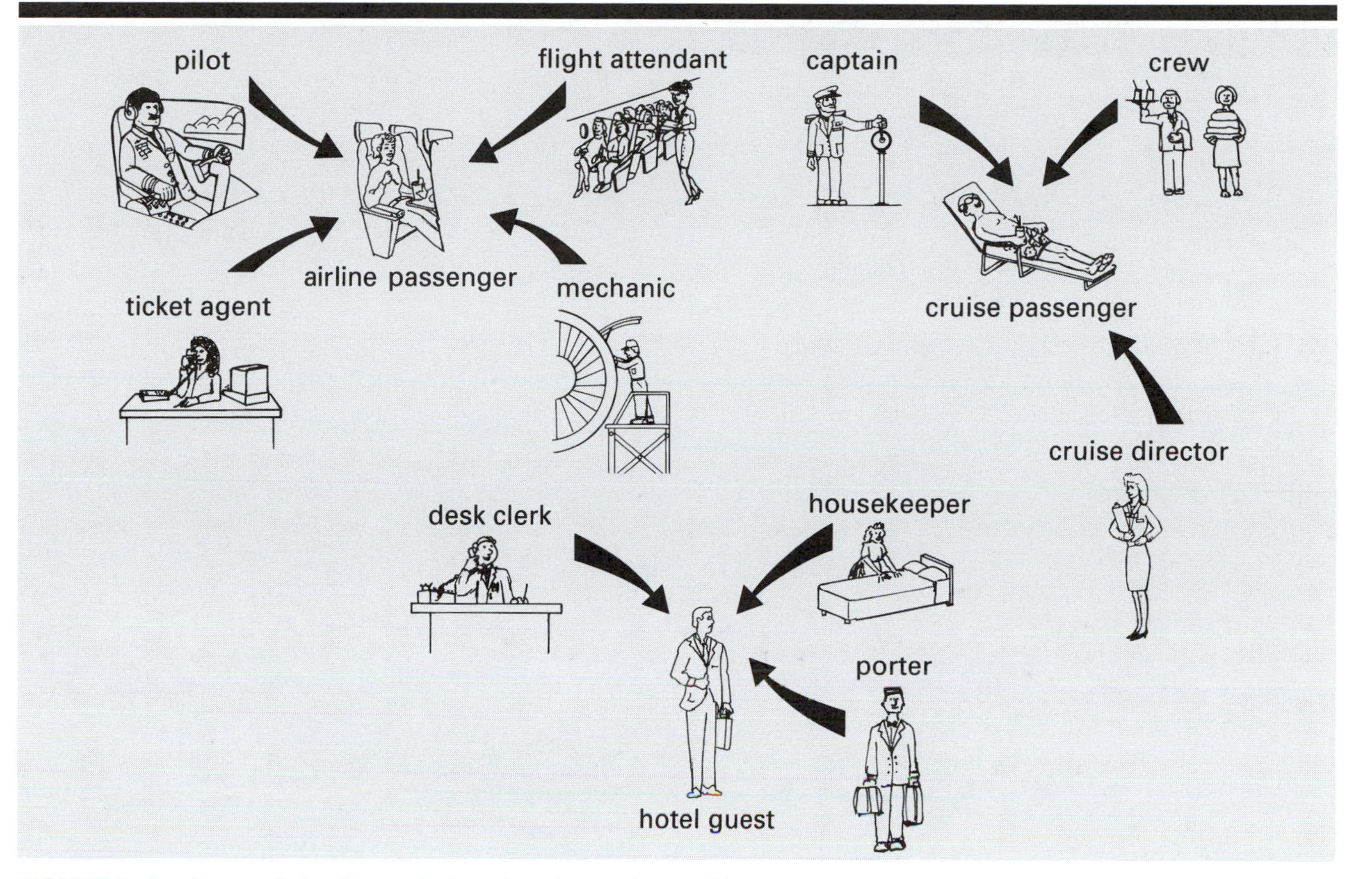

FIGURE 2–2 In many industries, products and services are inseparable.

ucts. One airplane seat is much like another. Similarly priced hotel rooms are likely to be similar in size and amenities. Often, therefore, the service quality makes all the difference in a customer's decision to purchase one travel product rather than another.

CHAPTER SUMMARY

* Characteristics of the travel product include intangibility, simultaneous production and consumption, perishability, seasonality, parity, uniqueness, and complementarity. Each characteristic influences how travel products are marketed.
* Unlike tangible products, travel products are consumed as they are produced. Also, suppliers and customers create the product together.
* Because of simultaneous production and consumption, travel products are difficult to standardize and their quality is unpredictable. No one travel product is exactly like another.
* Travel products can't be stored or inventoried—they must be used as they are produced, or else they perish.
* The season of the year, day of the week, and time of day affect the demand for travel products.
* The products of some travel companies are basically the same (parity), while other products are unique.
* Travel products are created through the efforts of employees who have direct contact with customers and provide excellent service. The attitudes and actions of service suppliers are extremely important in selling and marketing travel products.

KEY TERMS

tangible
intangible
simultaneous production and consumption
interdependence
perishability
seasonality
parity
brand loyalty
uniqueness
complementarity
service quality

DISCUSSION QUESTIONS

1. Give some examples of travel products not mentioned in the chapter. Why do people buy these products?
2. Why does intangibility make travel products more challenging to market and sell? How does the industry persuade customers to buy something they can't touch or test before buying?
3. What are two marketing strategies the travel industry uses to compensate for the perishability of its products? Do you think these strategies are effective? Explain.
4. Give an example of a seasonal travel product. What might the travel industry do to create a demand for that product in the off-season?
5. Give an example of a travel product that has parity. Then give an example of a nonparity product. How might the travel industry market and sell parity products?
6. Why is the travel and tourism industry referred to as a people-intensive industry? What significance does this have for marketing and selling?

Analyzing the Travel Product

Name: ______________________________ Date: ______________

Directions: Answer these questions as you read the chapter. You will be able to use these answers to help you review the chapter.

1. Identify seven characteristics that distinguish the products of the travel industry from those of other industries.

2. Why is it more difficult to market an intangible product than a tangible one?

3. How are production and consumption interdependent in the travel industry?

4. What is perishability and why is it important in the travel marketing process?

5. Give two examples of the way that seasonality affects the travel industry.

6. What are parity and nonparity products and what marketing challenges and opportunities do they present?

7. How can a travel business compensate for the problem of parity?

8. What role should the unique aspects of a travel product play in marketing a travel product?

9. How does complementarity affect the travel industry?

10. What is the relationship between travel products and services?

11. Why is the quality of service so important to the success of a travel business?

WORKSHEET CHAPTER

Analyzing the Travel Product

Name: ______________________________ Date: ______________

THINKING ABOUT THE PRODUCTS AND MARKETS

You have been working as a group sales representative for an established tour operator for over five years. Most of your clients are well-to-do couples, fifty to sixty years old. In recent years many younger families with children have moved into the residential area where your company is located, and some have dropped by for information on family vacations. Currently, your company is not really prepared to handle this growing market, but you have done some research and are considering starting your own tour company specializing in family vacations.

1. Describe the market you would want to reach.

____

____

____

____

____

2. Where should you be located?

____

____

____

____

3. What would you name your tour company?

____

____

____

____

4. Which travel products and services would be your specialty?

____

____

____

____

____

5. What services/products would you offer to appeal to families in which both husband and wife are employed full-time?

____

____

6. What promotional techniques would you use to reach your target market?

7. Describe the characteristics you would look for in your employees.

8. What special features and benefits do you think working families with children are looking for in vacation travel?

9. What special needs or problems might these customers have, and how would you address them?

10. How would you keep your new customers coming back to you for their future travel plans?

Selecting Target Markets

OBJECTIVES

When you have completed this chapter, you should be able to:

- Explain why markets are segmented.
- Know the four characteristics that determine the viability of a market segment.
- List the variables that may be used in demographic segmenting.
- Explain how marketers use geographic, psychographic, and behavioristic segmenting.
- Give reasons why companies do market research.
- Explain how people conduct market research.

The travel market includes the grandmother who travels two hours by bus to visit her grandchildren, the businessperson who flies across the country to attend a sales convention, and the young couple honeymooning in the Bahamas. Men, women, children, and teenagers; college students, singles, newlyweds, and senior citizens all make up the enormous and diverse market of travelers. Marketing professionals have the challenge of dividing this huge market into smaller groups based on the common characteristics that people share.

WHY TRAVEL MARKETS NEED TO BE SEGMENTED

The travel market as a whole is too large to reach efficiently and too diverse to communicate with in any single way, so marketing professionals break it up into smaller, more manageable parts. They develop travel products for specific groups of people who have things in common that can influence the travel decisions.

The process by which the total market is divided into groups of potential customers with shared characteristics is known as ***market segmentation***, and the groups themselves are called ***market segments***.

Breaking the total market into segments allows marketers to focus their efforts on particular types of buyers. When marketers aim their products and promotional messages toward one or several of these groups, they refer to the process as ***target marketing***. The segments they are focusing on are referred to as target markets.

Technically, each person could be considered a separate target market, defined by unique characteristics and special needs. It's not practical or economically wise, however, to think of the travel market as millions of unique individuals. The market segmentation process addresses this issue by grouping people who share common characteristics and are, therefore, likely to have similar needs or desires. Once marketing professionals target a particular segment, they develop and promote their product or service in a way that appeals most to that group of people, based on their shared characteristics.

Consider, for example, two couples planning a trip to California. One couple is in their thirties. Both husband and wife have high-paying professional jobs. He's a sales manager for a pharmaceutical company. She's a computer software engineer. They have no children. The second couple, a retired printer and his wife, live on a modest fixed income.

If your rental car company marketed luxury and high-priced sports cars, you would identify the younger couple as more likely to rent an expensive sports car than the retired couple. This is an example of how to use market segmentation to focus your marketing efforts on reaching young professionals with high incomes rather than retirees with fixed incomes.

Characteristics of a Market Segment

If one person is too small a market segment and the entire travel market is too large a market segment, what constitutes a meaningful segment? To test whether a market segment is viable, marketers ask four questions:

1. Does the segment or group respond similarly to marketing messages? Put another way, is the segment defined narrowly enough to act or respond as a group in a similar way?

   An amusement park could define its market segment as everyone under age thirty living within fifty miles. However, a twenty-five-year-old and a thirteen-year-old most likely would not respond to the same marketing message in the same way. That segment is, therefore, too broad to be meaningful or useful.
2. Is the segment sufficiently different from other segments? That is, is it defined in a way that includes only the people who share important characteristics and would respond to marketing messages in a similar way?

   If the amusement park aimed its message only at children aged ten, its segment would be too small. Children aged eight through ten probably belong in the same segment, since they would likely respond similarly to that marketing message.
3. Can the segment be reached effectively by communications media such as newspaper, magazine, television, and radio?

   An important aspect of segmenting is communicating a marketing message to groups with special shared characteristics. Just as an archery target is of no use without a bow and arrow, a target market isn't viable if there are no means to reach it efficiently and cost-effectively through marketing communication.
4. Is the revenue potential of the segment sufficient to merit investing the financial and marketing resources necessary to capture it? In other words, will the financial return be good enough to achieve marketing objectives?

This media photograph shows a public relations activity by a theme park. (Courtesy of Six Flags Great America®, Gurnee, IL)

A private cabin on the famed Venice Simplon-Orient-Express is appointed with beautiful woods, polished brass, and crisp linens. (Courtesy of Venice Simplon-Orient-Express, Ltd.)

For example, because tent campers who are serious backpackers tend to bring most of their specialized provisions with them, they may not be a viable segment for most commercial campgrounds. They simply don't spend enough money to generate sufficient profit.

Segmenting makes it more likely that marketers will communicate efficiently and effectively with groups identified as having outstanding potential for purchasing a particular product or service. If that requires too much expense in relation to potential sales, the market segment is not worth pursuing.

METHODS OF SEGMENTING TRAVEL MARKETS

Marketing professionals have a variety of ways to segment markets (see Figure 3–1). No single way is right or wrong, and the various techniques are often used in combination. Generally, four broad methods are used to segment markets:

* Demographic.
* Geographic.
* Psychographic.
* Behavioristic.

Demographic Segmenting

Demography is the statistical study of populations. ***Demographic segmenting*** groups people on the basis of objective criteria or measurable personal characteristics; age, income, occupation, family size/life cycle, and education are among the most widely used demographic segmenting variables.

Age. Marketing professionals know that people of different ages generally have different needs for comfort, economy, excitement, safety, and so on. Age usually has a major influence on buying behaviors.

Marketing professionals try to identify age groups that have similar buying habits. Age categories they commonly use are:

* Under 6 (preschoolers).
* 6 to 11 (children).
* 12 to 19 (teenagers).
* 20 to 34 (young adults).
* 35 to 49 (middle-aged adults).
* 50 to 64 (mature adults).
* 65 and older (senior citizens).

As people age, their priorities change. For example, a young adult backpacking through Europe in the

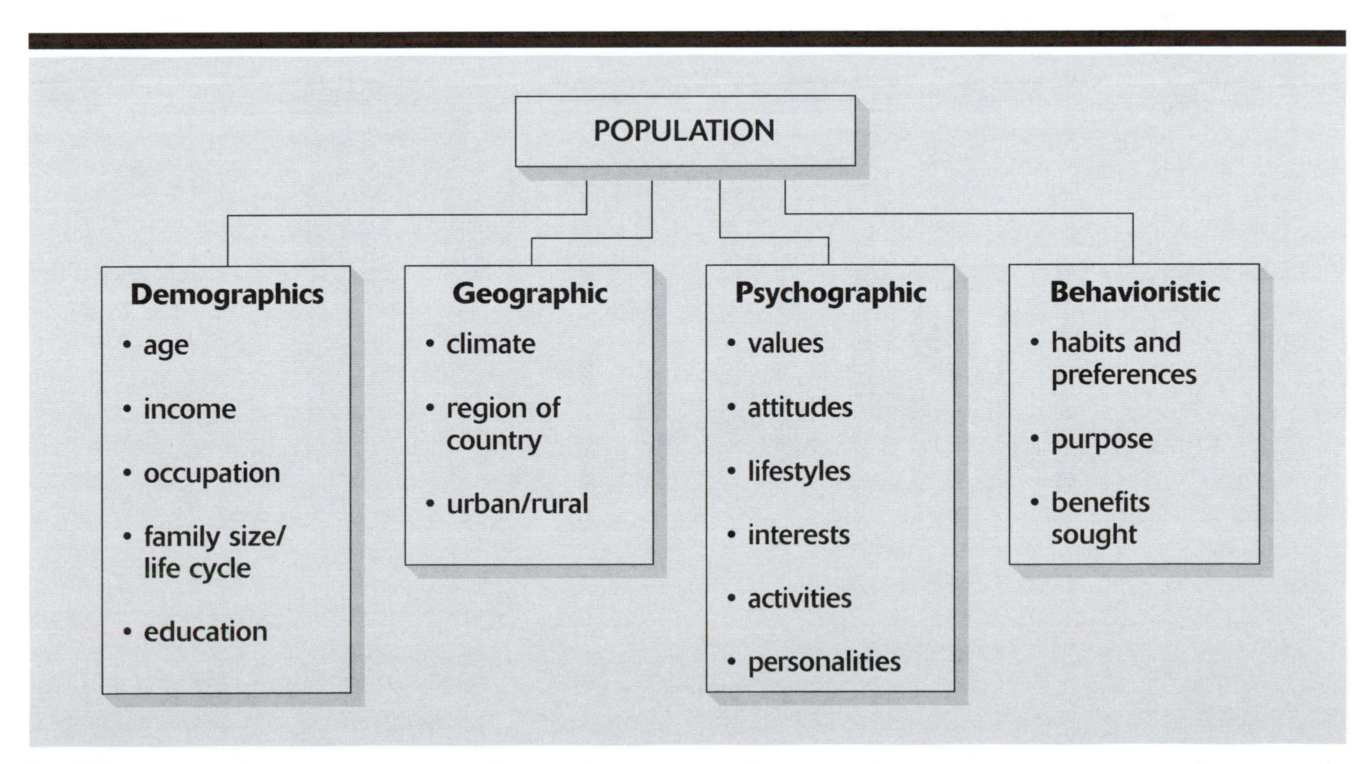

FIGURE 3–1 Marketers use a number of different techniques to break the general population into groups with shared characteristics.

summer is more interested in economy than luxury. On the other hand, a mature adult traveling through Europe may be looking for comfort and convenience in accommodations rather than low cost.

Income. How much people spend on travel is generally related to how much they earn. A young couple earning barely enough to pay for necessities such as rent and food is not likely to spend hundreds of dollars on a cruise to Bermuda. Generally, the more money a family earns, the more it can spend on travel.

Income is usually grouped into ranges, for example:

* Under $30,000.
* $30,000 to $44,999.
* $45,000 to $54,999.
* $55,000 to $74,999.
* $75,000 to $99,999.
* Over $100,000.

Since people who make more money can afford to travel more, upper-income segments are the focus of many travel marketers, especially those who promote expensive products. But lower-income segments can be excellent travel target markets as well. Budget motels are a good example of a travel product designed to appeal specifically to a lower-income target market. Their promotional messages, which usually emphasize economy rates, are aimed at individuals and families looking for an inexpensive yet comfortable place to stay.

An important measure of a country's wealth is gross domestic product (GDP), which measures a country's total economic output. Those countries with a higher GDP are usually designated as tourist-generating countries (see Figure 3–2).

Occupation. Although often related to income, occupation is a separate segmentation variable. Typical occupational categories include professional, manager,

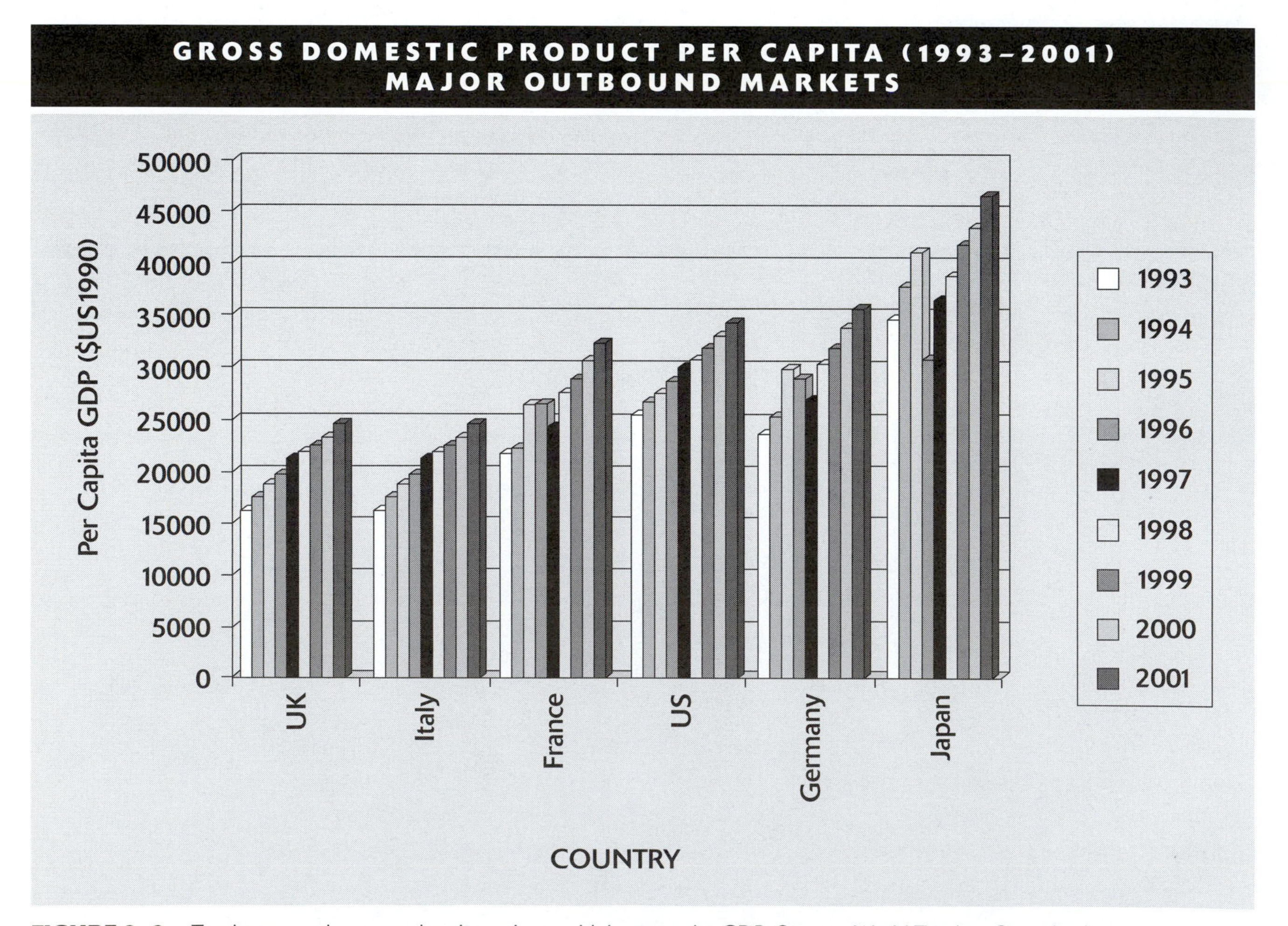

FIGURE 3–2 Tourist-generating countries always have a high per capita GDP. *Source:* World Tourism Organization

proprietor, clerical, sales, retired, student, and homemaker.

Often, for marketing purposes, even smaller occupational segments are created. For example, doctors, lawyers, and college professors are just three of the many subcategories of the larger professional segment.

Occupational segmenting gives marketers insights into income, education, and interests. It is also used to tailor specialized travel products for specific occupational groups. A tour operator, for example, may package a literary tour of Great Britain for a target market of high school English teachers.

Family Stage/Life Cycle. This method of segmenting a market incorporates age and marital status with the number and ages of children. For example, consider these possible segments: young and single; young and married with no children; young and married with preschool children; middle-aged and married with teenage children; middle-aged and divorced with teenage children.

There are many possible family stage/life cycle segments, each with its special travel needs and constraints. When families with small children travel, they may need the option of a crib or cot in their hotel room. They want to dine in restaurants where menus for children are available. These needs are very different from those of a couple on their honeymoon or a retired couple traveling without children.

Education. Generally, the more education people have, the more likely they are to travel. Education, therefore, is also useful as a market segmenting factor.

Educational categories are typically broken down by the highest level of education achieved:

- Grade school or less.
- Some high school.
- Completed high school.
- Some college.
- Completed college.
- Some graduate school.
- Completed graduate school.

Educational levels can be associated with certain types of travel as well. For example, destinations with major cultural attractions or events may choose to target a relatively well-educated market segment. College alumni associations often market seminars in exciting, and historic destinations to its members.

Other Demographic Variables. The travel market, like all markets, can be segmented demographically in other ways, too. Among the additional demographic factors marketers can use to isolate groups of people are gender, religion, race, ethnic background, nationality, and social class. Each can be used to identify groups of prospective travelers in ways that can be useful in certain applications. For example, the special needs of female business travelers are a focus of certain travel marketers. Ethnic background and nationality are segmentation variables that companies may use to package and promote tours to a "home country" of birth, and for reunions or ethnic festivals.

How Marketers Use Demographic Segmenting. Dividing the travel market into demographic groups makes sense for travel marketers. Groups of roughly the same age, for example, have certain things in common. So do people of similar income and people with similar jobs or educational backgrounds.

Within any one of these groups, there is still a great deal of variety, of course. No two people of the same age, for example, are exactly alike otherwise. But what is important from a marketing perspective is that these groups of people have more in common with each other than with the population as a whole and that, as a result, their travel preferences and buying tendencies are likely to have certain similarities.

Travel marketers often segment a market by combining more than one demographic factor in order to refine and focus their target market further (see Figure 3–3). For example, a cruise line may target not just the segment over sixty years of age, or just the middle-income segment, but instead focus on potential customers who are *both* over sixty *and* of middle income. The cruise line

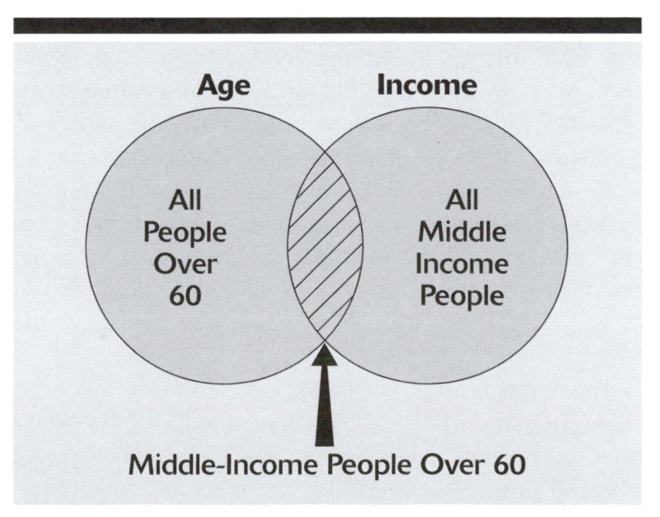

FIGURE 3–3 Marketers often use more than one demographic factor to define a target market.

Marketing Impressions

SALES AND SERVICE SEMINARS
TRAVEL MASTER SEMINARS

How would you like to sell Jeeps if you had never driven one? It would be pretty difficult, wouldn't you agree? They handle a certain way, the acceleration is not the same as with luxury sedans, and it's hard to describe the above-the-crowd feeling you have in comparison to sports cars. You'd either want to test-drive one to make sure you know the differences, or ask experienced users. Selling and servicing group motor coach tours presents the same challenge.

Most people who sell their destinations or their company's hotels, attractions, and restaurants to the motor coach tour industry are in their twenties and thirties. You see them every year at the American Bus Association Marketplace, the National Tour Association's Tour & Travel Exchange, and at regional travel shows throughout North America. We hear them on the phones when we call for reservations. These young people are bright, enthusiastic, and more than willing to help whenever and wherever they can. On the other hand, the average passenger taking a packaged motor coach tour, according to the National Tourism Foundation's Tour Traveler Index, is sixty-eight years old, female, retired from a white-collar job, and traveling with a spouse or friend. The problem? Most of the time, the sellers and the servers of the motor coach tour passengers don't fit that description, have very little in common with them, and very likely have never "driven the Jeep"—that is, been on a motor coach tour. It makes their jobs that much more difficult and frustrating when they think they're doing a good job, but they're not getting the reaction they think they deserve.

That's the reason Travel Master Seminars was established. The people who sell and serve the tour industry had limited opportunities to go to seminars at national conventions, and in most cases, those seminars just touched the surface. They needed a more in-depth, concentrated curriculum. I grew up on motor coaches: it was my family's business. I sat beside those sixty-eight-year-olds (and sometimes eighty-six-year-olds).

I learned through experience what they thought, what they liked and didn't like, and what they needed. That learning experience lasted for thirty-five years. I now travel the world doing workshops and seminars, teaching people how to "sell the Jeep" without having driven one. It's not a panacea, but it's close.

Travel Master Seminars workshops provide sellers and servers in the motor coach tour industry with an opportunity to concentrate on "thinking like the customer." It's a matter of putting themselves in the driver's seat. Tour operators who sell tours to their customers know what these customers want. Suppliers to those companies must adjust their thinking to provide those services, or they take the chance of losing or never even getting the business. For instance, tour takers like to be part of a group; but just that, a part, an individual, not the whole, not the herd. Most customers don't like to stand in line, but tour takers hate it. Avoiding long waits is why they bought the organized tour in the first place. They want to be treated specially. They don't want to handle their luggage themselves, but they want it to get to their rooms before they do. Unrealistic? Sometimes. Impossible? No. You just have to know how to handle each situation.

People take tours for six basic reasons: convenience, safety, security, companionship, education, and value, not necessarily in that order. Each passenger is different. The nuances of each of those reasons, and how they are delivered to the customer, can be the difference between success and failure, repeat business and "never again." That's why convention and visitors bureaus, state offices of tourism, travel organizations, hotel chains, and other companies find it so valuable to educate their suppliers on how to sell and service the tour industry and how to grow their group tour markets. Travel Master Seminars is proud to be an integral part of that process. We'd like to think we're a virtual ride behind the wheel.

would then intentionally try to heighten its appeal to this particular market segment, which is more specifically defined by two separate demographic variables.

Theoretically, the number of segmentation variables that can be combined to define a target market has no limit. Practically speaking, however, if too many factors are used to segment a market, the segment eventually becomes too narrowly defined, and thus too small, to be meaningful or useful. The goal of segmentation is to use enough variables so that the specific target market is clearly defined and remains large enough to be worth pursuing.

The concurrent use of different segmentation variables isn't limited to those that are demographic, however. Travel marketers also use demographic market segmentation in combination with the three other major methods: geographic, psychographic, and behavioristic.

Geographic Segmenting

Geography is an important tool for segmenting markets. Where people live has a tremendous influence on their buying patterns, especially in regard to travel, which is, after all, movement from one geographic location to another. Consequently, marketing professionals often target groups in particular regions of the country, climates, or types of environment (e.g., urban or rural). Whether people want to travel to the mountains or the beach, to New York City or Yellowstone National Park, the location of the destination in relation to the geography of their home plays a major role in their travel decisions.

Travel marketers use ***geographic segmenting*** in a variety of ways. A resort in the country may use it to target urbanites in its own region of the country. A warm-weather destination often targets potential travelers from geographic areas with cold winters. An airline might focus on a particular region of the country when developing new routes.

Take, for example, similar casino hotels in Atlantic City, New Jersey, and Las Vegas, Nevada. Although they offer travelers the same primary activities—gambling, entertainment, and recreation—their different locations lead them to target different geographic markets.

Atlantic City is on the Atlantic coast, in a temperate climate, within easy traveling distance of the millions of people living within the urban sprawl from Boston to Washington, D.C. Las Vegas, on the other hand, is located in the hot, sunny, and dry Nevada desert, more than two hundred miles from any other major urban area.

A casino in Las Vegas might target markets geographically by focusing first on prospective travelers in major western or midwestern cities who fly or drive into town for a day or two of weekend gambling. It might also focus on a nationwide market of suburban families who often include Las Vegas on the itinerary of a vacation in the western United States.

An Atlantic City casino may choose instead to ignore the nationwide suburban market entirely and to focus its marketing efforts exclusively on the major cities within 250 miles. Within those cities is a huge market of potential customers who can reach Atlantic City easily by either car or motor coach. When advertising to this geographic target market, the casino may target seniors living within a four-hour motor coach ride, or emphasize the attractions of the beach and boardwalk to appeal to urban residents who wish to gamble and escape the heat and humidity of the summer on the same trip.

In both cases, geography plays a significant role in determining whom the casino (destination) chooses as its target—the location of the destination in relation to the geography of potential travelers is the key element. The different geographic characteristics of the two cities dictate that the casinos use geographic market segmentation techniques to target markets that are distinct and best suited to their products.

Psychographic Segmenting

Segmenting markets on the basis of psychographic variables is a relatively recent practice in marketing. ***Psychographic segmenting*** is used to group people according to their psychological makeup—their values, attitudes, lifestyles, interests, activities, and personalities. One of the approaches for segmenting markets psychographically uses lifestyle as a way of grouping potential customers.

Lifestyle As a Measure of Values. Two important components of lifestyle are how people spend their time (their activities) and what interests and values they have.

In discussions about lifestyle, words such as "conservative," "liberal," "adventurous," "homebody," and "health nut" are sometimes used. Although no standard terminology exists, researchers from SRI International (formerly Stanford Research Institute) determined and labeled nine values and lifestyles (VALS) categories:

- Survivors—old, very poor.
- Sustainers—on the edge of poverty.
- Belongers—aging, conventional, stable.

* Emulators—youthful, show-off, trying to make it big.
* Achievers—middle-aged and prosperous, self-assured, materialistic.
* I-Am-Me—young, impulsive, individualistic, single, in a transition state.
* Experiential—young, artistic, inner-directed.
* Socially conscious—mature, successful, concerned with the environment.
* Integrated—psychologically mature, understanding, possessing a world perspective.

Of these groups, survivors and sustainers are not viable market segments for the travel industry because they have little money and few reasons to travel. In contrast, the achievers and socially conscious groups have been identified by many marketers as segments that travel frequently for business and pleasure.

Effective Psychographic Segmenting. It is important to understand why marketers have attempted to use psychology to identify market segments. People's personality types and beliefs have a great influence on their buying motivations and behaviors. But it's harder to put your finger on personality traits than it is on cold, hard facts like age. There's also almost no limit to the number of ways to look at psychological traits.

Psychographic segmenting can be a very effective tool, however. It helps travel marketers understand why a travel product appeals especially to certain personality types and how to tailor a message that is likely to appeal specifically to that type's psychology. Breaking the whole travel market up into smaller psychographic target markets can be extremely useful in matching products and services with potential customers.

Skiing is a good example of a travel-related activity that tends to appeal to certain personality types. To some people, skiing seems expensive, cold, and dangerous. To others, it is exhilarating, challenging, and rewarding. Using the VALS categories, one market research firm (National Demographics, Ltd.) has determined that 30 percent of those who ski fall into the Achiever category—people who are prosperous and materialistic. Ski resorts use this information by creating promotional messages that appeal especially to this particular psychographic group.

Behavioristic Segmenting

Marketing professionals rely on a fourth major segmentation technique that makes use of the behaviors of actual and potential customers in relation to a specific product or type of product. ***Behavioristic segmenting*** divides the market into groups that share particular buying habits, preferences, or purposes. Weekend travelers, repeat customers, and first-class passengers are examples of target groups defined by their behaviors.

Segmenting by buying behavior is powerful because it is based on what people *do* rather than who they are, where they live, or what their lifestyle is. A target group of business travelers who are known to stay in hotels five or more times a month is much more promising than a demographically defined target group of all salespeople.

Although it makes a lot of sense for marketers to use behaviors to focus on specific groups, reaching those groups can be more difficult than reaching market segments defined demographically or geographically. It is difficult and expensive, for example, to buy a mailing list of people who travel to Cape Cod every summer. But that doesn't mean that a resort operator in Hyannis can't focus primarily on these annual visitors by developing messages to attract them initially and activities to encourage their repeat business.

Travel markets can be segmented on the basis of several behaviors, including:

* Travel habits and preferences.
* Purpose of travel.
* Benefits sought from travel.

Travel Habits and Preferences. All people have travel habits and preferences, of which they may or may not be aware. Some families, for example, take a week's vacation every summer at the same resort. Other families go to a different place every year—one year to the mountains, another year to the beach, and so on.

Travel marketers use patterns of travel behavior to segment the market and to target groups that share certain travel habits or preferences. A target group may comprise those who share a preference for a certain hotel chain, those who customarily travel over the Memorial Day holiday, or those who always fly first class. Specific habits and preferences offer travel marketers one more clue for focusing on likely prospects.

Habits and preferences are both friends and foes to the travel marketer. If a couple usually takes a winter vacation in California, the hotel, restaurants, car rental company, and other establishments they patronize benefit from their habit. At the same time, their custom of taking California vacations makes it less likely that they will change their pattern and go to Arizona or

Florida. Similarly, a person's preference for a particular airline may be strong enough to make it extremely difficult for another airline to convince that customer to change companies.

Travel marketers look at any number of habits and preferences to divide the market, including season of travel (on- or off-season); method of payment (credit or cash); class of travel (first, business, or economy); and whether the person is traveling in a group or alone. Many companies in the travel industry define one of their primary target markets as heavy users of their product. For example, frequent-flier programs are one way airlines identify regular passengers and build brand loyalty by rewarding them for choosing their airline.

Other airlines, however, may target those who fly infrequently. U.S. Airways offers a special seminar for those who do not use airlines because they are fearful of flying or have had bad experiences in the past. Included in the free program is a discount coupon for a future U.S. Airways ticket. The airline's objective is to expand their market by attracting nonfliers, in addition to competing with other airlines for a larger share of the existing market.

Purpose of Travel. A widely used means of segmenting the travel market behavioristically is by its purpose. Most importantly, travel marketers distinguish between those people who are traveling for business and those who are not.

The business traveler has different needs from those of the nonbusiness traveler. For example, business travelers are likely to be more concerned about convenience than cost. Travel marketers use this distinction when they segment their markets by purpose of travel. When they target the business traveler, for example, they develop and promote their products and services with an emphasis on convenience.

Airlines, car rental companies, and hotels all offer special services to make business travel more convenient. An airline's members-only club in an airport provides a comfortable place to do paperwork, make phone calls, have a cup of coffee, or relax. Since business travelers are concerned about time, car rental companies have developed special express check-in and checkout systems to speed them on their way. And some hotels targeting business travelers offer preordered, in-room breakfasts, in-room telefacsimile (fax) service and computer connections, and a speedy checkout system.

In contrast to business travel, leisure travel may have many purposes. Relaxation and sightseeing, for example, are two different purposes for leisure travel. They dictate significant differences in the travel needs of people who travel for those particular purposes. Travel marketers know, for instance, that the groups that travel to relax and those that travel to see sights have different behavior patterns and expectations.

A resort located in a remote, rural locale may define its target market as travelers who want to relax, for example. These are people who want to go someplace to stay awhile and unwind, far from the bustle of their normal, everyday lives. A motor coach tour operator, on the other hand, may target the sightseeing market by offering guided trips through historic regions of the country, stopping at all of the major historic and cultural landmarks on the way.

Whether it is meeting new people or getting in shape, every purpose of leisure travel potentially offers marketers a means of segmenting the travel market. Many of them routinely use travel purposes as a productive, fundamental way of targeting markets by behavior.

Benefits Sought. Everyone who purchases a product or a service is seeking to benefit in some way from the money spent. A ***benefit*** is something that satisfies a need or makes someone feel better. The needs people wish to satisfy and the benefits they seek by traveling offer marketers another type of behavior by which potential travelers can be divided. Take, as an example, first-class, personalized service. Some travelers care about it a great deal and are willing to pay a premium for it. Others don't find it worth the cost, don't perceive any significant benefit to it, or are even made uncomfortable by receiving it.

For the segment that cares about service, travel marketers provide extras, from free champagne on the airplane, to concierge service at the hotel, to chauffeured limousine service. Cost is not a factor to this market; excellent service and value are.

For the segment that derives no benefit from such personalized service, travel marketers try to provide basic products and services at a competitive price. They may also try to provide a special benefit to a different target group as a way of gaining an edge on the competition.

Marketers keep a keen eye on various benefits travel provides and the needs it fulfills. Whether travelers seek entertainment and excitement or recreation and relaxation, the behavior associated with attempting to satisfy their needs divides them into useful market segments.

WHY COMPANIES DO MARKET RESEARCH

When travel professionals make decisions about which market segments to target for their travel products, they don't do it in a vacuum. They investigate the market to gather facts that help them make informed decisions. Acquiring information about the market in this systematic way is called ***market research***.

But target market decisions aren't the only marketing decisions that depend on research. Every stage of the marketing process—from product development to pricing—uses market research to provide the information necessary for good business decisions. And nearly every component of the market—sellers and buyers, products and services, distribution and promotion—can be the focus of systematic market research.

When used intelligently, market research can also reduce business risks. It provides managers with information to avoid costly mistakes. Market research lets them know with certainty what their customers' attitudes and behaviors are, as well as their willingness to pay. It also provides information on the competition and on new developments within their industry.

Personal interviews are a common technique for conducting market research. (Photograph by Michael Dzamen)

Good business decisions carrying fewer risks are one of the keys to running a profitable, growing travel business. To get a better idea of how market research makes this possible, consider its role in providing valuable information about four critical issues for a growing travel-related business: expanding into new geographic areas, recognizing growing markets, identifying lifestyle trends, and attracting more visitors.

Expanding into New Geographic Areas

One of several ways a company can capture new business is to offer its service in an area it has not previously served. For example, an airline's managers might look for new routes to a new destination. After hearing that the Ontario, California, airport may be expanded, they would conduct market research to help decide whether there are target markets in the region that would produce business. The managers would also want to know what kinds of travelers visit the area. To assist with the decision, they would ask such questions as:

- Who are they, in demographic, psychographic, or behavioristic terms?
- How much money do they plan to spend at the area's attractions, such as Disneyland and Knotts Berry Farm?
- Where do they come from and in what numbers?
- What percentage of the travelers just visit for the day and return home late in the evening?
- How do they currently get to California? Are they driving their own cars, renting cars, or taking motor coach tours?
- Which airline currently receives the most business from visitors to this area?

On the basis of this market research, the airline's managers would have a good idea of who's going to Ontario, California, region and how they get there.

They may discover, for example, that many visitors are from northern California, which could lead them to explore several possible routes for a new air shuttle service to Ontario for people from San Francisco, Sacramento, or San Jose.

Recognizing Growing Markets

Travel marketers look for geographic areas that are growing and able to support more business. A hotel chain, for example, would want to identify places where new hotels will be needed in advance of the actual need. It takes time to plan a hotel, purchase land, and complete construction. If a company waits until the area has already proven itself, land costs may already have gone so high that the hotel may not be able to afford to enter that market at all. That is why it is important to track population growth worldwide (see Figure 3–4).

A hotel catering to business travelers would look for areas of high anticipated corporate growth. It would conduct market research to find answers to such questions as:

- Where are corporations building large, new facilities?
- In what areas are local governments offering tax incentives to attract new businesses?
- Where are the customers and suppliers for rapidly expanding corporations?

Once it has identified some promising areas, its research would become more specific, asking a different set of questions, such as:

- What hotels currently serve the area? How many hotel rooms do they have? What conference facilities are available?
- What are the annual occupancy and average daily rates?
- What convention facilities are available?
- How many new jobs are expected to be created in the area?
- What transportation improvements are planned that could aid growth?
- Are new homes being built to help attract job seekers to the area?
- Have any major companies moved out of the area recently? Are any moving in?

The preceding example of market research might reveal that the area around Princeton, New Jersey, is booming with corporate growth and is possibly an excellent location for a new hotel for business travelers. Situated in the center of the state with a highly regarded university, equidistant from New York and Philadelphia, Princeton is easily accessible by road and by rail and is attracting many major companies.

To a hotel owner, all this corporate growth means that more business travelers will be needing overnight accommodations. If the results of the market research

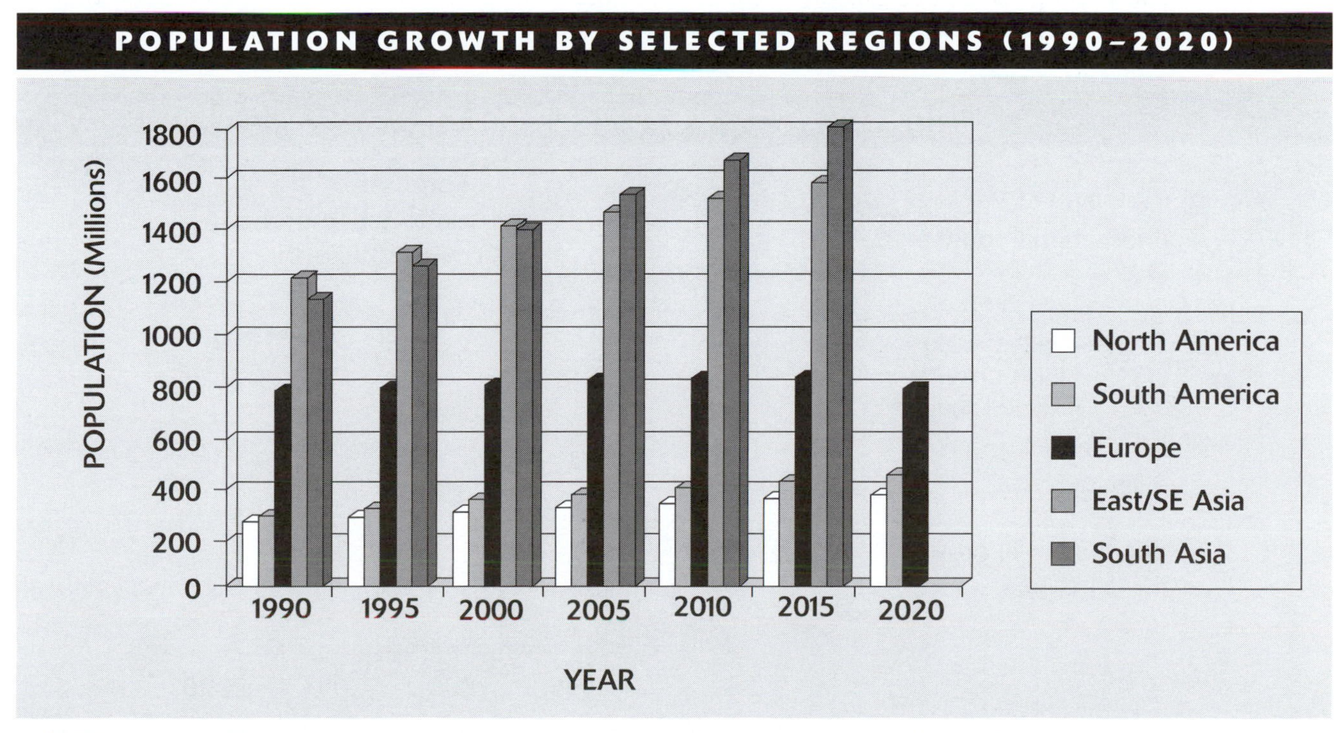

FIGURE 3–4 Increasing population can mean that new markets need to be considered. *Source:* International Marketing and Statistics/United Nations, 1997

are encouraging, a hotel company may decide to build a new property in the Princeton market.

Identifying Lifestyle Trends

Market research can help travel companies identify new opportunities, which can then be converted into new business. Consider the importance of such information to the operators of a cruise line. To stay competitive, they have to offer customers a vacation experience that is in tune with their lifestyle, one that offers the features and activities they want *this* year, not the ones they wanted ten years ago.

To stay current, they conduct market research to determine how lifestyles are changing. Do people have more leisure time for vacations or less? How have their eating habits changed? What kinds of music are they listening to? Are they exercising more or less, and when they do exercise, what are their preferred activities? Are they traveling more or less than last year?

The answers to all these questions and to a host of other lifestyle-related questions are critical to the cruise line operators, who want to optimize the appeal of their travel product.

Say, for example, that the cruises they currently offer average a week to ten days in length, feature gourmet French cuisine with heavy sauces, present big bands in the ship's lounge, and specialize in offering shuffleboard tournaments as exercise. But their market research reveals that lifestyles and preferences have changed. It indicates that people have less time for vacations than they used to and prefer cruises that last three to five days, preferably over a weekend. They also prefer healthful, low-cholesterol meals, jazz, classic rock and roll, and aerobics.

Smart cruise operators use this information to change their offerings. By doing so, they avoid potential financial disaster by staying in touch with the preferences of their market. They also may be staying ahead of their competitors who do not use market research as effectively. They use the information about lifestyle and preference to make good business decisions about changing their products and services. Good market research, then, is one of the keys to continuing profitability for any travel business. Knowing that global tourism is growing and that tourists travel for many reasons, consideration of lifestyle preferences is important to the success of tourism businesses and destinations (see Figure 3–5). Market research can identify specific lifestyle trends that can create new market segments.

Attracting More Visitors

Often a resort, an attraction, or a destination wants to attract more people. For example, a ski resort in the mountains of Colorado might boast beautifully

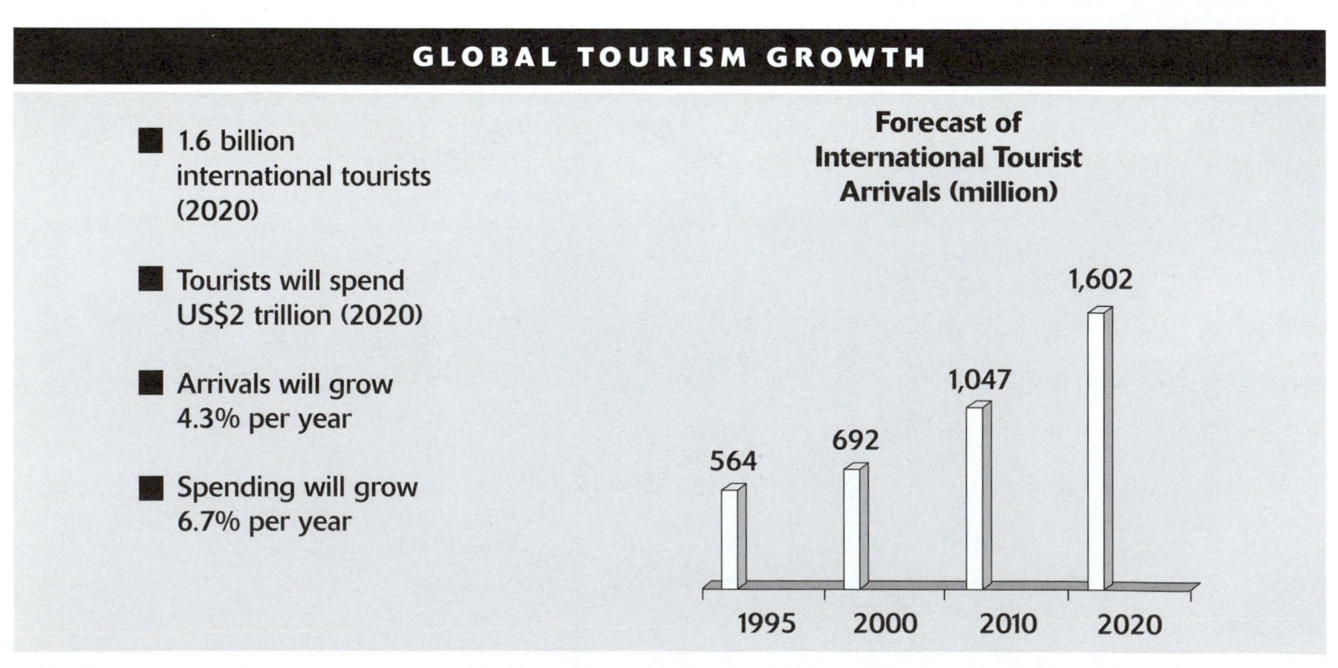

FIGURE 3–5 Tourists travel for many reasons, producing strong global tourism growth. *Source:* World Tourism Organization Vision 2020

groomed trails and all the amenities a traveler could want. Yet for some reason the area is never that busy. Before developing a plan to attract more visitors, it must conduct market research to learn about the people who *are* coming to vacation, seeking answers to such questions as:

- How far do visitors travel to reach the resort? From which regions of the country do they come? Do they live in large cities or small towns?
- How do they travel there?
- How many times have they visited the resort in the last five years? If not recently, why have they stopped coming?
- How did they first learn about it?
- Are the visitors predominantly men, women, young couples with children, or older couples?
- In addition to the great skiing, what attracted them to the area? What amenities did they especially enjoy?

The answers to questions like these can be surprising. The market research might determine that most visitors come from the Midwest, specifically around Chicago, because of the reasonable airfare to and from Colorado.

The heated outdoor pool might prove to be a big attraction since people like to relax, go for a swim, and view the slopes from an unusual perspective after a hard day of skiing. The research might also show that the gourmet restaurant with its fine wine list is another plus.

They must also determine why more Chicago skiers are not skiing at their resort and/or why they are choosing another resort (either in Colorado or elsewhere). These skiers may have "retired" from skiing, switched to another activity or prefer the lower cost and higher snow quality in Utah. Regardless of the reasons, it is as important to know why people have not returned to the resort (or never visited) as it is to determine why they have chosen to visit.

As a result of the market research, the ski resort might step up its marketing efforts in Chicago. To attract even more people from that area, it could advertise in regional Chicago magazines and newspapers and begin a public relations effort to get mentioned in travel articles. The resort could also bring more attention to its swimming pool and restaurant in its ads and promotional publications, thereby increasing customer and noncustomer awareness of the resort's offerings.

Market Research as a Tool

The major reasons that a company spends time and money conducting market research is to identify market needs, improve product quality, and generate increased business. Research serves as one of several tools that marketing professionals use to make informed business decisions that will ultimately yield more profit.

Through market research, travel companies find answers to questions about the various groups of people that are or are not using their product or service. Based on that information, marketing plans are designed, including the selection of target markets. Research gives marketers confidence that the course of action they are pursuing will produce the results they seek. In the end, the value of market research is often measured by the increase in business and/or the amount of additional profit it produces.

Database Target Marketing

The days of effective tourism mass marketing are waning. Today, effective marketers are using sophisticated databases that combine information from a number of sources to produce profiles of both their current and potential customers. By combining lifestyles, demographics, product preferences, buying habits, and values in a single database, marketers can measure and characterize their existing customer base (and unique expectations) and gain the power to track spending patterns and predict purchasing behavior. This technique of combining information about potential customers from different sources (databases) to create a profile for an existing or potential target market is called ***database target marketing***.

Analyzing these large and complex databases is called "data mining," and is usually conducted by market research companies that specialize in database marketing. An example of a target market that could be identified through this process and located by zip or postal code would be: male engineers over fifty who earn more than $100,000 annually; play golf, tennis, and ski; and who currently have a mortgage on their home. Such a segment would be very important for a four-season resort that was planning to sell condominiums on the golf course or next to the ski slopes and was constructing an indoor tennis center. The fact that this "data mining" process can identify where people who meet these criteria reside in high concentrations (neighborhoods) means that cost-effective advertising, including direct mail promotions, can be used by the resort to reach this segment.

HOW PEOPLE DO MARKET RESEARCH

Whether you realize it or not, you may have participated in market research. If you've ever filled out a form that asked how you enjoyed a meal and whether you thought the service was good, you've been the subject of market research. Many restaurants, hotels, airlines, cruise ships, and other businesses in the travel industry routinely conduct market research through customer surveys and other methods.

The market research process can be divided into four steps:

1. Defining the marketing research problem.
2. Developing and executing the research plan.
3. Producing useful results.
4. Drawing conclusions and making recommendations.

Defining the Marketing Research Problem

The marketing research problem is the focus of market research, which is designed to answer the important questions associated with the problem. Although marketing professionals refer to it as a "problem," this term can be misleading, since it can just as easily be an opportunity, such as the chance to open a hotel on a newly developed island. Whatever the nature of the "problem," it should be clearly stated. It should also be significant enough in financial returns to merit the expense of the market research. It should be specifically defined and not be so broad that it is impossible to use market research to adequately resolve the problem and provide recommendations.

Developing and Executing the Research Plan

Suppose that a resort is concerned that its operating costs are rising too quickly in relation to revenue. It is looking for ways to save money. The managers note that the cost of operating the ice machines on every floor of the resort is quite high. But before making hasty decisions, such as assuming that the machines are unnecessary or that they can get by with fewer machines, the managers decide to undertake market research.

They begin by determining what questions they need to answer, for example:

- Are the resort's costs higher than industry norms?
- Do competing resorts offer ice machines on every floor?
- Are other types of ice machines available? Are they less expensive to purchase? Are they less expensive to maintain?
- Do the guests use the machines? How often?
- Do the guests value them as an amenity the resort offers? If so, how much?

Just as the marketing problem dictates the questions to be asked, the questions are one of the primary factors in determining how the market research will be conducted. There are two basic ways to collect useful information.

The first and most common method uses secondary sources, or information that already exists. Secondary sources include a company's own records, government statistics, and published articles, reports, and studies completed by other companies and organizations. If the managers of the resort consulted a resort trade journal to find out what industry-norm expenses for ice machines were, they would be using a secondary source of data.

But some questions they formulated as a part of their market research plan would require more specific, direct information-gathering techniques. These methods use primary sources, that is, market research in which you collect information that isn't available from secondary sources. If you want to know how frequently guests use the machines or how much they value having them, you must ask them directly.

Much market research employs both secondary and primary sources: often researchers use and review secondary sources when they are deciding how to conduct their primary research. The three basic types of primary market research are observation, experimentation, and survey research. These can be used separately or in combination, depending on the scope and particular requirements of the research.

Observation. If the resort's managers posted a researcher near the ice machine on each floor for a specified period of time to count how many guests used it in a typical day (and when), they would be using a basic observational research technique. Observational techniques are particularly good at determining customer behaviors, but they can't tell you much about their motives, attitudes, or opinions. Resort managers often use this technique by sitting in the lobby and observing the interactions among guests and employees.

Experimentation. On the other hand, suppose the resort's managers decided to remove ice machines on certain floors and carefully monitor the reaction of their guests. The purpose of this research would be to compare the satisfaction level of guests on floors with ice machines with that of guests on floors lacking them. That would be an example of experimentation.

Another example of experimentation is test marketing a new product and monitoring the results before introducing it to the general marketplace. For example, an airline that hasn't traditionally offered first-class service may initiate it only on certain routes at first and then monitor customer reactions. The results would allow them to decide whether or not to introduce first-class service throughout their entire system.

Survey Research. Perhaps the most common of the three market research techniques is survey research. There are a variety of basic surveying methods, but they all do essentially the same thing: identify a group of people (referred to as a ***sample***) who were carefully selected to represent a larger group and ask them a list of questions that were equally carefully selected and worded. This can be done in a directed group discussion known as a focus group, in a face-to-face interview, in a phone interview, or by means of a questionnaire sent through the mail.

For example, the resort's managers, in order to determine how much guests value having an ice machine on each floor, would have to conduct survey research to find out. They may choose to gather a small group of them around a table for a group interview, or they may design a questionnaire to send out to a representative sample (five hundred) of their two thousand frequent guests. In either case—or in the case of observation or experimentation—their next step is the same: analyzing the responses and information they have gathered through surveys, observation experiments, or interviews, and interpreting the results.

Producing Useful Results

To be effective, market research must be conducted systematically. The particular techniques selected must be appropriate to the questions being asked. The questions themselves must be worded so that they will be clearly understood. The subjects must be chosen carefully, and the size of the sample must be carefully determined statistically and be the right size and composition for the research technique.

In order for the results of the research to have any meaning or predictive value, they must be statistically accurate and scientifically reliable. The data must be tabulated and edited carefully. Once this has been done, a statistician may look at the results to assess the research's reliability. Every element of the research: the data-gathering method, the number and nature of the questions, the quality and rate of the responses, and the size of the subject sample must be done correctly if the results are to be accurate and useful.

On the basis of these and other factors, a statistician can often report a ***margin of error*** for each research finding. This provides a scientifically determined measure of confidence (that the results are accurate) with which to interpret the results of the market research. For example, responses to surveys with an error rate of plus or minus 10 percent are not as accurate or useful as those with an error rate of plus or minus 1 percent.

Drawing Conclusions and Making Recommendations

When all the market research is completed, a final report is prepared to summarize the findings, draw conclusions, and make recommendations for actions to be taken in order to solve the original marketing research problem. It is important for this report to concisely and effectively address how the results can resolve the original problem. Management should be prepared to take the actions that the research indicates, even though it may not instinctively agree. The conclusions and recommendations in the report will be accurate if the research has been designed and conducted properly.

Next, a plan of action based on the recommendations in the report must be developed. Strategies should then be designed to meet the objectives of the action plan. After the plan of action has been implemented, its impact on business success should be reviewed to determine how accurate the market research findings and recommendations were. That way, refinements can be made based on actual experience, and more useful information will be available the next time market research is conducted.

Using Market Research

Because its findings must be statistically correct, market research may seem like an exact science. It is not. It is a useful tool for determining attitudes and preferences and predicting behavior of existing and potential customers. It is also useful for estimating how they spend their money.

Circumstances can quickly change, fads may pop up overnight, and people will change their minds. But ongoing market research can serve as a useful guide during changing business environments by providing management with information to help address marketing problems. Marketing professionals use the valuable information from market research in many ways, including product development, market segmentation, and product positioning, the last of which is the focus of the next chapter.

CHAPTER SUMMARY

- Market segmentation divides the total travel market, which is enormous and diverse, into smaller groups of people who are similar because they share common characteristics.
- Marketers use segmentation techniques to focus on particularly promising groups, a process known as target marketing.
- High-potential market segments can become target markets.
- Useful market segments must be composed of individuals who will respond similarly to marketing messages, who share characteristics which differentiate them from other segments, who can be reached effectively by communications media, and who have sufficient revenue potential to make focusing on them worthwhile.
- Demographic segmenting creates groups of potential customers on the basis of age, income, occupation, family stage/life cycle, education, or other measurable characteristics.
- Marketers use geographic segmenting to target customers in particular regions, climates, or types of environment (e.g., rural or urban).
- Psychographic segmenting identifies segments of potential customers on the basis of their personalities, lifestyles, and attitudes.
- Travel habits and preferences, purposes for traveling, and benefits sought from travel are three types of variables used in behavioristic segmenting.
- Database target marketing produces profiles of existing and potential customers.
- Market research gathers information from both secondary and primary sources to ensure good business decisions.
- Market research uses three basic techniques to gather information from primary sources: observation, experimentation, and survey research.
- The four basic steps of the market research process are defining the marketing research problem, developing and executing the research plan, producing useful results and making recommendations, and drawing conclusions.

KEY TERMS

market segmentation
market segments
target marketing
demographic segmenting
geographic segmenting
psychographic segmenting
behavioristic segmenting
benefit
market research
database target marketing
sample
margin of error

DISCUSSION QUESTIONS

1 What are the primary advantages market segmentation offers to travel marketers?
2. A motor coach tour operator has identified the market segment of widows over the age of 65 as a promising target market. Applying the four tests of a segment's viability, explain why this is or isn't a viable market segment.
3. Explain the basic relationship between educational levels and the tendency to travel. If you were an advertising manager for an international hotel chain, how would you use this fact in your direct-mail advertising and in your television advertising?
4. What are two major purposes of travel, and how do these purposes affect travelers' needs?
5. Describe a target market for a tennis resort using a VALS category.
6. Give an example of a specific business decision for which market research could reduce the risks. Explain how particular types of information would help do so in this particular case.
7. Imagine you are the marketing manager for an investment group considering building a new attraction in your town. List some questions you would include in a survey questionnaire.

Selecting Target Markets

Name: ______________________ Date: __________

Directions: Answer these questions as you read the chapter. You will be able to use these answers to help you review the chapter.

1. What is the difference between a market segment and a target market?

2. Why is it important to segment the travel market?

3. Explain how marketers determine whether a market segment is viable.

4. What are demographics?

5. How can income be used to segment a market?

6. How can more than one demographic factor be used to determine a market segment?

7. What is geographic segmenting?

8. What is psychographic segmenting?

9. How does behavioristic segmenting differ from other methods of marketing segmenting?

10. What is the most important distinction travel marketers make about purposes of travel? Why?

11. Identify four critical issues for a growing travel business that can be addressed by market research.

12. How can an understanding of lifestyle trends benefit a travel business?

13. What are the four steps for conducting accurate and useful market research?

14. Describe the three basic types of primary market research.

15. Explain why market research is not an exact science.

WORKSHEET CHAPTER 3

Selecting Target Markets

Name: ______________________________ Date: ______________

TARGETING THE MARKET

Each of the groups of people listed below belongs to certain market segments. Each is likely to find certain types of travel products and services more useful or appealing than others. Answer the questions about each group.

1. Computer manufacturer sales representatives making sales calls in several cities within one state

A. Describe the types of travel products and services that would interest this market segment.

____

____

____

____

B. Discuss how market research would be useful to help you decide how to promote these products and services to this market segment.

____

____

____

____

C. Choose one specific product or service, and explain how you would promote it to this market segment.

____

____

____

____

2. Doctors attending a professional conference

A. Describe the types of travel products and services that would interest this market segment.

____

____

____

____

B. Discuss how you would use market research to help you decide how to promote these products and services to this market segment.

____

____

____

____

C. Choose one specific product or service, and explain how you would promote it to this market segment.

3. Grandmothers with young grandchildren

A. Describe the types of travel products and services that would interest this market segment.

B. Discuss how you would use market research to help you decide how to promote these products and services to this market segment.

C. Choose one specific product or service, and explain how you would promote it to this market segment.

4. College seniors on spring break

A. Describe the types of travel products and services that would interest this market segment.

B. Discuss how you would use market research to help you decide how to promote these products and services to this market segment.

C. Choose one specific product or service, and explain how you would promote it to this market segment.

5. Couples who play in mixed doubles tennis tournaments

A. Describe the types of travel products and services that would interest this market segment.

B. Discuss how you would use market research to help you decide how to promote these products and services to this market segment.

C. Choose one specific product or service, and explain how you would promote it to this market segment.

6. Middle-aged opera fans

A. Describe the types of travel products and services that would interest this market segment.

B. Discuss how you would use market research to help you to decide how to promote these products and services to this market segment.

C. Choose one specific product or service, and explain how you would promote it to this market segment.

7. Just-married couples in their twenties

A. Describe the types of travel products and services that would interest this market segment.

B. Discuss how you would use market research to help you decide how to promote these products and services to this market segment.

C. Choose one specific product or service, and explain how you would promote it to this market segment.

8. One-income families with young children and relatives in several states

A. Describe the types of travel products and services that would interest this market segment.

B. Discuss how you would use market research to help you decide how to promote these products and services to this market segment.

C. Choose one specific product or service, and explain how you would promote it to this market segment.

9. Affluent singles with advanced degrees

A. Describe the types of travel products and services that would interest this market segment.

B. Discuss how you would use market research to help you decide how to promote these products and services to this market segment.

C. Choose one specific product or service, and explain how you would promote it to this market segment.

Positioning the Product

OBJECTIVES

When you have completed this chapter, you should be able to:

- Explain why a company must establish a position for its product.
- Show how establishing a position for a new product is different from maintaining a position for an existing one.
- Summarize what a positioning statement does.
- Differentiate among a product's position, image, and slogan.
- Contrast product features and product benefits as elements of a product analysis.
- Indicate why it is important to identify a product's current position when developing a positioning statement.
- Give reasons for formally writing a concise positioning statement.
- Understand how product positioning affects customer's expectations.
- Relate several examples of positioning strategies.
- Recognize the role that image plays in buying decisions.
- Identify why travelers' perceptions of a product are so important.

The world is literally full of travel products. Not only are travelers offered a huge variety of destinations, they also have many hotels, airlines, car rental companies, attractions, and other travel products from which to choose.

Many elements factor into a traveler's choice. Sometimes people visit a location because a friend or family member recommended it. Some people choose a destination because they see an inviting advertisement. Sometimes people are not conscious of the reasons for their choices.

Borrowing an example from consumer marketing, perhaps you've had the experience of being in the grocery store and looking at several kinds of ice cream. You choose a brand that has a European name and comes in an attractive gold and white package. You don't necessarily know why you chose that brand, but you have a good feeling about it. Whether you realize it or not, something about that ice cream or its packaging influenced you to purchase that product rather than the others displayed right next to it.

The perception of the consumer is a critical variable in the marketing process, one that has a great influence on purchasing decisions, especially decisions among similar products. For that reason, marketers pay a great deal of attention to trying to control—or at least influence—the ways in which their products are perceived by prospective customers.

THE PRINCIPLES OF PRODUCT POSITIONING

The process by which travel marketers address the issue of consumer perception is referred to as **product positioning**, or simply positioning. Perhaps the best way to understand the meaning of this term is to think of it as referring to the position of a single product in relation to competing products (its similarities and differences) and to prospective customers' perceptions of that product's position. Positioning is an attempt to clarify the former in order to influence the latter, thus gaining an advantageous position in the minds of consumers.

It is not sufficient simply to direct messages about a travel product at a well-selected target market. Instead, a position for that product must be established, both within the marketplace and in the perceptions of potential customers within the target market.

The main mechanism marketers use to establish a position for a product is the creation of an ***image*** for it. The image is meant to determine and influence how a product is perceived. Consequently, travel marketers devote a great deal of time and energy to developing and refining effective images of their products. When product positioning is used effectively, that image becomes a central and unifying influence on every aspect of the travel product. Everything—from the uniforms of the staff to the corporate logo to the advertising of the product—should relate to that image. They should all be consistent with and, ideally, somehow convey and strengthen that image in the minds of customers.

Suppose, for example, you are the manager of Pheasant Hollow Inn, a small bed-and breakfast establishment located in picturesque Bucks County, Pennsylvania, less than two hours by car from New York City. You have eight gorgeous rooms, all with queen-size beds, furnished with antiques and decorated with the work of local artists. A country breakfast served in the room is included in the basic room rate.

After research and careful consideration, you choose your target market: professional couples living in New York City who are in the mid- to high-income bracket, have no children, and are interested in art, antiques, and gourmet food.

The image you want to establish for your inn is one of an upscale, intimate, and elegant weekend destination where the hustle, bustle, and pressures of the city can be left behind. To help reinforce this image, you place a bouquet of fresh flowers in each room. You serve breakfast on fine china. You familiarize your staff with the origins of the inn's art and antiques. Everything—from the name of the inn to the advertisements placed in New York newspapers—contributes to the image you want to convey.

A product or service should be positioned in relation to the needs of the target market. To establish a position, marketing professionals try to convey their products' benefits by showing how they meet consumers' needs.

In the example of Pheasant Hollow Inn, the need of the target market is for an environment that is very different from the one they experience all week long. The weekending couple wants a natural, relaxed, beautiful setting in which to spend their leisure time. By demonstrating how your inn meets those needs, you create an image that helps establish the inn's position in relation to its chosen target market.

Consider the image of a similar product aimed at a totally different target market. The Drake is a large hotel in Chicago, very close to Lake Michigan and in the heart of the downtown business and shopping dis-

Logos are one way travel companies attempt to project a consistent, identifiable image. Hertz's signature yellow covers most of the world. (©1994 Hertz System Inc. Hertz is a registered service mark and trademark of Hertz System Inc.)

trict. One target market for this grand, elegant, conveniently located hotel is undoubtedly traveling business executives. Their needs are quite different from the couple weekending at a rural Pennsylvania inn.

Executives may need a suite, which has a living room separate from the bedroom, for private business meetings. Room service, in-house dry cleaning, and convenient access to photocopiers and computers are other possible services they may need. The Drake, in building its image, emphasizes the executive services it offers.

It is important to note the differences between establishing a position for a new product, maintaining a position for an existing one, and changing the current position of an existing product (repositioning). Each has different challenges.

When working with a new product, you start from ground zero in establishing your image. The public has no image of it. That means that you can't rely on former customers to spread the word or recommend your product to others. It also means, however, that you have no negative image to counteract.

For example, a new luxury resort on a little-known island in the Caribbean could capitalize on its location, but would have to build an image from the beginning. It could choose to appeal to swinging singles, to families with children, or to seniors with lots of free time and money, among other possible segments. Depending on its choice, it could tailor its facilities to match that segment's need. If it targeted singles or seniors, for example, it certainly wouldn't need a children's playground.

With an established product, a company must constantly assess its image and decide whether to maintain or alter it. It can't assume that the good feeling the public had about it in the past will continue. A company can't stop being conscious of its image. Its product or service exists not in a vacuum, but in relation to competing products and services that fulfill similar needs and project similar images. When the competition gets aggressive, a company often needs to counter it in some way. For example, if one major hotel chain decides to establish its position by offering new services to business travelers, the others targeting the same market segment may need to reassess the adequacy of their own positions. If they find that their current position remains strong enough to counter the new moves of their competition, they will maintain their current position. On the other hand, they may find the need to respond by developing a new image and position for their product that effectively counteracts the changes introduced by their competition (repositioning).

In the travel industry, unpredictable events can also change an image, and quickly. For example, when a major airline has a labor strike, the airline must work hard to address safety and reliability issues and reestab-

Different images establish positions aimed at different markets. (Top: Photograph by George Gardiner, courtesy of Beekman Arms Inn, Rhinebeck, New York; Bottom: Courtesy of Wingate Inn, Latham, New York)

lish public confidence. Similarly, if an island destination is hit by a hurricane, it has to work to restore its image as a desirable tropical vacation spot.

How consumers perceive the benefits of a product will determine whether they choose that product. By focusing on the benefits of the product and establishing a clear and compelling image for its product, a company can establish a favorable position in relation to its target market. It should also develop an image that differentiates its products from those of its competitors, in order to gain an advantage in the eyes of consumers.

ESTABLISHING A POSITION

Many people in a company or organization are involved in developing a product's image and establishing its position in the marketplace, ranging from executives to frontline staff. All of them need to know exactly how the company wants the product to be perceived by prospective customers.

A systematic approach in establishing a product position is the best way to develop an effective image for a product. Often, in the process of considering the image, valuable new marketing ideas emerge. This process provides an opportunity to look at the travel product intensely and objectively, as an outsider would. It is especially important to analyze what is unique about your travel product. An image that conveys uniqueness helps identify and differentiate your product in the minds of consumers.

The three steps in establishing an effective position are:

1. Analyzing your product by identifying the major features and benefits.
2. Identifying your current position and image.
3. Comparing your current position with your marketing objectives.

These steps should be undertaken because, to be effective, a position should be capable of being concisely communicated. This is the role of the ***positioning statement***, which is discussed later in this chapter.

Analyzing Your Product

A critical aspect of the development of a positioning statement is the analysis of the features and benefits of your travel product. Although this may seem like a step that could easily be skipped, it is important to the process.

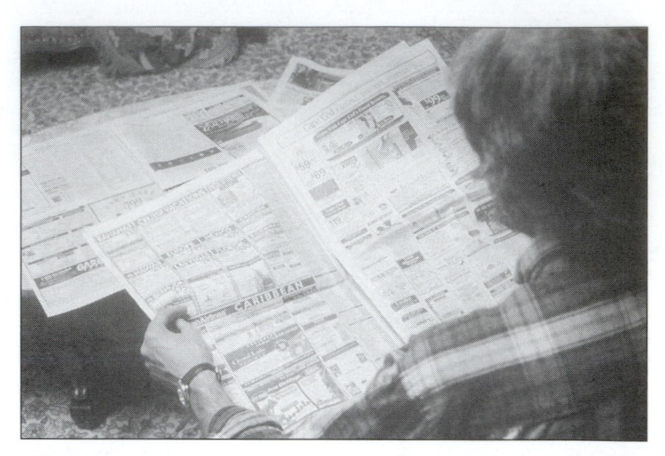

Emphasizing unique aspects of a travel product helps establish a position clearly differentiated from the competition. (Photograph by Michael Dzamen)

There are two distinct ways of approaching an analysis of a product or service (see Figure 4–1). One is in terms of its features, both tangible and intangible. The other is in relation to the ways that it meets the needs or interests of the prospective customer—the product's benefits. Both features and benefits are examined as part of a complete product analysis.

Product Features. Describing something you know well is not always easy. Think about a car you've driven. How would you describe it? You could easily list the model, the year, and the color, but what about some features of the car that make it unique? These are probably difficult to recall.

In developing a positioning statement, though, you must be able to describe your product or service very well. One way to focus your thinking is by compiling a comprehensive list of ***features***. The goal here is to develop a complete product description by listing every single feature and attribute of the product, whether you think it's important or not. Sometimes what one person thinks is insignificant is perceived by another as having great value.

Suppose, for example, you are marketing a resort in the Caribbean. What sort of list of features and attributes could you come up with for your resort? Here are some possibilities:

* 125 rooms, 70 with ocean view.
* Balconies in all rooms.
* Atmosphere of casual elegance.
* Private beach.
* Two swimming pools: one freshwater, one saltwater.

Features vs. Benefits	
Feature	**Benefit**
Refrigerators in hotel rooms	Allows for selecting own food, which may also save money; convenience
Motorbike rentals	Mobility; easy, inexpensive transportation
Lighted tennis courts	Tennis at night, when it is cooler
All guest rooms with balconies	View from balcony; outdoor dining, relaxation

FIGURE 4–1 Features are constant attributes of a travel product. Benefits, however, are specific to the individual. Not all features yield the same benefits to all customers.

- Two restaurants: one fine dining, one coffee shop.
- Two bars: one indoors, one on the beach.
- Four lighted tennis courts.
- Refrigerators in all rooms.
- Snorkeling and scuba diving equipment available for rent.
- Motorbike rentals available.
- Friendly and helpful staff.
- High staff-to-guest ratio.

Many other tangible and intangible features of this resort would be included in its description. Tangible features are often easier to list and describe; intangibles are often related to perceptions and feelings. When it comes to vacation choices, however, intangibles such as the resort's casual elegance can be very important decision factors, as you will remember from Chapter 2.

Customer Benefits. Another way to describe a travel product is by determining how it meets the needs or interests of the prospective customer. **Benefits** can indicate why customers choose a product and how customers might feel about the features of the product, and are therefore part of the complete product analysis.

To determine benefits, you can begin by looking at the features you already listed and imagining a prospective customer asking you, "What does that do for me?" or "How will that make my trip better?"

When looking for the benefits of a leisure travel product, consider the needs people satisfy by vacationing. Relaxation, recreation, fun, sun, exploration, and good food are just a few that may come to mind. Returning to the previous example of the Caribbean resort, try to restate the relationship between features and benefits, for example:

- Relaxation—enjoying a morning cup of coffee on a private balcony overlooking the ocean.
- Exercise—playing tennis until midnight on a lighted court.
- Luxury—eating in a restaurant with exceptional service, great food, and fine wine.
- Adventure—exploring the quaint village and surrounding countryside by motorbike.

The benefits of a business-oriented travel product or service would be quite different. For example, a downtown hotel might offer these benefits to businesspeople:

- Convenience—free limousine service to and from the airport.
- Flexibility—meeting rooms to accommodate both small groups and gatherings of up to 250.
- Special services—computer and audiovisual services available at no charge for that important presentation.
- Dining convenience—room service, twenty-four hours a day.
- Comfort—all rooms feature king-size beds and comfortable chairs.

Identifying Your Current Position and Image

The next step in establishing an effective position is looking at how your product is currently perceived. Two good questions to ask in order to identify your current position are:

- What is the appeal of my travel product or service?
- What characteristics of my product are being marketed as part of the current position?

Strengths and Weaknesses Based on Appeal. Different things appeal to different people. Just take a look at the cereal aisle of a supermarket. The number of breakfast cereals is incredible—flakes, nuggets, wafers, animal shapes; with and without sugar; with and without bran. When it comes to cereals, there really is something for everyone. So it is, too, for travel products.

You only have to consider the vast and varied geography of the world to realize that there are literally thousands of destinations to appeal to the many tastes of consumers. Their appeal ranges from the familiar to the exotic; historic to futuristic; nearby to faraway; frigid to tropical; and so on.

What one person finds appealing, another does not. Appeal is intangible and personal. Almost every product or service that is purchased appeals to someone. Usually, a product's appeal is based on the benefits consumers believe they will derive from it.

Sometimes the appeal of a product is luxury; for example, a first-class cruise in the Mediterranean. The opposite can also be true, where the product's appeal is its low price. A nonstop three-week advance purchase airfare to Cancun, Mexico has appeal because it's the least expensive, quickest way to get there.

To position a product, marketers begin by trying to understand its appeal to existing and potential customers. Maximizing the appeal of the product's image greatly enhances the way it is perceived and, consequently, its position in the marketplace.

Strengths and Weaknesses Based on Characteristics. In identifying the current position of a product, marketers look at the characteristics of a product that are part of its current image. Consider, for example, a small resort in Minnesota that is popular with older couples. One characteristic that contributes to its current position is its location on a quiet lake where no motorboating is permitted. In addition, as part of the room rate, the resort serves guests three daily meals of fresh, well-prepared American food. Guests on special diets can have meals prepared to their specifications. Every night classic movies are shown in the resort's lounge on a large-screen television. The resort has no disco or loud bar. These characteristics, which make the hotel such a hit with seniors, also make it unappealing to young singles.

Not all the characteristics of a product or service contribute to its current image. In the preceding example, numerous characteristics of the resort have nothing to do with its popularity with older people. The hiking trail up the adjacent mountain, the lake's excellent fishing, and the resort's superb wine cellar may be among the characteristics of the resort that are not very important to its current clientele.

Marketers need to identify not only the characteristics of a travel product that contribute to its current position, but also those that may meet the needs of groups other than the current target market. Later, they may choose to downplay some characteristics and emphasize others in order to reposition the product in a way that attracts a different target market.

The position that you establish for your travel product and the image it projects produce perceptions in the marketplace for both existing and potential customers. These perceptions, in turn, create expectations for your customers—they expect certain benefits and outcomes based on your marketing communications. If their expectations have been met and they are satisfied, it usually means that you have "delivered on your promises" and the reality of your product matches its marketing image. If, however, expectations have not been met, you face two problems—dissatisfied customers and a product image (including marketing promises) that does not match reality. The solution to these problems is complicated but essential. First, and foremost, your marketing communications must be adjusted to realistically represent the product's benefits and image, otherwise you are guaranteeing guest dissatisfaction. Second, you must determine whether your product's attributes will be able to satisfy your guests. Depending on what you find, you may need to adjust your position and image. Alternately, you may need to change the product to meet the needs and expectations of guests or to attract a different market whose expectations can be met. The latter also requires repositioning and new image development.

Comparing Your Current Position with Your Marketing Objectives

A marketing objective is a specific statement about what an organization expects to accomplish with its marketing programs. This includes future goals for its products or services. Accomplishing marketing objectives requires that all aspects of the marketing program be coordinated and operating in concert. Thus, it is critical that the product position be completely compatible with the marketing objective and vice versa. If they are not, then one (or both) must be altered. In some cases the objective is changed to reflect a new product position. In other cases, a new product position is required to accomplish the marketing

Marketing Impressions

DIRECTOR OF TOURISM
CITY CONVENTION AND VISITORS ASSOCIATION

Marketing and selling a city with as rich and diverse a history, and as high a worldwide profile as Washington, D.C., might appear to be one of the easiest jobs in the world. However, Julie Heizer, Director of Tourism for the Washington, D.C. Convention and Visitors Association will quickly say that isn't so.

"Because Washington, D.C. is the capital of one of the most powerful nations in the world, and because news made here is often news that both affects and is of interest to the world, it is seen on a daily basis all over the world," explains Heizer. However, the Washington, D.C. that's of most interest to the staff of the Washington, D.C. Convention and Visitors Association is often vastly different than the one portrayed in the daily news. The city is rich in history, culture, and diversity; teeming with attractions, restaurants, and accommodations; of interest to business travelers, student groups, convention attendees, families, reunion groups, etc., but at the same time, unique to each type of traveler—for as many reasons as they are unique themselves!

Fortunately, Washington, D.C. is all of those things—but finding the proper balance, getting the right positive image and message to the marketplace, and keeping the city fresh in the minds of those who may be contemplating a business or pleasure trip can be a daunting task.

Many people, both in the United States and abroad, have a very specific picture of what Washington, D.C. has to offer—usually developed at an early age by lessons learned in class, or movies or television programs. Their impression is that Washington, D.C. never changes, and once they've seen it, they've seen it.

These are the same people who would be surprised to learn that Washington, D.C. has added new monuments, memorials, and museums over the past several years, along with other impressive additions, such as the MCI Center, a downtown professional sports and special events facility. "This has required a repositioning of sorts of the city's tourism product—introducing new perspectives and new products to both first-time AND repeat visitors to Washington," says Heizer.

To sell the city, Heizer's staff qualifies the prospective travel trade client and determines which of Washington's many assets would, in turn, be the most saleable to their clientele. It's not always the venerable institutions that hook the client, though Washington is replete with these. Sometimes it's the small museum, historic home, garden tour, or other not so well known entity that captures their attention and their imagination. "We're trying to show our clients that Washington, D.C. is a city of many layers, of many faces, of many treasures. That it's NOT the same place many have frozen in their minds as 'capital of the United States,' 'stilted,' 'home of the federal government.' It is vibrant, ever changing, and ever developing. It's a city alive with diverse peoples, diverse cultures, diverse interests, and diverse opportunities. It's one of the most exciting cities in the world," Heizer points out.

With a limited budget, finding the right marketing and sales mix is also a challenge—particularly when the organization is responsible for both domestic and international sales and marketing to the travel trade. Wisely choosing the trade shows, sales missions, one-on-one sales appointments, promotions, and other activities that make up the annual marketing plan is critical to the success of the organization. This work is also critical to the members of the travel and tourism industry who depend on the Association to properly represent them in marketplaces where they cannot afford to represent themselves, or where it makes sense for the destination alone to work on behalf of the entire industry.

All the while, of course, the staff must keep the Association's bigger picture in mind, making strategic adjustments in the annual marketing plan as new and beneficial opportunities become available. They must also remain diligent about maintaining the right sales and marketing mix for their product.

objective. (Note: marketing objectives are discussed in more detail in Chapter 5.)

For example, Horizon Air offers the only commuter air service between Bend and Portland, Oregon. Thus, a marketing objective that Horizon Air will be the best airline flying that route is meaningless, since it's the only airline on that route. Here the marketing objective is not compatible with the airline's current position, which is determined to a large extent by its lack of direct competition.

Suppose, however, that a new airline received permission to serve the Bend-Portland route. In light of such head-on competition, Horizon Air's position might be adjusted to accomplish a new marketing objective: "To maintain current weekday passenger loads at 80 percent of capacity." To differentiate itself from its new competition, Horizon Air could emphasize the experience of its pilots, its reputation for reliability and fine service, or its frequent flier connection with Northwest Airlines.

Alterations, refinements, and restatements are all a necessary part of maintaining compatibility between a marketing objective and a position. Ideally, as managers consider the marketing objectives and the product position, they can sharpen their ideas and visions in a way that produces a powerful marketing program with a realistic goal for all to work toward.

CREATING THE POSITIONING STATEMENT

Once you've analyzed your product thoroughly, identified your current position, and compared it to your marketing objectives, you're ready to write the positioning statement. It's important to write the statement down formally so that many people are able to refer to it. In the travel business in particular, many people are involved in serving customers, and the positioning statement communicates a consistent viewpoint and a *unified* goal shared by all members of the organization.

The positioning statement takes into account many diverse elements. It considers what image the company now conveys and determines whether this is what management desires the image to be. For example, a small hotel may be quaint and folksy, but to increase its room rates, it would have to develop a more sophisticated, upscale image. Thus, its repositioning statement would have to be changed to reflect that new image clearly. Regardless of the product position, it is important the product's benefits are clearly communicated to the target market so that they understand what is good about the product and thus have a *positive perception* about its value.

A positioning statement should also indicate how a travel product is different from others that are available. Marketers call this difference the ***unique selling proposition (USP)***. If an airline is just like every other airline, there's not much to differentiate it from the others. If, on the other hand, the airline serves gourmet food and fine wines during the flight at no additional cost, it has a USP. Whenever a positioning statement uses words like "biggest," "smallest," "fastest," "least expensive," it's intended to differentiate the product in a way that helps potential customers distinguish it from the competition and to remember it. Marketers always look for a USP to weave into their positioning statements to help produce a distinctive image for their product in the marketplace.

Sometimes people confuse a positioning statement with a slogan; they are different. The positioning statement is created for use within the company. It is a concise theme or statement that is woven through all marketing communications. A **slogan**, on the other hand, is a phrase generated from the positioning statement that is designed to catch the attention of the target market and reinforce a travel product's image. The positioning statement also serves as a basis for many other marketing components, including the advertising campaign and slogan and virtually all other elements that contribute to a product's image.

Another element in the positioning statement—and consequently the product's image—is emotional appeal. Since buying decisions are based on emotion as well as hard facts, emotional appeal is an important aspect of positioning a product, especially a travel product.

Unlike televisions and many other tangible goods, travel products include many intangible elements. Since customers can't inspect or try out a travel product, they need to feel positive about it. How a customer feels about flying an airline, staying in a hotel, or visiting a destination is important: they need to be able to "see themselves there" and "identify" with the product benefits. The positioning statement should, therefore, convey a strong appeal that will elicit an emotion-based response from members of the target market.

The positioning statement should be designed to produce a distinct image of the travel product. Marketing efforts and expenditures are substantially wasted if potential customers confuse a product with its competition. The positioning statement should consistently convey the image that you want customers to have of your product. That image, in turn, creates a distinct and positive perception in customers' minds of the benefits of your product, thus establishing or maintaining its position. The positioning statement serves as the basis for all marketing efforts and is woven through all of your organization's communications with its customers. It is intended to establish a "special place" in the minds of your target market.

EXAMPLES OF POSITIONING STATEMENTS AND STRATEGIES

There are many ways to position a travel product or service. No single way is right or wrong. Often a company will stay with one positioning statement for several years because it is producing positive results. On the other hand, if a company is not meeting its objectives with one positioning strategy, then it should try another tactic.

In travel marketing, the success of a product's position is ultimately measured by how well marketing objectives are accomplished. For example, the best-written and most attractive positioning statement is of little value if it doesn't generate recognition, sales, and profit for the travel organization.

Positioning Relative to a Target Market

As you learned in the previous chapter, there are many possible target markets for travel products. To maximize its profit potential, a company identifies a target market, that portion of all potential customers that the company thinks will be attracted to its products and that it can serve well. The company then directs its marketing message to that particular group of people.

Perhaps one of the best travel industry examples of establishing a successful position in relation to a target market is Club Med. This company is the pioneer in the sector of the resorts industry known as ***all-inclusive resorts***. For one fixed price, these resorts provide guests with accommodations at a resort, meals, entertainment, and an array of activities and sports.

When they decided to enter the American market, Club Med's marketers looked carefully at the demographics of the population and decided to target baby boomers, those people born after World War II and before 1965, during a period of unprecedented growth in the population of the United States. With so many people in that age group, marketers have often found it profitable to identify the needs of that population segment in deciding how to position a product. Club Med did just that.

The need of the baby boomers in the 1960s and 1970s was for a casual resort that offered a combination of relaxation and sports. Their ideal vacation spot was conceived at the time to be one where you could escape from the cold and snow of winter to an island paradise. In the paradise environment, everyone would be pleasant to you and happily help you enjoy yourself. There would be plenty of food and entertainment. You wouldn't have to worry about telephones, newspapers, or money. You could sit on the beach for hours at a time if you wanted or play an energetic game of volleyball if you were so inclined. There would be no need to dress formally for dinner.

An important element of Club Med's appeal to this target market was that it was designed with an emphasis on the needs of single people, which most baby boomers were in the 1960s. Thus, Club Med intentionally positioned itself to appeal to young singles. Its environment was tailored to make those traveling alone feel comfortable and to make it easy to meet the many other singles at Club Med, often through planned group activities. During this time no other resorts positioned themselves so clearly to meet the needs of this target market.

Club Med recognized all the needs the baby boomers had for a vacation resort and met them with their specially designed resorts. Since their start, the number of specialized all-inclusive resorts has expanded greatly. Many other companies now offer resorts based on the same concept, due to continuing demand for the experience.

A few things have happened to the baby boomers since the 1970s. Many of them have married and now have children or grandchildren. As a result, their vacation needs have changed. But, what the older baby boomers want in a vacation now isn't all that different from what Club Med was offering previously, with one exception. Club Med's resorts used to frown on children as guests because children were incompatible with the singles image. The resorts also weren't equipped to handle kids, to keep them busy and happy while their parents enjoyed themselves. The baby boomers of the 1980s wanted to be able to bring their children with them on vacation. They wanted to spend time with their kids but still have some time with each other.

Club Med met the new needs of this large target market by developing the Mini Club. At many locations, as part of the regular Club Med, Mini Clubs offer special facilities and a full program of activities for children. From morning till night, parents can leave their children in the care of counselors at the Mini Clubs. If they would rather have the kids with them for a day on the beach, that's okay, too. But the Mini Clubs offer lots of planned and supervised activities for children. Many parents especially enjoy the chance to have a quiet, romantic dinner—something they don't often get at home.

In the 1990s, short "getaways" and "long weekends" of three to five days were what the lifestyle of the dual career baby boomers demanded. Club Med responded with short-stay packages that allowed baby boomers to provide their own air transportation (including free tickets earned through airline frequent flier rewards). Because baby boomers who had experienced Club Med's quality had become decisionmakers in corporations and organizations, Club Med created the "Rent a Village" program to attract both meetings and incentive travel business. And as this market segment began to show more interest in taking cruises, Club Med began operating luxury sailing cruises among islands in exotic destinations in the Caribbean, Mediterranean, and Pacific Ocean.

Having chosen a target market, Club Med positioned its products to appeal to the vacation needs of a generation. Recognizing that the needs of that generation were changing, it followed its early success with other products. This illustrates the need for marketers to pay attention to the changing needs of a target market and to adapt their products to better meet those changing needs.

Positioning by Product Benefits

Customers choose products consciously or subconsciously based on perceived benefits. Thus, a very direct way to position travel products is to show how a product or service feature or attribute will produce a benefit and/or value to the consumer. Multiple benefits can also be bundled to create slogans and images, although many positioning strategies focus clearly on a single benefit. If you want "the low-fare airline," fly Southwest Airlines. When you rent a car from Alamo "all the miles are free." Club Med is "the antidote for civilization," while Courtyard by Marriott is "the hotel designed by business travelers."

Positioning by Price and Quality

One of the more obvious ways that a company positions its product or service is by price and quality. Travel and tourism offerings are found at all points on the price and quality spectrum.

Consider hotels as an example of a travel product offered in a variety of price and quality levels. At the high end, hotels offer many elaborate services for their guests. From the uniformed bellhops and sumptuous lobbies with expensive carpeting to large fresh-flower arrangements and exquisite furniture, these hotels scream luxury. Their rooms are well decorated, spacious, and spotless. Such hotels usually have several restaurants featuring different cuisines. They also may offer a beauty parlor, a massage service, an indoor swimming pool, and an exercise room. Large hotel companies such as Marriott, Hyatt, Hilton International, Intercontinental, and Westin, among many others, offer luxury services and features. Many other hotels that are not part of a chain or franchise also cater to the luxury market.

At the opposite end of the spectrum are the economy hotels and motels. Some have the word "budget" or "economy" in their names, like Econolodge or Budget Motel. Other large economy chains are Red Roof Inn, Super 8, and Motel Six.

These hotels and motels offer the basics of lodging and a lower level of service. You won't find valet parking or a doorman to help you with your luggage. Their lobbies are sparse and utilitarian. Usually they offer no room service. But for people traveling on a budget, these hotels and motels fulfill a real need.

Many travel products are offered in the middle range of price and quality, often focusing on families. But positioning by price and quality is usually easier to accomplish and often more effective at the ends of the scale—high-priced luxury and low-priced economy.

Positioning Relative to a Product Class

A third way a company can position its product is in relation to a product class. This can be done either by likening the product to others in its class or by disassociating it from other products in its class.

A look at the large array of soft-drink products provides several examples. Many different colas are available on the market. There's cola with caffeine and sugar; cola with caffeine and without sugar; cola without caffeine and without sugar. Each brand of cola claims to be superior to other brands. They all are positioning themselves in relation to their own product class.

But for a soft drink that is not a cola, quite another position can be taken. Seven-Up increased its sales by positioning its soft drink as the "un-cola." Seven-Up contrasted its product with others in that class, thus disassociating itself from all colas. By stating that the product was different from colas, the marketers suggested that Seven-Up was a better alternative.

The same type of positioning is used in the travel business. A new airline might at first position itself by associating itself favorably with established airlines. By doing so, it can quickly shed the image of the inexperienced "new kid" on the block. However, once it has established a reputation, it may want to disassociate itself from other airlines. By showing how it isn't like everyone else, it differentiates itself, developing an image that will appeal to a certain target market.

The airline might cater to the needs of the well-to-do by serving gourmet meals on fine china, with a full complement of wines and champagne. Its seats would be roomy and its cabin appointments luxurious. It would attempt to create the feeling that flying their airline was like attending a sophisticated party in the air. Its fares would be higher than the competition, but it would offer more comfort and amenities. For a certain target market with a substantial amount of money, this airline would be very appealing because it is so different from the other airlines, offering much more than transportation.

Many hotels and resorts also position themselves in relation to a product class, frequently stressing how they are different from others. A large New York hotel ran many ads illustrating how it paid more attention to little details than did other luxury hotels. It provided plenty of thick towels, free premium soaps and shampoo, an extra pillow and blanket, and boasted of an especially courteous staff, for example. And with a lower room rate, it positioned itself as representing exceptional value.

When many products and services crowd a product class, travel companies often enhance their products in a way that makes them stand apart from the others. Consider, for example, the Deer Valley Ski Area, located in Park City, Utah. Like all ski areas, it provides a well-groomed mountain for skiing, lifts of various kinds, ski rentals, and all the other standard services. But Deer Valley, in looking to differentiate itself from other ski areas, added several special services to appeal to a more sophisticated skier.

For example, one big complaint of skiers is that lift lines are too long, forcing them to spend more time waiting to ski than actually skiing. In response, Deer Valley decided to limit ticket sales. Its management determined how many skiers could be accommodated without creating unacceptable lift lines and limited daily lift ticket sales to that number. This approach maximizes the amount of time a skier can actually spend skiing. Consequently, Deer Valley skiers do not object to paying rates slightly higher than average.

Another area in which ski resorts are often unimpressive is food service, which frequently is limited to high-priced, cafeteria-style food of mediocre quality. Deer Valley decided to position itself as an upscale ski area serving gourmet-quality food in its restaurants and in picnic lunches that could be enjoyed slopeside.

Still another service Deer Valley offers is ski valets who help you unload skis and belongings. Anyone who has trudged through an icy parking lot with unwieldy ski equipment can appreciate the luxury of being helped with unloading at an entrance gate. They also offer complimentary overnight ski storage.

Certainly all the added features that Deer Valley Ski Area offers to set itself apart from others in its product class cost money. But in the end, the enhanced position relative to the competition is well worth the economic investment.

Positioning Relative to a Competitor

Almost every travel product has competition for the consumer's attention and dollar. Sometimes the competition is direct, and sometimes it is indirect. ***Direct competition*** is between two or more products, like hotels, ski resorts, airlines, etc. ***Indirect competition*** is between travel products that are less similar but fulfill a somewhat similar need.

For example, two airlines flying from Los Angeles to Hawaii would be considered direct competitors. A traveler could choose one airline or the other. On the other hand, only one ferry boat operator may offer service to a small island, meaning the ferry has no direct competitor. However, an air shuttle service may also carry people to the same island. In a real way, the two companies compete for the same travelers' dollars, making them indirect competitors.

Often, the leader in an industry attempts to maintain its share of the market by positioning itself as the clear leader in its field. For example, an airline that states that no airline offers more nonstop flights from New York to St. Louis is positioning itself against its competitors as the leader on that route. An international airline would be likely to make a different claim, such as more direct flights from Toronto to Paris. Competing airlines,

40TH ANNIVERSARY TRANSCONTINENTAL JET SERVICE

IT FLEW 112 PASSENGERS ACROSS THE COUNTRY AND AN ENTIRE INDUSTRY INTO THE JET AGE.

Before the Internet. Before telephones that fit in a pocket. Before pizza-sized satellite dishes. There was a time when jet travel defined modern technology. So, on January 25, 1959, when 112 American Airlines passengers boarded the first transcontinental jet flight from L.A. to New York, the world took notice. In fact, Carl Sandburg, noted poet and biographer and one of the original passengers on that historic flight observed: "...we all know this is only a beginning, and a promise." Prophetic words indeed. More than 169,000 flights and 23 million passengers later, we're proud to say we still lead the way between New York and L.A. with more daily flights than any other airline. And today, we are dedicated to continuing to serve the New York area by committing more than $1 billion to expand and modernize our terminal at JFK Airport. So, here's to the first 707 Jet Flagship and to those passengers who turned something extraordinary into an everyday reality.

American Airlines tries to stand out among all major domestic airlines. (Courtesy of American Airlines)

with fewer flights on that route, would probably choose to position themselves against the leader by some other means. They may emphasize the comfort of their planes or their on-time record, in order to differentiate themselves from their direct competition.

Amtrak has positioned its passenger trains in the Northeast against its indirect competitors, the airline shuttles that fly the busy route between New York City and Washington, D.C. People traveling between those two cities have several transportation choices. They can drive the approximately 235 miles or ride an intercity bus. Another alternative is to fly nonstop on a shuttle. Shuttles are frequently scheduled airline flights, often running every hour, that allow passengers to either book ahead or simply show up at the airport to buy a ticket. Still another choice the travelers have is to take a train.

Amtrak has positioned itself to win customers by differentiating its product from the air shuttles. Its advertisements depict the air shuttles as harried and inconvenient. First, they usually require a taxi ride to the airport in the suburbs of the city and a wait at the airport for a flight that lasts about an hour. Then, after arrival, there's the problem of getting from the airport to wherever the traveler is going, presumably somewhere in downtown Washington or New York.

By contrast, Amtrak suggests that a train ride is quiet and peaceful. Its advertising reminds customers that the train stations in New York and Washington are conveniently located downtown in the business district, so long taxi rides are not required at either end of the trip. On the train, passengers sit in large, comfortable seats, which actually make it possible to get some work done. Amtrak concedes that, overall, the train takes slightly longer than the plane, but positions its product as a more civilized, less hassled alternative to air travel.

The competition for customers is also fierce in the car rental business. For many years, Hertz has held the number one sales position in the industry. Currently, Avis Rent-A-Car holds the second-place spot, followed by National Car Rental and Budget Rent-A-Car.

But it wasn't that long ago that Avis was in the sixth place. It had positioned itself directly against Hertz and was taking on the leader head to head. Then someone came up with a novel idea. Avis decided not to position itself against Hertz but to admit to its subordinate spot in the industry. As a result, the "We try harder" advertising campaign was born. Instead of saying it was larger, Avis was saying in a subtle way that it worked harder precisely because it was smaller. Its reservations clerks wore buttons proclaiming the "We try harder" slogan, and all the advertising for Avis mentioned in some way how it had to try harder to please customers because it was not in the number one spot. The Avis campaign created a clear image with an emotional appeal to customers—the underdog. It also differentiated itself from the bigger car rental company by implying that bigger was not necessarily better at serving their customers. Today, Avis is firmly in the number two spot and continues to challenge Hertz, often more directly.

THE ROLE OF IMAGE IN BUYING DECISIONS

Everyone perceives things differently. Maybe you've been with a friend looking for a restaurant to have lunch. You examine the menu displayed in the window and talk about whether you want to eat there. You like the choices and find the prices reasonable. Your friend, however, comments that the place is overpriced. Are you right or is your friend right? You both are; you simply perceive the restaurant differently.

Perception heavily influences buying decisions. A travel product that one person perceives as too inexpensive may be perceived by another person as just right. What is judged too fancy for one vacationer is certain to be perfect for another. For those who have not actually visited a tourism destination, perception is reality. Thus, building a distinct, positive, and appealing image in the marketplace is critical. The image should not, however, be created through illusions. A product's image must be grounded in its unique and appealing attributes and developed through the intentional and systematic product positioning approach described in this chapter.

The image that your product or service creates in a prospective customer's mind is often more important than the product reality. A customer may perceive a hotel to be too fancy or more expensive than its competition. The reality that the hotel is not either of those things doesn't matter if the customer has already chosen to stay elsewhere. That is why making certain that your target market has an accurate perception of your travel product is so important to its success.

CHAPTER SUMMARY

* A company establishes a position for its product by building an identifiable image that appeals to the needs of its target market.

* A positioning statement defines what is unique about a product and places it in the context of its competitors.
* A product's position is identified by analyzing its appeal and the characteristics of the product that contribute to that appeal.
* Features, both tangible and intangible, are the qualities of a product or service. Benefits show how a product or service fulfills a customer's needs.
* Written positioning statements for a travel product enable employees to better understand customers' expectations and to work toward the same goal: customer satisfaction.
* Companies position their products relative to their target markets and to those of their direct and/or indirect competitors.
* Positioning by price and quality is more effective at the high and low ends of the price and quality spectrum.
* When positioning relative to a product class, differences between your travel product and others can be highlighted by disassociating from the other products.
* The image that a company or destination creates in a prospective customer's mind can be more important than the actual attributes of the product.

KEY TERMS

product positioning
image
positioning statement
features
benefits
unique selling proposition (USP)
slogan
all-inclusive resorts
direct competition
indirect competition
perception

DISCUSSION QUESTIONS

1. Name two important actions a company must take to establish a product position.
2. Give a current example of travel product advertising that appears to be aimed at maintaining a position.
3. What are the two distinct ways of describing a product or service?
4. Give some examples of situations in which a current position may be incompatible with a marketing objective.
5. What is the purpose of creating a positioning statement for a travel product or service?
6. What is the purpose of formally writing a positioning statement?
7. Choose one of the following ways to position a product and give a specific current example:
   * Positioning relative to a target market.
   * Positioning by product benefits.
   * Positioning by price and quality.
   * Positioning relative to a product class.
   * Positioning relative to the competition.

Positioning the Product

Name: ______________________ Date: ______________

Directions: Answer these questions as you read the chapter. You will be able to use these answers to help you review the chapter.

1. To what two distinct concepts does the term "positioning" refer?

2. What is the difference between selecting a target market and positioning a product?

3. What actions must be taken in establishing a position for a new product?

4. What special actions must be taken in changing the position of an established product?

5. What are the three steps in establishing an effective product position?

6. What are product features?

7. Why is it important to compile a comprehensive list of product features in the product analysis?

8. What are product benefits?

9. Why are product benefits important to positioning?

10. Why is it important to analyze a product's strengths and weaknesses when considering its current position?

11. What is the ideal relationship between a marketing objective and a product's position?

12. What elements should a positioning statement include?

13. Describe the "unique selling proposition" (USP) of a travel product and discuss the role that a USP plays in the positioning process.

14. Briefly describe each type of positioning, including the importance of product benefits.

Relative to a target market:

By product benefits:

By price and quality:

Relative to a product class:

Relative to a competitor:

15. Describe the important role that image plays in buying decisions.

Positioning the Product

Name: ______________________________ Date: ______________

SLOGAN-SPEAK

Think about what each of the following slogans seems to be saying about the product's image, features, and benefits. Then answer the questions.

1. "The Fun Ships." (Carnival Cruise Lines)

A. What does this slogan convey about the product and its features and benefits?

B. Describe a market segment that might respond favorably to this product's positioning and image.

2. "We love to fly and it shows." (Delta Airlines)

A. What does this slogan convey about the product and its features and benefits?

B. Describe a market segment that might respond favorably to this product's positioning and image.

3. "Where all the miles are free." (Alamo Car Rental)

A. What does this slogan convey about the product and its features and benefits?

B. Describe a market segment that might respond favorably to this product's positioning and image.

4. "The antidote for civilization." (Club Med)

A. What does this slogan convey about the product and its features and benefits?

B. Describe a market segment that might respond favorably to this product's positioning and image.

5. "Spend your days like Butch Cassidy and your nights like Henry VIII." (Homestead Ranch)

A. What does this slogan convey about the product and its features and benefits?

B. Describe a market segment that might respond favorably to this product's positioning and image.

6. "Mother Nature made it perfect. We made it accessible." (Snowbird Resort)

A. What does this slogan convey about the product and its features and benefits?

B. Describe a market segment that might respond favorably to this product's positioning and image.

7. "It's where you go when you arrive." (Intercontinental Hotels)

A. What does this slogan convey about the product and its features and benefits?

B. Describe a market segment that might respond favorably to this product's positioning and image.

8. "The world next door." (Canada)

A. What does this slogan convey about the product and its features and benefits?

B. Describe a market segment that might respond favorably to this product's positioning and image.

9. "There's Hertz . . . and not exactly." (Hertz)

A. What does this slogan convey about the product and its features and benefits?

B. Describe a market segment that might respond favorably to this product's positioning and image.

10. "We try harder." (Avis)

A. What does this slogan convey about the product and its features and benefits?

B. Describe a market segment that might respond favorably to this product's positioning and image.

11. "The cost of the high life just got lower." (Holland America Line)

A. What does this slogan convey about the product and its features and benefits?

B. Describe a market segment that might respond favorably to this product's positioning and image.

12. "Something special in the air." (American Airlines)

A. What does this slogan convey about the product and its features and benefits?

B. Describe a market segment that might respond favorably to this product's positioning and image.

Creating Marketing Strategies

OBJECTIVES

When you have completed this chapter, you should be able to:

- Explain the role of marketing objectives in the development of marketing strategies.
- Identify the five elements of a good marketing objective.
- Explain the value of marketing strategies to a company and its travel products.
- Give examples of strategies for a market leader, market challenger, market follower, and market niche player.
- Describe the eight *P*s of the marketing mix.
- Describe the major forms of marketing communications and the differences among them.

So far you have learned about the importance of analyzing the strengths and weaknesses of travel and tourism products and matching them with various markets. You have also learned about market segments and the positioning and image a company develops for its products and services. In this chapter, you will learn how a company goes about achieving the objectives it has established. The "big picture" of what a company does to achieve its marketing goals is called the ***marketing strategy***.

A marketing strategy is to the marketing professional what a flight plan is to an airline pilot. A pilot knows a flight's destination; that's already been established. A flight plan tells the pilot how to get there. Similarly, for marketers, a marketing strategy lays out the path to follow to reach the stated marketing objectives.

MARKETING OBJECTIVES

In addition to developing a marketing strategy and creating the marketing mix, a company should establish specific marketing objectives for each of its target markets. **Marketing objectives** are expressions of goals in relation to target markets. Marketing strategies are always developed in the context of meeting these stated goals.

To be meaningful, marketing objectives must be specific. This is important because the success of marketing strategies is measured by determining whether the marketing objectives were met when the strategies were implemented. To make such determinations possible, marketing objectives must always include the following information:

1. What is to be changed or accomplished (desired result).
2. How will it be done (marketing activities).
3. To whom the activities are to be directed (target market).
4. When (time frame).
5. To what degree (measure of success).

Consequently, a resort's marketing objective which simply states "To increase occupancy" is too general. Even saying "To increase sales by 15 percent" is inadequate, since the marketing methods, a target market, or a time frame are not specified.

A meaningful marketing objective might be "To increase occupancy (desired result) by 15 percent (measure of success) during October (time frame) through a direct-mail promotion (marketing activity) aimed at senior citizens (target market)." The specific nature of this marketing objective makes three things possible. First, it provides a firm starting point for the development of the strategies that will be used to achieve the objective. Second, it is quite clear what needs to be done. Third, it is possible to measure the success of those strategies that are implemented. This specific approach to marketing assures that mistakes in strategy and tactics will be recognized immediately and appropriate adjustments can be made.

In addition to providing a means of measuring the progress and success of marketing programs, objectives are also useful for estimating the potential return on each of the company's marketing activities and identifying the range of marketing activities that will be implemented during a given time period. Objectives can also provide a common benchmark or frame of reference, which is helpful for all employees who are engaged in marketing the company's products.

In combination, these factors explain the importance of concise, measurable marketing objectives. Without such objectives, effective marketing strategies are unlikely to be developed.

EXAMPLES OF MARKETING STRATEGIES

The previous chapter described how marketers establish a position for their travel products after deciding on a target market. To do so, they establish a position that reflects the image they wish to convey. Thus, the product position must be consistent and compatible with their current and future marketing objectives.

After those objectives are stated, the next step is to determine the tactics that will be used to accomplish the objectives. All the various ***marketing tactics*** used to capture the company's share of the target market constitute the marketing strategy.

Specific tactics depend on a product's current market position as well as the level of competition, so deciding which marketing tactics and activities to utilize may be difficult. However, the goal of a marketing strategy may be viewed quite simply: to effectively communicate (through a marketing mix) with the target market(s) that has been selected. Described below are sample strategies based on four possible market positions: market leader, market challenger, market follower, and market niche player.

Market Leader

The organization in the leading position in its product category achieved its place of prominence by knowing the needs of the market and providing products to meet those needs. The ***market leader***, however, can't simply sit back and enjoy its superiority, because other companies are constantly working to close the gap between themselves and the leader. Market leaders, therefore, must continue to conduct market research to adjust their products and update their marketing strategies.

A market leader faces two related challenges. The first is to protect its position as leader. Just as in the children's game "king of the hill," in which everyone tries to knock the king off the hill, market leaders' products are constantly under siege by would-be leaders. The market leader needs to defend its position with good marketing tactics that maintain its image and market share.

The second marketing challenge a leader faces is expanding its share of the market, thus increasing its margin of leadership. To win customers from companies with competing products, a market leader must use aggressive tactics.

Starting with just one ship in 1972, Carnival Cruise Lines is now the leader of the North American cruise market. Its remarkable success resulted from a basic strategy of looking beyond the market of the 5.2 million who traditionally take cruises to the broader market of 200+ million Americans who take vacations. Carnival believes that basic strategy still makes sense for it from a leadership position as well, although it reexamines the strategy frequently.

But Carnival's success has created a marketing problem it never had before—imitators marketing to

Carnival's advertising reflects the trend toward packaging land destinations with cruises. (Courtesy of Carnival Cruise Lines®)

the same basic target market. Carnival has responded by devoting more energy to studying its competition. The company has become more vigilant than ever, according to Carnival President Bob Dickinson, but "we try to remain stoic and maintain a long-term perspective, rather than letting our imitators throw us off our own game."

The imitation by smaller cruise lines has made Carnival's image more important than ever. "Now that other companies have begun playing our tune, we have to work to find ways to play it more clearly, sharply, and loudly than before," says Dickinson. Every form of marketing communication is reviewed with this in mind in an attempt to reinforce and sharpen the unique aspects of Carnival's appeal to customers.

Market Challenger

A ***market challenger*** seeks to become the market leader, or at least to expand its share of the market by attacking the current leader. The challenger's strategy is aggressive and assertive.

One of the tactics a challenger might employ is to offer a product that competes directly with the leader's at a lower price. The idea behind this strategy is that customers are willing to switch loyalties temporarily if they can save money while buying a comparable product. Once people have tried a different product or service and found it satisfactory, they are then more likely to purchase it again, even without a savings incentive. The market challenger counts on increasing business volume and market share, albeit at a lower profit margin, by stealing customers from the market leader.

The crowded car rental market offers many examples of discounting as a challenging tactic. Hertz and Avis, the top two car rental companies in terms of volume, have large shares of the corporate car rental business. Smaller car rental companies such as Thrifty, General, and Alamo, however, compete aggressively with Hertz and Avis, especially for vacation car rental business. Their discount offers range from unlimited free mileage to free upgrades to larger cars.

One advertising campaign by Dollar Rent-A-Car challenged all the competition on the basis of price. The ads claimed that Dollar offered the lowest weekly rates with unlimited mileage. They included a chart of their rates for various kinds of cars and provided blanks for readers to fill in the rates of other car rental companies. Dollar even included the toll-free telephone numbers of all the other companies.

Another tactic used by market challengers is to offer better services. In offering more or better service at a comparable price, a market challenger tries to give customers more for their money.

Virgin Atlantic Airways has had an ongoing battle with British Airways to capture a bigger share of the England–United States transatlantic business. Included in the price of a ticket on Virgin Atlantic is access to a health club and library for pre- or post-flight relaxation, more comfortable seating, higher quality cuisine and video entertainment. Virgin Atlantic also uses advertising that features the results of passenger surveys from consumer travel magazines, and/or testimonials about Virgin Atlantic's service from former British Airways passengers to convince transatlantic travelers to try their airline.

Market Follower

Still another example of a marketing strategy based on market position is that of ***market follower***. A market follower may be quite content with its subordinate position in the market. Sometimes the leader is so strong that it just doesn't make sense for other companies to challenge it. At other times the follower is conserving finances by not disrupting the status quo. A follower fears that it stands to lose more than it might gain by challenging the leader and upsetting the market position order. Market followers acknowledge their position and expect that their business will improve as the whole sector of which they are a part gains business.

There are many examples of market followers piggybacking on the success of a leader. One such example is found in the all-inclusive resorts product category, in which Club Med is the longtime leader. Club Med pioneered the idea of a resort where one price covers practically all vacation expenses—airfare, lodging, meals, entertainment, and activities. The popularity of Club Med spawned many imitators, or followers. Today, for example, there are many all-inclusive resorts in the Caribbean Islands, Bermuda, and the Bahamas to choose from in addition to Club Med, including Couples, Hedonism, and Sandals.

Sandals kindles thoughts of romantic Caribbean vacations. (Courtesy of Sandals Resorts)

These all-inclusive resorts are not identical and each has its own individual appeal. However, their marketing strategy is largely that of a follower. Each offers alternative locations and slightly different programs to the same basic target market. To be a successful and viable travel product, these followers have determined that they do not need to be either a leader or a challenger. They believe that if the demand for all-inclusive resort vacations increases they will all share in the expanding market.

Market Niche Player

Because the travel market is so varied and broad, some travel companies choose to market products only to a very narrow part of the market. This strategy is that of the **market niche player**. Some specialized segments of a market may be largely ignored by big companies. These niches offer smaller companies opportunities to specialize in a way that avoids direct competition with big companies.

Consider, for example, a helicopter service from downtown New York City to nearby LaGuardia Airport. A large airline certainly has the capability of operating a helicopter service but for many reasons may choose not to. That leaves room for a small helicopter company to dominate that specialized shuttle market as a niche player.

A number of tour operators have been successful in the niche market of adventure travel. A pioneer in that market, Lindblad Travel, specialized in luxury tours to exotic places such as Antarctica, Easter Island, Bhutan, China, and Tibet. Lindblad carved out a specialized market for itself by offering tours to unusual destinations that most larger tour companies ignored. In contrast to the larger companies, which focused on volume business in choosing their destinations, Lindblad emphasized customized quality. Lindblad customers wanted travel to be an exciting, educational, culinary, and social experience. They knew that if anyone could offer a tour to destinations offering such experiences, it would be Lindblad.

The hotel market has its niche players, too. For example, Morgans in New York City may not be well known to the average visitor, but it has one of the highest occupancy rates of any hotel in Manhattan. Morgans is one of a specialized type of hotels called a boutique hotel. Boutique hotels are small, luxury hotels that emphasize personalized service. Typically these hotels have fewer than two hundred rooms, offer twenty-four-hour concierge services, and have a premier restaurant. Boutique hotels use niche marketing tactics to appeal to wealthy, discriminating travelers who want luxury accommodations and more individual attention than a large hotel usually provides.

MARKETING MIX

Another important element in the marketing of travel products is the **marketing mix**. The marketing mix includes all the variables a company can control in planning and implementing its marketing strategies and meeting its marketing objectives. Like the ingredients in a recipe, marketing variables must be used in just the right amount for success. For consumer product marketing, the four traditional variables—known as the four *P*s—are product, place (or process of delivery), price, and promotion. In recent years, some travel marketing experts have added four more *P*s: physical environment, purchasing process, packaging, and participation. They feel these additional *P*s are necessary to describe the processes involved in marketing travel services. Together these additional variables are referred to as the Eight *P*s (see Figure 5–1).

The *P*s of marketing have been compared to the controls in a car—the accelerator, brake, gearshift, and steering wheel. They must be used according to the road conditions (the market) and the actions of other drivers (the competition). Like the controls in a car, the *P*s must be constantly manipulated or adjusted to reach the destination (or goal).

Product

The product is what the company offers for sale in order to satisfy customer needs. Decisions about the characteristics of the product are based on the identification of its tangible and intangible aspects and their appeal to potential customers. This also includes determining what services will accompany the product. In many instances, of course, what a travel company sells will be a service. For example, by taking passengers from one destination to another, transportation companies are essentially selling a service. Selecting a name and developing an image for the product or service are also extremely important in presenting it to the public.

The *P*s	Definition	Example
Product	What a company is offering for sale	A cruise
Place/Process of delivery	Channels of distribution and delivery	Travel agency
Price	The amount of money paid for a product, based by seller on certain factors	$99 round trip
Promotion	Activities that stimulate interest in a product	Advertising
Physical environment	The environment in which the sale takes place	Travel agency Web site
	The environment in which the product is produced and consumed	Resort suite
Purchasing process	Motivations and information search	Selecting a destination
Packaging	Bringing together of complementary travel products	All-inclusive tour
Participation	The transaction or experience	Buyer, intermediary, and seller interaction

FIGURE 5–1 The eight *P*s are variables a company can control when trying to attain its goal of success.

Another part of this *P* is selecting and developing the right number and range of products and services. Most companies offer more than one. A travel agency must decide whether to offer a wide range of products or to specialize in products for a certain type of travel, such as vacation travel. A transportation company must decide what routes and levels of service (first-class, economy, business) to make available. A tour operator must decide how many tours to offer, when they will take place, and what the itinerary for each one will be.

Place/Process of Delivery

Process of delivery—also called place or channels of distribution—refers to all the activities involved in delivering a product or service to the customer. The seller must decide how and where to sell the product or service. For example, a resort belonging to a large chain can reach customers in several ways. Depending on the channels of distribution established by the resort's marketing department, a traveler could make a reservation in many ways. These include using a travel agent or tour operator, calling the resort's reservation desk or another resort in the company, visiting a Web site, and using an airline reservation system.

Sellers attempt to locate their distribution points where they are most likely to attract customers or be convenient for them. For example, a travel agency specializing in vacation travel might find that a location in a suburban shopping mall attracts more walk-in customers than a location in a downtown business district. Of course, sellers are limited in the number of distribution points they can afford to operate. Many airlines, for instance, have generally found it more cost-effective to distribute their products through travel agencies rather than through their own ticket offices and reservation centers. But the development of online reservation systems and airline Web sites have expanded the distribution points and reduced the airline reliance on travel agencies.

Price

Price means the amount of money the customer will be charged to receive the product or service. In establishing a price, a company must consider many factors: the actual costs to produce and distribute the product or service, the profit margin needed by the company, the current demand for the product, and the price of similar products and services offered by the competition. At the same time, the pricing strategy must appeal to the particular segment of the market for whom the product or service is intended—the traveler must perceive that the product provides value for the money.

As with the products of other industries, travel products usually have a predictable price range. There may, however, be discounted or promotional prices to stimulate sales when necessary or to respond to competitors' pricing. Discounted prices are frequently offered during off-peak seasons for leisure travel. For example, airlines may offer substantial discounts on regular ticket prices during low-demand periods, except during holidays, when few discounts are available. Most important, a travel company should have a comprehensive pricing plan that establishes standard prices and anticipates all fluctuations in demand, as well as competitors' "specials," and discounts.

Promotion

For customers, promotion is probably the most visible of the *P*s in the marketing mix. Promotional activities stimulate interest in products and services, furnish information that helps people decide what to buy, provide incentives to purchase, and, in general, attempt to persuade consumers to purchase particular products and services.

The ways in which a company can promote itself and its products are almost endless. Promotion includes paid advertising in print (magazines and newspapers), electronic broadcast (TV, radio, Internet), and outdoor media (billboards, kiosks). It also includes publicity such as press releases, feature articles in a newspaper, guest interview shows, and speakers' bureaus. Some techniques that salespeople use in working with customers are a form of promotion. These include special gifts and souvenirs, fliers, brochures, discount coupon books, letterhead stationery, business cards, newsletters, direct mailings, and many other promotional items which help to make consumers more aware of the travel products and services offered by the organization.

One interesting promotional program in the history of the travel industry has been the frequent-flier program devised by American Airlines in 1981. Since then, other airlines, hotels, and car rental agencies have created their own programs that reward frequent and loyal customers and create brand loyalty.

As part of their promotion strategy, travel companies and organizations use advertising slogans to help establish a clear identity. The advertising campaigns of United Airlines ("Fly the friendly skies"), Carnival Cruise Lines ("The Fun Ships"), and Tourism Canada ("The world next door") are among the successful campaigns of recent years.

Physical Environment

As mentioned, physical environment is especially important for the travel and tourism industry. This marketing *P* is important in two distinct ways: first, as the environment in which the sale takes place, and second, as the environment where the product is produced and consumed.

Since customers are more likely to make a purchase in a pleasant, comfortable setting, a marketing strategy should take into account the physical environment in which products and services are sold. In purchasing a product such as a TV or an easy chair, people are most interested in how the product looks, feels, or operates. Their attention is focused more on the product than on the surrounding environment. When purchasing travel products, however, customers cannot be sure they will enjoy the experience until the trip has been taken. In the meantime, their expectations and emotions are influenced by factors such as the layout of the room, the furniture, noise level, temperature, lights, and other factors. For those purchasing electronically, the appearance of the Web site, and how user-friendly and comprehensive the information is will make a difference.

In the travel industry, the physical environment—where the product is experienced—can be particularly important for securing repeat business. As an example, resort guests who find the design and decor of their rooms unattractive and uncomfortable are not likely to make reservations to stay there again. Dirty beaches or swimming pools, poorly groomed ski trails, and unattractive views from hotel balconies are additional examples of elements of the physical environment that can ruin a customer's experience. Consequently, travel companies and organizations devote a great deal of energy to enhancing the physical environment of their products in every way possible, in order to assure that visitors' expectations are met and their experiences are positive and memorable.

Purchasing Process

The purchasing process takes into account people's psychological motivations for purchasing travel and the way in which they make decisions. Why do people choose to spend their money on travel instead of on cars, boats, second homes, or new furniture? And why do they choose particular travel products out of the hundreds that are available? In addition to the broad purposes of travel mentioned earlier (business, leisure, and travel for special purposes), people might travel to gain prestige, to have an adventure, or to learn about other cultures. Some people travel to improve their health, to discover their ancestral roots, or simply to please family and friends. Customers' needs and wants, personality traits, and social and economic position help to shape their motivations. Companies that are able to discover buyer motivations can formulate products and promotions to meet customer needs and expectations.

Providing useful information in an appealing format to potential customers is crucial to the purchasing process. Before they can make a purchase, customers need to be aware of sources of information about travel products, how to access that information, and how to purchase products and services conveniently. Smart travel marketers supply customers with this information as a way of facilitating the purchase process.

In the purchasing process, information about products is not always perceived, or interpreted, as the travel companies had intended. Consequently, marketing sometimes must overcome negative stereotypes or misinformation about products. For example, during the 1990s, cruise sales increased tremendously only after the cruise industry convinced the public that cruising was not just for stuffy millionaires or senior citizens.

Finally, in considering the purchasing process, marketers also recognize that people don't give the same amount of thought to each travel product they purchase. Some travel products such as car rentals and accommodations may be selected easily. Other travel products such as vacation destinations and cruises may require a great deal of thought. Clearly, the complexity, timing, and price of the travel products influence how they are marketed and sold to consumers.

Packaging

In the marketing of travel products, the packaging variable is usually used to bundle separate products together to form travel "packages." The complementary nature of travel products, discussed earlier, is responsible for this approach. Most trips, whether for leisure or business purposes, are composed of many different travel products, often provided by different suppliers.

Packaging offers travel companies a mechanism to meet certain identified customer needs by bringing complementary products together in ways that address those needs directly. In the process, the appeal of each product is enhanced.

The all-inclusive, packaged group tour is probably the best example of this concept. These tours bring together numerous separate travel products into one comprehensive, complementary package. When put together properly, that package is likely to offer customers increased convenience and value, to reduce the hassles and surprises, to increase their sense of security and safety, and to provide them with the social benefits of traveling with a group of people. All of these benefits result directly from packaging, which heightens the appeal of each travel product by bundling it with complementary products into a unified trip that can be acquired in a single purchase.

Often the appeal of packaged products is enhanced through programming, which creates special events, experiences, services, or itineraries that add value to the package.

Participation

Participation refers to all the people involved in the sales transaction—the sellers, the intermediaries, the buyers, and even other customers. This *P* is especially important for the travel industry because of the close interaction between the seller and buyer and because the buyer's participation helps to shape the travel experience. In contrast to consumer products, the quality of the travel experience is dependent on the behavior and actions of the buyer as well as the seller during the course of a trip. In addition, buyers' perceptions of a sales transaction often determine whether or not they will purchase the product or service again. Since the travel industry depends heavily on repeat business, participation is an extremely important part of the marketing mix.

Interacting. An important aspect of participation is that the attitudes and actions of the participants in a vacation trip can enhance or ruin the experience. An airline passenger who is treated rudely by a flight attendant or who receives indifferent service will probably not enjoy the flight and will likely think twice about booking on that airline again. On the other hand, an ill or depressed passenger may not enjoy the trip no matter how excellent the service. And a screaming baby can ruin a flight for all of the passengers.

Although participation is a difficult variable to control, companies try to manage the behavior of their employees. Training programs, uniforms, and strategies for service excellence, including employee authority to "fix" service failures, are ways of doing this. The training program at Walt Disney World—known as "Disney University"—is famous for turning out thousands of polite, clean-cut, and customer-oriented employees. Many companies provide their employees with rewards such as free trips or bonuses for exceeding their customers' expectations. Some companies emphasize this practice as part of their ***internal marketing*** program. The goal of providing such incentives is to help employees feel good about the company and its products so that they will want to perform their jobs better and be more dedicated to satisfying customers.

Shaping the Experience. To understand how customer participation helps shape the experience, think about the last time you had your hair cut or styled. You and the stylist discussed what to do with your hair before any cutting began. The stylist probably suggested options, but you helped shape the outcome by telling the stylist to cut off an inch or two, to give you a trim, or to change the color. Of course, if the stylist did not ask for your suggestions or didn't follow your instructions, you were probably disappointed, and you probably would not return to that shop.

In a similar but even stronger manner, the preferences, expectations, and behaviors of travelers shape their travel experiences. Where travelers want to go, what they want to do, and what they think the destination will be like are among the factors that ultimately affect the quality of their travel experience. Thus, the image a destination projects and the desired benefits sought by a buyer play an important role in this process.

People working in the travel industry—especially in marketing and sales—need to be aware of and attuned to this interplay among customers, employees, and products. Travel agents, who help customers plan their travel and choose among alternatives, must develop specialized skills to clearly identify customers' expectations.

MANAGING THE MARKETING MIX

As mentioned, the *P*s of marketing are the actions, techniques, and systems a company uses to communicate with and satisfy customers. They must be used in the right amount, combination, and relationship to each other to achieve a defined goal.

The Product/Service Combination

Many elements, tangible and intangible, make up a product or service. Travel products combine tangible and intangible components, and customers usually do not differentiate among them.

The ***product/service combination*** is an important factor to consider in meeting the needs of the selected target market. If the combination does not meet their particular needs, then it will not be desired and must be altered. Adjusting the product/service combination can entail offering new services, eliminating services, or changing how they are combined.

Consider, for example, a resort in the mountains that attracts mostly families for weekend visits. The parents of these families may want to play tennis, soak in the Jacuzzi, or just enjoy quiet for part of a Saturday afternoon. To meet these needs, the resort obviously must provide these facilities for its guests. But since the families have children, the resort may need to initiate childcare services and children's activities to allow the parents to enjoy those facilities. On the other hand, the resort's flashy nightclub may not contribute significantly to the appeal of the property for families. If the club is underutilized, the space it occupies may need to be converted to something that provides benefits to family vacationers.

For another example of altering the combination of products and services, look at the airline industry. Although it may appear that an airline offers one thing—transportation between two points—in actuality, the airline offers a combination of products and services. The frequency and time of its scheduled flights and the type of aircraft all are one part of the service the airline offers. By adding flights or changing the time of the flights, the airline alters its product/service combination.

Some business travelers flying to a major city find it desirable to take an early-morning flight that arrives around 9 A.M., and an evening flight that gets them home before 9 P.M. This makes it possible to conduct a full day of work without requiring an overnight hotel stay. The airline that recognizes this need adjusts its schedule, type of plane, and service to better serve its target market.

In addition to altering the actual product/service mix, marketers can emphasize particular products or services in order to better appeal to their target markets. For example, an airline that identifies students and other people flying on a budget as its target market recognizes that they want the lowest possible fare and are willing to forgo some of the "frills" of airplane travel. To keep the fare low, the airline would provide limited food service on the flight. Then travelers have the option of bringing their own food. This also allows marketing efforts to emphasize the "no frills" aspect of the airline to budget-conscious people and turn the absence of a particular service into a benefit for the targeted group.

The Presentation Mix

It's human nature for people to want to know what they will receive in exchange for the money they will spend. Since so many aspects of travel products are intangible, marketing professionals must concentrate on making sure that the product is understood. Their purpose is to make its characteristics and benefits seem more tangible in order to facilitate customers' purchasing decisions.

The methods used to increase the tangibility of a product while differentiating it from its competitors are part of what is called the ***presentation mix***. Five major elements constitute the presentation mix:

1. Physical characteristics.
2. Location.
3. Atmospherics.
4. Price.
5. Employee behavior and attitude.

Physical Characteristics. Almost everyone forms opinions from what he or she sees at first glance. A traveler driving down a highway may come upon two motels right next to one another. One is a bit dilapidated, and part of its neon sign is burned out. A newspaper blows around its empty parking lot. The other motel has a freshly painted sign and potted flowers decorating the entrance. Most travelers would choose to stay at the second motel and not even consider the first. Initial impressions, therefore, are important.

Travelers draw conclusions from external appearances. What a hotel, resort, motor coach or ship looks like on the outside gives clues to the nature of what is inside. When people form opinions about a place and say, "I just don't like the way it looks," they are also indicating that they don't think that they would have a pleasant experience there. Travel marketing professionals, therefore, need to concern themselves with appearances and, as much as possible, make sure that what is initially seen gives positive clues about product quality.

In addition to external appearances, physical characteristics include the actual composition of the travel product and its layout. A resort's composition would include the number and type of its rooms and beds, the amount and types of public space (foyers, lobbies, etc.), and the facilities such as swimming pools, tennis courts, and golf courses. For business people, meeting-room design and audiovisual equipment might be among the significant physical characteristics or features of a hotel.

For a specific airline flight, many characteristics can increase its tangibility to potential customers and can differentiate it from other airlines operating the same route. Its physical characteristics could include the type of plane flown, its capacity, the size and configuration of its seats, and the kind of food served. More or less emphasis can be placed on any individual characteristics that suit particular target markets and help them better relate to the product.

Location. A second important element of the travel product presentation mix is location. Some people view location as a given, something that can't be changed. In a sense, this is true. However, travel professionals can change how customers feel about a location by managing the way they communicate information about the location.

Consider the importance of location to a fictitious destination ski resort in the mountains of Colorado—Mount Ski. Although the resort has some of the best trails and snow conditions, Mount Ski is far from most major population centers. Most skiers must first travel several hours by plane to Denver. Next they have to choose either another, somewhat expensive flight in a small plane or a several-hour trip by shuttle, motor coach, or rental car over snow-covered mountain roads.

The manner in which Mount Ski presents its location to potential customers is critical. The resort's marketing tactics can help determine how people perceive its remoteness. Mount Ski needs to present its remote location as a benefit, something that makes it special. Its location allows it to be a ski resort that's not for everyone; rather, one for skiers dedicated to their sport, who seek excellence "off the beaten trail."

In contrast, to ski enthusiasts in a major city, a nearby ski resort may present its location as a convenience. It will emphasize the short drive required to reach it and the availability of public transportation.

Marketers intend for the information they give customers to enhance their presentation of location. When the area surrounding a destination is beautiful and scenic, that fact becomes important and is emphasized. A hotel on a lake, for example, would certainly feature the lake when describing its location.

Similarly, hotels and restaurants located on well-traveled roads or at major intersections emphasize the accessibility of their location. Motels often describe their location in relation to a highway, an expressway, or an interstate exit, such as "just off exit seven." Location also can be stated in relation to a major attraction, such as "across from the main gate at Disney World."

Atmospherics. Those elements of the presentation mix that make the intangible aspects of travel products more tangible are called **atmospherics**. Terms like "elegant," "rustic," or "European style" are examples of those used to describe a resort or bed-and-breakfast. Atmospherics are meaningful descriptions that help communicate a feeling or benefit to potential customers.

For example, if restaurants want to convey a country atmosphere, they do so with rough-hewn wooden paneling and objects such as an antique washboard, farm tools, or framed advertisements from old magazines hanging on the wall. The intangible sense of country is communicated by tangible clues and decor.

For a hotel or resort presenting itself as luxurious, the atmospheric elements would be quite different. It might have plush carpeting or Oriental rugs in the foyer. Gilded mirrors, vases filled with fresh flowers, and crystal chandeliers are among the tangibles that might help communicate an atmosphere of elegance.

Airlines use atmospherics to communicate differences in class of service. In first class, passengers are served complimentary drinks in real glasses instead of disposable plastic, are given cloth napkins rather than paper, and when flying on transcontinental flights receive reclining seats, headphones and slippers, toothbrushes, and toothpaste. All these details help to make the first-class passenger feel special and to recognize the benefits and value of first-class travel.

Price. Another important element of the presentation mix is price. The price for any product must be set at a rate that will produce a profit. How high that profit will be depends on many factors, including the costs of providing and delivering the product and sales revenues.

Profit is the amount of total revenue left after all costs are paid—salaries, supplies, overhead, and other business expenses.

For example, an airline providing service between two cities on a predetermined schedule may have one flight with half as many seats sold as another flight. The airline must operate both planes even though one is only half full. As a result, it may lose money on some low-occupancy flights, but make up for the loss with the revenue from flights that are filled to capacity.

Similarly, hotels still bear the cost of upkeep for rooms that go unoccupied. Thus, room rates have to cover costs associated with low-occupancy, off-peak times as well as those of peak occupancy.

The price the competition is charging also plays a role in determining a product's price. If one bus company offers trips from Philadelphia to Atlantic City for $20, a competing bus company offering the same level of service won't have many customers if it charges $40.

When determining price, marketing professionals try to compare similar products of like quality. Sometimes it's difficult to compare products when intangible factors, such as the friendliness of employees or a comfortable atmosphere, are factored into the price. Consumers are also willing to pay more for the unusual or the exclusive. A small restaurant at the top of a mountain may be able to charge more for a cup of coffee than a similar restaurant on a dusty highway.

As much as consumers look for a good price in the products and services they buy, they also are concerned with quality. Often, price is seen as an indicator of quality, especially by someone unfamiliar with a product or service. It is important to remember that if something of high quality is priced too low, consumers may think that it is of low quality and, therefore, undesirable.

Employee Behavior and Attitude. In the service-oriented travel industry, employees are a critical part of the presentation mix. They have frequent contact with customers and influence their impression of a product. The behavior and attitudes of employees help determine whether customers will choose to purchase a travel product again.

An upsetting experience with a server or bellman can taint a traveler's perception about a resort, a destination, or even an entire trip. Imagine the reactions if a visitor's first experience with Mexico City is with a surly cab driver. The cabbie mumbles some incomprehensible words as he throws the luggage into the trunk, then slams the trunk lid shut. On the trip from the airport the cabbie drives too fast and hits almost every pothole. By the time the visitor gets to her hotel, she is in a foul mood and already has a negative impression of Mexico City. The same visitor would feel quite different about the city if the cab driver drove carefully and was polite, perhaps asking the visitor where she came from and what she was looking forward to doing while in Mexico City.

In many ways, employees are perceived to be part of the travel product. On a cruise ship the stewards, servers, and other employees set the tone for the passengers. Who wouldn't prefer to have the first cup of morning coffee poured by a bright, cheerful, and neatly dressed employee? Most people prefer to be treated as special customers, and when an employee recognizes a traveler by name, that small gesture of friendliness is pleasing to that customer, and increases the chance of repeat business.

Marketing Communications

There are many ways to communicate with the target market to increase the tangibility of the travel product or service, monitor consumer expectations, or persuade consumers to buy. All the forms of communications are included in the ***marketing communications*** component of the marketing mix. They must be carefully coordinated in order to contribute to the overall marketing objective. These communications take the form of advertising, public relations, sales promotion, and personal selling.

Advertising. Perhaps the most visible marketing communication form is ***advertising***: the paid, nonpersonal presentation of ideas, goods, and services by an identified sponsor. The sponsor purchases and controls the content of timed messages on a television or radio station, in a printed publication such as a newspaper or magazine, or on a Web site.

Advertising has several purposes, the most basic of which is to convey information. Just look at any ad in a newspaper. The circus is coming to town next week. That's a piece of information.

An advertisement might be intended to stimulate a demand for a certain product or service, to build or enhance a product's image, or to alter the public's perception of a product. Many advertisements openly call for or imply a request for the reader to take an action. An ad for an airline or destination may end by urging a call to an 800 number to place a reservation.

The importance of employee performance cannot be overemphasized.

If the purpose of advertising is not an immediate purchase, it may be designed instead to create or increase awareness of a travel product. For example, when a travel destination such as Bermuda advertises itself, its primary goal is to have people think of Bermuda the next time they are planning a vacation, even if it's many months later.

An acronym has been developed to describe the sequence of responses an advertisement should elicit—AIDA (see Figure 5-2). Each letter of AIDA stands for a concept of advertising.

- A is for the reader's or listener's ATTENTION, which must be captured by an advertisement.
- I is for INTEREST, which an ad should create.
- D is for DESIRE, which advertising should stimulate in the reader for the product or service being advertised.
- A is for ACTION, which is the end result of a successful ad, whether it's the action of making a reservation, purchasing the product, or requesting more information about it.

Advertising comes in many forms and has many uses, which you will read more about in Chapter 10. In general, the effectiveness of advertising depends on several qualities: quality of presentation, pervasiveness, and creative expressiveness.

Advertising is a highly public mode of communication. Its public nature suggests that the offer being made is legitimate and acceptable. Advertising capitalizes on the tendency of human beings to want to behave in a way that is publicly acknowledged as appropriate or acceptable. Since many people receive and respond to the same advertising message, customers infer that their motives for purchasing a prod-

The Four Concepts of Advertising

Attention - advertisement must catch audience's attention

Interest - advertisement must stimulate interest in product

Desire - advertisement must create desire for product

Action - advertisement must cause action, such as purchase of product

FIGURE 5–2 For an advertisement to be successful, it must elicit these four responses, known as AIDA.

uct are widely shared—and appropriate. In a sense, the public nature of advertising confirms their views.

A second quality of advertising that contributes to its effectiveness is its pervasiveness. Advertising is all around us. Messages are repeated many times in order to reach the largest number of prospective customers and to reinforce the message so the product will be remembered. Reinforcement is valuable because advertisers have no control over a prospective customer's receptiveness to an ad. Perhaps he or she has a headache or just got some bad news in an e-mail message. At another time, the same individual may be in a better mood and more able to respond positively to the message the advertiser is offering. Consequently, the frequency of advertising can help increase the likelihood of its being effective.

The pervasiveness of advertising allows advertisers to reach different target markets through different media. Consider for a moment which magazines you subscribe to or read regularly. Some of them are certainly different from those your parents read. Because advertisers want to reach specific target markets, they select the media that are most effective in accomplishing marketing objectives (for statistics on magazine advertising, see Figure 5–3).

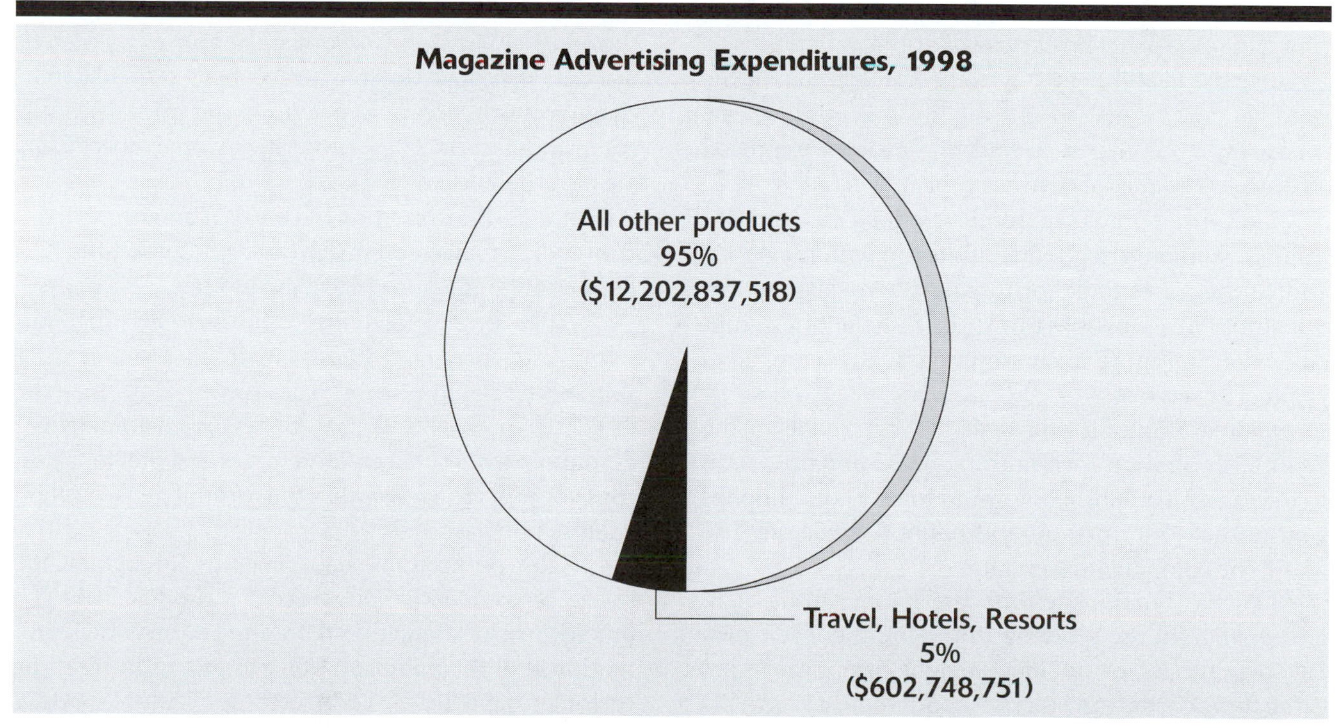

FIGURE 5–3 Travel organizations constitute a small but significant portion of the total market for magazine advertising. *Source:* Publishers Information Bureau, Inc.

The third quality of advertising that determines its effectiveness is its expressiveness through the creative use of the design, wording, artwork, sound, and photographic elements that make up the ad. Advertising is a means for a company to dramatize its products in ways that are intriguing, memorable, and pleasing to the consumer, while accomplishing the company's objectives.

Advertising can be conducted by individual companies and destinations or in partnership with other compatible and complementary companies. In cooperative advertising the costs of ads or the entire campaign are shared. An example of a private-public partnership would be Coca-Cola providing tickets to events it sponsored as prizes in a drawing, held by the New York Convention and Visitors Bureau. Travel advertising is aimed directly at target markets and at the travel trade (intermediaries), which influences consumer decisions on behalf of advertisers.

Public Relations. ***Public relations (P.R.)*** is the presentation of ideas, goods, or services. Unlike advertising, P.R. is neither purchased nor intended to directly generate sales. In most cases public relations content is controlled by the media, not the company. Some people think of public relations simply as unpaid advertising; it's much more than that.

A public relations program is designed to work with other elements of a marketing communications program. One general purpose of public relations is to increase the visibility and awareness of a company, its product, and/or its advertising in the public's eye. Increasing visibility is meant to lead to improved recognition by prospective customers.

Another purpose of public relations, as the name implies, is to build a good relationship with the public and/or the travel trade, or to strengthen existing relationships. When people think positively about a company, they are more likely to purchase that company's product or service.

For example, if you read a short article in the newspaper about a local tour operator donating food to the needy, you probably would form a good impression of that tour operator and might someday recommend the company to someone.

Public relations efforts are more subtle than advertising efforts. Working through either their own P.R. department or an independent firm, companies bring newsworthy information about themselves to the attention of the public. The information might be that a new hotel or resort is opening or that a travel company is sponsoring a college scholarship. Because the information is of interest to the public and because the message is not directly selling a product, the media are often willing to give free space or time to a public relations message. Grand openings, for example, are covered by newspapers and television as community news events. Often a celebrity or local figure attends the event to enhance its news value.

Companies use public relations as another way of reaching their target market. For example, an upscale hotel may cosponsor a charity ball and donate the use of its ballroom for a night. In return, the hotel will be mentioned in every news item about the charity ball—both in advance of the ball and in news coverage during and after. A specific type of P.R., publicity includes news releases or press conferences that might be used to announce new routes (airlines) or locations (resorts).

Sales Promotion. Specialized activities designed to stimulate demand for a particular product are called ***sales promotion***. Sales promotion is distinct from the more general term "promotion." The specific purpose of sales promotion is to encourage a sale, often in a very direct manner. For example, some frequently used sales promotions are coupons, gifts, vouchers, two-for-the-price-of-one offers, giveaways, merchandising (point-of-purchase displays) and contests.

The objective of all sales promotions is to provide short-term incentives to motivate people to try a product that they had not purchased before or had purchased only on occasion. Coupons and price discounts are examples of sales promotions that specifically prompt people to purchase a product or service. Whether purchasing a box of cereal or an airline flight, customers are given an incentive to try something new or unfamiliar in return for saving money.

Sales promotions also reinforce existing customers and encourage them to maintain their relationship with a product. A sales promotion may be designed specifically to benefit repeat customers. For example, a contest may require proof of a previous purchase or provide an award in the form of a discount on a future purchase.

Sales promotions also generally strengthen the image or competitive position of a product. Like the other forms of marketing communications, sales promotions put the name and the product in front of the customer many times. Every communication, whether advertising, public relations, or sales promotion, should contribute to the overall product image.

Marketing Impressions

HOTARD/GRAY LINE COMPANY PROFILE

In New Orleans, Hotard Coaches and New Orleans Steamboat Company proudly operate Gray Line tours. Hotard is a local charter transportation company, and the New Orleans Steamboat Company operates the world famous paddle wheeler SS NATCHEZ. These two companies joined forces in New Orleans to represent Gray Line, a name that has been known in the United States for over eighty years.

The history of New Orleans is one of adventure and intrigue. The Gray Line Super City tour offers a delightful trip back in time to learn about the events that have formed this charming city. The Gray Line Super City tour shares fun-filled facts and myths to give visitors that special acquaintance with the city's charm and splendor. Visiting a city without learning of its past means a person will be cheated. The charm and character of New Orleans is, in many ways, the draw that captures visitors.

Gray Line Sightseeing also offers daily sightseeing tours into the magical swamps of Louisiana. The sheer beauty of nature in the swamps is a must-see. Add an alligator or two, and the tour is a special treat.

New Orleans offers many diverse opportunities, such as large conventions. Hotard operates convention shuttle systems for meetings from 200 people to 20,000 people. As huge convention groups gather in New Orleans to do business, transporation is one of their essential needs. The delegates fill the city, and as the meetings get under way, special shuttle systems transport these important delegates from their hotels to meeting sites.

The customer base in the charter bus industry is a diverse one. One day, we may be transferring a group of first-graders on a field trip, the next day, a group of governors attending a governor's conference. The marketing challenge is to "invent" reasons groups will want to charter a motor coach. Since the business is not like a consumable product, much of our success depends upon our ability to create exciting outings.

The group dynamic of motor coach travel is quite something to witness. It is often said that when people ride a bus all day, they make friends for life. The time between destinations can be used for many things. For example, a sales training video can be shown to a sales team. School children can learn while playing several exciting games, watching videotapes, reading books, etcetera, all while enroute. When people are gathered in groups, a special bond develops for memorable experiences.

As marketing develops innovative excursions, the sales challenge is to convince random groups that motor coach outings will be fun, exciting, and educational. The dynamic of the group forming for the day is the Lagniappe (Cajun French for "a little something extra").

The largest sales and marketing challenge of the charter bus industry is to overcome the image of "the bus." Many people simply do not ever think of riding a bus for anything or, if the thought occurs, they recall an unpleasant memory of school days. The modern motor coach can be equipped with galleys, VCRs, CD players, and restrooms, all to make for an extremely comfortable ride. Load it up with snacks, a bar, videotapes, and the fun begins.

A new niche market, which is in the developmental stages, is the wedding market. As many brides and grooms have relocated to other cities, their families must fly into where the wedding is taking place. A chartered motor coach is a terrific way to transport the wedding participants to any and every party planned during the entire wedding event.

Our industry must reposition itself to attract groups of fun-loving people gathered for memorable excursions. As all charter companies in their own hometowns improve marketing of the concepts of motor coach travel, our industry will grow and prosper.

Sales promotion techniques can also be used to stimulate the productivity of the sales staff of an intermediary working as distributors of a supplier's products. For example, a car rental firm may offer awards tied to certain levels of sales by travel agents. (Note: When similar techniques are used for a company's own salespeople, they lie outside the area of marketing communications, which is primarily concerned with reaching and influencing prospective customers.)

Two-for-one offers are one type of sales promotion. Marriott hotels introduced an interesting twist on two-for-ones with a creative incentive program. The purpose of the program was to introduce business travelers to Marriott's resorts and to attract resort guests when occupancy was normally low. Business travelers who stayed at selected Marriott hotels during the week were given certificates for a night's stay at one of three Marriott resorts; the certificates were redeemable only at times when resort occupancy was low.

Personal Selling. An important opportunity for face-to-face, personal communication about a product occurs during ***personal selling***. As an ingredient of the marketing mix, a sales transaction provides an unmatched opportunity to introduce customers to a product, to arouse their interest, and to influence their buying decisions. Communication during personal selling is powerful by virtue of its one-to-one contact and its interactive nature, allowing for interaction (questions and answers) between seller and customer.

Personal selling allows for immediate responses from customers. (Photograph by Michael Dzamen)

A good example of communication through sales in the travel industry occurs between the client and the travel agent. Consider the example of Mr. and Mrs. Warner, who want to go on a two-week vacation this summer but don't know exactly where. Ideally, they'd like to travel to Europe, but their budget does not allow that. They like interesting countryside and touring historic buildings. The Warners visit the travel agency in the nearby shopping center and start talking to their travel agent, Maria, about their ideas. By listening to their needs and offering suggestions, Maria is able to suggest and describe a vacation to Quebec, Canada, based on the European flavor of its French culture and its great value due to an inexpensive Canadian dollar. Because her suggestion meets the Warners' needs so well, Maria can make a significant sale of travel products to them.

Because this type of marketing communications is so immediate and personal, it's a more flexible means than paid advertising or public relations. The major disadvantage of personal selling as a method of marketing communications, however, is the high cost of travel, salaries, and commissions paid to sales staff who meet directly with customers.

As mentioned above, two distinctive qualities set sales apart from the other components of the marketing mix: personal selling involves face-to-face communication and it provides an opportunity for immediate response.

As face-to-face communication, personal selling allows an interactive relationship. The salesperson makes a presentation to the customer and encourages the customer to purchase the product. However, good salespeople do not simply make a presentation. They first determine the needs of customers and then use their communication skills to tailor their presentation. The more personal the communication, the more likely the customer will respond positively.

The second characteristic of personal selling that distinguishes it from other components of the marketing mix is its immediate response opportunity. Personal selling, unlike advertising and public relations, may encourage the customer to respond because they have listened to the sales presentation. Good salespeople know that customer response is part of the sales communication process and either intentionally give customers an opportunity to answer or explicitly request a response.

Since travel industry success is based on service, good customer service is often an important personal selling strategy. When customers are pleased with the behavior and attitude of employees, they are more likely to increase their spending and become return customers. Sales to repeat customers generated by excellent service should be an important part of all marketing strategies.

Although every type of marketing communication is important, communication during the sales transaction can be the culmination of all marketing efforts. The interaction between a salesperson and a customer is a powerful form of communication. It can be used to answer questions, address concerns, suggest alternatives, set up the sale itself, and produce satisfied customers, which is the ultimate goal of all marketing strategies and communications.

A MARKETING STRATEGY IN PRACTICE

The following illustrates how the marketing mix might be used in establishing a travel business.

Ed Brewster lives in a midsize American city. He has worked as a travel agent for a large tour operator for ten years. About a year ago, Ed decided to open up his own business. Rather than establish a full-service operation, Ed thought it would be more profitable to start a cruise-only business. He knew that less than 15 percent of the North American population has ever taken a cruise. Thus, the market for first-time customers was tremendous. Furthermore, of all products sold by travel agents, cruises pay one of the highest commissions because they are complete vacation packages. Although several other cruise-only businesses were already in his city, Ed felt that by managing the marketing mix properly he could exceed the sales of his competition.

Ed's first maneuver was to position himself as the cruising expert in the local market. He realized that the name of his company could do much to create the image he was seeking. Instead of calling his agency "Brewster Tours" (which sounded dull), he chose the name "Cruise World." Since none of the other cruise-only agencies had a title that suggested their specialty, Ed knew right away that he had an advantage. People looking through the newspaper or yellow pages for a cruise vacation would be more likely to choose an agency with "cruise" in its title. Ed registered the name and had business stationery and cards printed.

A vacation-oriented business needs to be located in a conspicuous and easy-to-reach area. Ed was fortunate to find street-level space for rent in a shopping mall in an upscale residential area. He quickly set about redecorating the office space to give it a shipboard atmosphere. At the front entrance, Ed installed wood decking and a ship's rail and wheel. In the front window, he placed a VCR, computer, and television monitor so that people walking by would notice videotapes and compact discs that were playing (provided by cruise lines). He placed posters of ships on the walls and ship models on the sales representatives' desks. Ed even splurged on a computer-controlled map that would light up to show a customer's ports of call.

Another major part of Ed's strategy was deciding which cruise lines to represent. Rather than sell all the products of every cruise line, Ed chose a few suppliers for his 3-, 4-, 7-, and 14-day Mediterranean, Caribbean, and Alaska cruises. By going with just a few suppliers, he would be able to increase the volume of his sales with a particular cruise line. The higher his sales volume, the better position he would be in to negotiate extra commissions (called overrides). Ed could then use the additional income to give client discounts or employee bonuses. From his years in the travel business, Ed also knew that he could save money on promotional costs by partnering with the cruise lines and using the advertising that they provided.

The next step was to hire enthusiastic employees. Those Ed hired either had a working knowledge of the cruise industry or were anxious to learn. Ed arranged for representatives of his chosen suppliers to conduct in-house workshops to acquaint his employees with the cruises they would be selling. The employee training emphasized discovering prospective clients' wants and needs and then showing them how taking a cruise could meet their expectations. By joining the National Association for Cruise Only Agents (NACOA) and the Cruise Lines International Association (CLIA), Ed had access to publications, seminars, and other resources to help him with his business.

Ed timed the grand opening of Cruise World to coincide with the beginning of the heavy booking period for cruises. He sent out fliers describing his qualifications as the local cruise expert. He sent press releases to local newspapers, with pictures of the "Cruise World" offices and biographies of his sales representatives. Ed also persuaded one of his suppliers to donate a free cruise, which was awarded as the grand prize in a drawing on a local TV show.

In the year following the grand opening, Ed kept up his promotional efforts. He invited prospective customers to attend "cruise nights" where he showed suppliers' compact discs and videos, and explained the benefits of cruises. He convinced a local radio talk show to give him air time each week to answer questions about them, and he wrote a weekly column on cruises for a local newspaper. Ed also approached churches, civic organizations, and colleges with the idea of forming groups to go on cruises.

At the end of Ed's first year in business, his agency not only kept up with competitors, but outdistanced them in sales. What's more, his efforts raised the community's awareness of the fun and excitement of cruises.

CHAPTER SUMMARY

- Marketing objectives are expressions of goals in relation to target markets.
- The marketing strategy establishes the way a company will go about achieving its marketing objectives.
- Marketing strategies vary with the current market position of a travel product, for example: leader, challenger, follower, or niche player.
- Marketing strategies are developed by designing the marketing mix, which includes factors known as the eight *P*s of travel product marketing.
- In travel marketing, the marketing mix can be thought of as including the combination of products and services offered, the way that combination is presented, and communication with the target market.
- Marketing communications increase the tangibility of a travel product or service, monitor consumer expectations, or persuade consumers to buy. Effective marketing communications stimulate attention, interest, desire, and customer action.
- Advertising, public relations, sales promotion, and personal selling are the major forms of marketing communications.

KEY TERMS

marketing strategy
marketing objectives
marketing tactics
market leader
market challenger
market follower
market niche player
marketing mix
internal marketing
product/service combination
presentation mix
atmospherics
marketing communications
advertising
public relations (P.R.)
sales promotion
personal selling

DISCUSSION QUESTIONS

1. What is wrong with the following marketing objective: "To increase our leisure-market sales?"
2. What is the relationship between a company's marketing objecties and its marketing tactics?
3. Give a current example of marketing strategy based on one of the following market positions: leader, challenger, follower, or niche player.
4. Which of the eight *P*s of marketing do you think is the most important to a successful marketing effort? Why?
5. Describe the five elements that constitute the presentation mix for a travel product.
6. What are the major differences and advantages among the four forms of marketing communications discussed in this chapter?

Creating Market Strategies

Name: ______________________________ Date: ______________

Directions: Answer these questions as you read the chapter. You will be able to use your answers to help you review the chapter.

1. What is a marketing objective and what five categories of information should every marketing objective include?

2. What is marketing strategy?

3. What are marketing tactics and what is their relationship to the marketing strategy?

4. How does being a market leader affect a company's marketing strategy?

5. What is the strategic position of a market challenger?

6. What is the difference between a market follower and a market challenger?

7. How do market niche players compete with those travel businesses that use other marketing strategies?

8. Describe the important aspects of the "product" component of the eight *P*s.

9. How can the process of delivery affect a customer's satisfaction?

10. What factors will affect the price a business charges for its products?

11. What is the most visible of the eight *P*s? Why?

12. What is the effect of physical environment? How can an effective marketing plan accommodate it?

13. What are the key considerations for the purchasing process?

14. Why is packaging so important to travel marketing?

15. Describe the role that experience and interaction play in the "participation" component.

16. What is the importance of the eight *P*s to a successful marketing plan?

17. What is the difference between adjusting the product/service combination and emphasizing particular products or services?

18. Provide an example of how the location element would be important to the presentation mix of a travel product.

19. What are atmospherics and why are they important?

20. What is advertising?

21. What does the acronym AIDA mean when referring to advertising?

22. What is the difference between advertising and public relations?

23. What is the main objective of a sales promotion?

24. How is personal selling different from other components of the marketing mix?

WORKSHEET

CHAPTER

Creating Market Strategies

Name: ______________________________ Date: ______________

TRACKING THE MARKETING TACTICS

Answer the following questions as an observer of the current scene in the marketing of travel products. The newspaper travel section; consumer and trade travel and leisure publications; and television, radio, and print advertisements will help with these answers.

1. Explain what is meant by the term "marketing tactics."

____

____

____

____

2. What companies would you consider market leaders in the following product categories?

   A. Hotel: ______________________________

   B. Car rental: ______________________________

   C. Airline: ______________________________

   D. Luxury resort: ______________________________

3. What goals would all of these market leaders have in common?

____

____

____

____

4. What companies would you consider market challengers in the following categories? (There may be more than one answer in each category.)

   A. Hotel: ______________________________

   B. Car rental: ______________________________

   C. Airline: ______________________________

   D. Luxury resort: ______________________________

5. What goals would all of these market challengers have in common?

____

____

____

____

____

6. Choose two categories from Question 2. For each one, describe a tactic being used by the market leader to maintain the leadership position and a tactic being used by a market challenger to capture a larger market share.

Market leader 1: ______________________

Tactic: ______________________

____

Market challenger 1: ______________________

Tactic: ______________________

____

Market leader 2: ______________________

Tactic: ______________________

____

Market challenger 2: ______________________

Tactic: ______________________

____

7. How are a market follower and a market challenger alike, and how are they different?

____

____

____

____

8. What companies would you consider market followers in the following categories?

A. Destination: ______________________

B. Ski area: ______________________

C. Attraction: ______________________

D. Cruise line: ______________________

9. Why do these companies adopt the position of market follower?

____

____

____

____

10. In general, how do these market followers expect to gain business?

____

____

____

____

11. For each of the companies you have listed in Question 8, describe characteristics that will help it to succeed as a follower.

A. ______

B. ______

C. ______

D. ______

12. Describe what is meant by a market niche player.

______

13. Explain why some small companies choose this tactic.

______

14. What companies would you consider market niche players in the following categories? (There may be more than one in each category.)

A. Bed-and-breakfast or country inn: ______

B. Cruise line: ______

C. Tour operator: ______

D. Railroad: ______

15. Describe what each of the companies in Question 14 might offer to a specialized market.

A. ______

B. ______

C. ______

D. ______

16. For each example of the following marketing strategies, describe one advertisement that you consider an excellent example of communication.

Market leader: __________

Description of advertisement: __________

Target market: __________

Market challenger: __________

Description of advertisement: __________

Target market: __________

Market follower: __________

Description of advertisement: __________

Target market: __________

Market niche player: __________

Description of advertisement: __________

Target market: __________

CHAPTER 6

Implementing the Marketing Plan

OBJECTIVES

When you have completed this chapter, you should be able to:

- ✱ Describe the kinds of information contained in a marketing plan.
- ✱ Name four methods a company might use to establish its marketing budget.
- ✱ Describe the responsibilities of marketing professionals during the control phase of the marketing process.
- ✱ Explain why keeping customer records and sales records is important for the marketing process.
- ✱ List several types of information-gathering tools.
- ✱ Name four techniques marketers use to evaluate sales results.

"The Number One Walleye Spot in North America!" That's how Jim and Sally Dowler describe their wilderness fishing resort on Lake of the Woods. Drumshanbo Lodge, a main lodge with a dining room and eleven sleeping cabins, appeals to walleye fishing enthusiasts. Most of its guests purchase a package plan consisting of a room and meals, along with boat, motor, gas, bait, and fish cleaning. The daily fee for a fishing guide is extra.

Jim and Sally, who are approaching their third season of operation, have worked hard to position Drumshanbo Lodge as the spot for an outstanding fishing vacation experience. They spent time last winter promoting the lodge at hunting and fishing shows in Milwaukee, Minneapolis-St. Paul, Chicago, Toronto, and Winnipeg. They persuaded travel agencies in metropolitan areas to promote the lodge. Now business for the coming season looks good: their property is already completely booked for July.

At this point, with reservations coming in every day, Jim and Sally might be tempted to sit back, put their feet up, and watch the money roll in. But the Dowlers are only halfway through the marketing cycle. They still must take steps to ensure that everything goes the way they had planned. To accomplish this, they need to develop and implement a marketing plan.

THE MARKETING PLAN

Imagine that you want to drive your car to a distant part of the country that's unfamiliar to you. You know where you are and you know where you want to go, but you don't know how to get there. If you are adventurous, you might start down the first road you see. More than likely, however, you will stop at a gas station, an auto club, or a tourist information center and pick up a road map before you leave town. Without the map to guide you, you might waste a great deal of time and gas going off in wrong directions.

A marketing plan is a company's road map. It is a detailed written proposal that shows how a company intends to reach its marketing objectives. Like a road map, a well-conceived marketing plan can prevent an organization from taking wrong turns, wandering into blind alleys, and going down dead-end streets. It also makes it less likely that the organization will be wasting time and energy and squandering its budget.

In addition to keeping an organization on course, a marketing plan is important for several other reasons. It coordinates the efforts of the many people involved in the marketing process and serves as a point of reference and as a basis of communications with the target market. It helps to prioritize efforts and activities and ensures that marketing activities are consistent with the company's objectives for selected target markets. Finally, a marketing plan assists in measuring a company's success in the marketplace and provides continuity for the company's long-term operations.

Marketing plans vary in length and scope from company to company. A marketing plan for a small resort might be only one or two pages long, whereas a marketing plan for a large airline might fill several volumes. Some marketing plans focus on a single product or service, and others cover a range of products and services. A company can have a long-range, multilayer business plan—sometimes called a "strategic plan"—plus one or more product-based marketing plans, sometimes called "tactical plans." Marketing plans also vary in their content and format. Generally, however, a marketing plan contains three basic parts: introduction, rationale, and implementation (see Figure 6–1).

The Components of a Marketing Plan

I. Introduction (overview of entire plan)

II. Rationale (explains why and how plan was developed)

- A. Situational analysis (Where are we?)
  - Products and services
  - The competition
  - External environments
  - Market potential
  - Existing marketing activities
  - Strengths, weaknesses, opportunities, and threats
- B. Marketing strategies (Where should we go?)
  - Target markets
  - Product position and image
  - Marketing objectives
  - Marketing strategies
  - Marketing mix

III. Implementation

- A. Planning activities (How do we get there?)
- B. Setting the budget (How much will it cost?)
- C. Controlling the marketing process (How do we make sure we get there?)
  - Gather information and keep records
  - Monitor spending
  - Provide progress reports
  - Monitor employee performance
- D. Evaluating the marketing plan (How will we know when we get there?)
  - Performance standards
  - Measurement techniques
  - Evaluation follow-up

FIGURE 6–1 A marketing plan describes how an organization intends to reach its marketing objectives.

Introduction

The introduction provides a brief overview (often called an executive summary) of the plan as a whole. It is a simple way of letting the reader know what to expect and what is important. In summarizing the marketing plan, the introduction generally highlights the most important points of the two major sections that follow.

Rationale

The rationale explains why a particular marketing process is being undertaken. It summarizes all of the research, analyses, and decisions on which the marketing plan is based and provides a historical record of what actions were taken to develop the plan. The rationale is especially enlightening for people outside the organization, who are assisting with its market programs. An example would be public relations firms, who are called on to handle only one or two specific activities. In most cases, a rationale contains two primary components: a situational analysis and a marketing strategy.

Situational Analysis. A ***situational analysis*** is a statement of how things are now—the current status of a company, its products, and the marketplace. It is the end result of a company's systematic examination of a number of separate components that together determine the status quo. Among the more important factors considered in a situational analysis are:

- Products and services, with an emphasis on adjusting both tangible and intangible factors in order to maximize their appeal.
- The competition, especially an analysis of what new products or promotions to expect and an examination of the strengths and weaknesses of competing companies.
- External environments, including political, societal, and technological trends or changes and whether their impact is felt at the international, national, regional, or local level. The emphasis is on whether the impact of these changes is positive or negative in relation to the company's marketing efforts.
- Market potential, based primarily on what is known about current customers, their habits, preferences, and needs, especially whether or not changes are observed or anticipated.
- Marketing activities, including an analysis of what the company has tried in the past and an assessment of its effectiveness, noting implications for future activities.
- The company's strengths, weaknesses, opportunities, and threats, relative to its existing and anticipated competition and target markets, are analyzed in order to determine what products, services, activities, and strategies will be most effective and successful.

Once these factors have been examined thoroughly, the findings are summarized in the situational analysis part of the marketing plan's rationale. The point here is not to report everything that has been learned about each factor, but to provide an overview of what has been learned about the current status of the company and its travel products. What should always be emphasized are particularly important strengths and weaknesses and specific marketing opportunities or constraints (and threats) disclosed by the analysis. The emphasis of the situational analysis is to provide a firm sense of the current position and image of a company, to draw lessons from its previous efforts, and to suggest directions for the future based on conclusions about the past and the present.

Marketing Strategies. This section of the marketing plan's rationale describes and explains decisions about "Where should we go?" and the specific strategies and tactics to be used in the marketing plan. These include the following:

- Target markets, including what segmentation variables are to be used, and whether separately or in combination.
- Product position, including the image to be established for the product, the appeal of that image to the target markets, and methods to be used to distinguish the product from competing products.
- Marketing objectives, stating in specific terms the measurable goals of the marketing plan.
- Marketing strategies, establishing the overall marketing approaches to be used for each target market.
- Marketing mix, specifying how the eight *P*s are to be combined to present and promote the products.

The specific methods used to make these decisions and the principles underlying those methods have already been discussed in detail in Chapters 2 to 5. In the context of the marketing plan and its rationale, the emphasis is on providing a brief summary of the thinking that has gone into the particular decision about the strategies. In other words, what is the basis for believing that these are the best marketing strategies to take the company from where it is now to where it wants to go? The emphasis should be on identifying how to create the product's competitive advantage over the other travel products by exploiting its comparative advantage (product appeal superior to that of the competition).

Implementation

The implementation section specifies how the marketing plan will be carried out. It should be as detailed as possible. If the plan is too vague or open for interpretation, the people in charge of the various activities may go off in different directions, resulting in missed deadlines, unproductive spending, and general confusion. Most implementation sections contain the following information:

- Planning activities. Simply put, this section addresses "How do we get there and when?" The performance responsibilities of each employee involved in the plan's marketing activities are detailed and tied to a timetable, so everyone knows what is expected.

* Setting the budget. This section addresses "How much will it cost and what method of budgeting will be used?" The costs of each prescribed activity are determined within the context of the budget. This is usually a separate step in the plan and will be discussed in detail.
* Controlling the marketing process. This section addresses, "How do we make sure that we get there?" Details are given about what methods are to be used (including providing progress reports) by managers to monitor employee performance, timeliness, and progress toward goals, particularly those involving financial control of expenditures.
* Evaluating the marketing plan. This section addresses, "How will we know when we get there?" This information explains at what point and in what ways the overall success of the marketing plan is to be measured, based on measurement techniques, expected outcomes and performance standards. It also provides a basis for adjustments that may be necessary in future marketing plans.

Once these three components have been described by the marketing plan, what remains is the hard part: their actual implementation. Previous chapters have already described some of the specific methods that go into planning marketing activities and deciding who is to do what. The remainder of this chapter focuses on *how* to implement the remaining steps of the marketing plan: setting the marketing budget, controlling the marketing process, and evaluating the marketing plan.

SETTING THE MARKETING BUDGET

In a marketing plan, the marketing budget is an estimate of the cost to successfully implement the marketing strategies that are the key to achieving the marketing objectives. Setting a marketing budget can be an agonizing process, especially for a small company with limited resources, because the money is being spent "up front," or ahead of the actual revenue the product is expected to generate. Because the companies are, in a sense, gambling that they will recover their investment, they sometimes wait to create marketing budgets until other bills and invoices have been paid. The marketing budget, however, should be a top priority. Money spent on marketing can be a major factor in the success or failure of a company's product or service; it should be viewed as an investment to generate business rather than a cost. One benefit of a marketing plan that is grounded in solid market research is making a company more confident that its marketing budget is allocated properly.

Characteristics of a Good Marketing Budget

A good marketing budget is comprehensive and coordinated. The budget should show not only how much to spend to implement the total marketing plan, but also how the total should be split among each element of the marketing mix and the evaluation procedures. If the plan covers more than one travel product, or more than one target market, the budget should also show how the money will be split among these components. Of course, spending should be allocated appropriately, so that the organization does not designate too much for a minor component of the plan while a major part of the plan is underbudgeted.

A good marketing budget is also realistic and practical for the company. In other words, the budget should be logically related to the company's financial resources and its position in the industry. A goal of a good budget should be to create revenues that exceed the amount invested in marketing.

Finally, a sound budget has a ***contingency*** built in. It is usually recommended that 10 to 15 percent of the total budget be reserved for unanticipated increases in marketing expenses, such as the cost of printing cost overrun, an unexpected move by the competition, or an exceptional opportunity that arises.

Budget-Setting Methods

Marketing professionals generally use one of four methods in setting budgets (see Figure 6–2). Three of these methods—the arbitrary and affordable method, the percentage of sales method, and the competitive parity method—are relatively simple and straightforward, but generally do not consider marketing objectives. They establish the upper limits of expenditure, but usually do not provide guidance on how to divide money among the various elements of the marketing mix. The fourth method—the objective and task method—is more complicated and time-consuming, but it meets the requirements that budget setting should be done in a comprehensive and coordinated

The marketing budget should be regarded as an investment and not as an expense.

manner. It also allows objectives to be considered and resources to be allocated to specific elements of the marketing mix.

Arbitrary and Affordable Method. In ***arbitrary and affordable budgeting***, marketing professionals use their personal judgment and knowledge of the company's history to estimate budgets. They decide on an amount they think the company can afford. Often they use the same amount as budgeted in previous years, sometimes increasing it an arbitrary percentage from one year to the next. This budget method is used most commonly by small travel businesses that view marketing expenditures as a cost rather than an investment. Its main weakness is that it tends to maintain the status quo, making it impossible for a company to recognize—and therefore reach—its full potential.

Percentage of Sales Method. In ***percentage of sales budgeting***, marketers base their estimates on a percentage of the previous year's total sales or this year's expected sales. The percentage may be based on published guidelines of what a company "should" be spending on its marketing program (the rule of thumb). For example, several authorities recommend that a hotel, motel, or resort should spend from 2.5 percent to 5 percent of its total sales on marketing.

The most glaring problem with this form of budgeting occurs when sales decline. With percentage of sales budgeting, marketing budgets decrease in response to such a decline, which can then make the problem of decreasing sales even worse. In fact, a temporary increase in the marketing budget may be the appropriate response to decreasing sales, rather than a reduction in budget.

Competitive Parity Method. In ***competitive parity budgeting***, marketing professionals try to find out what their competitors are spending and then set their own budgets to correspond. Marketers attempt to determine this information by reading articles on competitors and

Budget-Setting Methods			
The Arbitrary and Affordable Method		**The Percentage of Sales Method**	
Pros	*Cons*	*Pros*	*Cons*
Simple	Doesn't consider marketing objectives	Simple	Doesn't consider marketing objectives
Straightforward	Maintains the status quo; company can't reach full potential	Straightforward	Budget decreases when sales decline
The Competitive Parity Method		**The Objective and Task Method**	
Pros	*Cons*	*Pros*	*Cons*
Simple	Doesn't consider marketing objectives	Comprehensive	Complicated
Straightforward	Reactive rather than anticipatory; to some extent allows competitors to determine budget	Coordinated	Time-consuming
		Considers marketing objectives	
		Sets objectives, then figures out tasks and costs	

FIGURE 6–2 Since money spent on marketing activities can be a major factor in the success or failure of a product, it is important to choose the most effective budgeting method.

their annual reports. The competitive parity method's disadvantages are that it is reactive rather than anticipatory and that, to a significant extent, it allows the level of the company's marketing budget to be determined by its competitors.

Objective and Task Method. In ***objective and task budgeting***, marketers construct the budget from the bottom and move up, rather than from the top down. They first set objectives and then figure out the marketing tasks necessary to accomplish the objectives. From there, they estimate the cost of completing each task.

To understand the objective and task budgeting method, consider the situation of a corporation that operates thirty hotels with a combined capacity of six thousand rooms. The corporate marketing department has set the following marketing objective: Use direct-mail advertising to sell one-third of the hotels' overall capacity (i.e., two thousand rooms) to families as weekend packages over twenty selected weekends between October and May.

The marketing department then projects the amount of revenue that would be generated by meeting this objective. Assuming that each package lasts for two nights and involves two persons at $45 per person per night (or $180 per couple per weekend), the revenue projection is as follows: 2,000 (rooms) x 20 (weekends) x $180 = $7,200,000.

Additional spending in hotels on meals, drinks, gifts, and so on @ $10 per person per day: 2,000 (rooms) x 20 (weekends) x 2 (people) x 2 (days) x $10 = 1,600,000.

Projected Revenue = $8,800,000

Next, the marketing department must decide how much money is required to achieve the projected sales revenue—in other words, what will the marketing budget be. Rather than simply taking a percentage of the projected sales revenue, the marketers use facts, experience, and personal judgment to itemize and project costs for the marketing tasks necessary to achieve the objective, including:

250,000 brochures =	$ 80,000
50,000 direct-mail postcards =	25,000
Advertising in consumer media =	250,000
Advertising in trade press =	20,000
Point-of-sale material (for travel agencies and hotels) =	25,000
Public relations campaign =	10,000
Travel agency commission =	180,000
Other =	50,000
Contingency =	60,000
Projected Costs =	$700,000

The marketing budget of $700,000 is 7.9 percent of the projected revenue, an acceptable figure for this hotel chain. If the marketing department had adhered to a more conventional percentage (perhaps 5 percent), the budget may have been too low to achieve its objective using these tactics.

CONTROLLING THE MARKETING PROCESS

It doesn't make sense for a company to spend money, time, and effort designing marketing strategies without being able to measure and manage what happens to them once they are set in motion. Implementation of a marketing plan must be controlled. The control phase includes all the steps a company takes to monitor and adjust marketing strategies and activities as they are progressing. These procedures are specified in the marketing plan.

During the control stage, marketing professionals gather information about customer response, monitor spending and sales, check employee performance and issue progress reports. Wherever necessary and possible, deviations from what was expected are corrected by modifying marketing strategies or tactics. Some marketing plans allow for certain contingencies, spelling out how strategies or tactics should be changed when objectives are not met.

Gathering Information and Keeping Records

Marketing professionals are constantly collecting information about a company's customers. As you already learned in Chapter 3, this is one of the primary functions of market research. In Chapter 3, however, market research was discussed primarily in relation to developing new products or refining for existing products, including initial decisions about target markets, product positioning, and other marketing strategies and tactics.

But the value of market research and information goes well beyond product and market analysis. Information is critical throughout the marketing cycle and is one of the keys to monitoring and controlling the implementation of the marketing plan. Marketing professionals gather and analyze information continuously in order to test the effectiveness of the various elements of the marketing mix.

Some information-gathering tools used for this purpose are similar to those employed at the market planning stage and have been described previously. Others are more specific to monitoring and controlling the marketing effort than to planning it and are described below. In most cases, the information that is gathered can be useful both in monitoring the performance of marketing efforts and in developing or adjusting products and services. Whatever the method to be used and whenever it is applied, recognizing the critical role up-to-date information plays in successful travel marketing is essential.

Registration Cards. Lodging companies within the travel industry need to know what percentage of their business comes from various geographic market areas. Registration cards, especially those used in hotels and motels, provide this important geographic information. The information should be extracted from the cards on a daily basis and categorized according to state and major metropolitan area. Season of the year could also be factored in, as well as how frequently guests stay at the property. An accurate geographic analysis aids in directing or modifying advertising and promotion efforts.

Self-Administered Questionnaires. Questionnaires are a popular and inexpensive way of getting feedback on guest satisfaction and marketing tactics. An example of questionnaires are the familiar comment cards that resorts place in guest rooms for return at checkout. Another is the survey mailed to the guest's residence after their stay is completed.

The disadvantage of self-administered questionnaires is that guests cannot always be depended on to complete them. To encourage participation, some businesses offer a gift as an incentive for completing the survey. To increase their response rate, some hotels now have guests answer questions as they are checking out either at the front desk or on their in-room television. The questions take about thirty seconds to answer, and the results are immediately recorded and tabulated by a computer.

Informal Interviews. Informal interviews with customers can yield useful information, especially for a small business. Managers of travel agencies, for instance, can have their sales staff routinely ask clients how they happened to choose the agency. Were they referred by a satisfied client? Are they responding to a particular sales promotion? Were the agency's location, parking facilities, or office hours the key factor? Were they attracted by the ad in the telephone book?

Client Files. Many companies keep files on their transactions with individual clients or guests. Tour operators, for example, might add to such a file each time a client books a trip. The file would include demographic information, such as the client's age, residence, and occupation, and information about the type of trips purchased, destinations selected, and the reasons for traveling. By reviewing client files on a regular basis, managers can get an idea of which products and services are most popular, and in which target markets the marketing efforts have been most effective. All information collected is compared to the specific expectations of the marketing plan to make certain the marketing plan is on track. If not, appropriate adjustments are made.

Response Mechanisms. Feedback mechanisms are used to test the effectiveness of direct-response advertising. They include systems such as a magazine ad with a mail-in coupon or card. If people want to find out more about an advertised travel product, they can send in the coupon, which includes a code indicating in which publication the coupon was printed. Television ads promoting travel to specific states feature special toll-free telephone numbers that viewers can call for more information or Internet addresses to browse. By tracking responses and their sources, marketers can get an idea of which advertising is working and the number of people their advertising is reaching.

Response mechanisms can also be designed to elicit more specific information about the respondents. For example, the same ad can be run in different regions of the country but with a different toll-free number for each region. Companies can then determine the geographic markets in which the advertising is most effective by noting how many calls each number receives. In a similar manner, marketers can test the effectiveness of one advertising placement over another—for example, by running the same ad in two different magazines, using different departments or box numbers as codes in the contact address.

The Texas Department of Commerce generates responses with this full-page magazine ad with response card. (©Texas Department of Commerce Tourism Division)

Inquiries. In addition to keeping track of inquiries generated by response mechanisms, travel companies record other requests for information, whether by telephone, letter, or personal visit. If a company sponsors a special event such as a cruise night or a lecture, inquiries will come from some of the people attending. While prospective customers seek information about travel products, marketers, in turn, seek information about potential and existing customers.

Marketing Impressions

TOURISM CONSULTANT

The first War Between the States ended in 1865. The second has heated up in recent years as states battle for their share of the tourist dollar. As the stakes get higher, tourism consultants like Bill Siegel and Karen Peterson get busier.

"When budgets were small, tourism promotion people did their thing without a lot of planning," says Siegel, president of Longwoods International, a Toronto-based tourism consulting firm whose clients include state and national tourist boards. "But these days, as the dollars get higher, the legislature gets nervous. 'Do we have a strategy? Is it working?'"

"The government feels like it has to have a scorecard," agrees Karen Peterson, president of Davidson Peterson, a tourism consulting firm headquartered in Maine. "What are our goals, and what resources are we using? Did we achieve our goals? Why or why not?"

Siegel points to the state of Colorado as an example. "They had done some research, but there was no consistency or overall plan. The program also didn't seem to have a strategy," Siegel recalls.

Analysis of Colorado's program, using a database Siegel's company had developed, revealed that the state was promoting the wrong product. Although it was tremendously successful in selling the Rocky Mountains, Colorado's wilderness image overshadowed its cultural and historic attractions and its many amenities. As a result, resorts sat half empty after ski season.

"First we recommended that they stop pushing mountains, mountains, and more mountains, and start promoting mountains and much more," Siegel says. Once a focus was established, the state could develop a coordinated campaign to achieve its goals, and Siegel could gauge the program's success against its objectives.

Although evaluating a program involves looking closely at research data, Siegel is quick to point out that "we're not in the number-gathering business. Our job is to be strategists, and to have enough background to know what it all means." To that end, he often will use qualitative research, such as a focus group or one-on-one interviews, to supplement numerical data gathered by field research.

"We base our key recommendations on the research, but beyond that we have to use our skills, judgment, past experience—that's what we get paid for, not research," says Siegel.

The consultant's job is made challenging not only by the problems posed by clients, but by the fact that each consultant may be juggling from five to ten projects at a time, and each will require a different type of research solution. Once the questionnaires have been drafted and approved and the information-gathering mechanisms put into place, data must be coded, entered into a database, and analyzed. The consultants put numbers into a graphic format for clearer communication and make their recommendations. Then it's on to the next one. Once an initial strategic marketing study has been developed, it serves as a model for others to track performance over time. In addition, smaller, more focused studies are used.

"If you're doing it right, you're constantly evaluating as you go along," Peterson says.

So, it seems, the tourism consultant's job is never done.

Of course, marketing departments should not be content to answer an endless stream of inquiries with no results. In the end the name of the game is ***conversion***: turning inquiries into sales. In fact, one evaluation measure a marketer often uses is calculating the ratio of inquiries to sales (see "Evaluating the Marketing Plan"). If a company is getting many inquiries but not many sales, then something in its marketing plan or product requires adjustment. It may indicate, for example, that the advertising is working to generate interest, but something about the product isn't appealing to customers as anticipated.

Personal Observations. Marketing managers can learn a great deal about how well a marketing plan is progressing by simply observing its implementation. They can walk through a hotel lobby, for example, to check how customers are being treated and how they are responding to the facility and its staff. Are the staff at the registration desk friendly and courteous? During the checkout process does the staff ask for future reservations? Managers can also observe the appearance of the facility. Is the hotel entrance clean and attractive? Is the lobby well lit?

Monitoring Spending

Another major way in which companies control the marketing process is by controlling their finances. This has two aspects. First, marketing personnel periodically check to see if the marketing budget is being spent according to the plan. Second, they periodically evaluate sales volume, costs, and profits to see if the company is cost-effectively achieving its marketing objectives. Thus, in addition to gathering information related to customer opinion and behavior, marketing departments (or, in some organizations, sales departments) are also keeping records on sales and expenditures. More is said about evaluating sales later in this chapter.

Progress Reports

It is important that the monitoring of the progress of each marketing activity be reported in a timely manner so that any necessary adjustments can be made. Many organizations have traditionally printed weekly or monthly reports. Today, creating an online database that is accessible twenty-four hours a day is the preferred option for providing accurate, up-to-the-minute information, which marketing professionals need to make decisions in the complex, fast-moving travel marketplace.

Monitoring Employee Performance

As you know, most travel products are, to some extent, intangible and perishable. Their quality depends in large measure on the people who deliver them to customers. Managing the performance of employees is difficult, but several useful steps can be taken. To begin with, a company can recruit and hire the people with the right skills and attitude for the job. Proper training, motivation, and orientation make control easier. This is especially true during the early implementation of a marketing plan, when employees need ongoing leadership and supervision. Managers also need to clearly communicate the critical elements of the marketing plan to employees, emphasizing the importance of their role in the success of each strategy.

Productivity. One way to monitor the work of employees is to establish productivity quotas. Marketing directors, or sales managers, monitor the work of salespeople by establishing a system of sales reports and sales quotas. Part of a director's or a manager's responsibility is to see that salespeople meet their goals within their budgets and to offer assistance if a salesperson is having difficulty. Managers might restructure a salesperson's tasks or retrain him or her. Sales meetings and incentives such as cash bonuses, awards, or free trips are designed to motivate salespeople to increase their productivity.

Team Spirit. An important responsibility of marketers is to build team spirit among employees so that they will be motivated to achieve the marketing objectives. Consider the situation of the Radisson Hotels and Resorts. In the early 1990s, the company, which was losing money, set about revamping its properties and image. As part of its marketing strategy, the company created the "Yes We Can!" advertising slogan. However, before introducing this campaign to the public, the management directed the message to hotel employees. Realizing that an enthusiastic and happy staff was the key to the success of the corporation, Radisson executives made every effort to gain the support of the company's employees. As part of their strategy, the president of the corporation met with as many employees as possible in person and in an effort to make each individual a committed member of the Radisson team.

This strategy, along with others, has been effective. Radisson has reestablished itself as a vigorous company with an ambitious building program and high service standards.

Frontline Training. Although travelers seldom meet a company's professional marketing staff—marketing directors, sales managers, and public relations officers—they do meet the company's frontline employees. Frontline personnel in the travel industry include hotel registration staff, servers, bellmen, travel agents, tourist information specialists, and many others who have direct contact with travelers every day. The actions and attitudes of these frontline employees can greatly influence how travelers perceive products and services. Therefore, these employees must receive proper training so they are knowledgeable about the marketing efforts of the organization and can recognize that their on-the-job performance and appearance are important to the success of the marketing strategies.

In addition to training employees for specific jobs, many travel organizations provide frontline personnel with service quality training. This training encourages and prepares employees to serve as enthusiastic and well-informed ambassadors of the business and the destination. Employees learn about their community's history, attractions, special events, shopping, and recreation. As a result of such training, frontline personnel are able to answer visitors' questions about what to do and see and even know how to provide accurate directions. This investment in employee performance produces more satisfied customers and makes it more likely that future marketing will be effective.

EVALUATING THE MARKETING PLAN

The final phase of the marketing plan is evaluation, where a company analyzes the results of the implementation of its marketing strategies and compares them with the objectives it had hoped to achieve. Evaluation is extremely important in helping the company prepare future marketing plans.

Performance Standards

A good marketing plan spells out when the formal evaluation will occur and which ***measurement techniques*** will be used. Since it is unlikely that the final results will match the objectives exactly, the marketing plan also specifies ***performance standards***. Performance standards that state what deviations from a marketing objective are acceptable or unacceptable are helpful in determining the success of the company's market plan.

For most companies the bottom line is whether they generate enough profit to stay in business. Therefore, the primary focus of evaluation is often on analyzing financial returns. Several measurement techniques are used to help a company achieve a clear understanding of the financial returns on their marketing investment. The results of each measurement technique should be compared to the expected outcomes through established performance standards.

Measurement Techniques

Total Dollar Sales. Some companies simply use total dollar sales as their evaluation base. They compare the amount of sales during one period with the amount of sales during another equivalent period. For instance, the current year's sales might be compared with the previous year's sales. Total dollar sales is the broadest and simplest measurement technique, but it is not very revealing. Although it does tell whether sales increased or decreased, it does not tell whether the company achieved its objectives, how the company is performing in relation to its competition, whether costs changed or how much profit the company made. Nor does it reveal which segments of the business are profitable and which components of the marketing plan were effective.

Sales Variance. Good marketing objectives are expressed in measurable terms—dollars or units (for example, the number of rooms occupied or seats sold). An analysis of ***sales variance*** compares actual sales with marketing objectives and tries to explain any discrepancies. Again, the more specific the objective, the easier it is to measure. An airline, for example, might set objectives for each class of service for each route for each week of the year. With the aid of technology, the airline can have the sales results within hours of a flight and compare them with previous levels in order to determine the amount of change (variance).

Market Share Variance. ***Market share*** refers to the proportion of a company's sales to an entire industry's sales. In an analysis of market share variance, a cruise line would compare its total sales with total sales for the cruise line industry over a period of time. For example, a company's share might increase from 9 percent in 1997 to 20 percent in 1999. The market share percentage is determined by dividing company sales by total industry sales.

An analysis of market share variance helps a company determine how well it is performing compared to overall industry performance, along with how well it is doing against its competitors. Sometimes the results of a market-share variance analysis provide an interesting picture of a company's performance. For instance, a theme park's sales may have decreased in a year's time, but during the same time its market share may have increased. This would indicate that the company is gaining on or outperforming its competitors, although it is part of an industry segment that is experiencing an overall decline in sales.

Marketing Cost Profitability. The analysis of a company's financial success isn't complete until the margin between the amount of revenue generated and the costs required to produce it are known. A company may have increased its sales volume, but its marketing costs may have increased to the point where its profits have actually decreased.

An analysis of cost and profitability should be focused on individual marketing components so that unproductive components can be altered, reorganized, or abandoned. This allows an organization to reallocate funds to more productive segments. Marketing professionals conduct what is called a ***segmental analysis*** in several ways—for instance, by looking at particular target markets, sales territories, or distribution channels. Figures for this type of analysis must be extracted carefully from revenue statements. The process is time-consuming but can be well worth the effort.

Effectiveness Ratios. A useful way to measure the performance of a promotional program is to calculate ***effectiveness ratios***. These are statistical measurements for determining the relative effectiveness of promotional and distribution strategies. They might include:

- Average number of sales calls per salesperson per day.
- Number of radio and TV stations using press releases.
- Percentage of sales through travel agencies.

Another type of ratio that is useful in direct response marketing (inquirers respond to advertising via coupon or toll-free numbers) is the ***cost per inquiry (CPI)***, which is the average cost of generating an inquiry. The CPI of an advertisement is calculated by dividing the total cost of the marketing activity by the total number of inquiries it generates. A CPI of 2.36 means it cost $2.36 for every inquiry produced by the advertisement. The ad's effectiveness can be further evaluated by figuring the ***cost per reservation (CPR)*** or ***cost per visitor (CPV)*** and the ***return on*** (marketing) ***investment (ROI)***, which is the amount of revenue generated for every dollar spent on marketing. CPR (or CPV) is calculated by dividing the total cost of the marketing activity by the number of reservations, or visitors, produced. It is important to note that CPR (or CPV) will always be higher than CPI, since not all inquiries are converted to reservations, visitors, guests, or passengers. ROI is calculated by dividing the total costs of the marketing activity into the total estimated revenue that it produced.

All of these ratios are very useful in determining the performance of each marketing activity as well as their relative performance, compared to all marketing activities. The latter can be accomplished by calculating a CPI, CPR (or CPV), and ROI for each and every marketing activity and comparing them. The worksheet in Figure 6–3 and the Marketing Evaluation Case which follows explain more about the calculation of these important ratios.

Marketing Evaluation Case Study

Jim and Sally Dowler decided on several promotional strategies to inform their target market about Drumshanbo Lodge. Their efforts focused on increasing occupancy during their slow period, which was indentified by an analysis of their guest records. As mentioned, included in their marketing activities were exhibits at several hunting and fishing shows. In addition, Jim and Sally distributed their brochures through travel agencies, advertised in several hunting and fishing newspapers and magazines, and ran ads on radio stations. They also participated in cooperative advertising with their local resort association.

The Dowlers wanted to know which promotional program components were effective in terms of generating revenue and which were not. With this information, they will have a better idea of how to spend their advertising budget in the future. Figure 6–3 shows the worksheet they could use to calculate effectiveness ratios for each program component. Effectiveness ratios allow the different promotional activities to be compared. Those with a low CPI and CPR (or CPV) and a high ROI, of

Uncontrollable factors, such as the weather, can influence what happens to a company in the marketplace.

course, would be most effective and, therefore, the best future marketing investments.

To see how effectiveness ratios work, the Dowlers compared the results for ads appearing during the same week last season in three different newspapers specializing in the "outdoors":

1. A small ad in *Sportsman's Weekly* cost $100. It yielded three inquiries and one conversion to a reservation.
   * Total revenue = $250
   * Total costs = $100
   * Total inquiries = 3
   * Total reservations = 1
   * Cost per inquiry (CPI) = $33 ($100 ÷ 3)
   * Cost per reservation (CPR) = $100 ($100 ÷ 1)
   * Return on investment (ROI) = $2.5/$1 ($250 ÷ $100)
2. An ad in *Outdoor News* cost $50. It yielded ten inquiries and five reservations.
   * Total revenue = $1,250
   * Total costs = $50
   * Total inquiries = 10
   * Total reservations = 5
   * Cost per inquiry (CPI) = $5 ($50÷10)
   * Cost per reservation (CPR) = $10 ($50÷5)
   * Return on investment (ROI) = $25/$1 ($1250 ÷ $50)
3. An ad in *Sportsman's Press* cost $75. It yielded fifteen inquiries and ten reservations.
   * Total revenue = $900
   * Total costs = $75
   * Total inquiries = 15
   * Total reservations = 10
   * Cost per inquiry (CPI) = $5 ($75 ÷ 15)
   * Cost per reservation (CPR) = $7.50 ($75 ÷ 10)
   * Return on investment (ROI) = $12/$1 ($900 ÷ $75)

By using these ratios, the Dowlers were able to determine that the most effective ad of the three was the one appearing in *Outdoor News* because it produced both the most revenue and the best return on investment.

When Drumshanbo Lodge closes in October, Jim and Sally will be able to look back at their third season of operation with pride. As a result of their

Effectiveness Ratio Worksheet				
Item	Program Component			Total Program
	Summer Ad			
1. Total costs =	100,000			
2. Total number of inquiries =	200,000			
3. Total number of reservations =	50,000			
4. Total revenues generated =	2,000,000			
5. Cost per inquiry (CPI) = $\frac{\#1}{\#2}$ =	$\frac{100{,}000}{200{,}000}$ = \$.50			
6. Cost per reservation (CPR) = $\frac{\#1}{\#3}$ =	$\frac{100{,}000}{50{,}000}$ = \$2.00			
7. Return on marketing investment (ROI) = $\frac{\#4}{\#1}$ =	$\frac{2{,}000{,}000}{100{,}000}$ = \$20.00			

FIGURE 6–3 The purpose of this chart is to compare the effectiveness of promotional programs. This information should be used to adapt current programs, if necessary.

recordkeeping and analyses, they will know why their season was a successful one, both in relation to the previous year and to their objectives for this year. They will know their margin of profitability and how well their lodge is keeping pace with the other resorts in the area. The Dowlers will have a good idea of which advertising and promotional strategies are worth future investment, and they should also have many well-founded ideas about how to improve the marketing of Drumshanbo Lodge. With this information, the Dowlers can look forward to an even more successful fourth season, thanks to their successful application and implementation of some basic procedures for evaluating the effectiveness of the components of their marketing plan.

Evaluation Follow-Up

After measuring the financial results of its marketing plan, a travel organization should attempt to determine the reasons for its success or failure. This is where customer records, surveys, observations, and more subjective information-gathering tools—like years of experience—can be most helpful. These measurements may indicate that, even though a company is making a profit, its success is due to some factor other than its marketing strategies. For example, most airlines' share of the Atlantic coast market will increase substantially as a result of a major, competing airline being on strike. By the same token, a company may fail through no fault of its own. External factors such as weather, civil war, a change in tax structure, currency fluctuations, or a price war among competitors can influence what happens to a company in the marketplace. Therefore, travel organizations need to be careful not to use outcomes that are the result of unforeseen, unpredictable, and uncontrollable circumstances as the groundwork for future plans.

At this follow-up stage of the evaluation process, several specific types of information are of interest to organizations in the travel industry. These include:

* How efficiently the marketing plan was followed and implemented.

- How effectively marketing objectives have been met.
- The accuracy and credibility of the reported results.
- Accountability for the money spent implementing the plan.
- Ways in which the marketing programs and strategies can be improved.

Travel companies also want to assess the effect of the marketing plan on customers by getting their feedback about the following:

- Their satisfaction with the travel product(s).
- How their actual travel experience compared with their expectations for it.
- Whether they would purchase the travel product(s) again.

With the evaluation complete, the marketing cycle begins again as the travel organization decides what to do next. If the route mapped by the marketing plan was smooth and successful, the company may choose to follow that road again. Several other options are also available:

- Continue with the same plan but with some major or minor modifications.
- Continue with the same plan and, at the same time, develop plans for identifying new markets and creating new products and services.
- Abandon all or some of the plan and start over again, based on the information about the current failures and successes.

If an organization has done a good job of controlling and evaluating the marketing process, its future course will be much clearer and the outcomes more predictable.

CHAPTER SUMMARY

- A company must have a marketing plan to achieve its objectives. A marketing plan describes where the company is now, where it wants to go, and how it will get there.
- The situational analysis and marketing strategies are the major elements of the rationale for a marketing plan.
- The implementation component of a marketing plan includes planning, budgeting, controlling, and evaluating phases.
- The marketing budget is an estimate of how much it will cost to implement the strategies described in the marketing plan. Since the amount of money spent on marketing helps to determine the success or failure of the product or service, budget setting should be a priority in the marketing process. Several methods are available for budget setting.
- During the control phase, a company is monitoring and adjusting marketing strategies and activities as they are progressing in order to make sure that strategies and tactics achieve desired results.
- Information about customers is one way the marketing professionals judge the effectiveness of the various elements in the marketing mix.
- Marketing managers support the efforts of employees through proper training, leadership, and supervision.
- Although the evaluation phase occurs after the marketing activities have ended, evaluation procedures are established in advance and specified in the marketing plan. To perform an effective evaluation, information on sales and customer response must be collected and monitored throughout the implementation of the marketing plan.
- The key elements of the evaluation phase are expected outcomes, accurate and reliable measurement techniques, and performance standards.
- Evaluation is extremely important, for both assessing current marketing efforts and determining future directions. To get a true picture of its success or failure, a travel organization should use several measures to calculate financial results and should determine the reasons behind its success or failure.

KEY TERMS

situational analysis
contingency
arbitrary and affordable budgeting
percentage of sales budgeting
competitive parity budgeting
objective and task budgeting
conversion
measurement techniques
performance standards
sales variance
market share
segmental analysis
effectiveness ratios
cost per inquiry (CPI)
cost per reservation (CPR)
cost per visitor (CPV)
return on investment (ROI)

DISCUSSION QUESTIONS

1. What types of information should a marketing plan contain?
2. Why is the objective and task method considered the best method for budget setting?
3. What are the major responsibilities of marketing professionals during the control phase of the marketing process?
4. Why is good recordkeeping essential for the marketing process? What are some tools for gathering information about customers?
5. Why might market share be a more important measure of success than total dollar sales?
6. Describe the differences between cost per inquiry and cost per reservation in terms of their calculation and their usefulness in marketing decisions.
7. To obtain a complete picture of a marketing plan's success, what types of evaluation can be done?

Implementing the Marketing Plan

Name: ______________________________ Date: ______________

Directions: Answer these questions as you read the chapter. You will be able to use these answers to help you review the chapter.

1. What is the relationship between a marketing plan and marketing objectives?

____

____

____

____

2. What are the three basic components of a marketing plan?

____

____

____

____

3. Name some of the factors considered in a situational analysis.

____

____

____

____

4. What four types of activities are commonly included in the implementation section of a marketing plan?

____

____

____

____

5. What are some of the characteristics of a good marketing budget?

____

____

____

____

6. Describe the four types of budget-setting methods generally used by marketing professionals.

____

____

7. Name five of the tools used to gather information as means of controlling the marketing process.

8. Discuss why each of the following is important to the success of a marketing plan.

Employee productivity:

Team spirit:

Frontline training:

9. How are performance standards used when evaluating a marketing plan?

10. Differentiate between the analysis of sales variance and market share variance.

11. Describe three examples of effectiveness ratios used by travel marketers to evaluate marketing plans.

12. The follow-up efforts that are the result of the marketing plan evaluation might include:

WORKSHEET

CHAPTER 6

Implementing the Marketing Plan

Name: ____________________ Date: ____________

MARKETING BY OBJECTIVE

The following companies need marketing plans to ensure long-term business success. Rewrite each of their marketing objectives in a more specific way, including the desired result, the marketing activities, the targeted market, the time frame, and the measure of success (see Chapter 5). Then suggest recordkeeping, information gathering, and evaluation methods that would measure whether this objective was accomplished.

1. *The Tulip Tree Bed-and-Breakfast Inn,* Elkhart Lake, Wisconsin. Current situation: The inn makes a small profit every year but is never completely occupied, even during the height of the summer season. Many customers who used to come to the inn every year have retired to the Sun Belt, and their children are now grown up. Goal: Attract more summer visitors.

____

____

____

____

Marketing objective: ____________________

Recommended recordkeeping or information gathering: ____________________

Suggested evaluation method: ____________________

2. *Mike's Red River Canoe Trips,* Crockett, Idaho. Current situation: The Red River offers perfect conditions for the experienced canoeist and the novice alike. Mike and his expert staff act as guides and supply instruction, safety equipment, and a wide range of one-day, weekend, and vacation packages. Although he is happy with the business he gets through canoe clubs, shows, and publications, Mike believes there is an untapped market of people who enjoy nature and water sports and who should see the river by canoe. Goal: Encourage more first-timers to try canoeing.

____

____

____

____

Marketing objective: ____________________

Recommended recordkeeping or information gathering: ____________________

Suggested evaluation method: ____________________

3. *Travel by Sandy,* Canton, Ohio. Current situation: Sandy runs a busy city travel agency. Her major source of business is leisure travel, but because she is located in an area with many small and medium-sized businesses, she has picked up some bookings from these sources as well. Sandy would like to retain all her leisure business while serving more business clients. Goal: Increase sales to corporations.

____

____

Marketing objective:

Recommended recordkeeping or information gathering:

Suggested evaluation method:

4. *Pine Hill Golf Resort,* Augusta, Georgia. Current situation: Pine Hill is in the heart of golf country, with outstanding playing conditions and accommodations. Once an estate, the main building has been converted to guest and meeting rooms and includes an excellent restaurant. Because the resort has always been popular with vacationers, the resort management recognizes the potential for increased revenue through sales of leisure activities to business clients. Goal: Generate more revenue from sales meetings and incentive trips.

Marketing objective:

Recommended recordkeeping or information gathering:

Suggested evaluation method:

5. *Overland Covered Wagon Excursions,* Billings, Montana. Current situation: Overland Covered Wagon Excursions offer individuals and families a unique opportunity to relive the past and see the sights throughout the West. Summer business has increased steadily, and because only a limited number of carefully planned and executed trips are available, bookings have actually reached capacity. However, trips in the late spring and early fall—when routes are specially chosen for mild weather and outstanding scenery—are underbooked. Goal: Increase revenue for spring and fall.

Marketing objective:

Recommended recordkeeping or information gathering:

Suggested evaluation method:

PART TWO

Selling the Travel Product

CHAPTER 7	Understanding the Traveler's Needs
CHAPTER 8	Identifying the Seller
CHAPTER 9	Evaluating the Travel Product
CHAPTER 10	Setting Up the Sale
CHAPTER 11	Personal Selling
CHAPTER 12	Satisfying the Customer

Understanding the Traveler's Needs

OBJECTIVES

When you have completed this chapter, you should be able to:

- List and describe the steps involved in the process of buying travel products.
- Explain the psychological needs of the leisure traveler.
- Describe patterns of travel psychology using personality, motivation, and behavior classifications.
- Identify barriers to travel.
- Describe the special needs of the business traveler.

To this point, the focus has been on strategies, systems, and concepts used by the travel industry to create, manage, position, and market its products and services. The remaining six chapters concentrate on the tactics, methods, and techniques for selling these products directly and indirectly to customers.

In order to successfully match suppliers' products with high-potential customers, it is important to understand what motivates them to purchase travel products, what benefits they desire, and what needs must be met.

Consider a busy intersection. You are at an office window on the twenty-first floor looking down at the rush-hour traffic. You see patterns of left turns, right turns, cars changing lanes, buses stopping for passengers. A woman waiting for the traffic light to change cannot see the same patterns you see from your vantage point. She sees instead an angry exchange between a taxi driver and a pedestrian that causes a minor delay. You see patterns from a distance; she sees close-up emotional causes and effects. The market comprising travel and tourism customers can be looked at in similar ways: from a distance and from close up.

The distant vantage point is the perspective of those who do market research. In Chapter 3 you learned about many ways to divide the travel and tourism market into segments based on certain characteristics—demographic, geographic, psychographic, and behavioristic—which are helpful in predicting the market's demand for travel. When considering groups of people in this manner, you can learn a great deal about how and why people use travel products. Such information is essential for developing a marketing plan that works.

For those involved directly in selling travel products, however, the close-up perspective of the market is equally important. Although you should know all

It is important for travel professionals to understand why customers choose various types of travel experiences. (Top left: Photograph by C. J. Ghormley; Bottom left: Courtesy of Carnival Cruise Lines®; Right: Photograph by C. J. Ghormley)

about external market conditions when you are selling a product, you must also understand what goes on *inside* the minds of individual consumers during the buying process. You need to focus your attention on what motivates people to buy products.

Motivations are the internal factors at work in individuals, expressed as needs and desires. Motivation is an intensely personal matter. No two people have exactly the same needs or buying motives because no two people are identical. And the same person can think, feel, and act differently at different times. But there are many similarities in the process of satisfying consumer needs. Each individual has desires and decides what he or she is willing to pay to achieve those desires. Consumers decide which benefits and advantages they want to enjoy, then select those products and services that they feel will deliver the chosen benefits.

It is important for marketing and sales professionals to understand how internal psychological processes influence an individual's choice of a particular vacation destination or of a specific type of product within the destination. By recognizing customer motivations and needs, travel professionals can sell more effectively and can influence buyer choices.

THE STEPS OF THE BUYING PROCESS

People choose specific travel products for all kinds of reasons, some rational, some emotional (see Figure 7–1). Rational decisions may be based on factors such as:

* Cost—A consumer chooses the less expensive of two hotels in the same city.
* Dependability—A customer has found a particular supplier reliable in the past and decides to stay with that supplier.
* Convenience—A customer selects a particular airline because it offers a flight at a convenient time.
* Service—A customer visits a resort known for its excellent service because service is important to that customer.

Purchasing decisions are rarely based on rational reasons alone, however. People's emotions also have a strong influence on their choices of travel products. These motivations concern such highly personal matters as pleasure, relaxation, status, and belonging. For example, one individual might choose a cruise line because he thinks he will fit in easily with the other passengers. Another might choose the same cruise line because she sees it as a status symbol that she can boast about to her friends. In general, rational and emotional motivations overlap when people buy travel products because they have more than one reason for choosing a particular product.

Although the buying motivations of travelers are complex and idiosyncratic, the process of buying travel products (the purchasing decision) can be divided into five general steps:

* Feeling and recognizing a need or desire.
* Seeking information.
* Understanding the value of products.
* Deciding whether to buy.
* Experiencing and evaluating the purchase.

Travel marketing professionals who understand the steps involved in a purchasing decision are better prepared to help customers to select a product and achieve a sale.

Feeling and Recognizing a Need or Desire

The buying process is sparked by feeling a need or desire. The potential customer becomes aware that he or she must travel or wants to travel. For example, an executive learns of an upcoming meeting that she must attend, or a family starts to think about its annual vacation. A psychologist looking at the buying process would explain that people have needs and desires that produce tension. Recognizing that a travel experience will meet these needs is important in addressing this tension, which is relieved when the needs and desires are satisfied. These needs and desires become motivators which require action to reduce the tension.

Needs and desires determine what types of benefits will be sought. The role of the travel sales professional is to identify those products that will produce the benefits that will satisfy the traveler's needs or desires.

Seeking Information

After recognizing the need or desire for a travel product, travelers seek information. They often draw on both personal knowledge and external sources of information. Personal knowledge includes past experience and information provided by friends and from the media (newspaper article, television news, etc.). Someone who has had friends recommend a particular

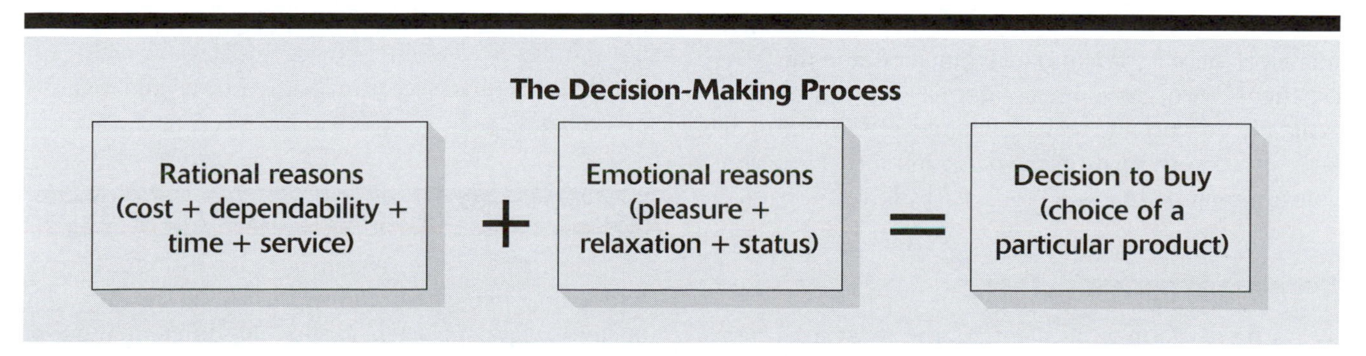

FIGURE 7–1 Think about the last time you went on vacation. Were you conscious of what went into your decision?

resort, for example, and has seen photos of it has personal knowledge (but not personal experience) of the resort. But when personal knowledge is insufficient to determine whether a travel product will meet certain needs, external sources of information are consulted.

External sources include travel agents, books, newspapers, magazines, videos, and Web sites, all of which provide information about travel products. Some people prefer to gather information from printed or electronic sources before making a decision; others are prepared to rely on a travel agent for advice.

When gathering information, people look for products that provide them with benefits that seem likely to satisfy their need or desire. They seek information about the tangible aspects of the product (in the case of a hotel, for example, the location, number and size of rooms, price, and so on) and about the intangible aspects (e.g., quality of service, ambiance, general atmosphere). If the potential buyer is satisfied with the information obtained from internal and external sources, the buying process will continue.

Understanding the Value of Products

People's attitudes and beliefs have a strong influence on the value they attach to products and on how well they think a certain travel experience will satisfy their needs. People value products based on the benefits they will receive by purchasing them. And of course, different people place greater value on different product attributes. Those who value familiarity, for example, would prefer to stay in a Holiday Inn because they know what to expect. Others, who relish new experiences, might favor an independently owned country inn instead.

The value of products is often based more on mental images than on its tangible features. Whether a prospective customer develops a positive or negative image toward a product determines the future direction of the buying process. A positive image will often result in the selection of a travel product, purchase, and the travel experience. A negative image may cause a consumer to avoid the product and seek alternatives. Clearly, the marketer's goal in this part of the decision process is to provide information that will produce a positive image.

Deciding Whether to Buy

The decision to purchase is the most important concern of travel sales professionals. Some purchases are made out of habit, some by conscious design. For all purchases, however, the consumer goes through some sort of decision-making process.

For travel sales and marketing professionals, the important concept to remember is that the decision to purchase is directly linked to motivations, which in turn are linked to the buyer's psychological needs. Motivations may be influenced through marketing efforts, especially product design and promotion.

At the decision stage, the consumer reviews the knowledge gained through the earlier steps of the process and makes a choice. The final decision to select a travel product is based on the traveler's confidence that it will produce the benefits that will satisfy the originally perceived need. This step includes selecting the type of product, the brand, the price, the time, and the distribution outlet. After the travel product is selected, the buying process is not yet completed. A critical step for both the traveler and marketer follows.

Experiencing and Evaluating the Purchase

After the decision to purchase is made, the trip is taken. During this experience, the traveler usually compares (often unconsciously) perceptions and expectations with reality. This includes whether the benefits sought (to meet needs and desires) have been realized. If the desired benefits are experienced, and the expectations and the reality (the actual trip experience) are very similar, then the traveler will be satisfied. Satisfaction leads directly to the final step in the process, which is evaluating the purchase. Did the hotel live up to the consumer's expectations? Was the flight as comfortable as it should have been? Did the resort provide the good time it promised?

The evaluation stage is particularly important in the travel industry. Customers benefit from it by purchasing products to suppliers who gave them good value and by avoiding those who did not. And the travel industry can benefit from this stage by acting on the feedback it receives from both satisfied and dissatisfied customers.

THE NEEDS OF THE LEISURE TRAVELER

The travel industry divides its market, as you know, into two distinct groups: leisure travelers and business travelers. Each group has different motivations, needs, and desires. This section of the chapter focuses on the needs of leisure travelers; those of business travelers are discussed later.

As a leisure traveler progresses through the buying process, several factors help shape the nature of his or her purchasing decision. Marketing has progressed rapidly in its understanding of the relationship between motivation and consumer behavior. Although many psychological aspects of consumer behavior are not fully understood, the following information will help provide a better understanding of the leisure traveler's decision making:

- The fundamental need to travel.
- The wheres and hows of travel.
- Barriers to travel.

The Need to Travel

Ask any group of people why they travel and you will probably hear several reasons. One person might cite a need for a change of pace; another might mention relaxation; another might express a desire to explore different locations.

These are among the more frequent motivations expressed for leisure travel. What they have in common—and what most theories of travel motivation focus on—is that there are basic human needs that travel can satisfy. In other words, the push to travel is intrinsic—it comes from inside a person.

Maslow's Theories. The theories of Abraham Maslow provide a logical starting point for discussing the psychology of need satisfaction. Maslow, a psychologist, developed a theory that explains human behavior in terms of its ability to satisfy needs. He divides these needs into hierarchical categories (see Figure 7–2), the first being ***fundamental needs*** such as thirst, hunger, and safety. Next in his hierarchy come ***psychological needs*** such as belonging, love, self-esteem, and the approval of others. The highest order of needs, according to Maslow, is related to ***self-actualization,*** or fulfilling one's full human potential.

Seen from Maslow's motivational perspective, leisure travel can be seen to satisfy needs toward the top of his hierarchy. People might seek travel as a means of enhancing their self-esteem, or gaining the approval of others, but they are unlikely to do so unless they have already met more fundamental needs. Travel is unimportant to those with inadequate food and shelter.

Maslow's hierarchy of needs is not, of course, specific to travel motivation. But most theories about basic travel motivation focus on how travel satisfies people's needs, and Maslow's theories offer a general psychological context in which to place other theories.

Kosters's Theory. A motivational theory specific to travel was provided by Marinus Kosters, a Dutch travel

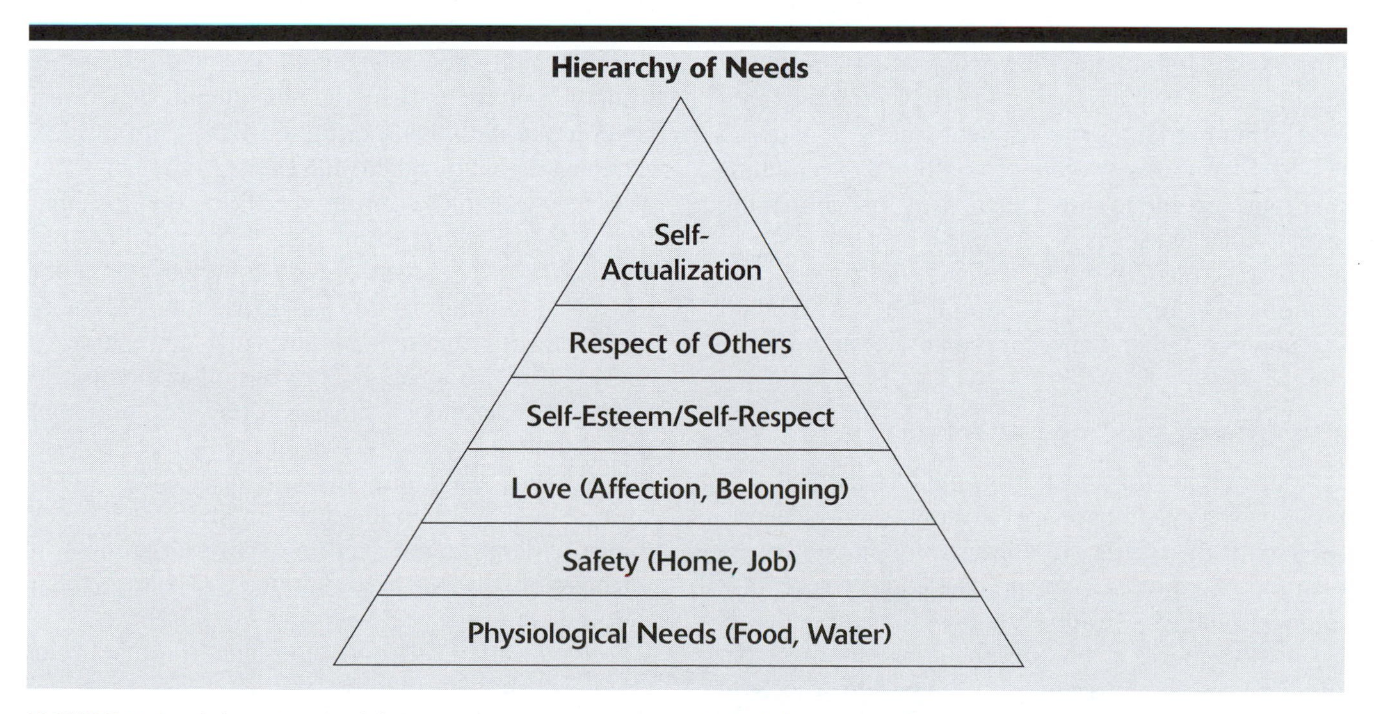

FIGURE 7–2 Leisure travel satisfies several needs as outlined in Maslow's Hierarchy of Needs.

researcher. Kosters divided all travel motivation into three basic needs:

- The need to compensate.
- The need to explore.
- The need for status recognition.

According to Kosters, the novelty of travel—the new people and experiences associated with new places—offers ***compensation*** for the routine of everyday life. The relaxation afforded by a vacation is a compensation for stress at work or at home.

The *need to explore* is related to the basic intellectual curiosity of human beings, to their need to learn. As people learn more about cultures and places they've never seen before, their natural curiosity leads them to travel. Travel satisfies their need to explore the unknown and expand their knowledge.

Travel also satisfies the need for ***status recognition*** by serving as a conspicuous demonstration of success and/or wealth. Travel destinations and the time and money spent on travel have definite status implications, and for some people, may be a basic motivation for a trip.

Mayo and Jarvis's Theory. Edward Mayo and Lance Jarvis explain the basic motivation for travel in a different way. Again, however, their theory is strongly linked to the basic notion of satisfying needs. They contend that leisure travel is motivated by curiosity combined with a basic human need to be productive. The need for productivity explains why people choose to satisfy their curiosity by traveling rather than, say, by watching television programs about different places.

Whatever the specific or combined motivations that cause people to travel, there is no doubt that the push to travel is strong. According to most surveys, over half of the American public now view an annual vacation of a week or more or a monthly getaway weekend as a necessity rather than a convenience or luxury.

The Wheres and Hows of Travel

For a travel sales professional, understanding what motivates people to travel explains only part of the psychology of the traveler. It is just as important—maybe even more so, from a sales and marketing perspective—to understand why customers choose the types of travel experiences they do. What distinguishes the mountain climber from the museum goer, the person who loves ocean cruises from the one who wants to tour the cities of Europe? Why does any given destination turn one person on and leave the other cold? What are the psychological characteristics that determine how people spend their time and money on travel?

Travel market research devotes a great deal of time and money to these questions and addresses them in a variety of ways. Some interesting studies have revealed useful patterns of travel psychology.

Personality Classifications. One of the most important studies in this area was conducted by Stanley Plog. Plog was trying to discover why so many travelers chose *not* to fly. He discovered that anxiety and fear played a larger role in determining travel choices than might have been suspected previously. Not only did anxiety and fear influence people's decisions about air travel, but those emotions were also significant in regard to people's choices of destinations.

Plog found that people with relatively strong feelings of fear and anxiety not only traveled less by air but, when they did travel, chose destinations that they perceived to be relatively safe and secure. Often, he found, they chose destinations with which they were already familiar and that offered products and services that were known as well.

At the other extreme, Plog found that people who were self-confident and outgoing tended to choose out-of-the-ordinary, adventurous destinations where they could learn about other cultures.

Plog labeled the first group ***psychocentric*** (self-centered) and the more outgoing group ***allocentric*** (other-centered). In between, he identified a much larger group with some of the characteristics of both extremes, whom he called ***midcentric***.

Plog went on to identify specific destinations that would be favored by each of the three personality types (see Figure 7-3) and to explain how perceptions of specific destinations could change over time. It is quite possible, for example, for a particular destination to appeal initially only to adventurous allocentric travelers. However, if enough allocentric travelers chose that destination and it expanded and became more accessible, it could, over time, become sufficiently "mainstream" to appeal to midcentrics and become a "mass tourism" (large volume and frequent tour groups). It might eventually become so familiar and common that it would even appeal to the fearful psychocentrics.

Plog's study is important because it explains one way in which the psychology of the traveler affects the choice of destinations. Travel professionals can use that

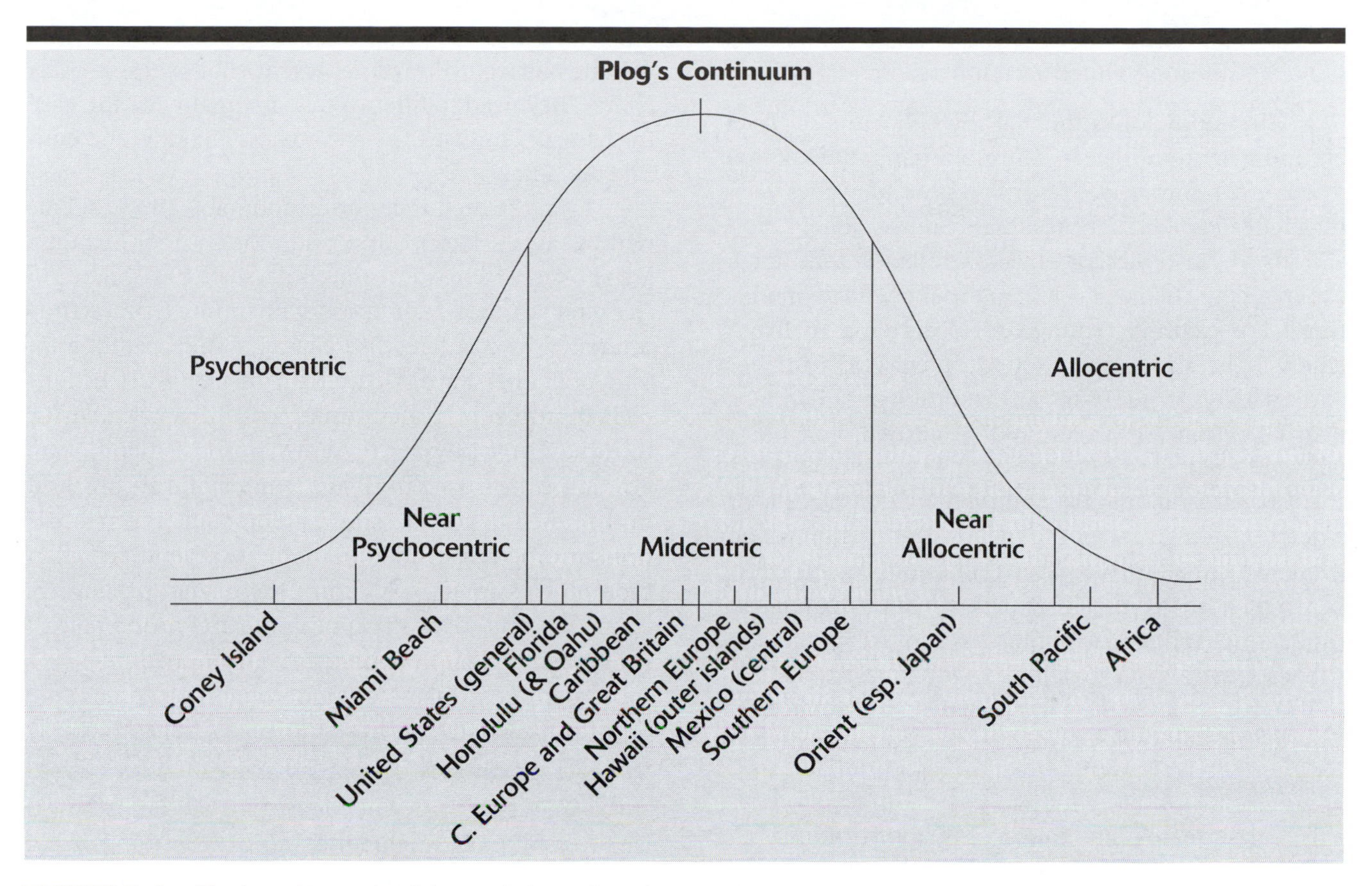

FIGURE 7–3 Plog's study examined the psychology of travelers and shows how it is reflected in their choice of destination. *Source:* Stanley C. Plog, Ph.D., "Why Destination Areas Rise and Fall in Popularity." The Cornell Hotel and Restaurant Administration Quarterly (Feb. 1974).

knowledge to suggest destinations most likely to suit individual customers.

Motivator Classifications. Other studies focus on various types of motivators that determine travel choices. McIntosh and Goeldner divide travel motivators into four basic categories:

* Physical.
* Cultural.
* Interpersonal.
* Status- and prestige-related.

Physical motivators all relate to the need to reduce tension, whether through rest, sports, entertainment, hiking, or any other activity. ***Cultural motivators*** are related to the impulse to learn about a new place, particularly about the music, art, religion, and folklore associated with that destination. ***Interpersonal motivators*** have to do with making new friends, meeting different people, and getting away from everyday life. And ***status and prestige motivators*** involve the need for recognition from others and the need to improve oneself.

Although these categories of psychological motivators are useful, specific destinations or types of travel can satisfy more than one category of travel motivator. (Travelers are usually motivated by more than one class of motivator.) But it's likely that at a particular time, one or more of these motivators will be more important to a potential traveler than others. People selling travel products need to understand the influence of these basic motivators in order to describe destinations and services as compellingly and specifically as possible.

Behavior Classifications. Another scheme for thinking about travel motivations was developed for the New York State Division of Tourism. It assigns leisure travelers to four basic categories:

* Outdoor enthusiasts.
* Young fun lovers.

* Sun resorters.
* Culture-oriented vacationers.

This study looks more at the behaviors of travelers and what they have in common than it does at their reasons for traveling. Nevertheless it identifies basic traveler categories that presumably reflect shared motivations. It also describes characteristics that might explain why the categories might share such motivations. For example, young fun lovers tend to live in cities, to be single and well educated, and to have a wide variety of interests; sun resorters also live in or near cities but are usually older, married, and not as well educated.

The various studies and theories that look at the psychology of travel choices focus on differing motivations. Although they may seem unrelated and even contradictory at times, they offer different ways of thinking about the same issue—what motivates people to choose their travel products.

Barriers to Travel

A complete examination of the psychology of the traveler must go beyond the pushes toward travel (motivations) and (perceived benefits) pulls toward certain types of travel experiences. It must also consider why some people choose *not* to use their discretionary time and money for leisure travel. Understanding the ***barriers to travel*** is one key to overcoming them.

Although most Americans do take an annual vacation, approximately 30 percent do not. Why? Some of them lack either the time or the money, or both, to spend on leisure travel. Poor health and family commitments also prevent people from traveling. Thus, many people may have the desire to travel but are unable to do so.

But psychological factors prevent people from traveling as well. A fear of the unknown inhibits some people: they are afraid of uncertainty, including new places and people.

Traveling also just doesn't seem worth the effort to some people. The packing and unpacking, the unfamiliar customs, the busy airports, and the need to find hotels and restaurants all seem to be too much trouble. It's easier and more familiar to stay at home. Then there are those who have never established the habit of traveling and those who are unaware of the tremendous benefits of travel. If you add all these nontravelers together, they represent a large number of people who don't travel now, and could be convinced to do so in the future.

For travel sales and marketing professionals, the various barriers to travel represent challenges to overcome. They need to find ways to assure the fearful, ease the hassled, motivate the habitual homebody, and educate the unfamiliar.

Even the seemingly insurmountable physical barriers to travel—lack of time and money, poor health—aren't conceded by some travel marketers. They develop weekend vacations for those with limited time. They promote low-cost fares and packages. And a number of tour operators have focused on people with health-related problems by developing vacations *especially* for those requiring physical therapy.

Thus, negative as well as positive forces are involved in the psychology of leisure travel. Travel professionals need to recognize and address both the negative forces, in order to find ways to overcome them, and the positive forces, in order to match appealing travel products with the travel motivations of prospective customers.

THE NEEDS OF THE BUSINESS TRAVELER

Understanding why people travel on business isn't difficult. Essentially, they must travel in order to meet their business objectives. Thousands of people in all kinds of professions are required to travel to meetings, conventions, and other places of business, in order to do their jobs. Nearly all business travel is nondiscretionary, in the sense that the travelers have little choice about where or when they will travel. Destinations and dates are determined by their companies. But that doesn't make psychology any less important for dealing with business travelers. It just means that different factors need to be considered.

The business travel market is enormous, accounting for a large share of the travel market as a whole. Business travel accounts for 60 percent of all domestic passengers in the United States. More than sixty-seven million Americans traveled on business in 1986, spending more than $300 billion in the process. Business travel, in other words, is big business.

The Need for Efficiency

The psychology of business travel revolves around one central fact: time is money. When people are traveling on business, every minute counts. They need to arrive at meetings on time; they must rely on airlines and hotels to supply the services they need; they want as little hassle as possible.

Marketing Impressions

TRAVEL INDUSTRY ASSOCIATION OF AMERICA'S U.S. TRAVEL DATA CENTER

Imagine you're an executive with a corporation that is considering building a resort community targeted to senior citizens along the coast of North Carolina. Before you invest a significant amount in the project, you'll want to know several things about travel and your target market. For example, is travel increasing or decreasing, especially on the east coast and in North Carolina, specifically? What is the forecast for travel in the coming year? Is travel among senior citizens on an upward or a downward trend, and what is the outlook for this segment? How do the travel patterns of older Americans differ from younger groups?

One place you can get such information is the U.S. Travel Data Center, the research department of the Travel Industry Association of America (TIA). Located in Washington, D.C., TIA is the national, nonprofit association that serves as the unifying organization for all components of the U.S. travel industry, the third largest retail industry and one of the largest employers in the nation. TIA's mission is to represent the whole of the U.S. travel industry to promote and facilitate increased travel to and within the United States.

One of TIA's major objectives is to serve as the authoritative source for travel industry research, analysis, and forecasting—an objective carried out by the U.S. Travel Data Center. Its research helps travel marketers better understand the needs of travelers, profile various segments in terms of trip and traveler characteristics, and monitor trends in traveler behavior. Data Center research provides a national perspective and a context in which to evaluate specific company research, as well as helps save travel marketers time and money by focusing on markets with the greatest potential.

The center publishes its research in a number of reports, which are sent to subscribers and sold to others. One of the center's primary publications is its National Travel Survey (NTS), results of which are published twice a year. The NTS is based on monthly telephone interviews with fifteen hundred U.S. adults, selected at random across the Untied States, and provides data on the travel patterns and habits of typical Americans. The data cover all major aspects of travel, including purpose of trip, mode of transportation, type of lodging, duration of trip, as well as demographics.

Similar data are also collected through the center's TravelScope® program, a monthly mail panel survey of twenty thousand households. The very large size of this survey's sample allows analysis at the state and local level. The results are also used to profile various traveler groups, such as historic/cultural travelers.

The U.S. Travel Data Center also conducts economic impact research at the national, state and county level, based on its proprietary, computerized model known as the Travel Economic Impact Model. Data from this model indicate that domestic and international travelers pumped $489 billion into the U.S. economy in 1997, creating more than 6.8 million jobs. Information such as this is invaluable in showing the importance of the travel industry and in making public officials aware of the positive impact of travel on the U.S. economy.

TIA and its Travel Data Center also provide forecasts for the travel industry through its annual conference, the Marketing Outlook Forum, and its proprietary forecasting model developed in close cooperation with Data Resources/McGraw-Hill (DRI). Forecasts, which are published quarterly, include travel volume forecasts of U.S. resident travel for the next four years, quarterly U.S. travel volume forecasts to the nine census regions, forecast of travel price inflation and total travel expenditures in the U.S. for the next four years, and international travel forecasts provided by Tourism Industry/International Trade Administration.

Much of the U.S. Travel Data Center's research can be accessed through TIA's Web site at <www.tia.org>.

In a nutshell, what business travelers want is efficiency and consistency. Their requirements fall into four general categories:

* Schedules.
* Convenience.
* Comfort.
* Special features.

Schedules. Schedules are critical in business travel. People travel to attend meetings at appointed times. Many airline flights, for example, are scheduled for early morning and late afternoon to make single-day business trips feasible and productive. Businesspeople need to be sure of getting to those meetings on time and wasting as little time as possible in doing so. A delayed flight, a missed connection, or a broken-down rental car can jeopardize their appointments. And missed appointments can mean lost business opportunities.

The travel industry knows about the importance of time and schedules. Airlines, for example, schedule as many direct flights as possible to major business centers, minimizing the need for time-consuming connections. They also try to schedule flights early in the morning to get travelers to their morning appointments and in the late afternoon and early evening to get them home again. Just as rush hours on the freeways are related to business schedules, so are rush hours in the airports.

Convenience. Given that time is money, convenience is often as important as schedule. Hotels understand the importance of convenience. Many are located near airports or convention centers for just that reason and offer complimentary shuttle service to and from those locations. Some offer conference and meeting rooms to make business appointments as simple and convenient as possible. They provide audiovisual equipment and cater lunches—anything they can do to make doing business in *their* hotel more convenient than in other hotels.

Comfort. Business travel is often difficult and exhausting. But businesspeople can't allow it to exhaust them. They need to be able to perform at their best to maximize their business opportunities. After all, their companies are spending money to allow them to meet clients face to face. To risk wasting that investment with a poor presentation is bad business.

So comfort, which is important to all travelers, is particularly important to business travelers. They can't afford to risk an uncomfortable bed or an overheated hotel room that might jeopardize sleep the night before a big meeting or presentation. Nor do they want to spend four or five hours in a cramped airplane seat. Many will gladly pay for a room in a deluxe hotel or an airline seat in business class or first class in order to be assured of their comfort. Most companies have policies about first-class travel based on time and distance to meetings.

Special Features. Although schedules, convenience, and comfort are especially important factors for business travelers, travel marketers have also developed several special features designed to enhance the appeal of specific travel products to this critical market.

Most business hotels, for example, now provide irons and hair driers. They know that personal appearance is especially important to business travelers and that these appliances will help them look well groomed and neatly dressed for their appointments.

Many business-oriented hotels have set aside special floors for business travelers, with rooms that include a desk or table for working and fax machine and computer ports to plug in a laptop computer, so that travelers can transmit documents to their offices. Other hotels have attempted to meet the fitness needs of businesspeople on the road by creating in-house exercise and health facilities or access to local health clubs.

Sometimes businesspeople are required to stay in a location away from home for an extended period. Or they may need to stay in a hotel for a while after being relocated while they search for a new home. To meet the needs of extended-stay guests, a new type of residence hotel has been developed. The "rooms" resemble apartments with maid and room service and often include kitchens for self-catering. The residence hotels ease the discomfort of business travel that extends to weeks or even months.

Credit-card companies address the needs of traveling businesspeople by providing special services. Some offer year-end statements, for example, listing and itemizing all charges for the year. Some provide emergency services, such as extra cash and travel insurance charged to their credit cards. And several now provide casualty and liability coverage for rental cars and flight insurance for air travel.

The fact that many businesspeople travel frequently has led suppliers to introduce several special features designed to ensure repeat business. Chief among these are the frequent-flier, frequent-guest, and frequent-renter programs that offer free flights and hotel rooms, discounts, and other privileges to repeat customers. In addition, airlines offer free drinks and special meals to business customers, car rental firms give away luggage and offer free upgrades to larger cars, and hotels have created special lounges and provide welcoming gifts for their business guests.

This preferential treatment helps business travelers prepare for meetings and makes them feel special. And if all other factors relating to schedule convenience and comfort are more or less equal, making travelers feel special can establish brand loyalty, thus influencing their choice of supplier.

The Special Needs of Women Travelers

Not so very long ago, the vast majority of business travelers were men. But within the last twenty years, more women have successfully entered the business world, and they now represent a sizable portion of the business travel market (see Figure 7–4). Today, in fact, one in every three business travelers is a woman.

This fact demands special attention from travel professionals. Most of the needs of women traveling on business are the same as those of men, but women *do* have some additional needs.

Foremost among these is their need for security. Women need to feel safe within their hotel rooms and when they travel back and forth to restaurants and meetings. If they dine alone or have a drink alone at the bar, they want to know that they can do so in peace.

Travel suppliers, keen to attract women business travelers, have introduced measures to heighten the sense of safety and security in their facilities. Some hotels have installed brighter lighting in hallways, and others employ a security escort to accompany women to and from the parking garage.

Most business travelers, male and female, spend large amounts for travel products they buy, and they expect good quality and service in return. Successful travel suppliers and intermediaries recognize the importance of meeting the needs of business travelers to ensure repeat business.

But whether customers are traveling for business or leisure, understanding needs and motivations is crucial to success in selling travel products. It constitutes the first half of the process of matching customers

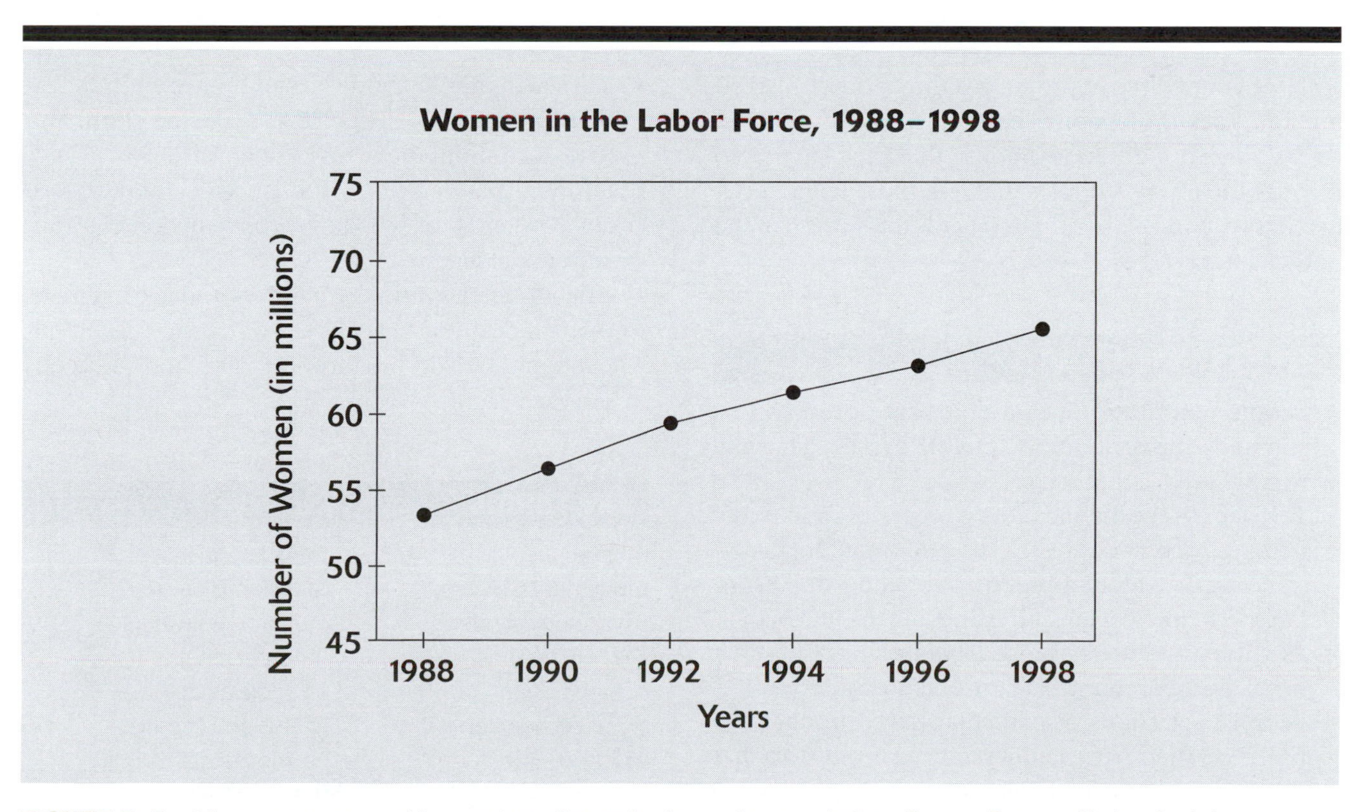

FIGURE 7–4 More women are working—and traveling on business—than ever before. *Source:* Bureau of Labor Statistics

One in every three business travelers is a woman.

with well-suited travel products. Once a travel marketing and sales professional has a good sense of a customer's needs and motivations, the next step is to identify the travel products that will provide the benefits that will best satisfy them. That is the subject of the next chapter.

CHAPTER SUMMARY

* People's motivation to travel is based on both reason and emotion, but the buying process generally follows predictable steps.
* The steps of the buying process are feeling and recognizing a need or desire, selecting information, understanding the value of products, deciding whether to buy, and experiencing and evaluating the purchase.
* Psychologists have developed theories suggesting that travel satisfies certain fundamental human needs.
* People's selections of particular travel products are based on their personalities, on the motivators that drive them, and on their expectations.
* Barriers to travel include lack of time or money, fear of the unknown, reluctance to make the effort, and ignorance about the benefits of travel.
* Business travelers look for efficiency and consistency in terms of schedules, convenience, comfort, and special features.
* One in three business travelers today is female. Women business travelers are very concerned about safety and security, quality and value, and courteous service.

KEY TERMS

motivations
fundamental needs
psychological needs
self-actualization
compensation
status recognition
psychocentric
allocentric
midcentric
physical motivators
cultural motivators
interpersonal motivators
status and prestige motivators
barriers to travel

DISCUSSION QUESTIONS

1. How can a travel professional go about discovering the rational and emotional motivation of a prospective customer?
2. Why is it important for travel professionals to understand the steps in the buying process?
3. Explain and give examples of internal and external sources of information for selecting travel products.
4. What can a travel professional do to help a customer decide to buy a particular travel product?
5. How can a travel professional use his or her knowledge of the theories about leisure travel as a means of need satisfaction?
6. Choose one of the barriers to travel described in this chapter, and explain how you would go about overcoming it.
7. Give examples of services that travel suppliers provide to satisfy the business traveler's need for efficiency.
8. In what ways are the needs of women business travelers different from those of men traveling on business? What can travel professionals do to satisfy those needs?

Understanding the Traveler's Needs

Name: ______________________ Date: ______________

Directions: Answer these questions as you read the chapter. You will be able to use your answers to help you review the chapter.

1. What are motivations and why are they important to travel marketing?

2. Briefly describe the five steps of the buying process.

3. How does Maslow's theory distinguish between types of needs?

4. How does Kosters's theory define travel motivation?

5. Describe Mayo and Jarvis's theory of travel motivation.

6. How did Plog classify people according to their personality?

7. Describe the four categories into which MacIntosh and Goeldner divide travel motivators.

8. Into what four categories did the New York State Division of Tourism divide leisure travelers?

9. What are barriers to travel? Give two examples—one physical and one psychological.

10. What are the psychological needs of business travelers and why is it important to understand them?

11. How can the travel industry provide high-quality service that caters to the needs of business travelers?

12. Why is comfort especially important to business travelers?

13. Give three examples of special features that can attract business travelers.

14. Describe how the travel market has begun to recognize the special needs of women business travelers and alter products and services to better serve them.

Understanding the Traveler's Needs

Name: ______________________ Date: ______________

INNER TRAVEL

You are a travel agent, and your goal is to increase your sales to leisure travelers and to establish a base of clients who will return to you for all their travel needs.

1. How might an understanding of what motivates a person to travel help you to reach your goal?

2. What are three questions you might ask clients to discover the needs they hope to satisfy by travel?

3. Describe a trip that might help a working parent compensate for a demanding, high-stress career, combined with caring for several children at home.

4. How can travel help satisfy a need to explore?

5. Suggest one trip that might allow a young professional from a large city in the northeastern United States to learn about a new culture and see a different part of the world.

6. How does travel satisfy the need for status recognition?

____

____

____

____

____

7. Suggest a destination that might meet the status needs of a moderately affluent retired couple from the southwestern United States.

____

____

____

____

8. Describe two travel-related needs and motivations in each of the following categories.

Physical: _______________

Cultural: _______________

Interpersonal: _______________

Status and Prestige: _______________

9. Which needs or motivations might be associated with the following travel destinations?

Four days attending the Aspen, Colorado, music festival: _______________

A walking tour of the Irish countryside: _______________

One week at a luxury spa in La Jolla, California: _______________

A tour of Vatican City: _______________

10. One approach to travel motivations classifies travelers on the basis of shared behavior, in the four groups listed below. For each group, suggest two possible destinations on tour packages. (Try to make your suggestions as varied as possible in terms of geography, cost, mode of travel, and so on.)

Outdoor enthusiasts: _______________

Sun resorters: _______________

Culture-oriented vacations: _______________

Young fun-lovers: _______________

11. What barriers to travel might exist in each of the following cases, and how might they be overcome?

A couple with two children under three years old: _______________

A middle-aged person who has never been on a plane: _______________

A young professional who is confined to a wheelchair: _______________

The owner of a small business who works six days a week and rarely takes a vacation: _______________

The members of a club for teens with diabetes: _______________

Identifying the Seller

OBJECTIVES

When you have completed this chapter, you should be able to:

- Identify the special characteristics of the travel product.
- Identify and explain the differences between the two basic categories of travel sellers.
- Give examples of the roles of different types of intermediaries.
- Explain the difference between direct and indirect distribution systems.
- Discuss the advantages to customers and suppliers of the two distribution systems.
- Describe how computer technology has increased access to travel products.

This chapter begins by examining the operation of various travel ***distribution systems***. These systems are responsible for making the travel products offered by the suppliers more accessible to the customers. Some travel suppliers sell their products directly to their customers; others distribute their products indirectly through intermediaries; but most use a combination of these distribution methods.

SPECIAL CHARACTERISTICS OF THE TRAVEL PRODUCT

When considering travel distribution systems, you should keep in mind the special characteristics of the travel product. Travel sales distribution systems have developed as they have because of the nature of travel products. This is true of the sales distribution systems of all products and services, because the way products are sold is directly related to the particular characteristics of *what* is being sold. For example, new cars are sold primarily through dealerships, because of the characteristics of cars—their size, their expense, their need for ongoing service, the relatively low number of automobile manufacturers, and so on.

In a similar way, the nature of travel products determines the ways that they are sold. For that reason, it will be useful to review a few of the concepts related to the nature of travel products that were presented in Chapter 2, including the characteristics of intangibility, perishability, and complementarity.

Intangibility

Most companies in the travel industry sell more than products. They sell a mix of products and services. This interaction of product and service is one of the main reasons travel products are basically intangible.

Buyers can't hold them in their hands to inspect them or "kick the tires." Customers may be able to inspect the tangible components of travel products, such as a hotel room and its furnishings, but the fact that they are going to pay to spend time in that room means that the hotel's services are going to be a large part of the bill. Beyond the hotel's services, customers are also concerned about other intangible aspects of travel products, such as ambience, entertainment, or luxury.

The intangible nature of travel products means that they can't be sold like tangible products, on shelves or in showrooms. It also means that sellers must be able to describe and categorize the products accurately and to emphasize their service components.

Perishability

Automobile dealers can leave cars on the lot until they sell. It costs money to keep them in inventory, but the opportunity to sell them doesn't disappear daily, since the products aren't perishable. Most travel products are perishable. Airlines with unsold seats and hotels with unsold rooms, for example, lose the opportunity to sell the seat on a particular flight once it takes off or the room on a given night once the next morning arrives.

The perishability of travel products creates a need to develop effective, convenient, and widespread sales distribution systems. It also creates an incentive to find different ways to sell those products if they remain unsold close to the time of their availability. Like seafood stores who lower their prices toward the end of the day because they know the fish won't be fresh enough to sell the next day, travel companies must consider unusual and creative measures in order to sell their products before they perish.

Complementarity

In Chapter 2, you learned about the complementarity of travel products, the notion that travel products are rarely purchased in isolation. Instead, most travel involves a combination of travel products that together constitute a trip. An airline flight, with car rental, resort accommodations, and sightseeing tour are examples of separate but complementary products that together create a vacation experience.

Travel industry suppliers tend to specialize in one general area. That is because there are only a few suppliers from whom you could purchase all of the complementary products that make up a normal vacation trip.

If customers with several different travel requirements were forced to purchase travel products only from each of the suppliers that provide or control them, they would face a complex task. The travel industry has, therefore, developed sales distribution systems that allow customers to purchase the numerous and separately provided travel products from a single sales source.

TYPES OF SELLERS

Imagine that you have been asked to organize a spring study trip to New Mexico for a group of college students. You will need to purchase airline tickets and reserve hotel rooms in Albuquerque. You will also need to arrange for transfer of the group and their luggage from the airport to the hotel and back. Then you will have to arrange sightseeing tours or visits to local attractions. Before you begin to make these arrangements, you need to know where you can go to buy the various travel products.

Like other industries, the travel industry has various ways of distributing its products and services. Sellers are those people from whom you can purchase the travel products necessary for the study trip. Travel customers can choose between two basic types of travel sellers: suppliers and intermediaries.

Suppliers

Suppliers own or operate the company or organization that produces the travel product that they are selling. Airlines, railroads, motor coach companies, cruise lines, car rental firms, hotels, restaurants, resorts, attractions, and sightseeing companies all control the products they make available to the customer. Suppliers want to distribute their products as widely as possible. Some suppliers only sell their products directly to customers. For example, many independently owned bed-and-breakfast establishments choose to sell their own rooms on an exclusive basis. But most suppliers sell indirectly as well, by using intermediaries. And a few suppliers, such as cruise lines, sell their products almost exclusively through intermediaries.

Intermediaries

An ***intermediary*** is a seller of travel products who acts as a link between a supplier and a customer. The travel industry intermediaries are divided into three

Many travel suppliers sell their products directly to customers.

general groups: travel agents, tour operators, and specialized distributors. All three sell travel products to customers on behalf of the suppliers who produce the travel product, but each type operates in a different way.

Travel Agents. Travel agents function as retail outlets for travel products. They provide a wide range of suppliers with a direct link to potential customers. Because they sell more airline seats, cruise reservations, hotel accommodations, and package tours than any other type of intermediary, travel agents represent the most important distribution system group for all travel suppliers.

An important difference between travel agents and most retailers (and from most other intermediaries) is that they are compensated differently. Traditional retailers buy goods or services from suppliers, then resell them to their customers at a higher price. Travel agents instead transfer products from suppliers to buyers; they neither buy the travel products they sell nor mark up the price. Instead, they act as transfer agents on behalf of suppliers who pay them a ***commission***, which is either a fixed fee or a percentage of the selling price. Most other intermediaries, on the other hand, receive discounts for buying in bulk from suppliers and make their profits by reselling the products at a higher price—like traditional retailers.

However, recent decisions by airlines to limit the commission paid to travel agents to a flat fee instead of a percentage of the price of tickets sold may force travel agencies to begin charging customers (buyers) for their services. It may also encourage them to reserve more travel packages on behalf of their customers through tour operators, who continue to pay travel agents a higher percentage commission than airlines or hotels do.

Tour Operators. Tour operators act as intermediaries by offering package tours for sale to the travel customer. A standard package tour includes some or all of the following individual travel products:

- Air and/or surface transportation.
- Hotel or other accommodations.

* Sightseeing tours.
* Services of a tour guide.
* Meals.
* Entertainment.
* Use of a rental car.

To create tour packages, a tour operator either buys travel products in quantity from a number of different travel suppliers (usually at a significant discount) or supplies them itself. It assembles those various products into a tour package that it offers to customers at a single, all-inclusive price. Since the tour operator has purchased cheaply in bulk quantities, it can usually afford to offer its customers good values for their money and still make a profit for itself. Customers who purchase tours consequently benefit not only from the convenience of purchasing the single, all-inclusive vacation but also from the relatively low price made possible by the tour operator's purchasing power. Tour operators may also sell packages created by other tour operators directly to consumers.

Specialized Distributors. In addition to travel agents and tour operators, several ***specialized distributors*** channel travel products from suppliers to customers. Each of these specialized distributors focuses on a particular type of travel customer.

* ***Incentive travel planners*** assemble or organize the trips offered by companies to their employees as rewards for achieving corporate goals.
* ***Meeting, convention, and event planners*** arrange travel, accommodations, and tours for people attending conventions, trade shows, or conferences.
* ***Ticket consolidators*** buy excess inventory of unsold travel products and sell them directly to individual travel customers and retail travel agents at discounted prices.

It is important to note that rapidly changing technology will create more opportunities for the distribution of travel products. Currently, both suppliers (airlines and hotels) and intermediaries (large travel agencies) use online Internet systems to sell travel directly to consumers, by providing user-friendly Web sites and sophisticated browsing software for those who visit their sites. They also conduct transactions (selling tickets or reserving rooms) with credit cards on secure networks.

DIRECT DISTRIBUTION

Travel products reach customers through travel distribution systems. These systems are organized and maintained in order to provide products to customers through convenient points of sale. Their primary function is to give travel suppliers access to potential travel customers and to increase their sale of travel products.

The travel industry employs two basic systems for distributing travel products to the consumer. The first, ***direct distribution***, involves the direct sale of travel products and services by the supplier to the customer. In the second system, called ***indirect distribution***, one or more intermediaries provide a link between the supplier and the customer. In this system, the customers make their purchases from one of the intermediaries discussed previously.

The direct distribution system is the simpler of the two, since it involves only the supplier and the customer. Many rail passengers, for example, buy rail tickets at the station just before boarding. In this situation, the railroad supplies a product—transport by train over a specified distance—directly to its traveling customers. No intermediaries operate between the supplier and the customer.

Suppliers may have more than one way to offer their products for sale directly. One of the simplest direct distribution systems enables customers to make reservations and purchase products over the telephone. Most major airlines, hotels, rail companies, and car rental agencies have toll-free telephone numbers that their customers can call for service, often twenty-four hours a day. Another simple means of direct sale is using sales agents to sell to customers in person. Many suppliers, especially airlines and car rental companies, do this by selling their products over the counter at major airports. They may also lease space at other locations visited often by potential customers, such as hotels, convention centers, shopping malls, major railway stations, and anywhere businesses are concentrated. Some suppliers also sell directly to customers by allowing them to make reservations and payment by mail. More recently, suppliers are also making their products available through Web sites on the Internet.

Supplier Advantages of Direct Distribution

Some industries have no direct distribution systems for sales. You can't buy an automobile from the manufacturer, for example; you have to buy it from a dealer. But the particular characteristics of travel products and customers combine to make direct distribution advantageous to travel suppliers in some significant ways.

Simplicity. Direct distribution cuts down on the number of steps involved in a transaction, so the sale is less complicated. The supplier receives payment from the customer and provides the product or service purchased. No payments need to be made to intermediaries, which cuts down on the amount of clerical work and administrative time involved in the transaction. Direct distribution is simpler, too, because it reduces risk. Only two parties—the supplier and the customer—are involved in the transaction. This is an advantage because, generally, the more people involved in a transaction, the greater the risk of miscommunication or complications.

Additional Sales Opportunities. Many customers prefer to buy their travel products directly from the supplier, so suppliers who want to reach such customers must maintain direct distribution systems. For example, many business travelers who plan to pick up a rental car when they arrive at an airport do not arrange the rental in advance. They expect to be able to walk up to a rental desk and do the transaction there and then. Obviously, only those rental agencies that maintain a direct sales outlet at the airport would be able to sell to such customers.

Direct distribution also provides suppliers with opportunities to make additional sales over and above a customer's original purchase. Suppose, for example, that Jane Smith calls United Airlines to book a seat on a flight from Denver to Chicago. The reservation agent may be able to persuade her to buy additional products, such as a rental car. The representative could ask if Mrs. Smith has plans for another business trip or a vacation trip in the near future as well. If she does, he could suggest she purchase her tickets early to obtain a lower fare.

Other types of travel suppliers can benefit from direct distribution in similar ways. When customers reserve a hotel room for a business trip, the hotel representative can inform them about the hotel's "Stay Three Nights, Get a Weekend Free" offer. They may then opt to extend their stay to take advantage of the special offer. Direct distribution enables suppliers to speak with their customers about promotions, current rates, and special services, which increases the possibility of additional sales.

Responsiveness. The more control a supplier has over its distribution system, the more responsive the system can be. If market conditions or customers' needs change, the supplier can react quickly to those changes. A price change, for example, can usually be implemented more quickly in a direct distribution system. Or consider how a hotel could temporarily increase the size of its own reservations staff to handle an increased demand for rooms resulting from a large convention.

Increased Profit. Suppliers that make direct sales to customers do not have to pay commissions or give discounts to intermediaries. Of course, the supplier must bear the full cost of maintaining the direct distribution system. Even so, the cost trade-offs may mean that a supplier can increase its revenue by selling travel products directly. Suppliers must determine whether the costs incurred in selling directly exceed the commissions to be paid to intermediaries.

For example, a customer might pay $250 for a ticket on a Southwest Airlines flight from Atlanta to Dallas. If the customer makes the purchase directly from the airline, the airline receives revenue of $250 from the sale. If, on the other hand, the customer buys the ticket from a travel agent, the agent receives a commission of 10 percent on the sale, or $25. The airline then receives only $225 in revenue for the same seat. But if it costs Southwest more than $25 to sell the ticket directly (e.g., in labor, overhead), it makes economic sense for the airline to sell through intermediaries.

Greater Control. In direct distribution, the supplier retains full control of the manner in which the product and supplier are represented to the customer. The supplier does not need to depend on the actions of an agent, who may or may not adequately represent the best interests of the supplier. Travel agents, after all, represent more than one competing supplier and sell thousands of different travel products. They can't reasonably be expected to have as thorough a knowledge of any single supplier's product as that supplier's own sales staff would. Nor can they be expected to sell it as forcefully against the products of competing suppliers.

Direct distribution also allows suppliers to monitor the way their products are being sold to a greater degree than they can with intermediaries. It gives suppliers direct contact with customers, which allows them to have more control over the quality with which their products are delivered to their customers.

Marketing Impressions

MCCORD CONSUMER DIRECT

In a time of commission cuts, closing travel agencies, and crowded flights, McCord Consumer Direct (MCD) credits their success to marketing, training, service fees, and preferred vendor agreements.

McCord Consumer Direct, a division of McCord Travel Management, is one of the country's largest leisure travel management companies in the United States. They specialize in direct phone sales to consumers seeking airline reservations and other related services. These services are marketed through toll-free "phone words" such as 1-800-FLY ASAP, 1-800-SKIN DIVE, 1-800-SKI CHEAP and 1-800-BEST CRUISE, to name a few. Their customers are consumer based and respond to marketing programs nationwide, such as fax marketing, the Internet, flyers, press releases, radio spots and word of mouth.

Training is a major focus in the MCD call center and they provide unique specialty training as well as travel career training. MCD constantly strives to develop and improve the programs throughout the company in this ever changing travel industry.

McCord Consumer Direct is open 24 hours a day, 7 days a week, 365 days a year. They have an employee base of 250, which includes their discount sales specialists, executive staff, and support staff.

Motivation, creativity and determination are key words describing the MCD call center. They believe in promoting enthusiasm in their center through games, recognition, theme dress-up days, and special company events.

It's very important to have an atmosphere that is lively when your job consists of answering over twenty thousand phone calls per day. Sales are projected to exceed $82M in 1998.

MCD's slogan is "A World of Possibilities," and the possibility of starting an on-site childcare center became a reality with the opening of the McCord Learning Center. They wanted to do something to benefit their staff and the community and the Learning Center was the answer. It's more than childcare; it's a center that promotes knowledge and guidance in addition to playtime.

McCord Consumer Direct, like many other companies, has a mission statement that they truly believe in. "The mission of McCord Consumer Direct is dedication to offering the highest quality travel experience at the lowest possible price. Our focus is to provide our services with skill, precision, and accuracy, delivered with a sense of warmth, friendliness, individual pride, and company spirit. Our goal is to treat all customers like we would want to be treated."

It goes without saying that a company is built based on the leadership it receives. Because of the vision and support of MCD's leaders, they've been able to move ahead and pursue opportunities that others only dream of.

McCord Consumer Direct is planning for the future. They anticipate building their center to 350 employees by the beginning of the new millennium and advancing their technology and services to new heights.

They believe that their spirit will drive them to reach their goals and they look forward to continued growth in this ever changing industry.

The choice to use a direct distribution system rather than an indirect system, however, also reduces the number of potential sales outlets for products and services and results in higher fixed costs of distribution for the supplier. Consequently, suppliers must carefully examine cost, availability, and quality-control factors in relation to the characteristics of the products they are selling when making decisions about which sales distribution system to use.

Customer Advantages of Direct Distribution

Direct distribution systems offer certain advantages to customers as well. As a result, some customers, particularly those who travel frequently, prefer to make their travel purchases directly from suppliers. They have several reasons for doing so.

Control. Many travel customers believe that buying travel products directly gives them more control over their travel plans. They do not need to depend on third parties to make their arrangements for them.

Time Savings. Purchasing travel products directly from the suppliers can be faster than going through intermediaries, especially when travel plans are simple and options in prices and fares are limited. Many suppliers provide toll-free telephone numbers for prospective customers. When customers speak directly to sales representatives, they can decide among various options on the spot. If an intermediary is involved, extra time may be required for an agent to relay travel options and decisions back and forth between the customer and the supplier.

Greater Accuracy. The more people involved in a transaction, the greater the chance for errors or misunderstandings. When travel customers use intermediaries, they have to depend on the accuracy of both the intermediary and the supplier. Some customers believe that purchasing travel products directly minimizes mistakes.

INDIRECT DISTRIBUTION

An indirect distribution system operates when one or more intermediaries provide a channel for the flow of travel products from the supplier to the customer. The supplier still sells travel products to customers, but does so indirectly through a third party acting on the supplier's behalf. Indirect distribution systems are the mainstay of the travel industry. According to the American Society of Travel Agents (ASTA), travel agents in the United States sell 95 percent of all cruises, 90 percent of all package tours, 80 percent of all domestic airline tickets, 50 percent of all car rentals, and 25 percent of all domestic hotel rooms.

The most common and straightforward example of an indirect distribution system is the use of a travel agent by a customer purchasing an airline ticket. The airline supplies the product: travel by air between specified points for a set fee. The customer purchases the product supplied by the airline but does not make the purchase directly from the airline. Instead, the travel agent acts as an agent for the airline by selling the product to the customer on the airline's behalf. The travel agent receives a commission from the supplier, in this case the airline, for acting as its agent.

Intermediaries in indirect distribution systems have access to a vast number of different travel products, offered by a variety of suppliers. Theoretically, all intermediaries have access to the same huge pool of travel products. With few exceptions, intermediaries do not offer unique travel products to their customers on an exclusive basis. They do, however, combine travel products in such a way that they can offer unique combinations of products to fill the needs of their travel customers.

Because of the variety and number of travel products, intermediaries often specialize according to the products they handle, the type of customers they serve, or their method of packaging combinations of travel products. As a result, travel intermediaries can be divided into four broad categories: travel agents, corporate travel departments, tour operators, and specialized travel distributors.

Travel Agents

Travel agents, for the most part, sell all types of travel products to anyone who wishes to use their services. Most travel agencies sell both leisure travel and business travel. However, different agencies may emphasize one area more than the other. Some may specialize in a particular type of travel, such as cruises, or a particular group of customers, such as college students.

Travel agencies operate much like any other retail outlet. They are usually located in areas where they are visible and accessible to the public, so they benefit from locations such as downtown areas and shopping malls. Agents who emphasize business travel may be located in office complexes or technology parks where they are close to their customers. The exceptions to this location issue are the online agencies with Web sites or those who use toll-free numbers for consumer access. Regardless, business travel agents often make leisure travel arrangements for the customers whose business needs they serve.

In their capacity as intermediaries, travel agents have relationships with both suppliers and customers, to whom they offer professional advice on the selection of travel products. When they sell travel products, they earn commissions from the suppliers of those travel products. If customers come to a travel agent to inquire about a cruise, first the agent finds out their specific requirements. What part of the world do they want to cruise? What ports of call do they wish to visit? What shipboard activities do they expect the cruise line to supply? How much money do they wish to spend?

After obtaining this detailed information, the agent selects several cruises that fit the criteria given by the customers. The travel agent gives the customers brochures, videotapes, and other pertinent information on each cruise. The agent may be able to advise the customer on the basis of personal experience or the reports of other customers or travel agents. The more information the customers receive, the more knowledgeable their decision will be, and the more satisfied they are likely to be with the travel purchase.

When the customers have chosen a cruise and decided to make a purchase, then the role of the travel agent changes. Now they become an agent for the cruise line selected by the customer. The agent takes the reservation and collects the deposit on behalf of the cruise line. The agent gives the customer information and advice free of charge; but the customer pays only for the cruise. The agent receives compensation in the form of commission from the supplier only when a sale is made.

Corporate Travel Departments

In today's travel-intensive business environment, an increasing number of large companies have found it beneficial to develop their own travel departments rather than use the services of an outside travel agency. Since they are salaried employees of travel buyers, corporate travel representatives aren't always considered to be intermediaries. But the people who work in corporate travel departments provide the same services as retail travel agents, except that they specialize in meeting the travel needs of their own companies. They are responsible for ensuring that the company's travel dollars are spent in the most efficient way possible. Often, corporate travel departments must work within the confines of a set travel budget.

Unlike travel agents, corporate travel representatives are compensated by the companies for which they work. Corporate travel departments do not receive commissions from suppliers. Their companies defray the cost of maintaining the travel departments by negotiating discounts and rebates directly with their suppliers, including airlines, hotels, etc.

In recent years, large corporations have begun hiring large travel agencies to handle all of their travel needs. Because of the large volume of business, these travel agencies are often located in the corporation's offices, and are viewed by their employees as the corporate travel department (because of their location). They are, however, a separate, private company (or satellite office) conveniently located in their customer's offices.

Tour Operators

Tour operators can be divided into two groups: outbound and inbound. The former group is the larger and more traditional tour operator who is located in the market (a city for example) and is selling tours that will take local citizens to far-off destinations. These tour operators often have staffed offices in the most popular destinations to coordinate activities and assure that customers (tour takers) enjoy their tour experience.

Increasingly, these outbound tour operators are opting to buy packages or services from a rapidly expanding group of inbound or ***receptive tour operators.*** These companies are located in popular destinations (Paris, Rome, Disney World, Colorado, etc.) and handle all of the needs of customers of outbound tour companies once they arrive in the destination. The advantage to this arrangement for the outbound tour operator is that the receptive operator can negotiate better prices (they are buying on behalf of many tour operators coming to their destination), is well known by destination businesses, and provides all the coordination and customer care so that the outbound tour operator does not need to staff and pay for an office in the destination.

Many of these receptive operators have expanded the size and scope of their services and have begun to call themselves ***destination management companies (DMCs).*** These tour companies play an important role in international tourism, where customers from Asia, Europe, and Africa fly to North American destinations, tour the area in DMC motor coach equipment, and are assisted by DMC staff. These receptive tour operators also are essential to small independent tour operators who are not large enough to own and operate motor coaches and support an office with staff in the destination.

Like travel agents and corporate travel departments, tour operators function as intermediaries in a system of indirect distribution. Their primary business is the creation and sale of package tours (see Figure 8–1). These tours may range from a two-day motor coach tour of a nearby city to an extended round-the-world tour. Tour operators assemble several discrete travel products into combinations that will be attractive to vacation and leisure travelers. These packages are then sold by various means to travel customers.

Some tour operators sell their packages directly to customers by using descriptive brochures or print (newspaper/magazine) advertising. Customers can then make their reservations directly with the tour operator. In many cases, however, package tours are sold through travel agents on a standard commission basis.

In most cases, tour operators create their products by negotiating block bookings for space on airline flights to a particular destination or by organizing charter flights. They also buy blocks of rooms or tickets from hotels and sightseeing tour companies. They then sell the entire travel package at one set price, often including optional extras for an additional charge. The exception to this approach is the few very large tour operators who own their own motor coaches, airplanes, and hotels and thus are able to supply the travel products directly to the customer.

Because of the variety of ways that these travel products can be packaged, tour operators tend to specialize. Types of specialization include:

- Destinations—the United States, the Far East.
- Type of customers—singles, retired people.
- Purpose of trip—nature study, history tour.
- Mode of travel—cruise, motor coach tour.

Specialized Travel Distributors

Specialized distributors may work on behalf of either the customers or the suppliers of travel products. In either case, they distribute travel products to a particular

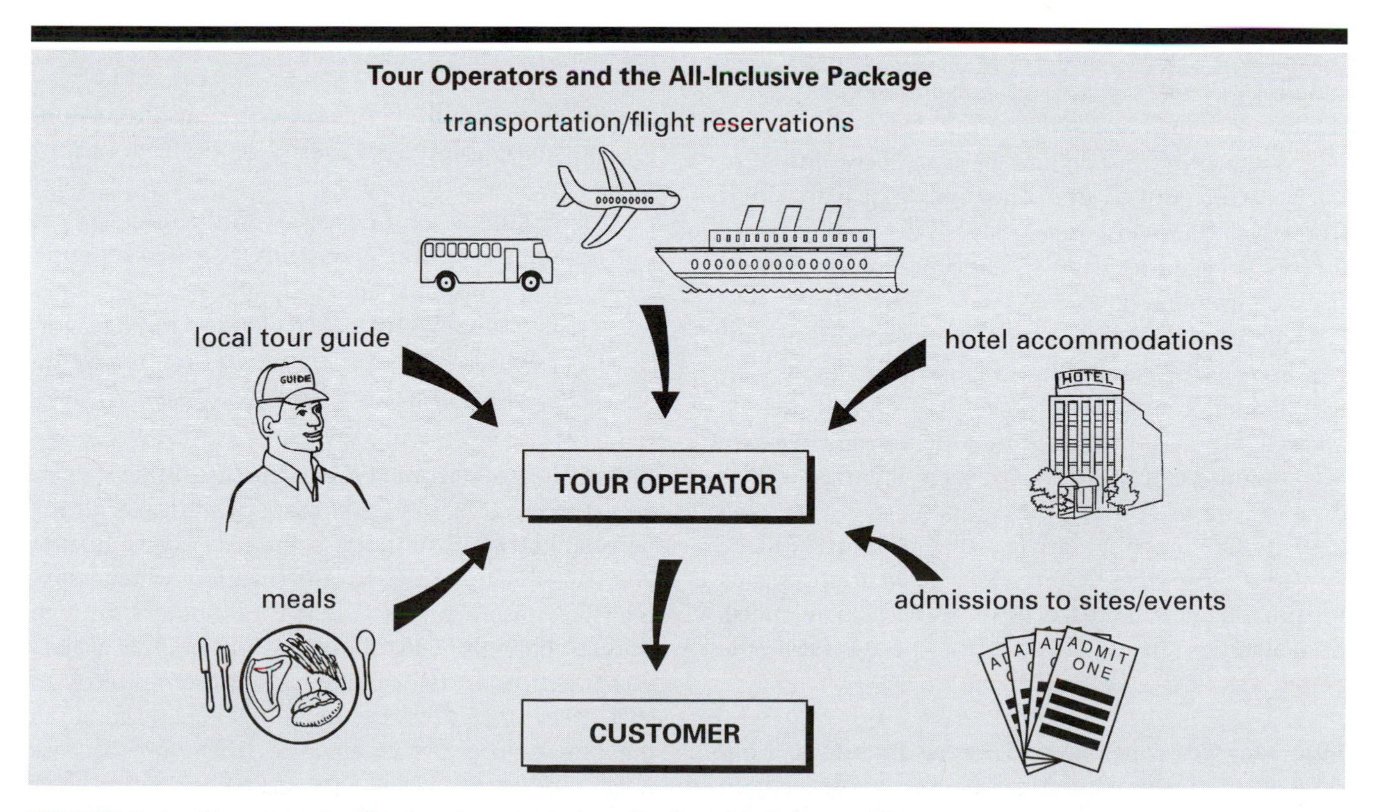

FIGURE 8–1 Tour operators offer the consumer the benefits of an all-inclusive vacation.

type or group of customers. Many specialized distributors are salaried employees of the group for which they make travel arrangements. Thus, like corporate travel department employees (but unlike travel agents), they do not receive a commission from the travel suppliers. As mentioned previously, specialized travel distributors are of three basic types: incentive travel planners; meeting, convention, and event planners; and ticket consolidators.

Incentive Travel Planners. These intermediaries organize the incentive travel programs offered by corporations to their employees as rewards for meeting or exceeding corporate objectives. Often these are salespeople and distributors who, because of the nature of their work, are the kinds of employees most likely to be offered incentive travel awards.

When incentive travel became popular some years ago, the purpose of the travel was strictly leisure. The employee enjoyed a week at a Caribbean resort, for instance, as a reward for achieving a sales goal. More recently, incentive travel planners have begun to create programs that mix business and pleasure. Business meetings held as part of a vacation allow a corporation to conduct training or strategy planning with its top employees at an exotic location.

Some of the largest companies that offer travel as a reward or incentive actually employ their own incentive travel planners. They may also spend some of their time on other tasks, such as convention planning or public relations.

Businesses that do not have in-house incentive travel planners often use companies that plan incentive travel programs exclusively. They may also use local travel agencies with special expertise in incentive trips or group travel.

Because incentive travel trips are used to reward employee performance, they are usually of high quality, including first-class transportation and deluxe, all-inclusive accommodations. Often, employees are accompanied on the trip by their spouses, whose expenses are also paid by the company.

If the company specifies that meetings will be part of the trip, the planner must make arrangements for suitable meeting space. In some cases, the planners also organize special activities for spouses while the employees attend meetings.

Meeting, Convention, and Event Planners. Constant changes in technology, increasing competition between companies, and rapid technological advances have fueled the growth of the meeting and convention industry. The current business climate places a high priority on the acquisition and dissemination of new information and the celebration of significant achievements. Meetings, conventions, and special events have proved an effective way to achieve these goals. As a result, the need for professional meeting and event planners has grown correspondingly.

Meeting, convention, and event planners are responsible for all the logistics of a meeting or special event. They decide on the best format and location for the meeting (or event), taking into account the budget available and the number of people attending. They negotiate with suppliers for meeting and display space, transportation, side trips, meals, and accommodations. They schedule the meeting agenda (event program) and provide technical support, such as technology and audiovisual equipment, where needed.

Many organizations, associations, and corporations schedule events (receptions, entertainment, golf tournaments, galas, etc.) as part of their meetings or as freestanding activities that meet sponsorship, public relations, and employee morale goals. In many cases, event management professionals plan, design, and implement these important programs, either as employees of the organization or as consulting companies.

Meeting-, convention-, and event-planning jobs fall into three categories:

- Association executives—full-time professionals employed by business, professional, or nonprofit associations.
- Corporate employees—coordinators of all major meetings and events for the corporation that employs them.
- Consultants—freelance planners hired by corporations or associations that do not have in-house planners; work on a fee basis.

Ticket Consolidators. One of the distribution channels developed by the travel industry to deal with the perishability of its products is the ticket consolidator. The consolidator acts as an intermediary when a supplier has unsold products that it cannot sell through normal channels of distribution. Consolidators usually buy travel products in bulk and sell them directly to customers, or less often, through retailers for resale to the public. This process requires them to purchase travel products in advance (versus retailers who act as transfer agents) and to sell a large volume, because the profit margin is smaller than for suppliers or other intermediaries. The largest group of ticket consolidators sell unsold airline tickets at a steep discount. They sell these seats through newspaper, telephone, and internet advertising.

Other ticket consolidators sell products such as tours and cruises at a substantial discount, most often through ***travel clubs***. For a small membership fee, travel clubs offer their members access to a variety of travel products. Because suppliers make these discounted products available to the consolidator only when the departure date is close, club members must be willing to choose from a limited selection of products and be able and willing to travel on short notice. Some travel clubs publish catalogs for distribution to all club members. Other clubs only give information and take reservations through a telephone number known only by members.

Unlike some intermediaries, notably travel agents, travel clubs do not give out information on their products to prospective customers free of charge. Only those who pay the membership fee have access to their specialized information and products. This limited publicity is meant to avoid offending customers who have paid full price for the same product.

Supplier Advantages of Indirect Distribution

Indirect distribution systems offer significant advantages to suppliers. Most of these advantages stem from the special characteristics of the intermediaries involved in indirect distribution.

Expanded Sales Outlets. By using intermediaries for indirect distribution, suppliers vastly increase the number of outlets in which their products are sold. A hotel, for instance, may have its own sales office in the hotel as well as at a desk at a nearby airport, along with a toll-free phone number and even its own Web page. But by making its rooms available to travel agents nationwide, the hotel has over thirty thousand sales outlets, each of which employs a number of agents. This principle of expanded sales opportunity applies to all the major types of suppliers in the travel industry.

No-Overhead Sales Force. Although an indirect distribution system expands a supplier's sales force, it does not add to the supplier's overhead expenses. For many suppliers, paying a commission to intermediaries makes more sense than maintaining a network of sales offices or reservation centers with full-time staffs. Small suppliers who do not have a sufficient product base to support a large sales staff can avoid the cost of additional salaries, benefits, and office space by using intermediaries. They also know for certain that they will incur sales expenses (in the form of commissions) only if the product is actually sold.

Customer Advantages of Indirect Distribution

If the advantages of indirect distribution mechanisms were confined to suppliers, customers might well opt to make their travel purchases solely through direct means. But indirect distribution offers customers a set of distinct advantages that increase its importance to the travel industry.

Choice. Customers who purchase travel products from intermediaries have more choices than they would if they were buying directly from a supplier (see Figure 8–2). The number of available choices is greater for two reasons. First, intermediaries offer the products of many competing suppliers, unlike individual suppliers, who generally offer only their own products. When purchasing through an intermediary, a customer can effectively choose from all the available flights to a destination or from all the hotels at that destination without making numerous phone calls. Second, intermediaries offer combinations of travel products that individuals would find difficult or impossible to assemble themselves.

Price. "Buy direct from the factory and save money" may be good advice for some types of products, but it is generally not true for travel products. In fact, the opposite is often the case. Customers who purchase products through intermediaries can take advantage of block purchases and bulk discounts. Tour operators, for example, can usually put together a package tour that costs the customer less than the sum of its individual product costs. Ticket consolidators also offer products at prices well below those usually charged by the supplier. In addition, travel agents use their knowledge of competing travel suppliers to identify the lowest price for a particular travel product.

Service. Intermediaries are especially efficient at narrowing down the number of possible travel products available to consumers. They play a key role in what is called "the double search process": customers looking for

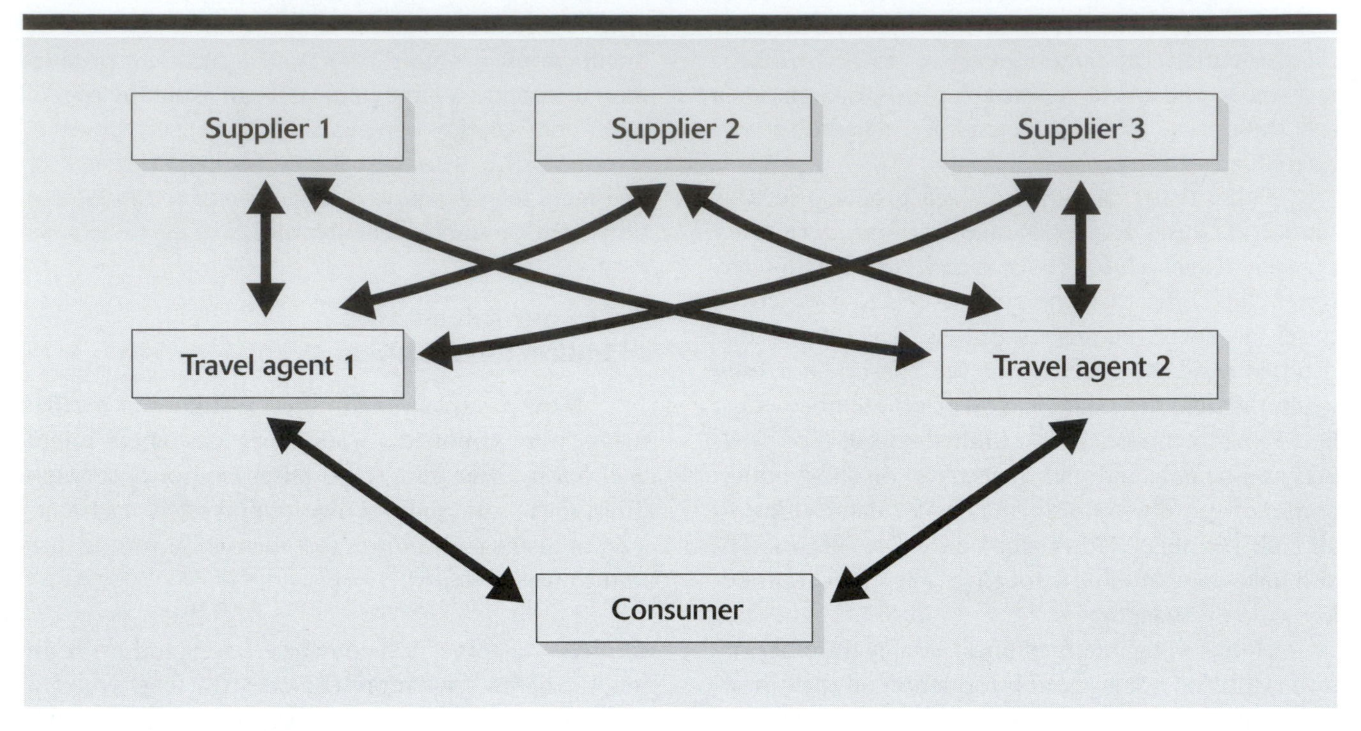

FIGURE 8–2 The indirect distribution system provides unlimited travel choices. Customers can consult multiple travel agents, each of whom deals with many suppliers.

products and suppliers looking for customers. Intermediaries are ideally qualified to identify and recommend the few travel products that will best meet their customers' needs, out of the enormous array of possibilities. Intermediaries offer both informed advice and special personal services. Local travel agents, for example, offer not only convenience but also a chance for customers to establish rapport through face-to-face conversations. Agents often take time to ascertain the travel needs and preferences of their customers. With this knowledge, they can select and recommend options that are best suited to their customers' needs and budgets. Since the deregulation of the airline industry, for example, the number of fares and restrictions on airline tickets has increased dramatically. In addition, there can be millions of price changes in a week. Travel agents are familiar with these special fares and restrictions and can advise their customers accordingly. Internet Web sites developed by large travel agencies allow customers to access fares and prices, which are continuously revised electronically and therefore always up-to-date. When customers have decided to buy a travel product, the agents can make the necessary arrangements for them or they can do so themselves electronically. These services, unlike many other professional services, are usually free of charge.

DISTRIBUTION MODELS

The direct and indirect distribution systems discussed previously are the basic types found throughout the travel industry. The following examples illustrate typical ways in which these systems operate. The one-stage model illustrates the direct distribution system. The two-stage model illustrates the simplest type of indirect distribution. The three-stage model shows how an indirect distribution system can become more complex.

One-Stage Direct Distribution

Dr. Michael Smith, a professor of philosophy at the University of Chicago, is attending a conference at Stanford University. His flight from O'Hare to San Francisco lands on time at 2:45 P.M. Dr. Smith needs a rental car to get from the airport to his hotel and to travel to various meetings over the next two days. He goes to a rental counter in the baggage claim area and orders a car for two days. Dr. Smith presents his credit card, signs the agreement, and walks outside to the company's shuttle van. A few minutes later, he is on his way.

This example illustrates the direct distribution of a single travel product (see Figure 8–3): the use of a

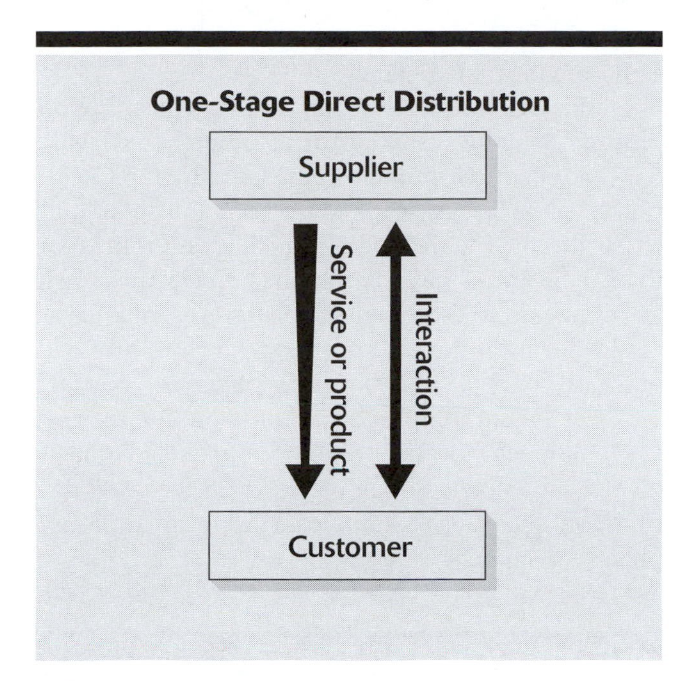

FIGURE 8–3 A customer can purchase a travel product directly from the supplier—an airline, a car rental agency, etc.

rental car for a specified period of time. The transaction between the supplier and the customer is simple and direct. Dr. Smith benefits from the simplicity, speed, and convenience of the transaction. Without a direct distribution system at the airport, the car rental company would not have been able to make this sale.

Two-Stage Indirect Distribution

Sean and Helen LaRoche will soon celebrate their tenth wedding anniversary. To celebrate the occasion, they plan to spend a long weekend in Philadelphia. They have already purchased tickets to a Saturday evening performance of the opera by calling the box office directly. For their hotel reservations, however, they decide to use the services of their travel agent.

They explain their requirements to the agent. They want to stay at a luxury hotel in the center of Philadelphia. Mr. LaRoche specifies a room on the first or second floor since he does not like heights. Mrs. LaRoche insists that the hotel have excellent room service, available twenty-four hours a day. Since they will be staying for a few days, they prefer a suite with separate sleeping and living room areas. Their budget for the hotel is generous.

Their travel agent has visited Philadelphia often and has inspected most of the downtown hotels. She describes three hotels that fit the requirements set by Mr. and Mrs. LaRoche. She also gives them brochures that describe the hotels in more detail. While the LaRoches look over the brochures, she checks the availability and the rates of suitable rooms in each of the three hotels. She discovers that each hotel offers a special weekend rate. After a brief consultation, Mr. and Mrs. LaRoche select the hotel of their choice. The agent makes their reservation, giving their credit card number to guarantee the room and the weekend rate.

This example illustrates the two-stage indirect distribution of travel products (see Figure 8–4), highlighting the benefits that customers receive from a travel agent. Mr. and Mrs. LaRoche benefitted from their travel agent's personal knowledge of the hotels. In addition, the travel agent was quickly able to tell them which of the hotels fit their requirements. They were able to look

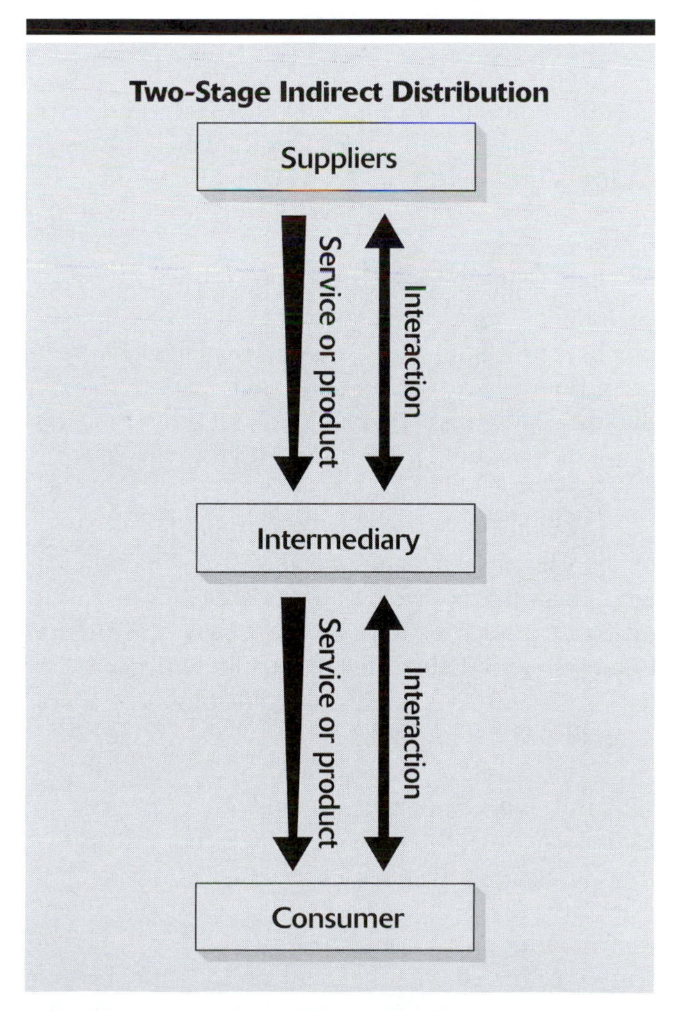

FIGURE 8–4 A consumer can utilize an intermediary—a travel agent or tour operator—who can contact any number of suppliers.

at the options and to compare rates and services. All of these services were provided free of charge, and the rate they paid at the hotel was not any greater as a result of using the services of the travel agent. In fact, the LaRoches probably saved money, thanks to their travel agent advising them of the reduced weekend rates.

The travel agent received her compensation in the form of a commission on the sale of the hotel space. She probably also earned opportunities to sell additional travel products to her satisfied customers, Mr. and Mrs. LaRoche, in the future. This is critical, since most intermediaries have access to the same pool of travel products and must, therefore, distinguish themselves by their superior knowledge and service. The hotel, as a supplier, benefitted from this transaction because it sold a hotel room and their only direct cost of the sale was the agent's commission.

Three-Stage Indirect Distribution

The Chesapeake Nature Society has decided to organize a group bird-watching expedition to Greece. Fifteen members of the society indicate their interest in participating in the tour. Sarah Williams, the president of the society, has the responsibility of making all the necessary arrangements.

Ms. Williams goes to a travel agency in nearby Fredericksburg, Virginia. She describes the type of bird-watching expedition that the group is interested in to an agent from whom she has purchased travel products in the past. The agent then contacts Seagull Tours, a tour operator specializing in nature tours. He knows that this particular operator offers several tours to Greece every year.

Seagull Tours does have a tour that fits the needs of the Chesapeake Nature Society. It includes a chartered flight from Washington, D.C.'s Dulles Airport to Athens, a passenger ferry to the island of Santorini, hotel accommodations, breakfast and dinner each day, use of a van on the island, and guided tours by a local naturalist who speaks English.

The travel agent describes this package to Ms. Williams and gives her the inclusive cost per person. He indicates that there are optional extras, such as side trips to areas of historical interest and the chance to extend the trip by two days in order to explore Athens, then returning to Washington on another of Seagull Tours's chartered flights. These options can be purchased for an additional charge. After discussing the package with her group, Ms. Williams forwards a deposit to her agent to secure the reservations. Having made the sale, the travel agent will receive a commission from the tour operator.

This example illustrates a three-stage distribution process, including a specialized distributor (see Figure 8–5). Some of the products purchased by the Chesapeake Nature Society would have been difficult to purchase directly. The members also paid less for the tour than they would have if they had made their own arrangements. In this example, the travel agent acted as a sales agent for the tour operator, which in turn had purchased travel products from suppliers.

Even more complex distribution models are possible, although not that common. Multistage models involve more levels of intermediaries in the travel distribution system, as products pass indirectly from suppliers to customers.

AUTOMATION AND TRAVEL SALES DISTRIBUTION

The use of automation has increased tremendously in the travel industry in the last two decades. Automation began when airlines developed computer systems to handle reservations. Since then, the capability of these systems has expanded. Today, travel agents can use these enhanced systems for:

- Reservations and ticketing (front-office).
- Accounting and management (back-office).

Today, nearly 100 percent of travel agencies in the United States use automated computer reservations systems, and over 70 percent have automated their accounting systems.

Computer Reservations Systems

A ***computer reservations system (CRS)***, also referred to as a global distribution system (GDS), performs two principal functions. It gives the agent instant access to information on schedules, fares, and seat availability, replacing old printed references that quickly become outdated. CRSs also allow the agent to use this information to book reservations, print tickets and itineraries, and generate invoices (see Figure 8–6). The entire process takes a fraction of the time it would take in a nonautomated office.

Several airlines have developed CRSs. Travel agents would have preferred that all airlines use one integrated reservation system, but that did not prove viable. Instead, several large airlines have developed CRSs that

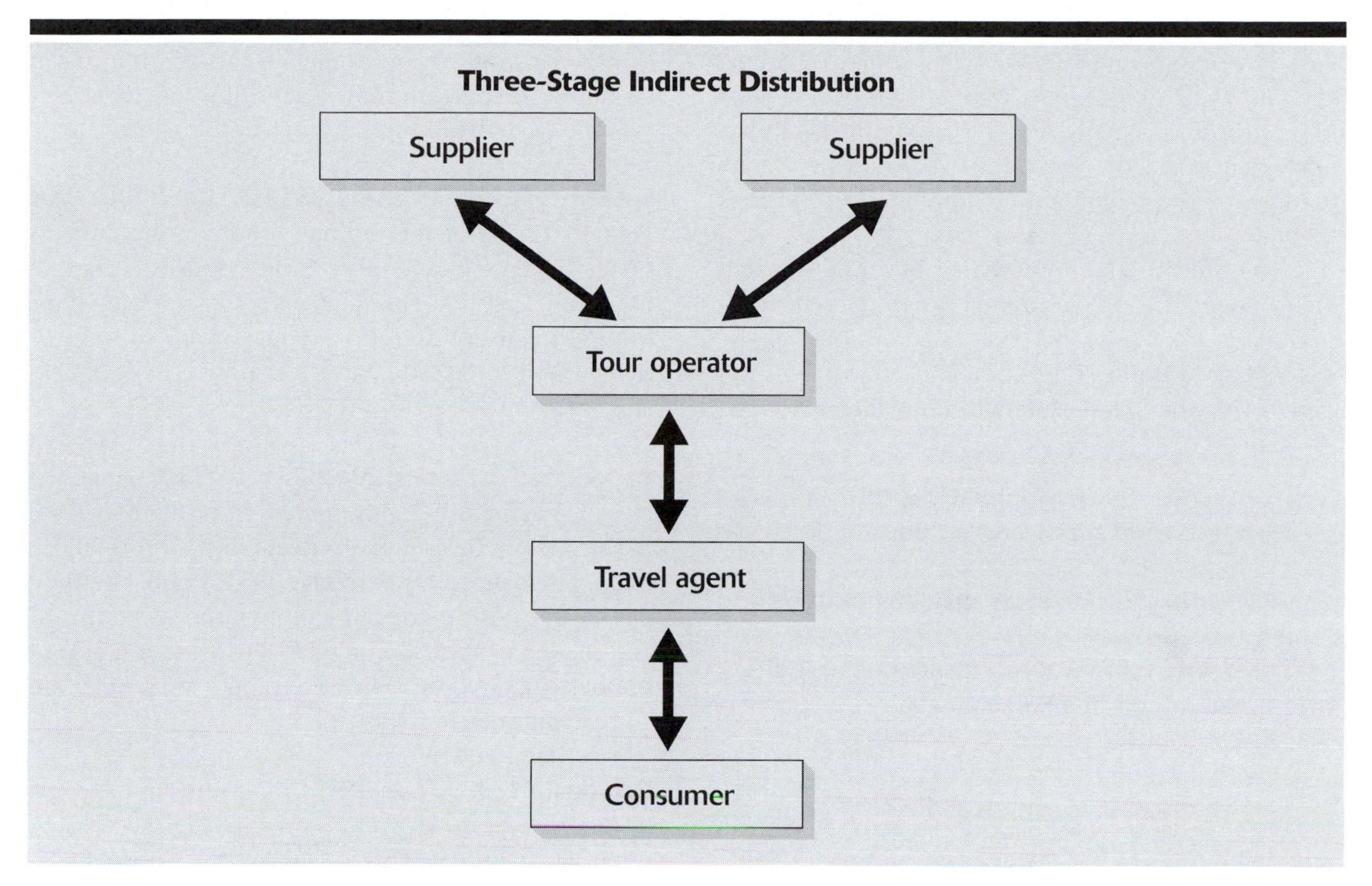

FIGURE 8–5 Sometimes a consumer will consult a travel agent who will have to consult a more specialized tour operator. This is an example of three-stage indirect distribution.

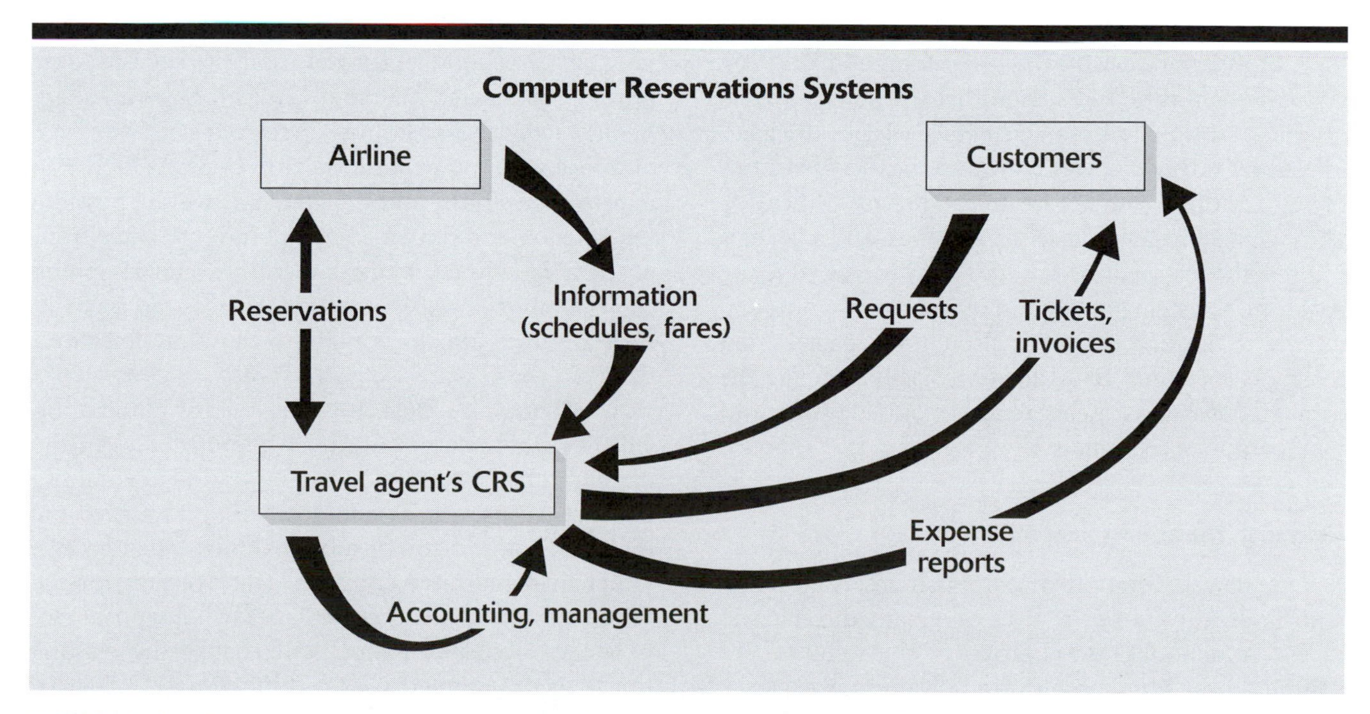

FIGURE 8–6 Computer reservations systems make the work of a travel agent more efficient.

are managed by subsidiaries, known as ***host vendors***. They have developed their own systems that give agents access to their products, as well as to those of most other airline and many non-airline suppliers. Today, most agencies in the United States subscribe to one or more of the major airline computer reservations systems.

The SABRE (Semi-Automated Business Research Environment) Group's computer system has the most subscribers of any of the systems. It is one of the world's largest nonmilitary computer networks. Travel agents using the SABRE system can provide the following services:

- Check airline schedules worldwide.
- Make reservations on over three hundred airlines.
- Book rooms at more than twenty thousand hotels.
- Reserve vehicles at over fifty car rental agencies.
- Sell Amtrak and Eurail tickets.
- Book tours.
- Book cruises.
- Sell tickets to Broadway shows.

Some hotel chains, car rental agencies, and other travel suppliers have developed their own systems. Unlike the airline systems, however, these systems are usually supplier-specific. They contain information and accept reservations only for one supplier's products and are rarely found in travel agencies.

In association with the reservation and ticketing systems, the airline CRSs and other software suppliers offer accounting and management packages designed for use by travel agencies and tour operators. Most of these back-office systems are linked directly to the CRS. Thus, when an agent makes a reservation and a ticket is printed, the information is automatically relayed to the back-office system for accounting purposes. Automation of accounting functions also allows agencies that focus on corporate travel to more easily generate the detailed travel and expense reports required by many of their corporate customers.

Current Trends in Automation

A new generation of computer reservation systems is already giving travel agents greater direct access to the entire pool of travel products. This trend toward computerized access to all travel products is expected to continue.

Most new developments, however, are aimed toward increasing the customer's direct access to travel products. Three recent innovations illustrate this trend toward direct distribution through automation.

Satellite Ticket Printers (STPs). ***Satellite Ticket Printers (STPs)*** are becoming a common sight in corporate office parks and other locations easily accessible to business travelers (like airports). These printers electronically deliver tickets from a travel agency directly to a client. Today, STPs are the fastest-growing type of ticketing machine.

Automated Ticketing Machines (ATMs). Operated by individual airlines, ***Automated Ticketing Machines (ATMs)*** allow customers to access flight information, make reservations, and receive tickets and boarding passes. The customer need simply insert a credit card and make the appropriate selections from a menu of options displayed on a video terminal. Most ATMs are currently located in airports.

Personal Computers (PCs). As the number of homes with personal computers increases, so will the use of PCs with modems to gain access to travel information. Today, customers can retrieve airline, hotel, railroad, and attraction information from several online travel Web sites, most of which allow for reserving and purchasing tickets.

The implications of these developments for the sale and distribution of travel products is clear. Most travel experts agree that suppliers will begin to share ATMs, giving the customer direct access to the type of information now found only on CRSs. As these systems are developed and integrated, it will be possible for a customer to buy a complete travel package from an ATM in a hotel, bank, supermarket, or shopping center. Online travel sites will also increase access to all travel products and are available on a twenty-four-hour basis.

What is also clear, however, is that automation will not eliminate the need for intermediaries in the distribution of travel products. The very nature of those products ensures that customers will always need the informed and sometimes subjective advice that people, rather than machines, provide. The question for the future is not whether intermediaries will disappear, but how increased automation will change the existing functions of intermediaries within the travel sales distribution system.

CHAPTER SUMMARY

- The special characteristics of travel products—intangibility, perishability, and complementarity—affect the way the products are distributed.
- Travel products are sold by two basic categories of sellers: suppliers and intermediaries.
- Suppliers own or control the travel products they sell.
- Intermediaries sell travel products to customers on behalf of suppliers.
- Travel agents, tour operators, and specialized distributors all serve as intermediaries.
- Two basic distribution systems channel travel products to customers: direct and indirect.
- Direct distribution occurs when the customer buys directly from the supplier.
- Indirect distribution occurs when the customer buys products through one or more intermediaries.
- Indirect distribution includes travel agents; tour operators; meeting, convention, and event planners; ticket consolidators; and incentive travel planners.
- Both distribution systems offer advantages to suppliers and customers.
- A one-stage distribution model illustrates a direct distribution system.
- Two- and three-stage distribution models describe distribution of travel products where intermediaries play a key role.
- In an automated travel agency, travel agents have access to information through computer reservation systems, which can make reservations and print tickets.
- Airlines are the principal vendors of CRSs, but other suppliers also have their own systems.
- The trend in automation is toward direct customer access to travel products, particularly through online (Internet) travel Web sites.

KEY TERMS

distribution systems
suppliers
intermediary
commission
specialized distributors
incentive travel planners
meeting, convention, and event planners
ticket consolidators
direct distribution
indirect distribution
receptive tour operators
destination management companies (DMCs)
travel clubs
computer reservations system (CRS)
host vendors
satellite ticket printers (STPs)
automated ticketing machines (ATMs)

DISCUSSION QUESTIONS

1. Describe the similarities and differences between the role of inbound and outbound tour operators.
2. Describe how intermediaries are important in the distribution of travel products.
3. Discuss how the various intermediaries differ in the way they distribute travel products.
4. Indicate how suppliers and customers benefit from an indirect distribution system.
5. Explain the difference between a two-stage and a three-stage distribution system, giving examples of each.
6. Suggest how automation will change customer access to travel products in the future.

STUDY GUIDE

CHAPTER 8

Identifying the Seller

Name: ______________________________ Date: ______________

Directions: Answer these questions as you read the chapter. You will be able to use your answers to help you review the chapter.

1. What is the difference between a supplier and an intermediary?

2. What is a commission?

3. Discuss the differences between a travel agent and a tour operator.

4. What are three types of specialized distributor?

5. Describe direct distribution.

6. Describe three advantages to the supplier of direct distribution.

7. How can a consumer benefit from direct distribution?

8. What are the major categories of travel intermediaries?

9. What is the purpose of a corporate travel department?

10. Describe four ways in which tour operators often specialize.

11. What is the job of an incentive travel planner?

12. Why has the demand for meeting and event planners grown so dramatically in recent years?

13. How does a travel club act as a ticket consolidator?

14. What is indirect distribution? What are its two main advantages to the supplier?

15. How do consumers benefit from indirect distribution?

16. What type of distribution is represented by the one-stage model? Why?

17. Give one example of a two-stage model of distribution.

18. How has automation increased direct public access to travel information?

WORKSHEET CHAPTER 8

Identifying the Seller

Name: ______________________________ Date: ______________

WHO GETS THE SALE?

The travelers described below need to purchase specific products and services. For each example, determine whether it would be better to buy directly from a supplier or to deal with an intermediary such as a travel agent; tour operator; meeting, convention, and event planner; or travel club. Briefly explain three reasons for recommending each seller.

1. Members of the Siberion Iris Society of Santa Barbara, California, have decided that they would like to tour some of the famous gardens and great houses of England.

A. What seller should the club choose? ______________________________

B. Will this sale be:

direct, from a supplier? ______________________________

indirect, from an intermediary? ______________________________

C. Give two reasons for recommending this seller. ______________________________

____

2. Sales of Tech-O-Matic Industry's new laptop computer have far surpassed company goals for three quarters. The company's chief executive officer has decided that the top five district sales managers should be rewarded with a luxurious free trip.

A. What seller should the company choose? ______________________________

B. Will this sale be:

direct, from a supplier? ______________________________

indirect, from an intermediary ______________________________

C. Give two reasons for recommending this seller. ______________________________

____

3. Michele and Peter Russo are high school physical education teachers who are avid skiers. They want to go on ski trips to a variety of locations, but their funds are limited.

A. What seller should the couple choose? ______________________________

B. Will this sale be:

direct, from a supplier? ______________________________

indirect, from an intermediary? ______________________________

C. Give two reasons for recommending this seller. ______________________________

____

4. The Mendoza family—two parents and two school-age children—have decided on a cruise as this year's family vacation. They want relaxation, exercise, sightseeing, and activities for the children.

A. What seller should the family choose? ______________________________

B. Will this sale be:

direct, from a supplier? ______

indirect, from an intermediary? ______

C. Give two reasons for recommending this seller. ______

______

5. The professional development committee of the American College of Orthopedic Surgeons has voted to hold its association's upcoming annual meeting in Orlando, Florida.

A. What seller should the association choose? ______

B. Will this sale be:

direct, from a supplier? ______

indirect, from an intermediary? ______

C. Give two reasons for recommending this seller. ______

______

6. Kay Gibson pays an annual fee of $50 to belong to AirAmerica's Golden Age Travel Plan. She lives in Arizona and is planning to visit her daughter in Connecticut and her sister in Alabama. Kay would like to take a sightseeing motor coach tour on each trip.

A. What seller should Kay choose? ______

B. Will this sale be:

direct, from a supplier? ______

indirect, from an intermediary? ______

C. Give two reasons for recommending this seller. ______

______

7. Justine Frazier, a buyer from Des Moines, Iowa, will be in New York City for business meetings Wednesday and Thursday. Her husband will join her there on Friday, and they will spend the weekend enjoying the city's restaurants, museums, theater, and other attractions.

A. What seller should the Fraziers choose? ______

B. Will this sale be:

direct, from a supplier? ______

indirect, from an intermediary? ______

C. Give two reasons for recommending this seller. ______

______

Evaluating the Travel Product

OBJECTIVES

When you have completed this chapter, you should be able to:

- Discuss the benefits and limitations of computer reservations systems (CRSs) in gathering information on travel products.
- Name the major reference books used in the travel industry.
- Cite other major sources of information about travel products.
- Evaluate the roles of quantity and quality in determining the price of travel products.
- Discuss factors that must be taken into account when calculating total travel costs.
- Explain why travel products may be perceived differently by different customers.

Everyone who sells travel products must be able to find those that specifically meet customers' needs. For those selling a variety of competing travel products, this is an especially vital skill. They must learn how to use a variety of information sources to identify those travel products that best meet their customers' needs. This chapter emphasizes that salespeople must take into consideration the needs of the customer when making these evaluations. It also focuses on the techniques available to identify the products that meet those needs.

Travel customers have two basic categories of needs. First, there are the specific, tangible specifications of customers' requests—their ***literal needs,*** such as schedule and budget. Second, there are the psychological needs that travel can satisfy. Some of the most important benefits of travel are intangible. Travel sales professionals must understand and take into account these psychological needs when they try to identify appropriate travel products for their customers.

Needs vary from customer to customer. However, what all customers want, whether they express it in these terms or not, is good value—travel products that are worth the expense, that offer the most travel benefits for the price that will be paid. Good travel salespeople keep this foremost in their minds as they search for the products that provide the most travel benefits—tangible and intangible, real and perceived—for their customers.

Although the principles of identifying travel products that meet the needs of customers apply to all travel sales, they are especially crucial to travel agents. Travel agents, after all, indirectly represent thousands of travel suppliers and consequently have access to an astounding array of travel products. As a result, travel agents face the greatest challenges when evaluating products. For that reason, this chapter focuses on the role of travel agents as it explains the travel product evaluation process. Other travel salespeople may have fewer products to evaluate and/or use slightly different evaluation tools, but the basic principles of identifying travel products that match the needs of customers are the same for everyone selling travel products.

But before travel agents can apply the principles of matching products with customers, they must be able to use the available tools for gathering information about travel products. The ability to evaluate travel products skillfully begins with the ability to get all of the relevant factors about them.

GATHERING THE INFORMATION

For travel marketing professionals to match customers with travel products, they must gain access to information which describes the wide range of travel products available. Travel agents, for example, rely on a variety of standard sources for essential information about destinations, accommodations, and means of travel. These sources provide descriptions and prices of travel products. Some sources may also provide subjective comparisons of the relative quality of selected travel products. Evaluating travel products requires a thorough knowledge of all these sources of information. Agents must be accurate and creative in responding to customers' requests, which may range from those of the customers who know where they want to go, how they want to get there, and what they want to do when they get there, to those of customers who simply say, "I want to go someplace warm for a week."

Computer Reservations Systems

Today nearly all travel agencies in the United States use a computer reservation system (CRS). For most travel agents, the CRS is their first and fastest source of information. They use it not only for flight information on the airlines that operate each system, but also for information on a variety of additional travel products. Most suppliers pay the host company that provides the system a fee for their listings in a CRS.

Computer reservations systems provide a variety of travel information quickly.

Although each is different, a typical CRS includes information on:

* Domestic airlines.
* International airlines.
* Hotels and resorts, primarily domestic but also many international (particularly chains or multinational companies).
* Car rental companies.
* Amtrak (USA), VIA (Canada), and Eurail (Europe).
* Foreign rail tickets.
* Cruise lines.
* Tours from large tour operators.
* Travel insurance.
* Theater and attraction tickets.

Types of Information Available. All of the major CRS systems enable travel agents to retrieve certain basic types of information and to execute the preparation of certain documents (reservations, tickets, etc.). Their capabilities differ for airline and non-airline products.

For airlines, travel agents can use a CRS to:

* Check the flight schedules of hundreds of domestic and foreign airlines.
* Display schedules and connecting service between most cities.
* Determine the availability of seats in various classes of service on flights of major carriers up to one year in advance.
* Check fares, including restrictions.
* Determine on-time performance.
* Make reservations.
* Print tickets, itineraries, and invoices.

Non-Airline Travel Products. As competition for travel agency subscribers has intensified among CRS host companies, an increasing range of non-airline travel products (e.g., hotels, rental cars, attractions) have been added to their systems. Non-airline suppliers have welcomed this trend. As the travel industry becomes increasingly automated, those suppliers whose products are not accessible on a CRS face a distinct competitive disadvantage. Industry sources expect the trend toward automation to continue, with the entire pool of travel products directly accessible to travel agents via CRSs.

Currently, agents can get information on several types of non-airline suppliers from their CRS. It gives them information similar to that found in the industry's standard printed reference guides (discussed subsequently). This typically includes a basic description of the products and their rates. Agents can also check the availability of most non-airline products, make reservations for the products of large tour operators and cruise lines via their CRSs, as well as rental cars, hotels, and sightseeing companies.

How to Use the System. Because the computer operating systems of each CRS vary, agents need to be trained on the specific systems they will use. The vendors usually provide training for travel agents at a regional location, as well as comprehensive user manuals and toll-free telephone assistance programs. Vendors allow agents to contact the vendors' assistance departments directly via the CRS itself.

The CRS automates many steps that agents formerly would have had to do manually (see Figure 9–1). For example, to make an airline reservation without a CRS, reservation agents would consult printed reference sources, call the airline to confirm a listed flight's availability and make the reservation, and then make additional calls if any changes are necessary.

Using a CRS, which is essentially a computer terminal linked to the host vendor's main computer, reservation agents can gain direct access to the airline, car rental, or hotel reservation system. They can display on their terminals all the information needed about the routes, schedules, fares, and availability of many different airlines. They can compare complex fare schedules and routing combinations, for example, in a fraction of the time it would take using printed resources. Once agents have selected appropriate flights for their customers, they can make their reservations. To do this, they create what is called a passenger name record (PNR) in the name of the customer. Into this record, agents enter the specific details of a customer's travel plans. When complete, the information is sent from the agent's terminal to the system's central computer in order to finalize the reservation.

For travel products that require tickets, the computer sends a series of commands, along with the passenger information, back to the ticket printer in the travel agents' office. The printer then generates the appropriate tickets and boarding passes. Depending on the agency's system, the printer may also generate a travel itinerary from the same information.

The CRS is a particularly valuable resource for agents who complete a high volume of similar transactions. In addition, the CRS is very efficient for

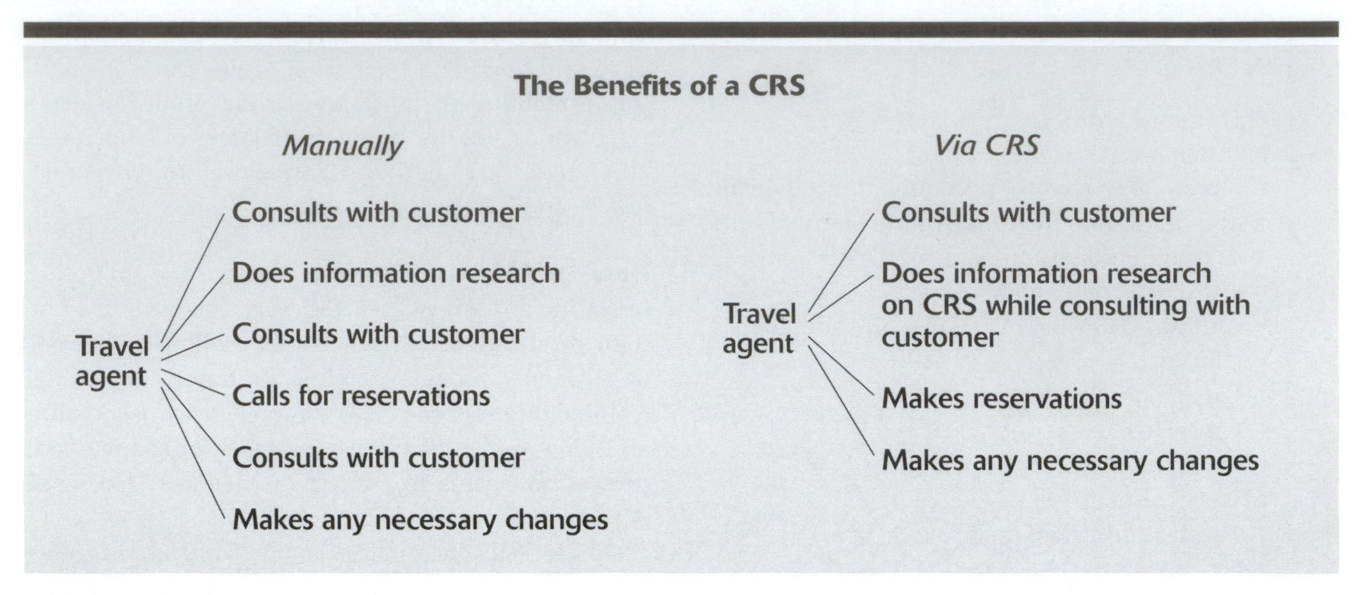

FIGURE 9–1 Getting information and making reservations manually requires more time and effort than using a CRS.

group sales. Using a CRS, a travel agent can make reservations and print tickets, itineraries, and invoices for a number of people traveling together. Changes, cancellations, and additions for airline, hotels, or rental cars can also be done relatively simply using the CRS.

Limitations. The development of computer reservation systems has dramatically changed the methods of operation in travel agencies. However, travel agents cannot rely on CRSs as their sole source of information. For example, these systems cannot provide the wide range of descriptive and evaluative information needed to select non-airline products, such as cruises. In addition, a few travel products (particularly in emerging destinations) are still not accessible through any CRS.

Computer reservation systems were developed primarily to serve the needs of the airline industry. Consequently, their primary function remains the automation of airline ticket sales. They are essentially transactional tools rather than informational resources. The information function of a CRS was initially designed to provide only the information necessary to sell airline tickets. Although new generations of CRSs are being developed with non-airline suppliers in mind, their particular needs will remain secondary to the needs of the airline host vendors. To overcome these biases, many non-airline suppliers have designed their own automated reservation systems which are compatible with and linked to existing CRSs.

Print Sources

Before the advent of CRSs, printed materials were the standard, first-line source of travel industry information. They are still relied on by travel agents, who use them every day to supply the kinds of essential detailed information about travel products, especially non-airline products, that automated systems cannot.

Industry Reference Books. When travel agents need information about products not in the CRS or linked systems or when they require more detailed information on a product, they turn to printed reference materials, known as ***industry reference books.*** Most travel

Print reference sources continue to play an important role in providing information about travel products. (Photograph by Michael Dzamen)

agencies have several standard travel reference materials for this purpose, including manuals, tariff and fare sheets, timetables, and maps.

The number of printed sources owned by an agency depends on its level of automation and its budget for purchasing reference materials. The few nonautomated agencies, for example, require a more extensive collection of reference sources. They must get the information normally available through a CRS from airline reference books instead.

Agents refer to these materials when gathering information on the products they are selling. Some of the references provide descriptions of products and their current prices. Others evaluate the relative quality of a certain class of travel products. For example, a reference source may classify hotels as deluxe, first-class, standard, or budget.

Listed below are some standard reference works found in many travel agencies and the type of information they contain. Please note that some of these will be available online through subscription Web sites that are constantly updated by the host company.

* Airlines
  Official Airline Guide
* Ground transportation
  Official Railway Guide (Amtrak and VIA schedules and fares)
  Thomas Cook Overseas Timetable
* Cruise lines
  Official Steamship Guide International (worldwide listing of cruise ship schedules and rates)
  Worldwide Cruise and Shipline Guide (worldwide listing of cruise ship schedules and rates)
  CLIA Cruise Manual (e.g., ship layouts, destinations, menus)
* Hotels and resorts
  Hotel and Travel Index (worldwide hotel listings)
  Official Hotel Guide (worldwide hotel listings, with evaluations)
  OAG Travel Planner and Hotel and Motel Red Book, 3 volumes (all provide accommodation listings and additional information)
  Official Meeting Facilities Guide
* Tours
  Consolidated Air Tour Manual (description of tours offered by major tour operators)

Each of these references has its own format and coding to make a huge volume of information manageable and understandable. They are written specifically for travel agents and designed to provide fast, easy access to information. Travel agents should become familiar with all of them if they are to use them effectively.

The *OAG Travel Planner and Hotel and Motel Red Book*, for instance, covers North America, Europe, and Asia and the Pacific in its three volumes. The North American volume provides information on:

* Ground transportation services in each area.
* Airport nearest to destination.
* Airport and city maps.
* Listing of special services available to handicapped travelers.
* Calendar of special events in each destination, with dates and locations.
* List of state and local tourist promotion agencies.
* Information, rates, and evaluations (one to five stars) of thousands of hotels and motels.

Suppose a customer wishes to plan a trip for his elderly mother and one of her friends from their homes in Washington, D.C., to Hot Springs, Arkansas. He asks his travel agent which airport is closest to Hot Springs. Are direct flights available, or will his mother and her friend need to make connections? What types of ground transportation are available to Hot Springs? Is a reasonably priced motel with kitchen facilities available there? What kind of weather can they expect in Hot Springs? Will any special events happen while they are there? What is the address of the nearest tourist promotion agency?

Agents familiar with the *OAG Travel Planner* can answer these questions quickly and accurately with up-to-date information. Using this reference, or the CRS, an agent could determine which travel products would meet the specific needs of this customer's mother and her friend.

Brochures. ***Brochures*** represent another important source of printed information available to travel agents. Many travel companies supply travel agencies with lavish brochures detailing tours, cruises, destinations, attractions, and accommodations. These brochures are designed to appeal to travel customers and assist agents in making sales. A good brochure will answer most of the customers' questions about the travel product it describes.

A specialized form of brochure describes a wider variety of travel products in a destination region in a more general way. These are the so-called lure books produced by state and city destination promotion agencies. These are another useful source of information about destinations, although of a less specific nature.

Agents should not rely on brochures to complete the sale for them, however. They need to explain to their customers how the product features described in a brochure will benefit customers and make their travel more enjoyable. Agents may also need to explain certain travel industry terminology used in brochures. For instance, some customers may not know that "round-trip transfers" means that they will be transported from the airport to their hotel and back again.

Brochures are an important source of information that must be interpreted carefully. They are designed by travel suppliers and tour operators to present their products in the best possible light. However, responsible travel companies and destinations take care not to misrepresent themselves in their brochures, and most will supply additional information over the telephone should questions arise.

Guidebooks. Most travel ***guidebooks*** are written with the traveler, rather than the travel agent, in mind. However, many travel agents use guidebooks as a valuable source of additional information on travel destinations. Almost all agencies have copies of these well-known books:

- Frommer Guides—list accommodations and restaurants; give sightseeing tips.
- Baedeker Guides—describe how to get there and what to see.
- Fodor Guides—contain maps and general information, list accommodations, restaurants, walking tours, museums.
- Fielding Guides—give grade evaluations of many travel products.
- Get Up and Go—lists tourist services and sources of information; describes sights.
- Michelin Guides—(primarily western Europe) rate hotels and restaurants; describe history, culture, and attractions of an area.

Trade Publications. Various professional groups in the travel industry, such as the American Society of Travel Agents (ASTA) and the Pacific Asia Travel Association (PATA), publish both magazines and annual guides. These, together with some commercial ***trade publications***, provide travel professionals with up-to-date information about travel destinations. Among the major ones are:

- *ASTA Agency Management.*
- *Travel Weekly.*
- *Travel Agent.*
- *Travel Trade.*
- *Travel Age.*
- *Tour and Travel News.*
- *Courier* (National Tour Association).

Because these publications combine destination descriptions with information about suppliers' products, they are especially useful to travel agents.

These publications also cover changes and developments in the industry as a whole. By subscribing to one or more trade publications, travel agents can stay abreast of general trends in the industry. For example, they can monitor the growth of travel to newly developed travel destinations or the changing interests of the mature market.

Trade Shows. Travel ***trade shows*** and conventions offer travel sales professionals an opportunity to gather a large amount of information in a short period of time. A trade show is a meeting that features freestanding supplier (including destinations) displays and booths. Some trade shows are run by private companies, but most are sponsored either by a professional association or by a ***consortium*** of suppliers. A consortium is a group of independent suppliers and intermediaries who cooperate in some enterprise or endeavor. A show may emphasize one particular sector of the industry, but trade shows usually include a wide variety of suppliers and intermediaries. Travel sales profes-

Travel trade intermediaries and trade publications. (Photograph by Purdue University Center for Instructional Service)

Marketing Impressions

MANAGER, VISITORS INFORMATION CENTER

From Tidewater to the Blue Ridge Parkway, Virginia offers travelers a mind-boggling array of destinations, attractions, accommodations, and services. Counselors at the commonwealth's thirteen highway welcome centers help travelers sort through all the possibilities to choose the products that suit their needs best.

"Late February through April is busy for us, because that's when the Canadians pass through on their way home from spending the winter down south," says Roger Carpenter, manager of the Lambsburg Visitors Center on I-77 just above the North Carolina border. Summers are busy, too, he says, with as many as 10,000 families a month stopping at the center for information.

"But we're not as busy as the centers on I-95, so we get more time to talk to people," he says. Which is good, because, "you have to be a detective. What people normally ask for is not necessarily what they really want. Then they'll mention that they're interested in the Civil War. *That* helps me suggest how they might have the best time."

The most important thing, he says, is that the counselors be familiar with the state, and this nine-year veteran is full of interesting information about Virginia.

"You ask them how much time they have and about their interests," says Jeanne Burton, manager of the Eastern Shore Visitors Center on Route 13 in New Church. "Whether it's scenery or history, events or outdoor activities. Most people have an idea of where they're going. Our objective is to recommend things to keep them in Virginia longer."

The tactic must work. According to a report from the Virginia Division of Travel and Tourism, 11 percent of visitors extended their stay by an average of 1.5 nights as a result of counseling at the visitors centers. This meant an additional $20 million spent in the state and $1 million in extra tax monies.

Visitors center counselors are not allowed to recommend specific hotels restaurants, attractions, or other travel-related businesses.

"We represent everybody," explains Connie Ford, manager of Virginia's Washington, D.C., Visitors Center on K Street. "So we give visitors several different options based on their interests, the amount of time they have, and their budget. We ask a lot of open-ended questions, and if we have personal experience with a place, we will share it."

Twice a year, on a rotating basis, the commonwealth sends its full-time travel counselors on six-day familiarization trips, each time to a different one of Virginia's six regions. On these trips, they get a chance to see the attractions, highways, hotels, and resorts firsthand. Occasionally, the managers escort travel writers and others on fam tours.

If a traveler is interested in an attraction or a hotel that the counselor hasn't had an opportunity to visit, that traveler might be put to work.

"We ask people to call us if they go and let us know how they liked it," Ford says. Most travelers oblige. "People are really good about it, and that's very helpful."

sionals who attend these shows can obtain printed information and view video and digital electronic presentations about new travel products. They can also speak directly with representatives of the suppliers and intermediaries. This direct contact can help agents evaluate and gather information on new products that they think may be of interest to their customers.

Travel Articles. Travel articles do not appear exclusively in travel industry publications. General-interest magazines and newspapers, such as *Time* magazine and *USA Today*, regularly print articles on travel topics, some with a news emphasis, others without. Many travel articles include accounts of the history, culture, or politics of different destinations. They may also contain current information on hotel rates, desirable destinations, or areas to avoid.

Electronic Sources. Many suppliers and destinations are marketing their products and services on Web sites that are accessed via the Internet. In some cases these sites are duplications of printed brochures, which were created by scanning the brochure copy into a file that was converted to Web site format by specialized software. Most sites include additional information categories, which are constantly updated, as well as the opportunity to purchase products via credit card on a secure network. These sites are excellent sources of information for travel counselors and other intermediaries.

Suppliers and destinations also produce CD-ROMs, DVDs, and videotapes of the products and services that are offered. These marketing products are very useful and informative, and some are produced in a virtual reality mode so that those viewing them feel as though they are actually visiting the site or property. The Atlanta Olympic Committee used the technology, for example, as part of their effort to secure the 1996 Olympics.

Most travel clubs produce a newsletter that describes travel options and upcoming trips. Many of them are provided to the club membership via electronic mail or on the club's Web site. Travel counselors can learn about frequent traveler preferences (club members) and destination choices by subscribing to newsletters or visiting Web sites.

Finally, many cable television companies include travel shows as part of the programming that they offer to subscribers. These shows provide an excellent opportunity for travel counselors to learn about popular and emerging destinations.

Word of Mouth. One of the best sources of information about travel products—word of mouth—is often underemphasized by travel sales professionals. Talking to someone "who's been there" is in many ways preferable and more reliable than any other source of information.

From Colleagues. Firsthand evaluations from other travel professionals constitute a valuable source of information on travel products. In most cases, the importance of these reports is not the objective information they contain. Any travel agent, for example, can look up the rates and a general description of the Seaside Hotel on Castaway Island. But well-informed travel sales professionals can also provide subjective evaluations of travel products. When a colleague returns from a vacation and reports that the Seaside Hotel is located right next to an oil refinery, the perception of its desirability and quality changes considerably. A colleague can also supply special tips about travel products—for instance, that a particular hotel is a superb property and that its best rooms are in its west wing.

From Customers. Often, customers make comments to agents about their previous trips. Some agencies routinely telephone or survey customers after they have returned from their trips. In either case, customers are a good source of current evaluations of travel products. These are particularly important when no one in the agency has visited a certain destination.

If customers' comments and feedback are verbal, agents should develop a method for making the information available to other agents. Options include:

- Passing along the information verbally.
- Using a comment file.
- Designating a regular time to exchange customers' reports.
- Using electronic mail or intraoffice memos for comments that would be helpful or relevant immediately.
- Creating a database with separate files for destination properties or airlines.

Firsthand Experience

Personal vacations give travel agents an opportunity to view the travel world from the customer's point of view. How luxurious is that new resort in the Caribbean that has been advertised so heavily? How relaxing are the new cruises offered by a major cruise line? There is no substitute for firsthand evaluation of travel destinations, accommodations, and facilities.

The most important means of gaining firsthand knowledge of travel products is the ***familiarization trip***, or "fam trip." These trips are sponsored by destination marketing organizations, airlines, resorts, cruise lines, tour operators, or other travel suppliers, often in conjunction with each other. During these trips, agents examine hotels and restaurants, visit local attractions, and get a feel for local culture. A fam trip may be designed to introduce agents to a particular product, such as a new hotel or resort. Or a trip may have a broader scope. If, for instance, an airline has recently opened service to Puerta Vallarta, Mexico, the airline may design a destination familiarization trip. After flying on the airline to Puerta Vallarta, travel agent and tour operator guests would inspect a number of hotels and restaurants in the area, visit Gringo's Gulch, and take a day trip to see where the movie *The Night of the Iguana* was filmed.

Often, suppliers offer familiarization trips to those who specialize in their particular geographic area. Suppliers use the trips to convince travel sales professionals to sell more of their products, while those participating use the trips to determine how those products would fit their customers' needs. They make note of particular restaurants, hotels, or attractions to recommend. The suppliers pay some or all of the expenses for fam trips. Often, a travel sales professional's company pays any remaining expenses. Travel sales professionals, in return, are obligated to attend all the functions and inspections planned by the supplier and often are required by their employers to write reports on their trips and to share their new insights with colleagues.

ASSESSING THE VALUE OF TRAVEL

So far, this chapter has focused on how travel sales professionals can gather up-to-date information on the many travel products available. The rest of the chapter deals with how they can assess the value of these products in relation to the needs of the customer.

Whatever their travel preferences and budgets, travel customers want good value. Travel sales professionals, therefore, must understand what constitutes good value and find products that represent it for their customers.

Value can be thought of as a function of the quality and quantity of the travel products as perceived by the customer, all in relation to the price of the travel. In other words, the more travel benefits per customer dollar, the greater the value. The ability to assess the real and perceived trade-offs between price and quality is an essential skill for anyone evaluating travel products.

Quality and Quantity

Quality and quantity are measures of the physical dimensions of a trip. The quantity factors are relatively simple to calculate. They include:

- Distance—How far will the customer travel?
- Duration—How long will the trip take?
- Activity—What will be done and how often?

The quality of travel products is usually determined first by the class of travel and accommodations. For example, customers who choose to fly first-class expect to receive a higher quality product than those who fly coach. A traveler who stays in a five-star hotel expects a better room and better service than someone who stays in a three-star hotel. Sources of such evaluative information include:

- Personal inspection.
- Industry reference guides.
- Evaluative travel guides.
- Government grading systems.

Quality ratings like these are specific to each source. A three-star rating in a Michelin hotel guide, for instance, is substantially different from a three-star hotel rating in a Mobil Travel Guide. In most guides, however, the following variables are taken into consideration:

- Location of hotel—seaside, airport, downtown.
- Location of room—poolside, luxury level.
- Fixtures and size of room—standard, suite, efficiency, penthouse.
- Meals—European, Modified American, or American plan.
- Features and amenities—health club, concierge, tennis courts, golf course, meeting rooms.

The best way to evaluate the quality of a hotel is to inspect it personally. Since it is impossible for agents to inspect even a small percentage of the available properties, they must rely on the evaluations of other travel professionals. Used carefully, such evaluations provide a sound basis on which to judge the value of a particular travel product.

Price and Value

Quality and quantity of the travel products are the major determinants of travel prices. Nevertheless, a host of other factors must be examined and weighed to determine the value of a trip. Travel agents must begin with a clear picture of the customer's travel needs and preferences and anticipated benefits. Only in terms of a particular customer's situation can distinctions between real and apparent bargains be made. When calculating actual costs (price) of travel products, thorough travel agents use the following techniques.

Shop Around. In today's fast-changing travel industry, it takes an agent skilled in the use of both a CRS and reference books, and who has contacts at suppliers and destinations, to search out and secure the best price for a customer. Since the deregulation of the airline industry, for example, myriad rates, rate structures, conditions, and discounts have complicated the price picture. Different airlines sometimes charge different fares for similar service between the same two cities, for example. Checking the latest rate information available on all possible options is the only way to ensure that customers receive the best price for a product.

Consider the Whole Trip. No single component of a trip tells the entire price story; the price of the entire group of travel products is what matters to customers. If a trip includes air travel, hotel accommodations, and a car rental, a discount airfare may not necessarily yield the best total price. For instance, special discount airfares might be offered on heavily traveled routes during peak travel seasons, when hotel and car rental rates are usually higher than at other times. Thus, adding up the total price for all the components of a trip is the only way to determine the best price and value.

Check Discount Trade-Offs. Most discounts offered in the travel industry come with certain conditions or restrictions. Discounts may require:

- Advance reservations or purchase.
- Immediate payment.
- No refund if product is not used.
- No changes in product specifications, for example, number in party or dates of stay.
- Out-of-season travel.
- Minimum or maximum duration of stay.

Each of these restrictions must be evaluated in light of its overall impact on the customer. For example, a married couple may be able to spend a week in the Caribbean during the summer for half the cost of a winter stay. But the summer trip may not fulfill their needs in the same way. If their primary reason for traveling is to explore new places, a summer trip may be a great value. But if they wish to escape the winter chill of Chicago, a summer trip would not meet their needs or be a good value, however low the price.

Check Hidden Costs. The total cost of a travel product may be difficult to calculate because of hidden costs that are not immediately apparent. The trend toward prepaid and ***all-inclusive*** vacations has helped to minimize these additional costs but has increased customers' expectations that the cost of a travel package is the total cost of the vacation. Travel sales professionals should explain to customers that all all-inclusive packages are not equally inclusive. Some tour operators require customers to pay membership fees in addition to the package costs. Others add a percentage for gratuities and service. Variations in national, state, and local taxes can make a substantial difference in total travel cost. Most car rental companies charge fees for fuel, insurance, and excess mileage.

Note Special Factors. Many travel destinations are affected by seasonal changes in the weather. Prices for accommodations, transportation, sightseeing, and even meals may be discounted during the so-called low season, owing to the lessened demand of travelers.

When the price of fuel increases, many travel suppliers pass along their additional costs in the form of fuel surcharges. These surcharges are common in the airline industry. Although the charges may increase the cost of a domestic ticket by only a few dollars, they may be much higher for international travel.

Exchange rates of currency must be taken into consideration for international travel. Because exchange rates can fluctuate significantly even during the course of a trip, their impact on the total costs of the trip can be difficult to predict. Different methods of paying for the trip, such as credit cards, traveler's checks, and cash, can also result in varying rates of exchange even if paid at the same time. Prepayment allows customers to make certain of the exchange rate that will be paid. Prepaying can save money when exchange rates are rising, but there is always the chance that the currency value will go down. In the latter case, customers can end up paying more for a trip by prepaying.

Exchange rates can have a great impact on the total cost of a trip.

Travel sales professionals and their customers can also take advantage of exchange rates. By looking at the currency rates of various countries against the U.S. dollar, travelers can find relative bargains. If the dollar is strong against the Spanish peso, a two-week vacation to Spain will cost less than a trip of the same length to a destination such as France or Switzerland, where the U.S. dollar may be less strong.

How to Compare Prices

Travel prices are not always as straightforward as they first appear. Experienced travel agents know this and are careful when evaluating the total costs of a trip and the trade-offs of similar products offered at different prices. The examples on pages 189, 190, and 191 demonstrate some of the factors that must be taken into account when comparing prices. As the comparison illustrates, a supersaver airline ticket alone does not make independent travel less expensive than traveling on a package tour. Astute travel sales professionals consider every component product of a trip before making recommendations to customers. Customers who wish to travel independently in spite of potentially higher prices

COMPARISON 1: TOUR PACKAGE AND INDEPENDENT TRAVEL

Travel specifications: one-week European vacation for two

	Independent Travel	Tour Package
Discount airfare for 2:	$1,500	included
7 days hotel:	$700	included
Transfers:	$36	included
City transportation:	$58	included
Guided tour:	$38	included
Attraction admissions:	$25	included
Discount meal vouchers:	N/A	included
Guidebooks and tapes:	$10	included
Total cost:	$2,367	$1,800
Benefits:	Flexibility in planning. Flexibility during travel. Wide choice of accommodations.	Prepayment—cost known in advance Arrangements guaranteed. Taxes and tips included. Volume discounts. No-wait tickets to attractions. Lower price.
Disadvantages:	Higher price. Total cost not known in advance.	Lack of flexibility.

COMPARISON 2: DIRECT AND CONNECTING FLIGHTS
Travel specifications: flight from Philadelphia to Chicago (Midway)

	Direct Flight	Connecting Flight (via Cleveland)
Price:	$250 Departs 7:30 A.M. Arrives 8:45 A.M.	$200 Departs 7:30 A.M. Arrives 9:45 A.M.
Benefits:	Shorter travel period. No chance of delay in Cleveland.	Less expensive.
Disadvantages:	Higher price.	Possible delay in Cleveland. Longer travel period.
Best value for:	Business travelers. Time-critical travel situations.	Those who want the least expensive fare. Those who will not be affected by delays.

COMPARISON 3: AIR TRAVEL AND AUTO TRAVEL
Travel specifications: one-way trip from New York to Tampa, Florida

	Air Travel	Auto Travel
Cost per person: Meals	$250 included	$240 (1,000 mi @ 24¢ /mi) Motel (one night) $45 Meals (per person) $54
Total cost: For one person For two persons	 $250 $500	 $339 $393
Benefits:	Shorter travel time. Comfort.	Flexible itinerary and schedule. Additional stops possible.
Disadvantages:	No flexibility.	Longer travel time. Possible fatigue of driver(s) on arrival.
Best value for:	Business travelers. Those who want to minimize travel time.	Families. Those who wish to visit other destinations. Those who have time to spare.

should be made aware that careful selection of travel products can help minimize the cost differential. In all cases, agents and their customers must evaluate what effect hidden costs may have on the total cost of a trip.

In a case like this, travel sales professionals, consulting with their customers, assess whether the advantage of the lower airfare is worth the increased travel time and the possibility of delay at the connecting airport. In this scenario, the method of travel chosen may be determined by the number of people traveling together. One person traveling alone can travel less expensively by air, but for a family of two or more, travel by car can be much more economical, although more time consuming.

This example shows the trade-offs a customer must accept in order to take advantage of discount

COMPARISON 4: SUPERSAVER AND STANDARD AIRFARES
Travel specifications: round-trip air travel from New York to London

	Supersaver	Standard Fare
	$750 round-trip	$1,450 round-trip
Benefits:	Lower price.	No restrictions. Can travel any flight on any day.
Disadvantages:	Advance purchase necessary. Minimum or maximum stay required. Penalty for changes. Limited departure dates. Nonrefundable. Limited seating on each flight.	Higher price.
Best value for:	Vacation travelers. Those who can plan in advance.	Business travelers. Those whose schedules may change.

fares. In most cases, the less expensive the fare, the greater the number of restrictions, especially during peak travel periods.

Together, these examples demonstrate the many factors that must be taken into account when comparing the prices of travel products. They also show that the less expensive options usually have several restrictions or disadvantages attached to them. In many situations, therefore, the less expensive option will not provide the best value to the customer.

Before comparing prices, travel sales professionals must know several other things about the customer's needs. To be in a position to recommend the best option for a customer, the agent must know the customer's:

- Reason for travel, such as business or vacation.
- Flexibility.
- Time constraints.
- Budget.

A travel sales professional and the customer must then weigh the cost of different options against the advantages and disadvantages associated with each of the travel products. A product is not good value if it does not meet the customer's needs and provide the benefits expected.

Perceived Benefits and Value

Products have value to travelers only to the extent that they satisfy some of their basic underlying needs. Travel customers perceive travel benefits as those features of a travel product that will fulfill these underlying needs. In other words, the customer's perception dictates whether or not a physical attribute or feature of the product is a benefit in a particular case. So, the value of a travel product can never be assessed except in relation to an individual customer's perception of that product.

Customers' perceptions are influenced by many factors. The following list identifies some of these factors and shows how they can affect customers' perceptions of travel products.

- Personal preference—If a customer prefers an aisle seat, then a window seat is not a benefit.
- Motivation—If a customer is trying to eat healthfully, a twenty-four-hour buffet is not a benefit.
- Knowledge—If a customer reads that the underwater views are great, free use of snorkeling equipment is a benefit.
- Interest—If a customer likes toy trains, a visit to a toy train museum is a benefit.
- Experience—If a customer enjoyed the tour of London, a tour of Paris may be a benefit.
- Hearsay—If a customer hears that Toronto should not be missed, including time to visit Toronto is a benefit.

Benefits are individual and personal. They vary from person to person and from trip to trip. Nevertheless, assessing the customer's perception of travel benefits is an essential part of determining the total value of travel.

Perceived benefits often relate directly to the tangible features of the product. For example, a hotel's tennis courts provide little benefit for a customer who does not play tennis.

Other perceived benefits may be entirely independent of the tangible features of the destination or product. These benefits are linked more closely to the underlying needs that a customer tries to fulfill in buying a travel product, as discussed in Chapter 7. For example, a particular destination may appeal to a customer because it appears to be the fashionable place to go. Its advertising might suggest that the social elite choose certain travel destinations and products. Although these perceptions may have no direct bearing on the features of the product under consideration, they can have a strong influence on the customer's view of the value of the product and decision whether to visit.

Perceived benefits, then, are an essential but varying element in the determination of value. A travel agent must recognize that the customer's perception, whether accurate or not, is the place where features become benefits. A customer's idea of total value is roughly determined by considering the tangible dimensions of the travel product, together with any additional benefits perceived by the customer, against the price of the product. Thus, the same trip at the same price can have radically different values to different customers. Determining precisely how the customer's needs and preferences affect the perception of benefit is part of the selling process, which is discussed in detail in Chapter 11.

CHAPTER SUMMARY

- Evaluating travel products requires a thorough knowledge of available sources of information.
- Information sources may be descriptive and/or evaluative.
- CRSs provide travel sales professionals with their fastest source of information on airline products and many non-airline products.
- CRSs provide information on rates and availability and expedite the reservation and ticketing functions.
- Reference books provide much information on non-airline suppliers.
- Other sources of printed material that provide important information include brochures, guidebooks, travel publications, and materials from trade shows.
- Travel sales professionals also get information by word of mouth and firsthand experience, the best way to find out about travel products.
- Familiarization trips provide travel intermediaries with an opportunity to experience a destination firsthand.
- The value of a travel product is determined by quality and quantity, plus additional benefits perceived by the customer in relation to price.
- Quality, quantity, and peak periods are the major determinants of the price of a travel product.
- Travel sales professionals must take into account several factors when determining total travel costs.
- Customers' perceived benefits also affect the value of a travel product.
- Perceived benefits are individual and personal. A benefit to one customer may not be a benefit to another customer.
- Benefits may relate to the features of a travel product or be independent of them.
- Electronic sources of information including Web sites, videos, Internet newsletters, and cable television programs are increasingly important.

KEY TERMS

literal needs
industry reference books
brochures
guidebooks
trade publications
trade shows
consortium
familiarization trip ("fam trip")
value
all-inclusive

DISCUSSION QUESTIONS

1. How can using a CRS ensure that a travel customer receives the best value when purchasing an airline ticket?
2. Describe the printed information sources that an agent should refer to when discussing cruises with a customer.
3. Discuss ways of collecting information, other than through CRSs and printed reference books.
4. Explain what constitutes good value in a travel product.
5. Explain the two major factors that determine the price of travel products.
6. What factors can affect the total cost of a travel product?
7. Explain why a travel product may be perceived differently by different customers.

Evaluating the Travel Product

Name: ______________________ Date: ______________

Directions: Answer these questions as you read the chapter. You will be able to use these answers to help you review the chapter.

1. Give five examples of the type of information available from a computer reservations system (CRS).

2. What is a passenger name record?

3. Contrast the limitations and benefits of CRSs.

4. Why do travel sales professionals use industry reference books?

5. Why are brochures a source of limited information?

6. What special information can be found in trade publications?

7. What is a trade show?

8. What is a consortium?

9. How can word of mouth from colleagues be especially helpful?

10. Why do intermediaries take familiarization trips?

11. Describe the relationship among price, quality, and value.

12. Provide examples of two quality and two quantity factors that a travel agent should consider when selling a product.

13. Why are perceived benefits the essential element in customers determining the value of a product?

14. Why is it more important for a travel agent to consider value than price?

WORKSHEET **CHAPTER**

Evaluating the Travel Product

Name: ______________________________ Date: ______________

INFORMATION, PLEASE

As a travel sales professional, you must help your clients choose the products that best meet their needs. Although computerized reservation systems provide the fastest access to ticket and tour facts, other background information is usually needed by customers if they are to make an informed decision. For each of the situations described below (1–9), choose the two most appropriate resources from the following list (A–H), then explain what information you would learn from each.

A. Thomas Cook Overseas Timetable
B. Russell's Official National Motorcoach Guide
C. Official Steamship Guide International
D. OAG Travel Planner Hotel and Motel Red Book (North American, European, or Pacific-Asian)
E. Consolidated Air Tour Manual
F. Mobil or Michelin Guide
G. Travel company brochure
H. Word-of-mouth customer or colleague

1. An avid golfer from Detroit wants to fly to Scotland with a friend who is also a golfer. They want to play several courses, stay in interesting places (such as an old castle or bed-and-breakfast inn), and see some of the countryside.

Choose two key sources of information (A–H), and explain what you would learn from each.

____
____
____
____
____
____

2. Parents of a Korean executive who works in New York want to fly to San Francisco and meet him there for a one-week vacation, then fly back with him to New York for an extended visit and tour of the East Coast.

Choose two key sources of information (A–H), and explain what you would learn from each.

____
____
____
____
____
____

3. A family from New Jersey is looking for a guest ranch in Montana, Wyoming, or Idaho with rustic, comfortable accommodations for two parents, two grandparents, and two children, aged ten and thirteen.

Choose two key sources of information (A–H), and explain what you would learn from each.

4. An engaged couple from Green Bay, Wisconsin, is getting married on Valentine's Day and want a warm place to spend their honeymoon. They want a reasonably priced villa, access to water sports, and informal atmosphere.

Choose two key sources of information (A–H), and explain what you would learn from each.

5. Two college roommates from Boston want to travel Europe by train, linking up with other school friends in Milan and Innsbruck. They would like to spend much of their time outdoors, meet young people from other countries, and travel on a restricted budget.

Choose two key sources of information (A–H), and explain what you would learn from each.

6. A seventy-year-old widow from Philadelphia has always dreamed of sailing from New York to San Francisco (via the Panama Canal) on a luxury cruise ship. She enjoys swimming, playing bridge, and meeting people.

Choose two key sources of information (A–H), and explain what you would learn from each.

7. A public relations account manager must attend a four-day trade show in Tokyo. Her husband will accompany her, and they will spend an additional six days touring Japan. They need hotel reservations in Tokyo, Kyoto, and points in between, as well as rail transportation and guided tours.

Choose two key sources of information (A–H), and explain what you would learn from each.

8. A family of four (including two teenage boys) from a small town in eastern Tennessee wants to travel by train to Nashville for a five-day visit to the city and surrounding area. They need two connecting rooms in a moderately priced motel, preferably with a kitchen, as well as information on attractions to visit.

Choose two key sources of information (A–H), and explain what you would learn from each.

9. A professor from Seattle wants to travel to Alaska by boat, spend several weeks exploring the entire state, and sail back home again. The professor is a nature buff who wants to see as much unspoiled territory as possible in the most remote locations. Cost is not the most important factor.

Choose two key sources of information (A–H), and explain what you would learn from each.

Setting Up the Sale

OBJECTIVES

When you have completed this chapter, you should be able to:

* Give reasons why travel suppliers and intermediaries need to provide information about travel products through persuasive communication.
* Identify the three components of the communications mix.
* List the guidelines for creating an advertising message.
* Evaluate the advantages and disadvantages of different advertising media.
* Outline the methods used to evaluate advertising campaigns.
* Develop a strategy for a public relations campaign using a variety of public relations tools.
* Distinguish between trade and consumer sales promotion methods.

When a travel company introduces a new product, it must make travel customers aware of the product and its benefits. It must also make certain that those who sell the new product are aware of its features and how they will benefit travel customers. To communicate this information, the company uses three primary promotional techniques: advertising, public relations, and sales promotion. These three activities are part of the ***communications mix*** and are intended to communicate information about products that will either meet expressed demand or create new demand for a product by convincing potential customers of its value.

Since the market for any travel product can change quickly, travel companies must be able to adjust their communications mix to reflect current sales and revenue needs. When evaluating the balance of the communications mix, marketing specialists consider the following:

* The type of customer to be reached.
* The geographic location of the customers.
* The communications mix of competing companies.

This chapter examines how each element in the communications mix contributes to the sale of travel products.

ADVERTISING

Do you know which airline is "something special in the air," which car rental agency says "We try harder," and which hotel offers to "leave the light on for you"? Advertising is such a common element of our

Double Double
Miles Miles
On On
American
American.

Now through August 25, AAdvantage members can earn double AAdvantage miles anywhere American Airlines, American Eagle or Reno Air® fly – including 250 cities in over 40 countries. All you have to do is purchase and fly on a qualifying, unrestricted, full-fare ticket on any American, American Eagle or Reno Air flight. Just register for the double-mile offer by July 31.† For reservations, call your Travel Agent or American at **1-800-433-7300**. Or visit **www.aa.com** to purchase tickets online or become an AAdvantage member instantly. And be sure to use our convenient **AA Electronic Ticket**™ option.

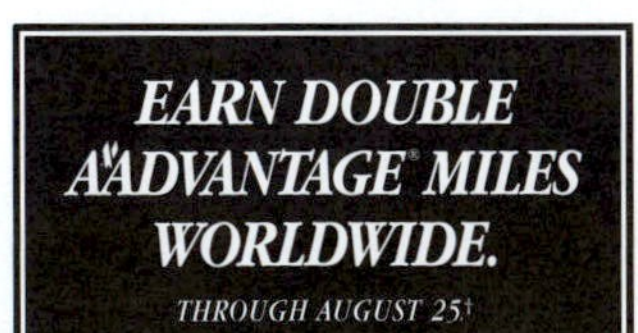

To qualify, AAdvantage members must register before departure and before 7/31/99 by calling AADVANTAGE DIAL-IN® at ***1-800-882-8880****, pressing* **1, 2, *, 4, *** *and, when prompted, entering Promotion Code* ***DBMLS****.*

AmericanAirlines®
American Eagle®

Advertising slogans promote product recognition and recognition promotes sales. (Courtesy of American Airlines)

Advertising messages aimed at the travel trade differ from those intended for consumers. (Courtesy of Lee County Visitor and Convention Bureau)

daily life that few of us give much thought to what makes a particular advertisement appealing or effective. Advertisers, on the other hand, carefully research how to convey information to the public in a way that will elicit the desired response—in most cases, the purchase of a product. The purpose of advertising, according to the American Marketing Association, is threefold:

* To give customers information.
* To develop positive attitudes toward products.
* To encourage the sale of products.

However powerful advertising may be, it does not close sales. Rather, the goal of advertising by the travel industry is to motivate a potential customer to contact a travel supplier or intermediary for information about a travel product. It also prepares the customer to purchase it electronically or receive the personal selling message. That message is the focus of the next chapter.

Steps of the Advertising Process

Travel advertising takes many forms, from expensive network television advertising by major travel suppliers to Yellow Pages listings placed by small, family-owned resorts. Regardless of the audience, medium used, or budget, however, the basic process of advertising remains the same.

Selecting the Audience. Before an advertiser can create a message or select an advertising medium, it must target an audience. ***Trade advertising*** is designed to communicate information to the various members of travel distribution channels, especially between suppliers and travel agents and/or tour operators. ***Consumer advertising***, on the other hand, focuses directly on customers who buy travel products. Because these two audiences have very different needs for information, advertising messages directed toward them will differ considerably.

Trade advertising attempts to stimulate demand for a company's product and encourage sales by appealing to travel intermediaries, based on the benefits the product will provide to travel customers. This advertising usually contains details about the product, including suggestions for presenting the product to the general public and descriptions of how the intermediary will benefit from selling the product. This strategy is based on the assumption that if intermediaries know the product well and are convinced of its benefits, their knowledge and enthusiasm will make the personal sales process more effective.

Regardless of how well informed travel intermediaries are, the success of travel sales depends on the attitudes of the general public. For this reason, most travel advertising is directed toward prospective travel customers. Consumer advertising often makes a more emotional appeal than does trade advertising, focusing attention on how travel products can meet the needs and desires of travel customers. Often, it targets specific types of prospective customers, for example, frequent business travelers, skiers, or travelers to a specific destination. Suppliers must be careful to match their products with potential buyers.

Because these appeals are made through mass media, the cost of consumer advertising can be extremely high. As a result, travel suppliers often spend 5 percent of their overall revenues on advertising. Some tour operators and other intermediaries who rely heavily on costly brochures, catalogs, and television advertising spend as much as 15 percent of revenues on advertising.

With small profit margins, intermediaries like travel agents or tour operators cannot afford to bear the total cost of a large-scale print or electronic advertising campaign. For this reason, the travel industry has developed a system of ***cooperative advertising***, whereby a travel agency and a supplier (or another intermediary) jointly sponsor an advertisement. Cooperative advertising is particularly popular in the print media because of the ease with which both sponsoring organizations can be featured. A cruise line, for example, may provide a complete newspaper advertisement, to which an intermediary's name, phone, and fax number or e-mail address may easily be added. Intermediaries can also add their names and contact information to radio and television advertisements prepared by suppliers. Some cooperative advertising may emphasize a particular travel destination; for example, the Detroit Metropolitan Convention and Visitors Bureau and Northwest Airlines (whose hub is in Detroit) may jointly promote Detroit as a tourist destination.

Creating the Advertising Message. Having selected the target audience whose needs can be met by their products, advertisers must decide what the advertising message should say. Creating the message is the heart of the advertising process, since the message must make prospective customers aware that they have a need for travel products and that certain products will best fill those needs. The more specific the target audience, the more focused the advertising message can be. But how does an advertiser determine what message will appeal to its target audience?

Consumer research, a component of the market research discussed in Chapter 3, analyzes consumer preferences, buying patterns, and the influence of various forms of advertising on the public. This research can be done by the supplier's research department or by specialized market research organizations, which provide advertisers with detailed profiles of their intended audiences. These profiles can be used to determine what information is relevant to a given customer and create a message that will address the target market's specific needs and interests.

Once a target audience profile has been established, the advertiser can then decide on the intended purpose of the message. An advertising message may be intended to:

- *Inform* customers about unique features, new locations, or improved or enhanced services.
- *Establish, reinforce, or change attitudes* about a product, destination, or company.
- *Persuade* customers to try a new product or to switch from another supplier's product.
- *Elicit response* by offering incentives to those who inquire about travel products and services.

Two other factors affect the content of the advertising message: the prospective customer's perception of benefits and the role of psychological factors in buying decisions. Clearly, travel needs and desires differ among individuals within a target audience; they may even differ from one time to another for the same individual. Nevertheless, advertisers use their research profiles to highlight those aspects of the product that each group is most likely to regard as a benefit and respond to quickly. The same airline, for example, may advertise its hourly service to major cities in *Forbes* magazine, but focus on its nonstop service to the Caribbean in *Travel and Leisure* magazine. Even when the supplier remains the same, advertising messages can change to suit different intended audiences based on the characteristics of the product that is offered.

Understanding the psychology that underlies purchasing patterns (as discussed in Chapter 7) is important when developing an advertising message. Research has repeatedly shown, for instance, that customers are usually motivated by the idea of a bargain, by familiar product names, and by positive images they have of products or destinations. The psychological factors that enter into the creation of an apparent bargain affects the prices used in advertising. Products are rarely priced at an even $100.00; instead, they are more likely to be priced at $99.95. Even though the price difference is insignificant, customers often choose the product with the lower price. Other psychological factors that enter into the creation of an advertising message include the appeal of products that will impress friends and acquaintances, the appearance and/or endorsement of celebrities, and the use of language and artwork that reflect the latest trends.

Combining all these elements and emphases into a compelling advertising message is not an easy task. For this reason, many travel professionals who are responsible for their company's advertising turn to advertising agencies for assistance in the development of creative and effective advertisements. Certain guidelines, however, should be followed by anyone writing an advertising message:

* Make the message clear, direct, and concise.
* Be sure the product's benefits are clearly described.
* Call for specific action by the customers.
* Use current product information.
* Use only high-quality photos and artwork.
* Know what legal restraints affect advertising.

Selecting and Scheduling Media

Once the basic message has been determined, an advertiser must decide which media will reach the target market most effectively. The advertiser evaluates six primary avenues to find the one with the highest likelihood of achieving the marketing goals:

* Print—newspapers, magazines.
* Broadcast—radio and television (often cable TV).
* Direct-mail marketing, including fax and broadcast e-mail.
* Out-of-home—billboards and signs on buses and taxis.
* Directories, including the Yellow Pages.
* Internet Web sites.

How does an advertiser select from among these different media? The following factors help determine the best medium for the situation:

* Level of coverage (reaching customers).
* Selectivity (reaches target market).
* Consumer acceptance.
* Reproduction quality.
* Flexibility.
* Cost per customer contact.

Each medium has its own particular strengths, making it capable of meeting certain advertising requirements. Each also has disadvantages that must be considered in light of the objectives of the advertising program. In general, however, the cost of placing an advertisement increases as the level of coverage by the medium increases.

Newspapers and Magazines. Most print advertisements for travel products appear in newspapers and magazines. Typically, they account for about half of all travel and tourism advertising expenditures.

About 75 percent of the people in the United States look at a newspaper each day. Because newspapers appeal to such a wide audience, they are a potentially important avenue for any travel supplier or intermediary. Major national and international travel suppliers, such as airlines and car rental companies, advertise regularly in the *New York Times, USA Today*, the *Washington Post*, the *Los Angeles Times* and many other major daily papers with circulations in excess of one million. Local travel companies and small suppliers usually advertise in smaller-circulation dailies, local weekly papers, or the travel sections of large-newspaper Sunday editions. Compared with other media, newspapers have several advantages:

* Wide readership.
* Frequency of publication.
* Low cost, particularly in small newspapers.
* Good geographic segmentation, based on readership profile.
* Short lead time (prior to publication), allowing flexibility for late changes, updates, and additions.
* Good response options via printed coupon, toll-free numbers, e-mail, or Web sites.

Advertisers must also bear in mind the disadvantages of newspapers:

* Waste circulation—Newspapers reach many readers who are not potential customers.
* Short life—There is little or no repeat exposure.
* Little retention—Newspapers are often scanned rather than read.
* Unpredictable print quality—This is especially true for color ads.

General-circulation magazines, such as *Time* and *Newsweek*, attract many of the same travel advertisers as do the major newspapers. Many travel advertisers also place advertisements in smaller specialty magazines, such as *Travel and Leisure* and *Travel/Holiday*, whose readers are already predisposed to travel. Magazines offer travel advertisers several advantages:

* Large circulation.
* Excellent print and color quality.
* Regional and subject specialization.
* Good psychographic segmentation possibilities.
* Association with prestigious publications.
* Extra reach owing to many secondary readers.

Magazines have certain disadvantages as well:

* Long production lead time (up to two months).
* High production costs, especially for color advertising.

* Less frequent schedule of publication than newspapers.
* More difficult to revise, update, etc.

Radio and Television. Radio and television reach more homes than any other advertising medium. Radios are found in 99 percent of all homes in America; the figure is only slightly lower for television, at 98 percent. In both media, advertisers rely on creativity and repetition to help their message reach potential customers.

With a few exceptions, a radio advertisement reaches a relatively small geographic area. Yet many travel advertisers find the specificity of radio attractive—for example, when an airline wishes to advertise new service between two cities. The different station programming formats (e.g., classic, rock, country, easy listening) attract different types of audiences, allowing advertisers to further define their target audiences. The advantages of radio include:

* Geographic, psychographic, and demographic selectivity.
* Relatively low cost.
* Contact with people other media cannot reach effectively, especially in cars.
* Appeal of the human voice.
* Short production lead time, allowing last-minute changes.

The accompanying disadvantages of radio advertising are:

* It often does not receive listener's full attention.
* Visual appeal is absent.
* Competition for listeners is heavy.
* Message is not available for review by listener.
* Search and seek buttons make station switching easier.

Nationwide network television gives big-budget advertisers an opportunity to reach many people with their messages. Local television fits the needs of companies that serve a small area, and cable channels give both types of advertisers the ability to focus on a particular type of viewer. In fact, many cable systems now carry a channel devoted exclusively to travel-related content. This allows destinations and suppliers to produce television programs which are devoted to their products and services. These programs, which are a blend of documentary and promotional efforts, include frequent display of contact information, including toll-free numbers, Web sites, and e-mail addresses to encourage immediate response. These programs can also be shown as part of in-flight programing on airlines or in motor coach video systems. As an example of how television can target specific markets, a tour company offering packages to the Olympics in Sydney, Australia might advertise on ESPN, the all-sports cable channel. For travel advertisers, television offers these advantages:

* Stronger impact than that of other media (moving images with sound).
* Visual demonstration of product or destination.
* Large and/or selective audience.
* Theme linked to television program (Superbowl, golf tournament, etc.).

The disadvantages of television should not be overlooked by prospective advertisers. They include:

* High cost of production (particularly commercials shot on location) and air time.
* Short life, with ads unavailable for review by viewer.
* Long production lead time (up to several months).
* Message usually restricted to 15, 30, or 60 seconds.

Direct-Mail Marketing. Many travel advertisers send catalogs, brochures, fliers, and other information directly to prospective customers through the mail. They can obtain mailing lists from mailing list brokers, local directories, associations, clubs, or their own listing of past customers (including those who responded to previous advertising by phoning a toll-free number or returning a coupon). ***Direct mail*** has several advantages:

* Production and mailing flexibility.
* High selectivity, offering good behavioristic segmentation.
* Ease of response as a result of reply cards, coupons, toll-free numbers, e-mail, fax, or Web sites.
* Attention drawn by creative packaging and personally addressed mail.

Direct-fax marketing is similar to direct-mail marketing except that the "address" is a telephone fax number selected from a directory or through a computer system that randomly dials phone/fax numbers. The message sent is usually limited to a few pages, which the recipient's fax machine will print.

Many organizations and companies have e-mail addresses listed in their directories (print and electronic) or Web sites. This makes it relatively easy (although tedious) to contact a large number of targeted individuals quickly through broadcast messages that are part of a database of contacts.

Out-of-Home Media. The most common forms of ***out-of-home media*** are billboards, kiosks, and the transit signs that appear on the sides of buses, streetcars, subways, and taxis. In many cases, these advertisements can reach people who are already traveling. The main advantages of out-of-home media advertising are:

- Relatively low cost.
- Repetition (travelers see signs day after day).
- Location (in prime areas or circulated via transit vehicles).
- Geographic selectivity.
- High impact achieved by good reproduction.

The disadvantages are:

- High waste coverage caused by low percentage of potential customers among those who see ads, and low attention in some markets. Message size restrictions (including the number of words for billboards).
- Long production lead time, making it difficult to change and update quickly.

Directory Advertising. Unlike other forms of advertising, directories do not impose themselves on prospective customers. People who seek information about a particular travel product often look in the Yellow Pages, travel atlases, and maps, or in a travel business directory produced by a local tourism promotion agency (often as part of a direct-response brochure), or some other group of travel businesses. Because the prospective customers are already predisposed to purchase a particular item, ***directory advertising*** often provides more specific information on the products or services offered by a travel supplier or intermediary. Directories offer excellent geographic selectivity at a relatively low cost.

Advertising on the Internet usually takes two forms. The first, and most frequent, includes promotional messages in any (or all) of the previously discussed media (print, broadcast, etc.) that direct readers or viewers to send messages to an e-mail address to request additional information, or to visit a Web site. On such sites, destinations or companies can provide high-quality pictures, video footage, music, information-request systems, reservation options, etc.

The second form of advertising involves key words that describe your destination (Example: RESORT, GOLF RESORT, UTAH GOLF, RESORT UTAH, would be key words for a golf resort located in Utah). These words are included in the directories for the "search engines" that locate information sources (often Web sites) available on the Internet. These "search engines" will find all sources of information that can be found on the Internet, based on the key words you enter. The entering of key words that locate various information sources, including Web sites, is often referred to as "surfing" the net.

The combination of all of the key words selected by individuals, companies, and organizations effectively creates an ever-expanding directory of products, services, and information resources. Thus, potential travel product consumers can access supplier Web sites through their listings (key words) in an electronic directory.

PUBLIC RELATIONS

Public relations, in its broadest sense, is the process of building the goodwill of customers toward a business or product. By emphasizing the news value of various aspects of a company and its products—a job promotion, corporate support of a worthy cause, or a reception marking a new resort opening for business—travel companies can convey information of a positive nature to customers, thereby bringing attention to themselves and their products. In many cases, then, the public relations effort focuses on those organizations and travel editors, writers, and journalists who are in a position to influence public opinion via the news media.

A strong emphasis on public relations has several distinct advantages. Most public relations campaigns cost far less in the long run than do advertising campaigns. The principle is a simple one: advertising time and space must be purchased, whereas time for a television feature story or space for a travel article does not (although there are costs for production of public relations). Furthermore, the context in which information about a supplier or product appears can positively

Marketing Impressions

AD AGENCY CREATIVE DIRECTOR, TRAVEL ACCOUNTS

There was the wonderful state that everyone drove through without stopping on their way to someplace else. There was the incredible country inn that couldn't get noticed by people in the big city next door. The fabulous restaurant no one believed was fabulous because it was in a shopping mall. The family ski resort with great summer activities but no summer visitors. The hotel with a view of seven other almost identical hotels. The food service corporation wading through local politics to land concessions contracts at airports.

"See? Working in advertising isn't about cute jingles, it's about being a *problem solver,*" says Susan Daugherty, a twenty-year veteran of the business. Daugherty spent thirteen years as a writer and creative director at Earle Palmer Brown, a mid-Atlantic advertising firm, and then went on to found her nearly decade-old freelance copywriting company. "Every business has some problem . . . some challenge that's standing in its way," Daugherty observes. "And often a smart, creative marketing plan can be the solution. Maybe it's finding a radio station that reaches more of the right customers . . . getting a public relations story placed in an influential newspaper . . . coming up with an involving promotion . . . or creating a TV commercial that's so drop-dead funny or beautiful or outrageous that everyone talks about it. The secret is making sure the solution is rooted in what the customer out there really needs and wants. When you find a way to solve a true consumer problem—bingo—you've also solved your client's problem."

Marketing can also be the key when a client's product is blending into the crowd. "These days," Daugherty notes, "there are so many 'me-too' products out there. We're all buried under an avalanche of competing travel and tourism opportunities. They all look alike until *one* of them does an amazing advertising campaign. Suddenly, *that one* has a personality. They're unique. We remember them."

Thinking up that "amazing" campaign is the job of the copywriters, art directors, and creative directors who develop the ideas, words, and pictures that convey the client's message, usually under considerable deadline pressure. "You have a huge head start if you can do research to understand what's going on in consumers' minds," says Daugherty. "I love sitting behind a one-way mirror, listening to real live customers talk about what turns them on and off. I love hearing the language they use when they describe a product. I love going out and seeing consumers in action at the hotel, restaurant, tourist attraction, whatever it is. *That kind* of intimate understanding of consumers is what great advertising is made of, not ideas that are dreamed up in a vacuum on the fourteenth floor of an ad agency."

So what's a typical day in advertising like? "There isn't one," Daugherty claims. "You always find yourself becoming an 'instant expert' about something new. Learning everything you can about a subject you'd never even heard of the day before. It's kind of like being a psychologist, business analyst, detective, emergency room doctor, poet, and guerilla fighter all at the same time. Crazy? Sure . . . but it's never boring."

Royal Caribbean's *Crown & Anchor* provides a good example of a customer-directed newsletter. (Courtesy of Royal Caribbean International)

affect the potential customer's perception of that information. Advertising, being sponsored, is an effort to persuade consumers to purchase a product, and viewers or readers know it as such. But a newspaper column describing a resort in the Bahamas, for example, has an air of objectivity and credibility about it, regardless of the initial source of that information.

Some articles and news stories are long enough to provide more detailed information on a company or product than an advertisement can, making public relations an ideal companion to advertising. One objective of a public relations campaign is to create a positive image for a company and its product in the minds of prospective customers, making them more receptive to the company's advertising. In this way, good publicity can distinguish a supplier from its competition. This is particularly important in a highly competitive market.

One drawback of this unpaid publicity in the news media is that companies must relinquish control of the message content, and potentially the travel product's image, to a third party with its own separate interests in mind. The article mentioned previously about the resort in the Bahamas could end up making the resort less desirable to prospective customers, for example, if it observed that the resort shares a beach with two other properties, whereas a similar resort nearby has a private beach for the exclusive use of its guests. An astute public relations professional considers this possibility and takes steps to maximize media exposure while minimizing risks of having the message altered by the publisher.

In many cases, however, the public relations goal is simply creating a positive image of a company, its products, and its employees. For example, United Airlines' sponsorship of a golf tournament does not bring specific attention to its business-class service, but is intended instead to create goodwill in the minds of prospective customers when they read about the United Airlines' tournament, whose proceeds benefit charities. Companies using public relations for this purpose must choose carefully those organizations with which they are associated and identified.

What, then, are the basic principles underlying a successful public relations effort? Since the goal of public relations is getting information into the media, public relations professionals need to know:

* The kind of information or activities that will be considered "news."
* The people in the media organization who control the flow of news and other timely information.
* The basic techniques of public relations—that is, the means by which newsworthy information is conveyed.

Newsworthy Information

A careful survey of major travel magazines and the travel sections of large newspapers gives a sense of what kinds of stories or events interest travel writers and editors. But public relations need not be limited to stories that describe the best resorts or the newest travel destination. The following list, though not exhaustive, indicates some types of information that may be of interest to the media.

* Professional certifications or degrees earned by employees.
* Staff appointments and promotions.
* Innovative products or operating procedures.

* Unusual services not offered by competitors.
* Company involvement in community service activities.
* Election to office in professional or trade organizations.
* Opening of new or renovated facilities.
* Human interest stories.
* Consumer tips.

Media Contacts

Newsworthy events become news only when editors or producers decide that the information is of interest to their readers or viewers. For that reason, good contacts with organizations and the media are crucial to the success of any public relations professional. It is also important for media personnel to know travel professionals, because the travel industry can be a frequent source of news. When, for example, Congress began to deregulate the airline industry, reporters needed access to travel industry sources who could explain the changes in simple terms and describe their impact on specific groups of travelers and travel companies. Those travel industry sources benefitted not only by being identified in stories, but also by making new contacts with editors and reporters who could potentially convey newsworthy information to the public in the future. Public relations professionals cultivate all such contacts in the media because they are critical to the success of public relations campaigns.

Public Relations Techniques

When a travel company has newsworthy information and knows which media sources to contact, how does it convey the information to them? Public relations professionals have several basic tools for this purpose.

Press Releases. A ***press release*** is an announcement or a news article, written by or for a travel company, that objectively describes something newsworthy, such as the appearance of a celebrity, the work of an employee who has made a special contribution to the community, the introduction of an innovative product, or the introduction of airline service to a destination. Press releases should be written in a journalistic style that maximizes the news value of the particular event. Many public relations departments, particularly in large companies, employ trained journalists for precisely these reasons. Most travel professionals learn to write an effective press release in a lively but simple narrative style that covers the "five Ws": who, what, where, when, and why.

Newspapers usually prefer articles that make liberal use of quotations, focus on the human side of a story, and emphasize the local impact of the subject under discussion. A well-written article includes the name of the company and all relevant information about its products and services, presented in a way that emulates what an unbiased reporter might write. A press release, after all, is a news story, not a paid advertisement.

The purpose of a press release is to make information available to the media in a form that the media can use. Even so, travel companies should try to make the media's job as simple as possible, by including with all press releases the date when the information should be published, the name of the person who prepared the article, and the telephone number or e-mail address at which the writer can be reached for questions or more information. They should be available in digital form (on disks) so they can be incorporated in a story or article by the media.

Press Conferences. A ***press conference*** is another means of disseminating information through the media about a special occasion or event, such as a new product launch or an award. At a press conference, a company makes a presentation or an announcement to invited members of the media and then answers their questions. Often, press conferences are used to announce upcoming events, in order to increase media attention (particularly broadcast) and customer awareness and curiosity. For example, a company may hold a press conference to announce that it will be sponsoring a travel fair and to encourage area residents to attend the event.

Press conferences can be expensive, partly because the conference itself is usually supplemented by complimentary press kits that are distributed to the members of the media. These kits usually contain a printed news release prepared by the supplier's public relations staff, a fact sheet, videotapes, photographs, and other information.

Staged Events. Travel companies and organizations may also choose to plan a **staged event** for members of the media, invited guests, and sometimes the general public in order to increase their visibility and develop goodwill in the community. The sponsored appearance of a celebrity, the showing of travel films, performances by musical and drama groups, and the staging of a food festival are examples of events that might well be covered by local news programs.

Because the reputation of the company and organizations depends on the quality of the staged event itself, careful planning is critical to the success of this type of public relations effort. All contingencies must be anticipated, from a celebrity's not arriving on time to a shortage of punch glasses. When properly conceived and executed, however, a special event can return a substantial measure of community goodwill and name recognition for the time and money expended. That is why special event coordinators are often hired.

Receptions. **Receptions** are designed for the purpose of promoting contact between travel companies and organizations and media representatives such as publishers, producers, editors, writers, and reporters. Thus, many of the same people who attend a press conference go to a reception, but the atmosphere is designed to be conducive to establishing contact between the supplier and the press, rather than conveying information. For that reason, receptions are usually held in luxury hotels or restaurants so that both the location and the complimentary food and drink will attract the media representatives, who will presumably react favorably toward the organization sponsoring the reception.

Familiarization Trips. Perhaps the most effective way to generate goodwill among the media is to make it easy for them to examine travel products firsthand. These subsidized (or all-expenses-paid) "fam trips" can, of course, be expensive to the sponsor. But the opportunity to influence the media directly can justify the cost. Convention and Visitors Bureaus, airlines opening service to a new city, and hotel chains opening a new property frequently use familiarization trips to generate publicity and awareness among the media. The return on investment in this public relations method may not be immediate or obvious. For instance, the agreement of a journalist to participate in a fam trip to a resort in Cancun does not constitute an agreement to write a favorable article about the resort. Nevertheless, media representatives do use familiarization trips as one method of evaluating travel products, and they usually pass these evaluations along to their readers or listeners.

It is important to note that fewer editors, writers, publishers, freelance journalists, and reporters are accepting free "fam trips" from travel companies and destinations. That is because accepting subsidized or all-expenses-paid trips gives the appearance (accurately or otherwise) that the fam trip invitees are being unduly influenced or "bought" by the host company or destination. Thus, many invitees pay all or most of the expense of participating in these trips.

SALES PROMOTION

Sales promotion is the third component of the communications mix, extending the impact of advertising to the point of sale. The way in which advertising, public relations, and sales promotion combine to form an overall communications program varies to suit a company's particular needs. In an effective program, each element of the mix enhances and supplements the other elements.

Sales promotion techniques are used to achieve four primary objectives:

- Motivating people to make an initial product purchase.
- Encouraging repeat sales.
- Maintaining overall customer loyalty.
- Maintaining product competitiveness.

Because every sales transaction involves at least two people, a buyer and a seller, sales promotion techniques can be directed at both. They provide specific, usually tangible incentives, both for the buyer to make the purchase and for the seller to close the sale. This section looks first at sales promotion strategies directed by suppliers or intermediaries toward their prospective customers, and then examines sales promotion efforts directed by suppliers toward the intermediaries who sell their products.

Customer-Oriented Sales Promotion

In a sense, customer-oriented sales promotion completes the work begun by the advertising or public relations campaign. If advertising paints the product picture with broad strokes designed to stimulate the imagination and pique the interest of prospective customers, then sales promotion attempts to stimulate action by those customers. Travel companies and organizations use several promotional strategies to encourage customers to purchase travel products.

Point-of-Purchase Displays. Most prospective customers respond positively to visual displays that picture travel products and destinations. How could a person who enters a travel agency in Detroit on a snowy winter day see a poster of a beach in the Caribbean and *not* think about a vacation, even if he came to make business travel plans? Most travel agencies use some or all of the following point-of-purchase displays:

* Brochures and other printed materials.
* Posters and photographs.
* Displays of handicrafts and souvenirs from travel destinations.
* Slide shows, videos, and compact discs (CDs).

Some of these materials are used for interior wall decorations or window displays; others appear in special stands and racks made especially for promotional materials. Attractive and highly visible displays of brochures, most of which are provided by travel suppliers, are prominently placed in most travel agencies. These brochures vary from a small leaflet describing a single hotel to a large catalog listing a company's entire range of products, such as those of American Express or Club Med. In most cases, the brochures are carefully designed and written and feature glossy photographs of glamorous travel products and destinations. Not only are brochures used by agents to show customers what products are available, but they have the added benefit of continuing the selling process after the customer takes them home.

Videotapes are an increasingly popular means of promoting travel destinations and products to customers. Some videos, because they are short and focused on a particular product, can be viewed by the customer at the travel agency. Others, such as videos and CDs that thoroughly examine many aspects of travel to a destination, are designed for home viewing. National tourist offices, major tour operators, and large cruise lines have led the move to this electronic sales promotion, which will become even more important in the future.

Often, a travel agency coordinates its point-of-purchase displays to emphasize a special promotion or event that is taking place. If one of its suppliers is offering a new package tour to Japan, for example, an agency may designate one week for a special promotion of the Japan tours. During that time, posters and displays will focus on Japan, videos will show customers what they would see on the tour, and agency personnel may even wear special pins or articles of clothing related to the Japanese theme. These visual displays help to create an atmosphere in which the customers will respond positively to the overall sales promotion effort.

Hilton, Diners Club, and American Airlines use tie-in promotions to increase business for all companies involved. (Courtesy of Hilton HHonors Worldwide)

Price Breaks and Special Discounts. In general, travel sellers find that reducing the price of a product increases its sales, all other things being equal. The art of promotional pricing is to use discounts to initially attract customers to products they will buy again at nondiscounted prices. Toward that end, suppliers often use promotional pricing to stimulate interest in a new or revitalized product or to attract new customers. Many cruise lines, for example, offer a substantial discount on the first season of cruises on a new ship.

Suppliers often use discounts to attract the business of students, retired people, and other groups for whom price is an important consideration when making a travel purchase. Discount pricing can also help overcome sales declines during slow travel periods.

One means by which travel suppliers have increased the scope of their promotional effectiveness is by using a ***tie-in*** between the purchase of widely distributed consumer products and discounts on travel products. A tie-in of this type is a promotional agreement between a travel company and a consumer goods company. For example, an airline may offer fare discounts to people who have purchased a certain brand of camera, stereo system, or luggage.

Free Travel Products. Customers often respond positively to an offer of a free product with the initial purchase of a nondiscounted product. Major hotel chains often use this strategy, offering an additional night free to a customer who has paid for a three-night stay, for example. Suppliers of different types of travel products sometimes agree to offer tie-ins involving free products. For example, customers may qualify to receive a free weekend car rental by renting a car for three weekdays and possessing a recent boarding pass from a particular airline.

Sweepstakes, Gifts, and Prizes. Sweepstakes are a popular way to attract the attention of new customers and keep regular customers interested by giving away free prizes, often expensive ones. By law, a person need not make a purchase to enter a sweepstakes, but many companies make entry automatic upon the purchase of a travel product. British Airways, for example, once offered the chance to win a Rolls-Royce to everyone who purchased a ticket to London within a defined period of time.

Many tour operators and cruise lines offer free gifts to customers who purchase their travel products. These gifts include tote bags and luggage, audio or videotapes, travel books, coffee mugs, and miscellaneous items of clothing. Sometimes companies offer free prizes to customers who are among the first to purchase a new or promotional product.

Loyalty Marketing. Ever since American Airlines introduced its AAdvantage frequent-flier plan, loyalty marketing has been an increasingly important part of sales promotion in the travel industry (see Figure 10–1). The goal of loyalty marketing is twofold: to attract new customers for the travel company and, more important, to keep established customers coming back.

These plans have several benefits to frequent travelers, including free air travel after accumulating a certain number of miles or credits and special ground services, such as preferential check-in and exclusive airport lounges. Most frequent-flier plans now have agreements with major hotel chains, cruise lines, and car rental companies, whereby members receive discounts on hotel rooms and car rentals while they collect additional credits on their airline frequent-flier plans.

Examples of Loyalty Marketers	
American Airlines	AAdvantage
Continental Airlines	One Pass
United Airlines	Mileage Plus

FIGURE 10–1 These types of programs offer a number of benefits, such as free air travel and preferential treatment. All these benefits are aimed at the frequent traveler, in the hopes of getting their business. This is why the programs are so popular with competing airlines.

After American Airlines' promotional breakthrough, all other major U.S. carriers and many international airlines introduced frequent-flier plans of their own. Smaller domestic airlines and many foreign airlines joined forces with the major carriers to offer frequent-flier bonuses as well. Many hotel chains and car rental companies have also initiated similar programs to encourage customer loyalty in a competitive market.

Currently, some airlines are creating partnerships that allow customers to earn mileage on one airline while traveling on another. Canadian Airlines and American Airlines are an example of this strategy. In addition, airlines are banding together to create a consortium that will honor the frequent traveler points/mileage accrued by customers on all members of the consortium. The star alliance, which includes Air Canada, Lufthansa, United, Scandinavia Air Lines, and Varig, is an example.

Finally, most frequent traveler programs offer newsletters as well as special prices and availability on their products and services and those of their partners.

Trade-Oriented Sales Promotion

For travel suppliers, an effective program of sales promotion must consider more than direct contact with customers. It should also consider the intermediaries who, in most instances, link the travel suppliers to their customers. An important part of the sales promotion strategy focuses on the intermediaries who actually sell or transfer the products and services to consumers. Trade-oriented sales sometimes are conducted for the following purposes:

* To generate enthusiasm for the supplier's products.
* To develop and maintain supplier loyalty among intermediaries.
* To provide intermediaries with materials and incentives to complete the sales process.

Suppliers direct two distinct types of sales promotions toward intermediaries. One encourages a high volume of sales by rewarding intermediaries when they reach a specific sales goal, and the other helps agents become more familiar with the travel products so they can sell them more effectively. The following discussion identifies some methods employed by travel suppliers to accomplish these two objectives.

Sales Incentives. Suppliers use several sales incentives to motivate intermediaries to sell more travel products. Suppliers may, for example, offer gifts of merchandise, tickets to concerts or other events, or free travel to intermediaries who reach supplier-set sales goals. Some car rental companies, for instance, offer intermediaries a free one-day car rental for each car rental contract they sell.

Some suppliers pay cash bonuses to intermediaries who sell a certain quantity of their products within a specified period. These bonuses may take the form of extra commissions on all products sold in excess of a certain sales volume. Or they may be ***overrides***, which are cash payments made to the agency above the standard commission rate.

The manager of a travel agency in Denver may, for example, receive a call from the sales promotion office of a major airline that wants to increase its share of the Denver-to-Los Angeles market. The agency is asked to increase its sale of seats on the airline by a certain amount. If it succeeds, the airline will give the agency an additional commission on the extra seats sold or provide an override.

Trade Shows, Parties, and Receptions. Suppliers can use a trade show as a forum for introducing new products, informing intermediaries of changes in established product lines, and generating wide-ranging enthusiasm for their products. Many suppliers hold parties or receptions for intermediaries at these trade shows. Regardless of the specific purpose of the show or reception, these events help increase the visibility of the suppliers' products. Because intermediaries' enthusiasm is such a critical element in the total sales effort, travel suppliers have found trade shows to be a key venue for sales promotion.

Familiarization Trips. The objective of familiarization trips offered to intermediaries is the same as for those designed for the media: to make it easy for participants to examine travel products firsthand, in order to produce a positive impression and generate goodwill. Intermediaries who visit destinations or properties, or experience cruises or airline service under these circumstances become more knowledgeable and familiar with the product and services and can become a more effective "sales force" for suppliers. In contrast to the media, who pay most of their own expenses for "fam trips," intermediaries' participation is usually complimentary or highly subsidized. And because fam trips are expensive, it is important to creatively and efficiently plan the participant's itinerary and carefully select who will be invited.

In the context of sales promotion, suppliers offer familiarization trips to intermediaries to increase their motivation to sell a product. Fam trips put intermediaries in a better position to describe the product to customers (because they have experienced it) and to make them aware of its features and benefits, based on their firsthand experience.

Sales Contests and Sweepstakes. Over the past few years, sales contests and sweepstakes have been used as a means of encouraging agents to sell more products. Usually the contests are simple to enter, since the completion of a certain number of bookings automatically makes the intermediary eligible to win sweepstakes prizes. The prizes may include expensive cars, vacations in exotic places, or large cash prizes, as well as a number of prizes of lesser value. Some suppliers run sweepstakes for their intermediaries in conjunction with contests aimed at travel customers. This gives them additional incentive to close the sale by encouraging customers to buy the products.

Whether directed toward the travel trade or the travel consumer, advertising, public relations, and sales promotion all have one purpose: setting up the sale of travel products. Selling, the focus of the next chapter, is the ultimate objective of the marketing process because it produces sales revenue and profit.

CHAPTER SUMMARY

* The communications mix is a key element in implementing an overall marketing strategy.
* Advertising disseminates information, develops positive attitudes, and encourages customers to inquire about products.

* Trade advertising provides detailed product information for sales professionals and suggestions (usually to intermediaries) for increasing sales.
* Consumer advertising appeals directly to the needs and desires of travel customers.
* The advertising message informs, influences attitudes, persuades, and elicits responses.
* Cooperative advertising involves a supplier and an intermediary jointly sponsoring advertising.
* Consumer research, the perception of benefits, and the psychology of buying all affect the nature of advertising messages.
* All advertising media have advantages and disadvantages.
* Public relations is achieved primarily through media attention to newsworthy events.
* Information about travel products in an article or a news story usually has more credibility with consumers than does advertising.
* Companies often do not have control over how the media use public relations materials.
* Good media coverage depends on a supplier knowing what is newsworthy, whom to contact with the information, and how to convey it.
* Sales promotion efforts seek to translate customer interest into sales and produce customer loyalty.
* Customer-oriented sales promotion enhances the work begun by the advertising campaign.
* Customer-oriented sales promotions include point-of-purchase displays, price breaks and special discounts, sweepstakes, free travel products and loyalty marketing.
* Trade-oriented sales promotion provides intermediaries with information to help them sell the product and with special incentives to encourage more sales.

KEY TERMS

communications mix
trade advertising
consumer advertising
cooperative advertising
direct mail
out-of-home media
directory advertising
press release
press conference
staged event
receptions
tie-in
overrides

DISCUSSION QUESTIONS

1. Explain the communications mix, and indicate its importance.
2. Describe the relationship between the three aspects of the communications mix.
3. Write a one-line advertising message for a specialized tour, and discuss the objectives of the message.
4. How would you select the media that should be used in an advertising campaign?
5. Why are advertising campaigns difficult to evaluate?
6. Describe the public relations tools a tour operator might use when it begins to offer tours.
7. Discuss the similarities and differences between sales promotion methods for consumers and intermediaries.

Setting Up the Sale

Name: ______________________________ Date: ______________

Directions: Answer these questions as you read the chapter. You will be able to use these answers to help you review the chapter.

1. What three activities make up the communications mix?

2. What are the three purposes of advertising?

3. What are the four basic steps in the process of advertising?

4. What is the difference between trade and consumer advertising?

5. How does cooperative advertising benefit both the supplier and the intermediary?

6. What are four basic goals for an advertising message?

7. Compare the advantages and disadvantages of magazine and newspaper advertising.

8. What are the advantages and disadvantages of television advertising?

9. What is direct-mail marketing?

10. How is directory advertising different from other types of advertising?

11. What are two ways to use the Internet for advertising?

12. What is the basic public relations goal?

13. What types of information do public relations professionals need to know?

14. What are five tools that can be used to improve public relations?

15. What is the difference between trade- and consumer-oriented sales promotions?

16. Describe five types of consumer-oriented sales promotions.

17. Describe four types of trade-oriented sales promotions.

Setting Up the Sale

Name: ______________________________ Date: ______________

ADVERTISING TO THE TRADE

Companies advertise differently to intermediaries than they do to leisure travelers, as the following advertisements demonstrate. Think about these differences as you answer the questions following each ad.

"TWA'S LAYAWAY PLAN"

Increase your commissions. Sell your clients a seven-day Hawaiian vacation starting at only $26 a month. When your clients use TWA's Getaway Credit Card, paying for a trip to Hawaii, Caribbean, Paris, or anywhere else TWA flies is no problem. Your clients can charge their airfare and even a Getaway Vacation and pay for them in easy-to-manage monthly installments. And with a TWA Getaway Credit Card as a separate line of credit, other charge cards remain open for additional vacation purchases.

Give your clients credit fast. If your clients don't already have a TWA Getaway Credit Card, it's a snap for them to obtain one. By calling TWA's exclusive number for travel agents, 1-800-821-7910, you will know whether they are approved for credit within one business day. Best of all, the TWA Getaway Credit Card is free. . . . Easy credit. Easy sale. The layaway plan that can earn you money.

1. What is the purpose of this advertisement?

2. What product advantages are stressed in the ad?

3. Describe a target market that TWA would want intermediaries to pursue with the product described in this ad.

4. List three key phrases from the ad that make it effective in influencing an intermediary.

"LOW RATES GUARANTEED"

Avis's low SuperValue Plus Weekly Rates are guaranteed. Guaranteed for all rentals through this year. So you can be assured the low rates you quote your clients today are the low rates they'll get tomorrow. *Guaranteed.*

And that's not all we guarantee. *"We'll make sure you get your commission promptly."*

SuperValue Plus Rates are available on a full range of low-mileage, professionally maintained GM and other fine cars. And Avis offers your clients everything from the economical Chevrolet Spectrum to the elegant Cadillac Sedan de Ville. Low rates guaranteed, quick commissions, and a wide selection of popular cars are just a few ways the employee-owners of Avis, Inc., are trying even harder than ever to make your job easier and more rewarding.

Call 1-800-555-2212 for more information on Avis's guaranteed low SuperValue Plus Weekly Rates. Or, using your automated system, enter /SI-RC SA in your booking.

>>FOR TRAVEL AGENTS ONLY: *"Meet the Fleet" rates for as little as $17 per weekend day (Call for details)*<<

1. What is the purpose of this advertisement?

2. What product advantages are stressed in the ad?

3. Describe a target market that Avis would want intermediaries to pursue with the product described in this ad.

4. List three key phrases from the ad that make it effective in influencing an intermediary.

"SPACE. THE FINAL FRONTIER ON A CRUISE SHIP TOO"

Your clients will like the way we conquered space. We give them much more of it. Consider: Our first ship, SEABOURN PRIDE, is a full 440 feet long by 63 feet wide with nine decks. But our passenger list is small. Only 212. Comparably sized ships carry closer to 400. This means your clients enjoy suites—all on the outside with a 5-foot-wide viewing window. Sitting area. Large bath. And, yes, a walk-in closet. They dine when they want and with whom they want in our "open-seating" restaurant. And no gratuities are expected. Or accepted. Seabourn Cruise Line. Let your clients explore space. And all the advantages that go with it. *Please send me more information. . . .*

1. What is the purpose of this advertisement?

2. What product advantages are stressed in the ad?

3. Describe a target market that Seabourn would want intermediaries to pursue with the product described in this ad.

4. List three key phrases from the ad that make it effective in influencing an intermediary.

Using Personal Selling Techniques

OBJECTIVES

When you have completed this chapter, you should be able to:

* Define personal selling and explain why travel products and services require this sales technique.
* Compare order taking with creative personal selling.
* Give examples of in-house sales representatives and outside sales representatives.
* Identify the basic steps of personal selling.
* Describe techniques used to gather information from the customer.
* Differentiate between open probes and limited-response probes.
* List the six questions used to qualify the customer.
* Explain the importance of turning features into benefits when making sales recommendations.
* Identify techniques for recognizing how and when to close a sale.
* Understand the important role of sales proposals and sales presentations in travel sales.
* List additional aspects of personal selling essential for success in group and corporate sales.

It is nine o'clock on Monday morning—the beginning of another busy workweek. In offices throughout a major metropolitan area on the west coast, people are settling into their jobs.

At a midsize travel agency in a suburban mall, Linnea Borg is putting the finishing touches on a customized itinerary for a new customer. The customer, an affluent retired gentleman, has purchased an expensive trek through exotic Tibet. Linnea is pleased with her work on this trip. Although it took a good deal of time to make the complicated arrangements, she feels she has helped her customer with his dream of an adventure in a faraway place. After several years as a travel agent, she has developed the ability to quickly size up clients and translate their ideas and desires into appropriate, tangible travel plans.

Meanwhile, at the convention center downtown, Tim Parensky is making a presentation to corporate travel planners attending a regional conference. Tim, who works for the corporate sales department of a major hotel chain, is informing the planners about his company's new executive suites and its frequent-guest plan for business travelers. Tim's main responsibility is to boost the hotel chain's corporate business. In addition to keeping travel planners up-to-date on all of the hotel chain's products and services, Tim makes sure that booking procedures are customer friendly and run smoothly.

What do these two professionals have in common? They sell travel products. The companies they work for—a midsize travel agency and a hotel chain—have carefully positioned themselves in the marketplace and developed marketing strategies. Time and money have been spent on advertising and promotion. However, if their travel products and services are not purchased, all of the preceding marketing efforts will have been in vain. Consequently, effective personal selling is a critical element in the success of the entire marketing process.

Both of these sales representatives are involved in personal selling. They sell travel products and services—either face-to-face or on the telephone—on behalf of suppliers and intermediaries. (Photograph by Michael Dzamen)

PERSONAL SELLING DEFINED

Because of the unique characteristics of travel products—especially their intangible and perishable nature—customers usually depend on the assistance of travel sales professionals. A flight on an airplane, a stay at a hotel, a trip to Europe, or a weekend at a resort can't be selected from a convenience-store shelf or inspected in a showroom. Potential buyers must, therefore, rely on the expertise of salespeople when purchasing travel products or services.

Travel sales often result from the personal selling process. Personal selling is defined as sales resulting from personal interaction between buyers and sellers, either face-to-face or by telephone. It ranges from order taking to creative selling. In order taking, the salesperson processes routine requests from customers for travel products and services. Order taking occurs when customers are already familiar with travel products and services and know exactly (or nearly so) what they want to purchase.

Creative selling, on the other hand, is more complicated. Prospective customers are often unfamiliar with the travel products available and may have only a vague idea of where they want to travel. In creative selling, the salesperson must determine the needs of potential customers, recommended appropriate travel products, and motivate customers to buy them.

Personal selling is a powerful element of the promotional mix. Despite the millions of dollars spent for advertising and sales promotion, personal selling is usually superior in converting demand for travel products and services into actual purchases because its message can be tailored to individual customers and it allows for immediate feedback and reaction. Person-to-person communication is a potent and persuasive sales technique.

Have you ever heard friends and acquaintances joke about their lack of resistance to sales presentations? For many people, selling seems to be a mystical art. They suspect that sellers work some kind of magic to induce them to buy every product they see. Although some salespeople may possess a certain charisma that charms buyers, most successful salespeople rely on their training and experience, along with an understanding of their customer's needs. Through study and hard work, they have developed a thorough knowledge of the products they sell, the benefits they can produce, and they have learned a variety of specific sales techniques.

In presenting their travel products to buyers, successful salespeople follow a structure that is designed to encourage progress toward a sale. This structure consists of a minimum of three basic steps: gathering information from the customer, making recommendations, and closing the sale. Although the steps are discussed separately, in reality they often overlap.

These three steps are common to virtually all personal selling, which can be divided into two basic types: ***inside (in-house) sales*** and ***outside sales.*** The terms refer to where the selling generally takes place, although this can sometimes be misleading.

In the travel industry, much selling is done by in-house salespeople. For example, the agents sitting behind the desks at a travel agency, the reservations agents answering an airline's toll-free phone line, and the person behind the counter renting cars at an airport are all examples of in-house sales staff. All depend on the inquiries of customers to initiate the selling process.

Outside sales are used in the travel industry primarily to sell travel products to large groups, organizations, or businesses, which may sometimes be a part of the travel industry as well. Large travel agencies use outside salespeople to sell their services to companies booking business travel, for example. Airlines use them to sell their products to tour operators, and some tour operators use them to sell to travel clubs. Resorts and attractions use outside sales representatives as well, often to follow up leads from promotional activities, consumer travel, or travel trade shows. Destination marketing organizations (including state travel offices and convention and visitors' bureaus) use outside sales to persuade tour operators, associations, government agencies, and corporations to visit their destination or hold conferences, meetings, or events there. In most cases, outside sales representatives initiate the selling process, including follow-up leads provided by advertising.

But for both outside and in-house sales—whether they are conducted in person or over the phone, on behalf of a supplier, destination, or an intermediary, to an individual, group, or business—three steps lie at the heart of the personal selling process (see Figure 11–1). In this chapter, they are explained in the context of the most typical travel transaction: creative personal selling to an individual customer.

BASIC STEPS OF PERSONAL SELLING

As you read about the steps of personal selling, it is important to keep in mind another element of successful marketing. Underlying the methods and techniques of selling should be a genuine desire to serve the customer and provide value for the dollar spent. In a crowded and competitive marketplace, salespeople who can deliver high levels of service and value have a distinct advantage. This has been a recurring theme of this text because it is important to the marketing process, and particularly crucial for personal selling in the travel industry, where companies often compete with each other to sell a nearly identical collection of travel products.

Gathering Information from the Customer

Imagine this situation. A young man with two small children enters a travel agency. An agent greets him pleasantly and introduces herself. The man says

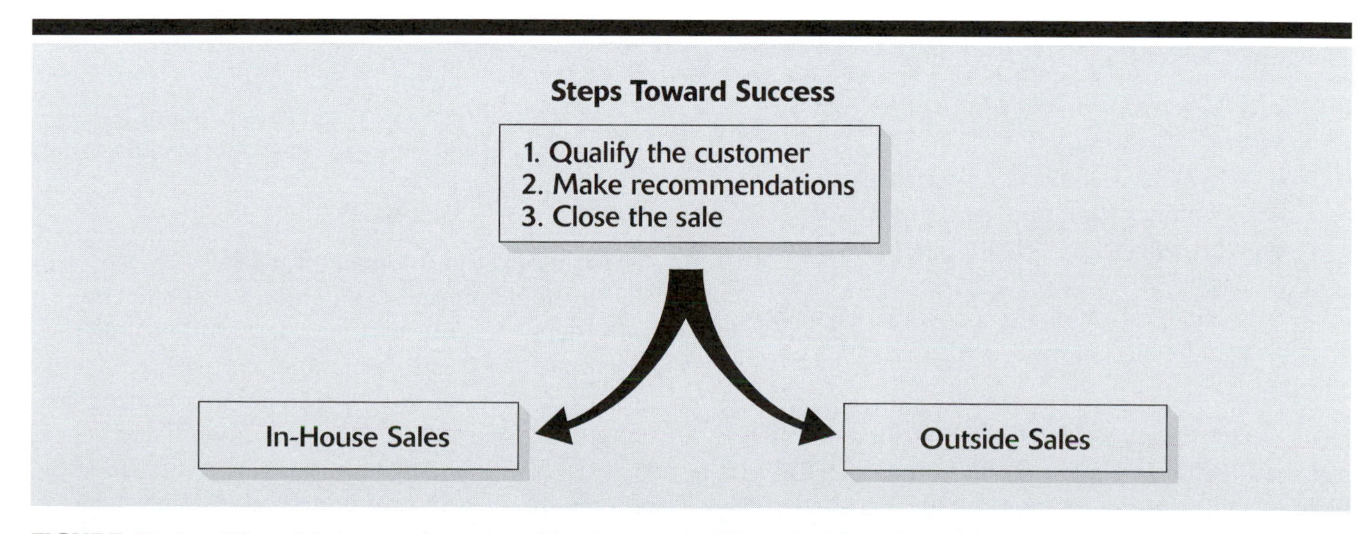

FIGURE 11–1 Although in-house sales and outside sales occur in different locations, they require the same basic steps.

that he wants help planning a trip to Mexico. Assuming that the man is thinking of a family vacation, the agent immediately begins digging through her files for brochures on family-oriented destinations in Mexico. But the man stops her to explain that he is a professor who needs to travel by himself to a remote archaeological site.

Or consider this situation. A woman telephones an airline reservations number and asks how much it costs to fly to Phoenix. The reservations agent immediately replies, "Our lowest fare is $99." The woman says, "Great! I'd like to book a flight." However, in the process of executing the reservation, the agent discovers that the woman won't be traveling until October, and the $99 rate to Phoenix applies only to summer travel.

In both situations, the salespeople have wasted time with irrelevant information and perhaps have embarrassed or disappointed potential clients. They have gotten off to a false start by omitting the first step of personal selling: qualifying the customer. ***Qualifying the customer*** means finding out as much as possible about the customer's preferences and needs before providing information about or recommending specific travel products and services. Like a physician diagnosing a patient's illness, salespeople determine the customer's needs by skillfully asking a series of questions and paying close attention to the answers.

Using the Six Questions. To begin helping the customer, the sales representative needs to ask some basic questions. Sometimes potential customers will volunteer this information right away. If not, the salesperson must ask for it. The following questions (usually known as the "six questions") are commonly used by sales representatives in the travel industry.

- Where would you like to go? (destination)
- When? (timing)
- Why? (needs, benefits, experiences)
- How long? (duration)
- Who will be going? How many? (number in party)
- What level of service do you prefer? (Price, value, expectations)

Although salespeople want to find answers to the basic questions as quickly as possible, they should not ask them brusquely or hurriedly. Even over the telephone, questions should not be asked in such rapid-fire order that customers feel rushed.

Phrasing Questions. In addition to gaining information, travel sales representatives benefit in several other ways from asking basic questions. The questions get the conversation started and provide a logical direction. By asking questions, the salespeople can control the conversation, not in the sense of dominating it but in the sense of leading it toward a successful conclusion.

When qualifying customers, salespeople can control the conversation by phrasing, or asking, the questions in a certain way. Questions can be of two basic types: open-ended questions and limited-response questions. Because salespeople are attempting to uncover client needs, the questions used in personal selling are often referred to as probes.

An open-ended question, or ***open probe***, encourages the client to respond freely. Salespeople use this type of question when they want to get more information about customers' attitudes, experiences, and needs. Customers who merely say "I want to go someplace warm on my vacation" need to be drawn out to say more. Examples of open probes include:

- What did you have in mind?
- What did you like about your last vacation?
- Why do you think you might enjoy a cruise?
- Tell me about the kinds of service you prefer.
- How have you arranged for your business travel in the past?

A ***limited-response probe*** is more specific and is intended to restrict the customer's response to yes or no or some other short response. Salespeople use this type of question when they want to obtain precise information, move the conversation along, or help customers narrow down their choices. Examples of limited-response probes include:

- Do you require a rental car?
- How long do you plan to stay in Seattle?
- Would you prefer to leave on a weekday or on the weekend?

Asking about the Budget. In general, sales representatives should postpone questions regarding budget until later in the conversation. For one thing, until they feel comfortable, customers may not wish to discuss how much they are willing to spend. For another, customers may not know how much a trip is likely to cost. They need to gain a better understanding of the value of travel products in relation to their benefits. By locking into a price category too early in the selling process, customers may not learn about the products that are best suited to their needs.

Listening. The critical companion to effective questioning is effective listening. Research indicates that most people are not good listeners. Travel sales professionals must become good listeners in order to accurately assess customers' needs and preferences.

Improving listening skills is largely a matter of better concentration. In a personal selling situation, salespeople can do several things to improve their concentration. To begin with, they should try to conduct the conversation in an environment free of distractions and interruptions. Taking notes can help increase concentration while also providing a record of a conversation. When speaking to customers on the telephone, sales agents should not be sorting through their mail or doodling on a notepad. Good listening requires a concentrated focus on the words of the customer.

Salespeople can also do several things to indicate that they are listening. They can give occasional verbal signals such as "I see" or "I know what you mean." Paraphrasing, or repeating what a customer has said but in slightly different words, can be reassuring. A face-to-face conversation allows for nonverbal signals such as nodding, smiling, and maintaining eye contact. Of course, in either a telephone or a face-to-face conversation, salespeople should never interrupt a customer or jump to conclusions before the client has finished speaking.

Leisure/Business Differences. In order to effectively qualify customers, sales representatives usually need to spend more time questioning leisure travel customers than they do business travelers (see Figure 11-2). Because leisure travel is discretionary, the motivations underlying it are more complicated and varied than are those of business travel. As you already know, vacationers travel to satisfy a variety of psychological, emotional, and intellectual needs. Uncovering these motivations requires the salesperson to ask probing questions and interpret the responses. Furthermore, in contrast to business travelers who must be at a specific destination at a specific time, leisure travelers have more choices of where and when they want to travel.

This is not to say, however, that salespeople should limit their questioning of business travelers. The needs of business travelers may be more specific and demanding in some respects. They may need to know, for example, what specific business services a hotel offers or which hotel is most convenient to their business meeting. When companies restrict the travel budget of employees, sales representatives may have to work harder to locate suitable transportation and accommodations. By qualifying business customers, travel salespersons can also reveal opportunities to sell them products for leisure travel. In fact, a growing trend among travel companies is to develop the leisure side of their corporate business, including adding on a short minivacation before or after a business meeting or appointment.

Making Recommendations

The heart of the personal selling process is making recommendations. Sales representatives must apply principles of psychology, as well as knowledge about products, in making recommendations. They think about the client's underlying motivation for travel and consider what type of traveler the client is likely to be. Using information from computer systems, print sources, colleagues, and their own experience, salespeople must then identify the products and services that match their analysis of the client's needs.

Acknowledging Needs. After the complete picture of the client's needs has emerged, travel sales professionals should verify that they understand those needs correctly. They can do this by paraphrasing what the customer has said and using a limited-response probe. For example, a hotel reservations agent might say, "So, you'll be in Milwaukee from March 7 to March 11, and you'd like a room to accommodate two adults and three children. Is that correct?" Or a travel agent might say, "Let's see, you want to travel with a group, but you also want free time to pursue your own interests. Am I getting that right?" By acknowledging needs, salespeople demonstrate that they understand what is wanted. Customers, in turn, then feel more confident that what the salesperson recommends will meet their needs.

Introducing Features and Benefits. Every product or service possesses features. A feature is a specific aspect of the product or service that is always associated with it—it is an inherent characteristic. For instance, the features of a major hotel specializing in business travel might include:

- Suites with living rooms for business meetings.
- Free daily newspapers.

Leisure Traveler	Business Traveler
Q: Where would you like to go? A: Somewhere warm.	Q: Where do you need to go? A: New York.
Q: Do you have a specific destination in mind? A: Place with beaches, palm trees, white sand, casinos.	Q: When would you like to be there? A: I will need to leave here Wednesday evening during the second week in December. I need a flight back here that Friday evening.
Q: When would you like to go? A: I have one week available. I'd like to go during the winter, probably January.	Q: Will anyone be accompanying you? A: No.
Q: It's least expensive in December. Especially if you leave on a weekday and return on a weekday. Is there a week in December during which you would like to go? A: Let's make it during the first week in December. I'll leave on Thursday and return the following Thursday. If I change my mind, I'll call you.	Q: In terms of cost, there are two choices. Will you have a preference? A: Of course my company would prefer the cheaper rate, but it is more important that I get there on time and return on Friday by 8:00 p.m.
Q: Who will be going with you? A: It will be my wife and I and our two children. We'll need a place where we can each have our privacy. And maybe a day camp for the kids.	Q: Can you think of any special accommodations or services you'll need? A: A room with a fax and computer connection.
Q: How much money would you care to spend on this vacation? A: Of course as little as possible, but between $2,000 and $2,500.	Q: Would you like to stay on the line while I work on this? A: No, but could you call me back?
Q: Would you like to stay on the line while I work on this? A: No, but could you call me back?	Q: When can I call you back with some suggestions? A: Tomorrow at 10:00 in the morning.
Q: When can I call you back with some suggestions? A: Tomorrow at 10:00 in the morning.	

FIGURE 11–2 Leisure travelers have more choices than business travelers. But it takes a lot of effort on the part of a travel agent to satisfy any traveler.

- Express check-in and checkout.
- Guaranteed corporate rate.
- Full-service business center, including personal computers, a fax machine, and a business library.
- Exercise room and swimming pool.
- Cocktail lounge with nightly entertainment.

Salespeople should point out the features of travel products to persuade travelers to buy them. However, it is not enough to simply present information. On the basis of their understanding of the client's needs, travel sales professionals must go on to translate those features into benefits. (For similar reasons, travel marketers translate features into benefits in the course of establishing a product position; see Chapter 4.) A benefit is the value the client seeks to derive from a feature. If a business traveler has expressed dissatisfaction with conducting meetings in crowded, noisy restaurants, then a hotel room with comfortable space for business meetings is a benefit. If a traveler exercises regularly, then a hotel with exercise facilities will provide a benefit. Of course, features provide different benefits to different people, and sometimes features produce no important benefits. For example, when talking to a family traveling with children, a salesperson is not

A conference center meeting room is an important, attractive feature. (Courtesy of International Conference Resorts)

likely to emphasize the hotel's nightly entertainment in the cocktail lounge.

The ability to translate features into benefits is extremely important in personal selling. Sales representatives who help a customer understand a product's benefits make the product seem meaningful and distinct from similar products, (and often more personal), and are, therefore, more likely to achieve a sale.

Emphasizing Benefits. Salespeople use several techniques to emphasize benefits to their customers. One technique is to incorporate a client's earlier statements into the recommendation. For example, a travel agent might say, "You mentioned that on your last tour you didn't have enough time to go shopping. I'm recommending this tour, which has more free time built into the schedule." Another remark might be, "I'd like to make a reservation for you at the Marriott. It's located downtown within walking distance of your convention." This technique also has the advantage of showing clients that the salesperson is listening to them and treating them as individuals with unique needs.

In a face-to-face situation, sales representatives can use brochures to make the benefits seem more tangible. The salesperson reviews the brochure with the customer, pointing out interesting features and relating them to the customer's needs. (Note: the salesperson—not the customer—holds the brochure. When customers have control of the brochure, they can become more involved in leafing through the literature than in listening to a recommendation.) To personalize the brochure, the salesperson can underline, draw circles around, or place asterisks by features that are potential benefits to the customer. No more than two pieces of literature should be shown at a time. Otherwise, the customer may become distracted and unable to make a decision.

Sometimes salespeople can refer to a third party to support their recommendations. An agent might say, "Mr. and Mrs. Healy have just returned from a similar trip to Scandinavia, and they really enjoyed it," or "The Hillcrest Company has always been satisfied with the travel arrangements we've made for them." Of course, the salesperson should have permission to use the recommendation of the third party, and the third party should be someone with similar interests, preferably someone the client knows and respects. Sometimes an anonymous recommendation is equally effective, such as, "We've booked a half-dozen couples on that cruise, and they all had fun."

Sales representatives should always try to convert travel jargon into everyday language. Customers can't recognize the benefits of curbside check-in, round-trip transfers, and dine-around plans, if they don't know what the terms mean.

Recapping. After presenting the recommendation and discussing it with the customer, the sales representative summarizes the benefits of the product to the customer. ***Recapping*** gives the customer an opportunity to comment on or ask questions about any of the details of the conversation and helps to ensure mutual understanding. If the client seems satisfied with a travel product's benefits, then the salesperson can begin to close the sale. Any disagreements or objections revealed during the recap process, however, must be resolved before the salesperson can proceed with the booking.

Overcoming Resistance. A customer may resist a sales recommendation for a variety of reasons. Salespeople should not panic or become defensive when this happens. Instead, they should react positively by trying to determine the reason for the resistance and then applying an appropriate technique to overcome it.

Sometimes customers resist a recommendation because of a misunderstanding resulting from poor communication. This type of resistance might begin with a customer saying, "Well, I'm not sure about . . ." or "I don't get what you mean by. . . ." When they hear such phrases, salespeople should probe to find the obstacle and then offer appropriate clarification.

After listening to a sales presentation, customers may point out a drawback or an objectionable feature. In this case, a salesperson might agree with the objection as if it were the only one standing in the way of the sale and then go on to try to convert the drawback into a benefit. For example:

> **Customer:** This tour seems to spend too much time in London and Paris.
> **Salesperson:** The tour does spend more time in those cities, but that's so you can visit all the sights you want to see. It also means you won't be packing and unpacking every day.

Another type of resistance is skepticism. The customer questions or doubts that a product will provide all the benefits the salesperson suggests. Skepticism is best countered by making a proof statement citing an additional source, such as an impartial third party, a magazine article, or personal experience. In the long run, the best method of countering skepticism is to build a reputation for providing outstanding service, thereby increasing customers' confidence and trust.

A final type of resistance is indifference, or a customer's lack of interest in a recommendation. In this case, a customer's needs or intent in a travel product have been misjudged. More probing is needed to uncover what the customer really desires.

Upgrading. Another element of the recommendation process is upgrading. ***Upgrading (upselling)*** occurs when a sales representative recommends a more expensive product than the one currently being considered by a customer. Salespeople recommend upgrades when they believe that a more expensive product offers more value to the customer, even though it costs more.

Consider this example of upgrading. A traveler who wishes to purchase a three-week grand tour of Europe is mainly interested in visiting the historical and cultural attractions of its major cities. In most instances, these attractions are located in the downtown areas. Two tours are appropriate and offer virtually the same itineraries. The customer chooses the less expensive tour. But her travel agent knows that the hotels on that tour are generally located in suburban areas or near airports. The hotels on the other tour, however, are within walking distance of most of the attractions the customer wishes to see. Believing that she would not want to waste time and cab fare in each city, the agent recommends the more expensive tour as providing more benefits and better value.

Marketing Impressions

WESTERN LEISURE COMPANY PROFILE

Western Leisure, Inc. was established in Salt Lake City, Utah in 1979, and is the oldest full-service receptive operator in the Intermountain West. Originally formed as a convention service company, Western Leisure now also provides a complete range of personalized group travel services including: meeting service, tour planning assistance, incentive programs, bilingual and step-on guides, and tour programs of varying lengths.

Western Leisure's Mission Statement is as follows:

"We create, package, and manage customized travel programs for the hospitality industry. In providing these services we will always strive to:

1. Meet and exceed the customer's expectations,
2. Provide innovative ways to offer the best possible product,
3. Make customers feel welcome in a foreign place,
4. Treat customers as our guests and exemplify Western Hospitality, and
5. Provide superior service at a fair price."

For the first two years, Western Leisure concentrated entirely on convention services. Then, says Keith Griffall, President and CEO, "Our business evolved, and we began to customize inbound tours for operators bringing groups into the western United States. We acquired a much broader range of customers, and our business began to grow dramatically." In 1985, the company's market mix expanded to include international tour operators.

"We began by serving the European market," says Griffall, "but it quickly became clear that it would be easier for us to gain a share of the Japanese market than to compete against large and well-established receptive operators for Europe." The Japanese business now comprises more than a third of Western Leisure's gross income; over the past five years, it has grown faster than any other department in the company.

The other dominant market, Inbound Domestic Tours, has benefitted from Western Leisure's sharp focus on territory. "We concentrate on a very specific area," says Griffall. "We specialize in tours of the Western United States including the Rocky Mountains, Southwest Desert, California, and the Pacific Northwest. And we really know our territory—we are up-to-date on new roads and hotels, fine dining, top evening entertainment and all the other components that add up to create an enjoyable, successful tour. When we operate a tour, the customer doesn't have to worry about any of the details."

Rather than selling directly to the public, Western Leisure wholesales tours to other operators, who then sell the tours under their own companies' names. This strategy, called 'private branding,' allows the purchasers to provide their customers with a wider range of products than they could produce on their own. The private branding of tours is especially useful as more and more groups demand tours that are specific to their members' particular needs. "We deal with a lot of tour operators who have preformed groups," says Griffall, "and the customers in these groups are smart and sophisticated. They know exactly what they like, and are open to unusual and rewarding experiences. These groups are the fastest growing segment of the domestic tour market." To accommodate the demand, Western Leisure's latest product line of Active Adventure Tours, called 'Pathfinder Vacations,' is a way for small tour groups to experience and explore the West by foot, horseback, raft, jeep, boat, and minicoach.

Western Leisure's international customers demand even more variety in their products. In addition to custom group tours, they require FIT products, adventure tours, and incentive programs, and the company has carved its own niche in the market by providing these services.

Western Leisure's marketing is aimed directly at the travel professional through direct mailings of factual brochures, as well as associations and trade shows. "We do produce a catalog for our Asian products," says Griffall, "and we provide operational support and detailed written information for all the tours we sell."

In closing, Griffall says, "This is an exciting time to be in the travel industry. Challenges and rewards are greater now than they ever have been before. As a knowledge-based company, Western Leisure sells its expertise and creativity, and I can't think of a more dynamic marketplace in the world."

Selling Additional Products. Opportunities should not be overlooked to sell more products and services than customers originally intended to buy. Of course, travel sales professionals should attempt to do so only when it would truly benefit customers and when the additions are compatible with their customers' budgets. For example, a tour operator sales representative might suggest that a retired couple would enjoy a tour of Scotland and Ireland after completing their tour of Britain. Requests that seem like routine orders for travel products can be turned into sales opportunities by creative personal selling. For instance, an enterprising airline reservations agent might suggest that a person calling to book a flight also reserve a rental car and hotel room through the airline.

Closing the Sale

A man telephones the reservations department of a major cruise line. He explains to the agent that he has a one-week vacation coming up, and he would like to take a cruise. The caller says he must leave on August 7 and return no later than August 14. He has a budget of $2,000 for the trip.

After asking several questions, the agent discovers that the man's parents were Greek immigrants. He then suggests that the man might enjoy the company's Aegean Holiday, a cruise from a port near Athens to several Greek islands. The man likes his suggestion. The sales agent then proceeds to locate a cruise that fits his time schedule and determines that minimum accommodations on the cruise are within his budget.

In response to this information, the caller says, "Great! Thanks for the information!"

"It's been a pleasure," replies the agent. "I'll send you our Aegean Holiday brochure and my business card. Let me know when I can be of service."

This sales agent has made one of the great mistakes of personal selling. He had an opportunity to ***close the sale***—to get a commitment from the customer—but he let it slip by. He should have said, "Minimum-rate cabins on our cruises fill up first. Why don't I make a reservation for you so you don't miss out? All I need is a credit-card number." But he didn't, and now the man may or may not call back, or he may even decide to book with another cruise line. Although sales representatives must be friendly and helpful, they cannot simply dispense information all day long. If the company is to remain in business, travel sales professionals must close sales!

When to Close. Knowing when to offer to close a sale can be a dilemma. Salespeople do not want to close too soon for fear of appearing pushy or high-pressure. On the other hand, if they delay too long, they might lose the sale.

For help in deciding when to close, sales representatives need to learn to recognize signals from customers that indicate their readiness to make a commitment. These include comments such as, "Well, this sounds like what I'm looking for," or "Will I need a passport?" In a face-to-face situation, salespeople can observe a customer's physical actions and facial expressions. Touching a brochure, sitting in a relaxed position, or smiling can indicate a willingness to buy. By contrast, customers who remain silent, reread a brochure closely, sit with arms folded and fists clenched, or frown, are probably not ready to buy.

Salespeople should be constantly on the lookout for buying signals. The opportunity to close can come surprisingly early in the interview. Customers who travel frequently and are confident about their travel plans may even close the sale themselves. They might say, for example, "That's all I need to know. You can sign me up." Indecisive customers may even appreciate being nudged toward a decision, since extending the conversation may make them even more uncertain.

A sales representative should not feel timid about asking for the sale. After all, in most cases of selling travel to individuals, customers initiate the contact, meaning they must already have some interest in traveling. Realizing this, salespeople should not feel they are twisting people's arms to buy travel products.

How to Close. Knowing how to close a sale can be perplexing. In general, closing begins by summarizing the product's benefits to the customer. The summary provides reasons to commit. Then the salesperson puts forth an action plan. The action plan is a concrete way customers can demonstrate their commitment, such as signing a contract or writing out a check for a deposit. When the salesperson has a commitment from the customer, the sale is "nailed down." The salesperson can then go on to provide details about deposits or payments, picking up tickets, applying for a passport, and so forth. At this point, the salesperson is also writing up the order, being extremely careful to record all information accurately.

Types of Closings. Sales closings can be classified according to the various techniques used to execute

Knowing when and how to close a sale is a critical skill for those selling travel products. (Photograph by Michael Dzamen)

them. Customer behavior during the selling process may influence the type of closing technique selected for use by the salesperson.

In the direct approach, the salesperson asks the customer if he or she is ready to purchase—"Shall we go ahead and reserve space?" This type of closing is used when the presentation has been logical and direct and little resistance has been encountered. Self-confident customers usually appreciate the direct approach.

Another type of closing is the assumptive approach. The salesperson acts as if the sale has been made—"I'll just write up this reservation for you." This approach can be useful with an indecisive client.

When the sales conversation has gone on for a while, the selling agent might begin closing the sale with the summative approach. The sales agent would begin by summarizing past points of agreement—"Okay. Now we've agreed that. . . ." The summative approach reinforces areas of harmony between the sales agent and customer and reviews facts that may otherwise have been forgotten or misunderstood.

Finally, the sales representative might offer an incentive to close the sale—"If you reserve the convention center this week, you'll be able to take advantage of a 10 percent discount." Whether or not customers decide to buy, they should always be informed of deadlines for special rates. If they should return later to buy, they could be disappointed or upset to learn of a missed opportunity to save money.

When prospective customers balk, salespeople can use open probes to determine the nature of the obstacle, or they can offer to do something—get more information or work out an estimate, for example—to keep the sales possibility alive. They might suggest making tentative arrangements with no obligation on the part of the customer to follow through. This technique should be used sparingly, however, because conditional arrangements are sometimes difficult to undo and may just waste a salesperson's time.

Sometimes customers have legitimate reasons not to commit to a purchase, such as the need to consult a spouse. When this happens, salespersons should make arrangements to contact the prospective client later, not wait for them to "get back" to them.

What to Do When the Closing Fails. The closing fails when a customer refuses to make a commitment. But this does not mean the sales representative will never sell to that person. It just means that this particular opportunity for a transaction has been missed. Salespeople should not take failure to close a sale as a personal insult but instead should learn from the experience and look forward to the next opportunity to make a sale. The conversation should end on a pleasant note, with the salesperson thanking the customer and inviting him or her to call again. Whatever happens, the salesperson should never be the first one to hang up, end the presentation, or walk away.

ADDITIONAL ASPECTS OF GROUP AND CORPORATE SELLING

Although selling to individuals is the most common form of travel sales, the industry offers many other sales career opportunities as well. Here are a few examples of group and corporate sales efforts:

- A sales executive of a car rental company negotiating a deal with a major airline to offer a fly/drive package to the traveling public.
- A salesperson for a midsize travel agency trying to convince a local business to let her agency handle all of its business travel arrangements.
- A sales representative from an incentive travel company trying to persuade a corporation to establish an incentive travel program for its employees.
- Representatives from airlines, hotels, and destination marketing organizations attempting to sell their products and services to tour operators so they will be included as tour components.
- A salesperson for a major hotel chain offering a discounted rate to the corporate travel director

for a client company, tied to the annual dollar volume of business booked by that company.

Selling to groups and businesses is often more complicated and time consuming than selling to individuals, sometimes requiring additional steps in the personal selling process. These include prospecting for customers, writing sales proposals, and making sales presentations.

Prospecting

In general, sales representatives selling to groups or businesses, on behalf of either a supplier or an intermediary, have more responsibility to initiate the sales transaction than do those selling to individuals. Like miners searching for gold, these salespeople must conduct research to identify likely customers. ***Prospecting*** is the process of looking for new customers. It is an ongoing process; even successful salespeople must continue to prospect as old customers move away, go out of business, switch to the competitor, or develop different needs. As a company grows, new customers must be found to develop new sources of revenue.

Prospecting consists of two main steps. The first step is simply gathering leads, or the names of individuals, groups, and businesses that might be interested in purchasing travel products and services. This is the "suspect" group.

Many methods turn up possible sales leads. One way is to ask satisfied customers to suggest names of people they know who might also be interested in purchasing the product or service. Known as the "endless chain," this method could theoretically go on forever as one customer recommends another customer, who in turn recommends another, and so on. Another way of gathering leads is to ask satisfied customers to provide a referral. This goes beyond simply suggesting a name, because the customer does something such as writing a letter of recommendation or setting up a meeting. A third way is to ask for help from influential people—friends and acquaintances in a position to influence the travel decisions of others. Additional methods of gathering names include mail-in or telephone responses to advertising and promotions, business directories and other listings, canvassing by telephone or in person, and searching on the Internet using key words that will locate the companies, organizations, or associations that fit your customer profile.

The second step of prospecting is to narrow down the suspect group. Salespeople try to prioritize and focus by determining which leads are most promising. These leads are the "prospect" group of a high-potential sales target. Sales representatives also follow up on leads by making cold calls, telephoning for an appointment, sending a letter and making a follow-up telephone call, or by employing a combination of these techniques.

Cold Calls. ***Cold calls*** are made when salespeople arrive unannounced at the office of a prospect with whom they have had no previous interaction. They take a risk that the person who makes travel decisions will not have time or be willing to talk with them. Nevertheless, many salespeople feel that by actually being on the premises rather than phoning they have a better chance of getting to talk to their prospect. They believe that people are less likely to say no face-to-face than over the telephone. Cold calls to small and medium-sized companies, where decisionmakers are more accessible, are generally more productive than cold calls to large companies or organizations.

The first obstacle in making a cold call is usually the receptionist or staff assistant. When a receptionist (whose job includes screening out salespeople) inquires about the purpose of the call, sales representatives should not respond that they want to sell someone something. Instead, they should make a benefit statement such as, "I'd like to discuss a plan to save your company 10 percent in travel costs and reward top customers."

Once past the "first obstacle," the salesperson should strive for a "tell-me" rather than a "sell-you" session. In other words, salespeople should discover as much as possible about the company's travel needs so that they can respond immediately or return with a detailed recommendation for meeting those needs. Of course, salespeople who have researched their prospect and can demonstrate that they already know a great deal about the company are more likely to be well received.

Telephoning for an Appointment. Telephoning for an appointment has several advantages over cold calls. For one thing, the salesperson can make many more contacts in the same amount of time. Also, the prospect may view a telephone call as less of an intrusion and, therefore, be more inclined to speak to the salesperson.

As with the cold call, getting past the receptionist or staff assistant is the first hurdle. When the prospect is reached, salespeople should not ask immediately for

New customers can be found by asking satisfied customers to suggest people they know who might be interested in purchasing the product or service.

an appointment. Instead, they should begin with a carefully worded, attention-grabbing statement and then lead into the request for an appointment. They might say, for example, "One of our clients recently saved 10 percent in travel costs and increased revenue by 8 percent with our incentive program. I am confident that I can do the same for your company. Would it be convenient for me to stop by your office tomorrow morning at ten, or would you rather see me in the afternoon?" If the prospect presses for details over the phone, the salesperson should hold out for an appointment in order to explain things more adequately unless it is essential to provide details in order for the prospect to consider your product and services at all.

Sending Out a Letter. Many sales representatives prefer to send a letter to a prospective client and then follow it up with a telephone call. They find that being able to refer to a letter makes it easier to get past the "first obstacle" ("I'm calling in regard to the information that I sent") and start the conversation with the decisionmaker ("Did you get a chance to read the letter that I sent to you?"). The introductory letter should stress the potential customer's needs and benefits. It should close by indicating the intention to follow up by telephone.

Writing a Sales Proposal

When selling to individuals, representatives can often open and close a transaction and present their recommendations informally in a single meeting with a customer. When sales are geared toward major accounts—perhaps involving millions of dollars in potential sales—they usually require more preparation and more than one meeting. Before making recommendations, sales representatives will study prospective customers' operations and needs, sometimes devoting a considerable amount of time and money to a detailed needs analysis. Or they may have to respond to bid specifications (meetings, conventions) or a ***request for a proposal (RFP).*** After assessing a potential client's needs, salespeople create a formal written proposal outlining how their products and services can meet customers' needs while providing benefits and value. This proposal should include any special services or discounts that can be provided.

A well-written sales proposal can be an important and effective tool in winning an account or closing a sale. It should demonstrate attention to detail and sensitivity to the prospective customer's needs. The proposal should be written in a positive tone and be well organized. It should be concise, so that the prospective customer does not have to waste time wading through irrelevant information. It should be sent by courier, not regular mail, as a printed document or as a file on a computer disk, or it could be faxed or sent as an e-mail attachment to speed up the response time. Graphics, good-quality paper, an attractive cover, and a handsome binding all help to create a professional image for the selling company.

In a situation in which a travel supplier or intermediary is competing for an account, a written sales proposal that effectively communicates recommendations is even more crucial. Often, sales proposals are written in response to the RFP. The company usually supplies all competing bidders with the same background information about its operations and a format for the proposal. Decisionmakers look unfavorably upon proposals that deviate substantially from the prescribed format. Within that format, however, each sales representative must be creative and clear in order to distinguish the products and services that they offer from those of the competition.

Making Sales Presentations

In a sales presentation, the salesperson presents the sales proposal in person. An effective presentation can greatly enhance the selling company's image and convince a prospective customer to make a commitment. Salespeople making presentations must appear professional and possess a pleasing voice and style of speaking. Since some presentations are made at the client's office, salespeople need to learn appropriate techniques for handling interruptions and distractions.

Regardless of where the sales presentation is made, a summary of the key points, which is distributed to those listening to the presentation, should be developed. This will make it easier for them to follow your presentation and better understand the important benefits of your products and services.

Since sales presentations are generally geared toward a group of people—a community, professional, or religious association; a business or corporation; or another travel organization—they should include audiovisual aids. Color slides, films, videotapes, compact discs and computer projections (presentation software programs), flip charts, or graphs help to improve the quality of the presentation and hold the group's attention. Time is needed to prepare the visuals and to integrate them smoothly into the presentation.

The ability to sell to a group of people requires special skills and experience. In particular, sales representatives must appear confident and at ease and be able to deal with a variety of questions and responses.

But the basic steps of personal selling apply whether sales are to individuals, groups, or businesses, or are in-house, outside, or both. These steps are particularly important to the travel industry and travel sales professionals never lose sight of this fact. They learn to execute every step of the personal selling process with an emphasis on the value and benefit of the travel products they sell and—always—on service to their customers.

CHAPTER SUMMARY

- Travel sales usually depend on personal selling. Personal selling differs from self-service reservations or brochure/catalog shopping because the customer depends on a salesperson to recommend and sell the product or service.
- Personal selling is considered part of the promotional mix because of its information-gathering and -providing role in advance of the sale. It can be more persuasive than advertising and other forms of promotion because the message can be tailored to fit the customer.
- Personal selling may be as simple as order taking or more demanding, as with appointments, proposals, and presentations. Both types are necessary for the sales of travel products and services.

* Both suppliers and intermediaries use personal selling. Personal selling occurs in-house when a potential customer telephones a sales representative of a supplier or intermediary or visits them on the supplier's or intermediary's premises. Outside sales occur when sales representatives of the supplier or intermediary telephone or visit prospective customers by appointment or to provide a sales presentation.
* In general, travel companies sell in-house to individual leisure and business travelers. They are more likely to use outside sales to sell travel products and services to groups, organizations, corporations, and associations.
* A successful salesperson follows a system designed to move a sales transaction toward a conclusion. To gain an edge on competitors, the successful salesperson also strives to provide the client with better service and travel products that provide benefit and value.
* The basic steps of personal selling are qualifying the customer, making recommendations, and closing the sale.
* In qualifying customers, the travel sales professional uses the "six questions" to get prospects to describe their needs, likes and dislikes, and previous travel experiences. This information is needed to begin forming recommendations.
* In making recommendations, salespeople translate product features into benefits for the customer. Upgrading (upselling) and selling additional products and services are special elements of this step of the personal selling process.
* In closing sales, salespeople observe clients for signals that they are ready to make a positive buying decision. Salespeople close by moving toward a conclusion by summarizing benefits and formulating an action plan.
* Outside sales representatives must locate their own customers. They follow up on sales leads with in-person cold calls, telephone calls to make appointments, letters with a follow-up telephone call, or a combination of all of these methods.
* Because group, association, and corporate sales generally involve large sums of money and affect many employees, salespeople spend more time studying the needs of these types of customers. This includes prospecting—looking for new customers.
* Salespeople prepare a more formal recommendation for a group than in a sales transaction with an individual customer. The recommendation with group and corporate customers may be made in the form of a written sales proposal, a verbal sales presentation, or both.

KEY TERMS

inside (in-house) sales
outside sales
qualifying the customer
open probe
limited-response probe
recapping
upgrading (upselling)
close the sale
prospecting
cold calls
request for a proposal (RFP)

DISCUSSION QUESTIONS

1. What is personal selling? Why do travel products and services require personal selling?
2. When is personal selling more like order taking? When does personal selling become more creative and demanding?
3. Who sells travel products and services, and to whom do they sell?
4. What is the difference between an in-house sales representative and an outside sales representative?
5. What are the ways in which inside salespeople obtain information from customers?
6. What is meant by turning features into benefits, and why is this important?
7. What are some signals that a client is ready to close? How can salespeople begin to move toward closing a sale?
8. What additional steps in personal selling are necessary for groups, sales to associations, and corporations?

Using Personal Selling Techniques

Name: ______________________________ Date: ______________

Directions: Answer these questions as you read the chapter. You will be able to use these answers to help you review the chapter.

1. What is personal selling?

____

____

____

____

2. Compare order taking and creative selling.

____

____

____

____

3. What is the basic difference between inside and outside sales?

____

____

____

____

____

4. To what types of markets are outside sales usually geared?

____

____

____

____

____

5. Describe how you can use questions to qualify a customer.

____

____

____

____

____

6. What is the difference between an open probe and a limited-response probe? How are they used to gather information?

7. How can identifying features and benefits help a salesperson to make recommendations to a customer?

8. Describe three ways a seller can make recommendations and overcome hesitation in a customer.

9. What is upgrading (upselling)?

10. How can you tell when it is the right time to try to close a sale?

11. Describe four methods of closing a sale.

12. Describe three methods of prospecting used by outside sales.

13. Describe five qualities of a well-written sales proposal.

WORKSHEET

Using Personal Selling Techniques

Name: ______________________________ Date: ______________

IT'S YOUR MOVE

For each situation described, supply the question or response that will help close a sale.

1. You are a travel agent in a busy shopping mall agency. An elderly woman approaches you, accompanied by an elderly man in a wheelchair. She says: "I need information on a cruise to South America."

   A. You respond: ______________________________

   ____

   ____

   ____

   ____

   After answering your questions and discussing possible cruise arrangements, the customer says, "I really must speak to my husband's doctor about this vacation."

   B. You say: ______________________________

   ____

   ____

   ____

   ____

2. You are the sales manager for the newest edition to a major hotel chain. Your hotel is located next to the convention center in a busy midwestern city, and you have been traveling around the country making proposals to potential customers and meeting with considerable success. Next month you will be traveling to the east coast, and you are trying to make an appointment with the director of a trade association that has booked the convention center for its international trade show and conference next year. When you call the association, the receptionist says, "The director is in a meeting. What is the nature of your call?"

   A. You say: ______________________________

   ____

   ____

   ____

   ____

   You call again at a specified time, and the director says, "I have five minutes between meetings. Tell me what your hotel has to offer us."

   B. You say: ______________________________

   ____

   ____

When you finish your five-minute speech, the director says, "You know, when a hotel is so close to the convention center, it gets so crowded with convention-goers that you feel like you're in Grand Central Station."

C. You say:

3. You are an independent tour operator specializing in creating custom tour packages for travel groups with special interests. Last week you had a preliminary meeting with the travel committee, and tonight you will be making a presentation to a hundred-member nature hobbyists' group considering a three-week tour of Australia. The itinerary will include trips to the Great Outback, Great Barrier Reef, and several wildlife reserves and natural attractions such as Ayers Rock and the Olgas.

A. What sales aids will you bring to help you in making the presentation?

B. At the conclusion of the presentation, you say:

C. Many of the group's members have questions about various aspects of the tour. Why is it important for you to listen to each one?

D. What do you say and do to show that you are listening to the group members?

4. You are a travel agent in an agency that handles mainly leisure travel. A single woman in her thirties sits down at your desk and says, "I run my own business and I need a vacation. I'm under a tremendous amount of stress because my business has tripled over the past year. A friend of mine spent a week on St. Thomas, and it sounds like just what I want."

A. You ask the following questions: ____________________

As a result of your conversation, you find out that your customer wants to travel alone and that the week she has chosen will be a school vacation time, when many families will visit the reasonably priced resort she is interested in. However, you have been on a fam trip to a more luxurious resort nearby, which you sense would be a better choice.

B. You say: ____________________

C. You take out a brochure describing the resort you have recommended. How do you use it? ____________________

D. After discussing transportation, costs, and features and benefits of the trip, you see that the customer is smiling and looks relaxed.

You say: ____________________

5. You are the owner of a restored inn in Santa Fe, New Mexico, and you are meeting with the representative of a major tour operator. Your goal is to be included in the itinerary of the company's popular motor coach tours of the southwest. You have sent the company representative photographs of the inn, plus a concise description of its features: location in a historic district, intimate atmosphere, authentic furnishings, gourmet dining (including in-room breakfasts), and proximity to art galleries and museums, shops, and places of interest. The company representative says, "Your inn is very attractive, but what makes you think it will appeal to our customers? They're mostly over fifty, and they have very specific likes and dislikes."

A. You say: ____________________

After listening to your description of the hotel's benefits, the company representative says, "Of course, many other people are after our business, and those we choose stand to gain a lot. In return, we expect a break that will help us sell more tours."

B. You say: ______________________________

Tour conversation with the tour company representative has gone on for nearly an hour, and she seems undecided. After recapping what you have said, you attempt to close. She says, "No, I really can't make that decision at this point. I still have to see some other people and hand in my report to the vice president."

C. You say: ______________________________

Satisfying the Customer

OBJECTIVES

When you have completed this chapter, you should be able to:

* List the principles of good customer service.
* Describe ways in which travel sales professionals provide service with the sale.
* Give examples of value-added services and amenities that accompany travel products.
* Name ways in which a sales representative follows up on a sale.
* Describe ways of maintaining a professional level of service.
* Identify how technological innovations can be used to improve service to customers.
* Use marketing information in an ongoing way to stay abreast of technological changes, industry trends, and changing preferences.

The sale has been successfully concluded. The customer's signature is on the dotted line. Now the salesperson can sit back and relax. Right? Wrong! Just as salespeople must have a plan to close the sale, they must also have a plan to retain customers' business. To be financially successful, travel companies—both suppliers and intermediaries—depend on repeat business. And the key to establishing repeat business is providing superior service. Satisfied customers not only will remain loyal themselves, but also will encourage their friends and acquaintances to do business with companies that they favor. Satisfied customers are the key to the growth of travel businesses.

PRINCIPLES OF CUSTOMER SERVICE

Not too long ago a major airline ran a series of television ads showing airline employees interacting with customers. In one, an airline ticket agent races through the airport terminal to catch up with a passenger and return the gift that the passenger left at the counter. In another, a baggage handler reassures a little boy that his dog will be safe and comfortable in the plane's cargo section. In a third, a flight attendant waits outside the terminal with an elderly woman until the woman's son arrives to pick her up.

By emphasizing caring behavior by their employees, the advertisers demonstrated a clear understanding of what it takes to meet customer expectations and to gain repeat business. Travelers demand—and deserve—clean hotel rooms, on-time flights, well-tuned rental cars, and other basic services in the products they purchase. But travelers crave something more: they want to feel that the company and its employees care about their satisfaction and are willing to do whatever it takes to deliver quality service. This special attention to customer needs is often referred to as ***customer service***. Although it is the responsibility of all travel industry companies and employees to promote goodwill among customers, from the perspective of travel sales and marketing, the responsibility to serve customers falls most directly on travel sales representatives.

This chapter addresses service excellence by providing examples of customer service techniques that are important to specific types of travel suppliers and intermediaries. However, the principles of customer service on which these examples are based are critical to the success of all travel businesses. From cruise lines to tourist attractions, visitor and convention bureaus to tour operators, success depends on winning repeat business. And superior service to customers is the way to win it.

Actions

Customer service begins with the fundamental recognition that the customer is the most important person in the marketing process. Travel salespeople demonstrate this attitude with a pleasant manner, courteous and attentive behavior and speech, and an understanding of customers' needs and desires. They make a conscious effort to remember customers' names and preferences. Successful travel salespeople work quickly and efficiently and are willing to spend extra time and effort to satisfy their customers' needs. Salespeople also understand that travelers, especially business travelers, often have to change their plans at the last minute. Travel sales professionals take extra steps to meet their customer's expectations and make themselves indispensable so that their customers won't consider taking their business anywhere else.

Appearance

Just as you want to look your best for the important people in your personal life, trained travel salespeople also strive to be well groomed for their customers. Although a salesperson need not be handsome or beautiful, he or she should dress neatly, avoiding fashion extremes. When a salesperson looks healthy and neat, a customer is likely to feel more confident and comfortable about making a purchase.

Communication Skills

While interacting with customers, travel sales professionals must demonstrate good communication skills. They must be able to express themselves clearly, in both speaking and writing. They must also be able to listen to and empathize with customers. A travel salesperson's manner of speaking should be easy to listen to and free of annoying habits, such as constantly saying "you know" or coughing nervously. Finally, the focus of the salesperson should steadfastly remain on the needs of the customer and what he or she is saying.

PROVIDING SUPERIOR SERVICE

Faced with increasing competition and consumer demands, many travel companies find it necessary to demonstrate the superiority of their products. As you already know, however, many travel products are virtually identical. It is sometimes difficult to distinguish, for example, between two airplane flights to the same destination, or two overnight stays in competing hotels. As a result, travel companies work to improve and maintain service quality or to add new services in order to capture customer interest and loyalty. They use service excellence to differentiate their products and services from those of competitors.

Providing Service with the Sale

To induce customers to make a purchase and to plant the seeds for future sales, travel sales professionals and the companies they represent provide special services. Providing superior service with the sale includes making travel products convenient to purchase, counseling the client, anticipating special needs, and going the extra mile.

Convenience. Travel organizations work to make it easy for customers to purchase travel products and, when necessary, to change their travel plans. Travel agencies and airlines often locate their offices in downtown business areas, in airports, or in suburban malls, where busy customers can drop in, saving them time and effort. Airlines and travel agencies provide toll-free numbers for customers and mail their tickets to them. Travel agencies servicing business accounts often employ couriers to hand-deliver tickets to clients' offices.

Some special services can enhance the convenience of making travel plans—or of travel itself. Some travel agencies, for example, sell travel insurance and passport photos. They may even have a small travel boutique in a separate area of the agency, where luggage, travel books, travel accessories (e.g., foreign electric conversion plugs, immersion heaters, travel alarm clocks), and travel notions (e.g., small sewing kits, emergency rainwear, tiny clotheslines and clothespins) are sold.

Hotels, resorts, rental cars, attractions, and tour operators also provide toll-free numbers for the convenience of customers making reservations and prepaying for travel products and services. An increasing number of destination marketing organizations are accepting reservations on behalf of their membership. They also provide toll-free numbers for that purpose.

Counseling. Customers enjoy their travel more when they know what to expect. Sales representatives who take the time to prepare their customers for a trip are more likely to gain repeat business. For example, salespeople should describe the destination to customers, especially if the customers are likely to encounter unfamiliar laws, rules, or customs. Many first-time travelers to Latin countries are taken aback when they discover a museum or shop closed in the early afternoon to accommodate the customary siesta. Customers taking their first cruise also appreciate being familiarized with the protocol for dining and other aspects of shipboard life. Salespeople can help their customers by advising them about what kind of weather to expect at their destination and what clothes to take along. In addition, they should advise customers about passport and visa requirements and inform them of any required inoculations. Travelers should also be warned about any possible health risks at their destination.

Anticipating Special Needs. Many travelers—especially the disabled, senior citizens, and families with young children—have special needs. When travel sales professionals anticipate these needs and make appropriate arrangements, they do a great deal to build customer loyalty. For example, a sales representative might arrange for a rental car with hand controls and a hotel room with wheelchair access for a disabled customer. Allowing a family with small children to preboard a flight is a special service offered by most airlines.

Successful travel salespeople and their companies maintain customer files for their regular clients, especially business travelers. These files list the customer's special needs or preferences, such as airplane seat location, dietary restrictions, or desired class of accommodations. Both intermediaries and suppliers maintain these customer files, particularly for frequent-traveler programs. Most files are stored in sophisticated databases that allow companies to develop customer profiles, including special needs that have to be met consistently. Having this information on file eliminates the need to ask the same questions every time a customer requests a reservation.

Going the Extra Mile. The expression "going the extra mile" aptly describes travel sales professionals' special efforts to provide additional services. They go beyond the normal requirements of their jobs to increase their customers' satisfaction. A good example is the travel agent who prepares a "subitinerary" for his or her escorted-tour clients. The subitinerary suggests activities for clients when they are not formally touring and tells them how to get from place to place. It also may list attractions, restaurants, and current theater productions at each destination.

Sales representatives of destination marketing organizations, such as visitor and convention bureaus, routinely go the extra mile to secure convention business.

Most airlines provide special assistance for disabled passengers. (Photograph by Michael Dzamen)

They may, for example, arrange for an organization's convention planners to attend a special rehearsal of a local chorale or orchestra when the planners are there for a familiarization trip or a preconference visit to their city. Such an extra not only helps them sell a convention initially, but also increases the likelihood that satisfied groups will return to their city in the future.

Providing Service with the Product

Providing exceptional service along with travel products is the other major factor determining whether customers will purchase them again. All travel products include basic services. Every hotel room, for instance, should have a comfortable bed, clean linen, and hangers or hooks for clothes. But to increase customers' enjoyment and to make them feel special, travel companies add services and amenities. The number and kind of extras depend on how the company has positioned its product in the marketplace. Customers, for example, do not expect the same services from a budget hotel as they do from a luxury resort. Even so, the extra services provided by one budget hotel chain can give it a decided competitive advantage over other hotels that offer fewer services. This is a key principle that all types of travel companies need to recognize as they strive to secure repeat business.

Airlines. Airlines typically provide economy-class passengers with preassigned seating and baggage handling at check-in. Travelers with some airlines, however, can check their baggage when they drop off their rental cars, rather than drag the suitcases to the terminal. Passengers normally receive complimentary meals, snacks, and nonalcoholic beverages. But they may also order kosher, salt-free, or other special-diet meals ahead of time at no extra charge. Magazines, including complimentary copies of the airline's in-flight magazine, are available to help pass the time. Headsets for watching movies or listening to music either are provided free of charge or can be rented for a nominal fee. Also available are telephones and connections for laptop computers, providing Internet and e-mail access. Flight attendants help passengers with carry-on baggage and provide special assistance for elderly and disabled passengers and families with young children.

Many of these services seem commonplace. Yet, you only need to recall the approach of any of the defunct "no-frills" airlines to realize how much they add to the enjoyment of a flight. Although not devoid of services, some of these "no-frills" flights were so spartan that passengers joked about having to bring their own bag lunch and folding chairs.

Airlines pamper their business-class and first-class passengers even more. These sections tend to have more spacious seating than economy class. Business-class and first-class passengers receive more individualized attention from flight attendants. They are given more meal options; they may even be served gourmet meals on fine china. Their cocktails and headsets are always complimentary. Many now have video screens, computer ports (faxes and e-mail) and telephones.

Car Rental Companies. The major car rental companies make it convenient for customers to rent a car by providing rental counters in airport terminals and key downtown and suburban locations. Most also provide a courtesy bus to take customers from the airport to wherever the cars are kept. Special services offered with many car rentals include maps and personalized driving directions, twenty-four-hour emergency road service, and drop-off privileges allowing customers to leave the car at any location owned by the company. Some companies also provide satellite-based mapping systems in their vehicles to reduce the likelihood that customers will get lost. Some companies now offer portable cellular phones and free insurance. And many have clubs for frequent customers that provide members with special services such as express pickup and drop-off.

Hotels, Motels, and Resorts. Traditional services in finer hotels and resorts include room service, laundry and dry cleaning, limousine service to and from airports, shopping facilities, and one or more restaurants. Special check-in (based on frequent guest profiles) and checkout (via in-room television) services are also available in these properties. In reaction to the strong interest in physical fitness, many hotels and resorts now provide elaborate recreational facilities, some with instructors.

Many deluxe hotels employ a concierge, whose primary function is to satisfy the special needs of guests. A concierge may be called upon to secure theater tickets, arrange for babysitting, recommend a dentist, or satisfy any specific requests from guests who require special, personalized service.

Hotels specializing in business travel will provide a business center furnished with personal computers, photocopying machines, computer connections, and other equipment. The services of word processors, receptionists, translators, and notary publics may even be available.

Most hotels and motels are expanding the number and kinds of services that they offer. (Photograph by Michael Dzamen)

Almost all hotels, motels, and resorts are expanding the number and kind of amenities they provide. A few years ago, typical amenities might have been a few bars of soap and a color television. Now they include hair driers, toiletries, bathrobes, telephones in the bathroom, VCRs, remote-control TV, fax machines, and additional telephone jacks for computer modems. With more women business travelers, amenities such as skirt hangers, full-length mirrors, and robes are becoming common. To help all guests feel more secure, many hotels now provide escorts to accompany them at night to and from parking lots.

Travelers who belong to frequent-guest programs receive additional services to entice them to return in the future. These include preferential reservations handling, express check-in, late checkout privileges, check-cashing privileges, complimentary cocktails or continental breakfasts, free newspapers, and more. The decision to provide these special services demonstrates how critical travel managers and salespeople believe them to be in satisfying customers and earning their repeat business.

Attractions. Many attractions provide special prices for frequent visitors, or for local residents who can visit during off-peak periods. They also provide guides, special tours for different groups (schools, sponsors, travel industry professionals, etc.) and interpreters in order to make the visit to the attraction a memorable experience.

FOLLOWING UP THE SALE

The selling process has been compared by some marketers to courtship and marriage. As in courtship, much time and effort is spent in wooing the first-time buyer. Unfortunately, once the sale has been made, there is a tendency to neglect the buyer. But a sales relationship, like a good marriage, requires ongoing and deliberate efforts to keep it intact.

Communicating

From experience, you realize the importance of communication in a personal relationship. Business relationships are basically similar. For a relationship between a travel salesperson and a customer to flourish, the parties involved must be able to talk to each other and be understood, to express their preferences, and to resolve misunderstandings and disputes. To ensure repeat business, travel salespeople must work hard to keep the lines of communication open and current.

Expressing Appreciation. No one likes to be taken for granted. Customers, too, like to feel valued. They want to know that their patronage is important. Following the close of a sale, sales representatives should always express their appreciation with a brief note or a phone call.

In addition, giving customers a small gift is an effective way of saying "Thank you for your business." Travel agents, for example, might have flowers delivered to a customer's hotel room. Customers embarking on a cruise are delighted to find a bottle of champagne and a bon voyage card from the tour operator waiting for them in their cabin. Many visitor and convention bureaus routinely sponsor receptions to welcome organizations that are convening in their city.

Soliciting Customer Feedback. Another important part of following up on a sale is to solicit customers' reactions to the travel products they purchased. Requesting customer feedback is essential for several reasons. For one, it demonstrates an interest in customers and lets them know that their opinion is valued. For another, customer feedback can be an important source of information. Feedback can uncover problems a company would not otherwise know about. Perhaps accommodations in a certain city have deteriorated, or a tour escort was consistently late or inattentive. A company or destination is able to identify problems that need to be solved and can also get ideas for new markets and new products from this information. Finally, if customers did have problems, postsale feedback allows them to air their dissatisfaction before it produces the possibility of a company losing their business in the future.

At the end of their stay, visit, or trip, or after returning from their trip, customers should be requested to complete a questionnaire soliciting their reactions. Salespeople might also send them a personalized welcome-back note inviting them to call within a few days to discuss their travel experience. Some travel agencies and tour operators even hold reunions for their customers. In addition to reminiscing about their trip, the tour-goers frequently make suggestions that help the travel agencies and tour operators improve future trips.

Handling and Resolving Complaints. Dealing with the complaints about travel products can be difficult. Unlike defective cars or washing machines, a defective trip cannot be repaired or exchanged. Travel products are not sold with warranties. Furthermore, sales representatives often have no direct control over the delivery of the products that they sell to their customers. (Most intermediaries try to compensate for this fact by dealing exclusively with suppliers who are known to be reliable and reputable.) Travel agents are frequently blamed for blunders such as canceled flights or lost luggage that are actually the fault of suppliers. Some travel agencies have had to resort to having their customers sign disclaimers agreeing that the agency is not to blame if certain elements of a trip turn out badly.

The best way to avoid complaints, of course, is to prevent problems from occurring in the first place. This can be done by selling customers travel products that meet their needs and by being in agreement as to what is expected of the product. For example, travelers requesting the least expensive rate at a seaside resort should be advised that they will not be getting a room with an ocean view. Whenever possible, customers should be alerted to any unusual conditions that might detract from their enjoyment of a trip. For example, if a transit strike is snarling traffic in London, travelers bound for England should be informed so that they can prepare themselves (at least mentally) to deal with delays. Finally, sales representatives must be absolutely certain that customers understand company (suppliers or intermediaries) policies about cancellations.

If complaints arise, handling them efficiently and effectively can do a great deal to build a sound relationship with the customer. Salespeople or customer service specialists (depends on the size of the company) should resolve complaints immediately. If the settlement is prolonged, the customer will only become angrier and more vocal. Complaints should also be handled pleasantly, since employees with unprofessional attitudes that are not customer-friendly can create ill will toward a company.

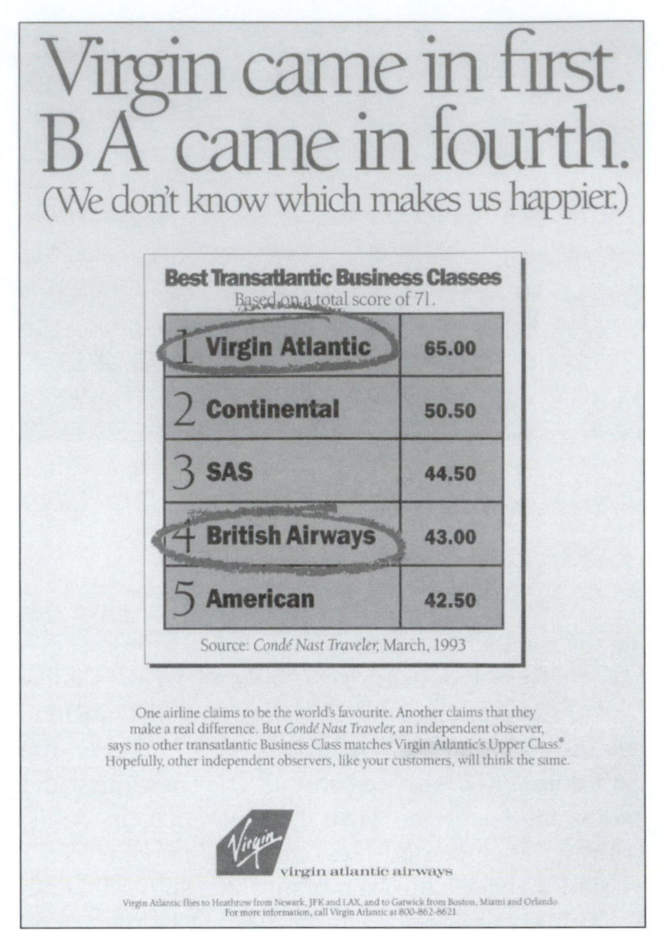

Many airlines have feedback mechanisms to determine the level of customer satisfaction and to identify complaints and problems that need to be addressed. (Courtesy of Virgin Atlantic Airways)

Employees also need to give courteous attention to and express genuine interest in a customer's problem. If necessary, irate clients should be allowed to vent their frustration until they calm down. Sales/customer service representatives should attempt to gather all the facts of the situation. Whenever possible, they should agree with the customer and offer a fair adjustment (usually an apology), a promise to do better in the future and either a reduction in the bill or a voucher for future purchases of travel products. Sales/customer service representatives have an opportunity to increase goodwill if the adjustment is more liberal than the customer expected. But even if a customer's complaint is unjustified, salespeople should attempt to find a compromise that will satisfy the customer without hurting the company.

Sometimes salespeople need to help customers seek remedies for their grievances from other sources.

For instance, travel agents might write a letter to an airline on behalf of a customer. Salespeople should inform customers in advance of their rights in the event of canceled or delayed flights or lost resort reservations. They should encourage customers to contact appropriate customer service representatives (including providing them with contact numbers) if they have problems while traveling. Many suppliers hire customer service troubleshooters to handle problems on the spot. Customer service representatives for airlines, for example, can arrange meals and hotel accommodations for stranded passengers, authorize luggage repairs, and write checks to resolve complaints involving small amounts of money. Professional associations such as the American Society of Travel Agents and the American Hotel and Motel Association also have complaint referral services to help consumers.

Staying in Touch. If salespeople forget their customers, their customers will certainly forget them. Travel sales professionals need to maintain ongoing contact and communication with their customers. This ensures that when customers are ready to purchase travel products again, they are aware of the special opportunities, discounts, new products, etc., and know that the salesperson is still there, ready to serve them.

Several methods can be used to stay in touch with customers. Quarterly newsletters and monthly promotional mailings are an excellent way of maintaining contact, as are frequent-traveler guest publications. Even when clients don't read these, they still see the name of the sponsoring travel organization regularly. Travel salespeople can also telephone customers from time to time with news about products that might interest them. Sending holiday greeting cards is another personalized way of staying in touch. (One travel agent sends Thanksgiving cards because they are uncommon and, therefore, apt to be remembered longer.) Congratulatory notes can be sent when customers become engaged, get married, have babies, or receive promotions and other honors.

Successful travel sales professionals often maintain "tickler files." A tickler file consists of a book, calendar, or some other date-tracking system that reminds salespeople when to send cards for clients' birthdays or wedding anniversaries. A resort where a couple spent their honeymoon could then send an anniversary card with a special offer to visit the resort again. Tickler files can also be used to remind representatives that it is time to telephone or make an in-person call again.

Providing Incentives

Another way to promote repeat business is to reward regular customers. An outstanding example of this is frequent-traveler programs. Frequent-traveler programs are currently used by virtually all major airlines and by many hotel chains and car rental companies as well.

As mentioned, participants in frequent-traveler programs receive special services. The programs also offer the opportunity for members to earn points that can be applied toward discounts on future purchases, free upgrades (going from one level of service to another), or free services or products. Members earn points each time they purchase a company's products or the products of a company with which a tie-in agreement exits. For example, members of one airline's frequent-flier program can also accumulate points by renting a car from Hertz or Alamo; staying at a Marriott, Hyatt, Hilton, Renaissance, Sheraton, Omni, Radisson, or Westin hotel; and flying internationally on Northwest, Air France, British Airways, All Nippon Airways, Alitalia, Qantas, Sabena, and Swiss Air. The underlying premise of frequent-traveler programs is that, as they earn points, customers become increasingly likely to choose travel products participating in that particular award program in order to qualify for free products and services or upgrades from the partner travel companies.

Servicing a Business Account

Handling the travel arrangements for a corporation or small company has definite advantages. Repeat business can be built right in, which tends to lower the costs of selling and to increase profit.

However, many business accounts require certain services long after a sale has been transacted. Pressure to maintain the customer service standards that were promised when the account was first sold can be great.

Max Talbot owns Corporate Travel, a midsize travel agency. He recently negotiated an agreement with CompuData, Inc. In addition to making all business travel arrangements for CompuData's employees, Max's agency has agreed to provide free visa processing, travel insurance, and ticket delivery. His agency is expected to monitor CompuData's travel practices, obtain the lowest airfares available, and submit regular reports, summarizing CompuData's travel expenditures. Max's agency is also to keep track of each employee's frequent-flier points.

Max knows how important it will be to get off to a good start with CompuData. A favorable first impression will help ease any apprehension CompuData executives might have about transferring the company's travel business to Corporate Travel. In bringing the new account on board, Max has decided to take these special measures:

- Arrange for key personnel from the agency and from CompuData to meet each other in order to establish good working relationships.
- Have his staff create computer profiles covering the travel preferences and needs of individual CompuData travelers.
- Distribute a brochure to CompuData travelers explaining how to expedite their travel arrangements, detailing credit-card and payment policies, and listing the range of products and services provided. The brochure will also list the agency's office hours, its toll-free service number, and names of personnel.
- Educate his staff about CompuData's business operation so that they will better understand the company's travel requests.

Max and his staff recognize that it will take from three to six months to establish a good working relationship with CompuData. After this initial period, however, he does not intend to relax and put the account on automatic pilot. Max has specific plans for maintaining a high level of service. For example, he intends to meet regularly with the CompuData staff who process the reports and billings provided by Corporate Travel, in order to make sure CompuData feels that its expectations have been met and that it is receiving satisfactory service. He will insist that his staff double-check all reservations and billings to make sure there are no errors. Max knows that if his agency fails to deliver the quality of service promised in the sale, he can lose the account to a competing agency that might be offering better service.

MAINTAINING A PROFESSIONAL LEVEL OF SERVICE

Like many other professionals, travel sales and marketing professionals need not only to develop good skills initially, but also make special efforts to maintain them. This is especially critical in a field as competitive and quickly changing as the travel industry. More than an enthusiasm for serving customers is required to successfully sell travel products. It requires an understanding of the ongoing need to polish skills, to stay informed, and to be aware of and subscribe to professional standards of behavior. The need to improve is another critical element of travel sales professionals' commitment to satisfying the needs of their customers.

Continuing Education

The fast-changing nature of the travel industry makes it important for travel sales professionals to keep up-to-date with its latest developments. Continuing education is one of the best methods of keeping skills sharp and learning about current issues in the industry.

Salespeople can enroll in courses in sales and marketing at colleges, universities, and vocational schools. Alternately, they might enroll in a certification program sponsored by a travel-related institute or by a professional association for people employed in the travel industry. An example of an industry association certificate program is the Certified Tour Professional (CTP) program offered by the National Tour Association. The CTP program is available to the tour operators, suppliers, and destination marketing organizations that comprise this international association. In addition, to find out about current trends and other pertinent industry-related issues, travel sales and marketing professionals can attend seminars, workshops, and conferences sponsored by professional associations and industry organizations or subscribe to newsletters and reports that track trends and identify future opportunities.

Travel sales representatives should also read professional journals and newspapers regularly. They should make a point of studying the product information furnished by their company (or by suppliers if they are intermediaries), including training tapes and newsletters. Of course, one of the best ways for travel professionals to stay current with the world of travel is to travel themselves.

Legal Responsibilities

Travel sales professionals should know what laws prohibit and require, and how laws apply to their activities. Although no legislation exists pertaining to travel sales per se, legislation regulating selling in general does apply to the travel industry. For example, federal legislation forbids any of the following practices:

- Price fixing (Sherman Act, 1890)—A company cannot agree with a competitor to charge a certain price for a product.

- Exclusive dealing (Clayton Act, 1914)—Sellers cannot prevent their customers from buying the products of other companies.
- Tying (Clayton Act, 1914)—A buyer cannot be required to purchase one product in order to be allowed to buy another.
- Unfair methods of competition and deceptive practices (Federal Trade Commission Act, 1914)—Sellers are prohibited to engage in misleading advertising and certain other questionable practices.

In addition to such general federal legislation, travel sales are subject to a variety of more specific laws and regulations on local, state, federal, and even international levels. The particular laws vary, not just by legal and regulatory jurisdiction, but by particular types of business within the travel industry, for example, accommodations and transportation.

For obvious reasons, travel sales professionals must make it their business to become aware of all laws and regulations pertaining to their own activities. To attempt to describe all such legal requirements in this chapter would be nearly impossible and beyond the scope and intent of this book. The various associations for professionals in the travel industry are a good starting point for obtaining such information.

These laws are mentioned here for an additional reason. They define a level of performance that is required as a minimum to meet legal and regulatory standards. For travel sales representatives who want to earn repeat business, meeting such standards is necessary but not sufficient to satisfy their customers.

Ethical Behavior

Sales representatives also have an obligation to maintain ethical standards, in regard to both their customers and their companies. Unethical behavior violates the rules or standards of an organization or goes against the salesperson's conscience. For example, any of the following actions would be considered a breach of ethics:

- Selling a package tour to a person who can't afford it.
- Deliberately misrepresenting a destination (telling customers that a resort has its own private beaches when it actually only has access to a public beach).
- Recommending a course of action because it benefits the salesperson rather than the customer (pushing a certain cruise line in order to win a prize from the supplier).
- Passing confidential information on to others.

One good way to reduce the likelihood of unethical behavior is to think about possible ethical dilemmas in advance and try to decide what actions and behaviors are appropriate and acceptable. Talking to colleagues facing similar dilemmas can help resolve ethical doubts. Salespeople should always follow the ***code of ethics***, or guidelines for behavior, provided by their company or professional association. Both the American Society of Travel Agents and the National Tour Association, for instance, have developed a code of ethics that emphasizes professionalism and ethical behavior in the travel industry and is dedicated to protecting consumers.

HIGH-TECH SERVICE

During the last forty years, travel sales professionals have used a variety of tools to help them meet people's travel needs. With each succeeding decade, their equipment has become increasingly sophisticated:

- In the 1950s, travel salespeople used manual typewriters, carbon paper, and rotary-dial telephones (with few toll-free numbers) and consulted separate timetables published by individual airlines and railroads. When agents requested reservations, suppliers noted their request and called back after determining availability.
- By the mid-1960s, travel agents had the Official Airline Guides and electric typewriters. Airlines and hotels were starting to automate.
- By the late 1970s, salespeople used photocopying machines, touch-tone phones, and teleticketing machines. Most rental car agencies and hotels installed reservation terminals.

Each wave of new technology and equipment has helped sales representatives serve their clients more efficiently. Today, even more technologically advanced equipment is on the horizon. This equipment will undoubtedly change the ways travel products are sold. Although some salespeople view these developments as a threat to their job security, the new technology offers many advantages to those who can adapt to it. Most important, the new technology will automatically handle much of the routine work of order taking and information processing. Sales representatives will be freed to

Marketing Impressions

DEFINING THE PREMIUM CRUISE LINE HOLLAND AMERICA LINE

Call it perspective, but after 125 years in the cruise business, we have made the ability to cut through all the hoopla about "the more the better" and focusing on "more that matters" a cornerstone of the Holland America Premium Cruise Line philosophy.

Holland America Line is in a unique position as the only major premium cruise line. Most passengers and travel agents can easily identify the extremes of the marketplace and know mass-market lines and the ultra-luxurious lines. But defining a premium line to our audience requires our full-fledged marketing and sales efforts to deliver a cohesive and effective premium message.

There are many features and amenities which differentiate Holland America Line from the larger-ship, mass-market lines, but more than any other quality, it is the tradition of service and genuine hospitality which our Indonesian and Filipino staff deliver that distinguishes our brand and has earned us top recognition from the discerning readers of *Condé Nast Traveler* and *Travel & Leisure* magazines.

One of our guests wrote us to say, "memories are of the cabin steward who tucked in a three-year-old's beloved stuffed animals. Imagine her delight to discover them thus! And ours, as grown-ups, to observe such an endearing bit of thoughtfulness."

Another wrote that "our dining room steward learned of our fondness for iced tea and had it waiting for us each evening when we arrived. Years later, on another ship, he remembered us and also our iced tea."

In addition to superior quality service, accommodations distinguish Holland America as the world's best and only major premium cruise line. On every Holland America Line cruise, guests can expect roomier accommodations with more public area per passenger than any other cruise line in our class, staterooms that have more personal space, and spacious verandahs. These are carefully designed aspects of the product.

Add to this award-winning cuisine and entertainment, fresh floral bouquets throughout the ship, full bathroom amenities kits, exquisite art and antiques valued into the millions, and a value-oriented price that leaves passengers with the feeling that not only did they get more, but that they received more of what matters. Also, Holland America Line has consistently maintained our "tipping not required" policy as a guarantee of genuine, gracious, and unconditional service, while other lines automatically add tips to guests' bills.

Holland America Line further defines a premium cruise line as one with the leadership experience and expertise to offer worldwide itineraries, such as our Grand World Voyage, in addition to traditional Alaskan and Caribbean sailings. Holland America Line has expanded our repertoire lately with our new Explorer cruises to South America, the Orient, and the Pacific. Moreover, these cruises include special features like gentlemen hosts and famous lecturers to enrich guests' appreciation of each magical destination's culture, hsitory, and art.

Being a successful premium line means delivering more than you promise, standing by your commitment to excellence and value, and doing it all over again week in and week out on eight ships around the world.

do even more customer counseling and creative selling, thus becoming less clerical and more professional. Consequently, understanding travelers' needs and providing essential personal service to customers is likely to become even more important to selling travel products.

By the late 1980s, airline computer reservations systems (CRSs) had expanded to include hotels, resorts, rental cars, tour operators, and attraction admissions. Most destinations offered toll-free numbers. Many printed reference manuals were replaced with computer databases. By the late 1990s, Web sites like Travelocity and Priceline allowed consumers direct access to travel products. Most airlines, hotel companies, and rental car agencies also provided Web sites that accepted reservations. Electronic (ticketless) tickets became more common and were delivered by facsimile machines (fax).

In the Office

Travel sales offices are becoming increasingly automated. As you know from Chapter 8, this is especially true for travel agencies, the vast majority of which now depend on computer reservations systems and Internet Web sites for much of their work. You've also read about newer technology developments, including satellite ticket printers, automated ticketing machines, electronic ticketing, and personal computers through which customers can access travel companies' Web sites and make their own reservations.

The advances in electronic technology are relentless. Even faster and more user-friendly systems are already in use or will be before long. Travel sales professionals in all areas of the industry need to stay informed about these technological developments. The reason is simple: they have an impact on the way travel products are sold. Travel salespeople who want to expand their sales and increase the likelihood of repeat business need to utilize new technologies in ways that can help them improve their level of customer service.

Facsimile Machines. Facsimile machines, or "fax" machines, have improved technically and are now commonplace. Travel sales personnel use this electronic communication device to send clients copies of letters, flight itineraries, reservation confirmations, and invoices. Faxes are key elements in the electronic ticketing process.

Sales representatives who recognize the power of fax machines have a tremendous competitive edge over those who do not. Compared with overnight mail or other delivery systems, fax machines provide a much faster, less expensive way of communicating in writing with corporate and leisure travelers. Communicating by fax, which is as fast and convenient as a phone conversation, also reduces the chances of misunderstandings by providing written documentation.

Travel sales professionals can also communicate via computer messages sent as electronic mail to customers' computers. Customers can respond to these messages and/or initiate contact themselves. Because electronic mail can be sent and received anywhere, it is particularly useful for maintaining communication with customers who are "on the road." By creating a file of all of the e-mail addresses of its customers (called a listserv), a company (or sales representative) can communicate directly with those customers electronically—the computer is instructed to send the same message to everyone in the file. This allows the customers to be easily and simultaneously contacted about special prices, tours, etc.

Videocassette Recorders. In addition to tapes for staff training, videocassette recorders (VCRs) are being used to show customers videos portraying travel destinations. In certain applications, videos are replacing brochures as a sales tool. Customers often feel better informed and more comfortable with a destination after viewing a videotape. Videos can also save salespeople time in conveying information. Often, prospective travelers take the tapes home to view them with family and friends before making a decision about a trip.

Compact Discs (CDs). CDs allow companies and destinations to portray their products and services and special offerings to customers and intermediaries. Since the images, words, and sounds are digitally recorded, they are of higher quality than videotapes. CDs also can hold an enormous amount of information that can be organized clearly and accessed easily. Because they are digital, they can be viewed on multimedia computer systems, including laptops, which makes CDs extremely portable and convenient.

Other Technologies. Whereas fax machines and VCRs are a reality in many travel offices, other equipment is still in the development stage or not yet affordable. Most of the new technology affects the ways information is handled internally or provided to customers, which are critical aspects of high-quality service.

Outside the Office

New technology is affecting the way in which travel products are sold not only inside the office, but outside the office as well. By enabling customers to access information about travel products and services and to make their own reservations, the Internet, video kiosks, multi-media online travel services, and other devices will add a growing element of self-service to travel sales. Travelers, however, will still depend on travel sales representatives for advice and counseling, especially as the marketplace for travel products becomes more competitive and complex.

Video Kiosks. Video kiosks are already in place in a number of metropolitan areas. Developers predict that these "electronic sales representatives" will be widely accepted and used within the next few years. Installed in locations with a heavy volume of pedestrian traffic, such as airports and shopping malls, video kiosks can advertise a sponsoring company as well as open new markets.

A video kiosk resembles a small newsstand and houses an interactive video terminal. Customers step up to the kiosk to view a colorful, fast-moving travelogue depicting a variety of vacations, destinations, and packages. When they see something that particularly interests them, they can touch a spot on the screen that takes them to the reservations section of the program. (An on-screen narrator or written guide prompts them throughout the process.) Often, a telephone is attached to the kiosk so that users can call the sponsoring company for more information. Most kiosks also have a printer to type out itineraries, confirmations, and other information.

Internet Web Sites. As mentioned previously, online travel information and reservation services are becoming more popular. Some specialize in destinations (e.g., California), while others provide access to most of the travel products and services available worldwide. Using sophisticated software, these sites search their product databases to find the lowest available price or the most direct route, depending on the needs of the customer. To encourage use of these sites, airlines may offer, for example, frequent-flier bonus points or discounted airfares if a customer makes reservations on line. All such sites are electronically interactive but self-service, because they are not staffed by reservationists or salespeople.

Multi-media Online Travel Services. These electronic services, which combine the word screens of personal computers with full-color graphics, enable people who are too busy to shop for travel products in person to do so at home via computer.

These multi-media services work something like cable television. Customers must first subscribe to an Internet package that includes a shopping service offered by an Internet service provider. The service is linked to home computers via phone lines. Subscribers can choose to view a variety of products, including travel products, from a menu of options. They can also get news and weather updates, find out the latest Dow Jones average, and order dinner. They can even receive personal messages, check the balance in their checking accounts, and pay their bills! Shoppers can place an order on the spot and pay by credit card. Tickets and other documentation are mailed or picked up at the airport or hotel. In general, these subscription-based online services provide better service and are more reliable than Web sites that can be accessed via the Internet without a subscription.

On one hand, the increase in electronic travel sales raises the specter of less human involvement. But overall, technology has freed salespeople to give customers more personal service by allowing them to become more efficient and faster in acquiring and disseminating information and making reservations. The likelihood is that future technologies will continue to increase the efficiency of travel sales professionals, which means that the ability to offer superior service will continue to depend on the prudent and timely implementation of new technologies.

MARKETING INFORMATION AND MARKET TRENDS

Using marketing information in an ongoing way not only ensures that travel companies will stay abreast of technological change, but also provides a means for them to keep up with all sorts of trends and changing preferences. Doing so is critical in order to continue to satisfy customers and earn their repeat business. Travel marketers looking forward to the future recognize a number of significant trends with implications for nearly all travel professionals.

Recognizing Market Trends

Many authorities predict that travel and tourism will be the world's single largest international industry early in the twenty-first century. As such, it will be a very competitive industry. To remain competitive, travel organizations and companies must satisfy their customers by offering superior service and quality products. They will need to use marketing techniques to stay in tune with market trends so that they can offer products and services that best meet consumers' needs and wants. Here are just a few examples of current market trends and how travel and tourism organizations are adapting to them.

Shorter Vacations. Not so long ago, the typical family vacation consisted of Mom, Dad, and the kids piling into the car and heading off for two or three weeks. Although this type of vacation still occurs, more people are choosing to go on shorter trips. Many people are finding shorter but more frequent excursions more beneficial than a single trip of longer duration. Also, with two parents working and children involved in school activities or part-time jobs, many families find it difficult to coordinate extended vacation time or simply are unable to be away from their jobs for more than a few days. As a result, family vacation habits are changing.

Dual-career families without children also are choosing to take more frequent trips of shorter duration. Coordinating work schedules is often challenging, and the increased frequency of breaks from the normal routine are more appealing and beneficial than waiting for a single, longer vacation. In addition, the potential for disappointment due to inclement weather, family, health, or job demands is reduced if there are multiple get-aways.

In response to the trend for shorter vacations, some cruise lines are selling three-, four-, and seven-day cruises. (This strategy also permits travelers to sample this type of vacation for the first time without investing a great deal of time and money in the process.) Ski resorts and attractions are now offering discounts on tickets for three and four days to encourage and capture the long weekend and get-away market segments. Hotels are offering special weekend packages, with discounted room rates and a variety of special features such as meals, tours, and theater tickets. Some weekend packages are even built around themes. As an example, Canadian-Pacific's Royal York Hotel murder-mystery weekends provide guests with an opportunity to participate in and solve a fictitious murder.

Today, approximately 75 percent of the vacations taken at major resorts in the United States total three or fewer days. Nearly 60 percent of these short pleasure trips were taken on weekends. If the four-day workweek becomes more common, weekend travel is likely to increase even more.

International Tourism. The economies of several European countries are showing steady growth as a result of increased industrialization and restructured economies. Pacific Rim countries have also shown improvement in their economic growth after faltering in the late 1990s. Several Latin American economies are also starting to become more stable and predictable. Sustained economic growth and tourism historically go hand in hand. With increased leisure time and money, middle- and working-class Europeans, Asians, and Latin Americans are traveling more.

Some are traveling within their own area of the world, and American companies are taking advantage of this increased tourism. With strong demand for travel to the United States but with evidence of overbuilding, hotel companies, especially, are looking overseas for most of their growth in the next decade. Holiday Inn, for example, has launched a new budget hotel chain in several smaller cities of the United Kingdom.

The rise in the standard of living in Europe, Latin America, and Asia, along with a strong American economy, is bringing more foreign tourists to North America, as well as other regions worldwide (see Figure 12–1). The travel industry is beginning to realize that inbound international tourism provides outstanding business expansion opportunities. Tour operators, for example, are packaging specially tailored two-week vacations in Florida aimed at British travelers. The travel industry is also working to become more accommodating to foreign visitors. Hotels in Vancouver, San Francisco, and Seattle, for example, now offer their Japanese guests a back-home breakfast of miso soup with seaweed, marinated fish, and fried bean curd.

Baby Boomers. In the early twenty-first century, the baby-boom generation will reach middle age. This huge segment of the world population will have reached its peak earning years and acquired more discretionary income. Because of its size and earning power, the changing tastes and interests of baby boomers will continue to have a great deal of impact on the types of travel products offered. Already, new products to match their lifestyles are being developed. Not content to lie on a beach somewhere, eating greasy food and gaining weight, many goal-oriented baby boomers want to make their vacation time as productive as their work time. They may choose to improve their skill at tennis, golf, or some other sport; learn more about nature or foreign culture; or improve their physical fitness. One response to this trend has been an increase in the number of

FORECAST OF INTERNATIONAL TOURIST ARRIVALS 1995–2010

	Tourist Arrivals (Millions)		
Regions	**1995**	**2000**	**2010**
Europe	335	390	527
East Asia/Pacific	80	116	231
Americas	111	134	195
Africa	20	27	46
Middle East	14	19	37
South Asia	4	6	11
Total			1,047

FIGURE 12–1 International tourists will become a bigger factor in marketing all destinations. *Source:* World Trade Organization Vision 2020

resorts positioning themselves as health and fitness centers complete with full-service spas. These health-oriented facilities offer a variety of programs, including aerobics, nutrition counseling, massage therapy, stress management, and hydrotherapy.

It is important for travel organizations and their sales and marketing professionals to track trends and monitor changes in consumer preferences. Doing so allows them to anticipate the impact of change rather than be forced to react to it.

THE ONGOING VALUE OF MARKETING

All changes affecting the travel industry potentially affect the ability of travel sales and marketing professionals to meet the needs of the customers. Some changes improve sales opportunities, while others make selling travel products more difficult. Fortunately, the marketing process provides ideal mechanisms for staying abreast of changes and constantly improving service to travel customers. When marketing plans are reviewed regularly and refined and adjusted in light of anticipated changes, identified through market research and competitive analysis, companies are not likely to lose sight of the needs of the marketplace. When they consistently evaluate the results of their marketing efforts and repeat the entire marketing cycle in an ongoing manner, they improve their chances of satisfying customers more effectively than competing companies and travel products.

Travel products and services must meet the goals and needs of today's travelers. (Photograph by Michael Dzamen)

Travel sales professionals can never lose sight of the fact that the travel needs and preferences of their customers lie at the very heart of buying decisions. Marketing offers travel marketing and sales professionals a systematic way to identify, understand, and address those needs with their travel products and services.

CHAPTER SUMMARY

* To be financially successful, travel organizations and companies must develop repeat business, which not only generates revenue for a company, but also reduces its costs. Time and money do not have to be spent prospecting for or qualifying clients.
* The basis for repeat business is satisfied customers. Satisfied customers are a valuable business resource

because they promote travel products through positive word-of-mouth advertising.

- In general, customers will buy products again if they feel they are getting their money's worth and if they receive good customer service. In the competitive travel marketplace, however, travel organizations and their sales representatives must go beyond providing basic services. To assure repeat business, they must provide added services and amenities, at the time of sale with the product itself and during post-sale follow-up activities.
- To capture repeat business, sales representatives must maintain communication with their clients and offer them incentives to remain loyal. They must be able to resolve complaints effectively.
- Travel sales representatives cannot expect to gain repeat business if they are not knowledgeable about the products and services they sell. They must keep up-to-date with what is happening in the travel industry. Salespeople and the companies they represent also must be committed to obeying the law and practicing ethical behavior.
- Travel sales professionals use various tools and techniques, including technology, to help them serve their customers better. The high-tech equipment of the 1990s will increase agents' speed and efficiency in helping their customers. New technological advancements such as the video kiosk will increase the visibility of travel products and, to some extent, free salespeople to do more creative selling and counseling.
- Interactive Internet Web sites, with multi-media capability (both subscription- and non-subscription based) will provide customers with better access to information and allow them to make their own reservations.
- Another factor in maintaining loyal customers is to provide people with products they need and want. To remain competitive, travel organizations must perform ongoing marketing research and be willing to change their marketing plans to accommodate travelers' changing preferences and expectations.

KEY TERMS

customer service
code of ethics

DISCUSSION QUESTIONS

1. What are some principles of good customer service?
2. What are four ways in which travel sales professionals provide service with the sale? Give an example of each.
3. Give two examples of a value-added service or amenity for each of the following travel products: an airplane flight, a rental car, a stay in a resort.
4. What are the general ways in which a salesperson follows up on a sale?
5. What tools and technology are likely to be found in the electronic sales office of the new millennium? What do video kiosks, online travel Web sites, and satellite ticket printers have in common with convenience stores?
6. Why is it important to review and update the marketing plan on a regular basis?

STUDY GUIDE — CHAPTER 12

Satisfying the Customer

Name: ______________________ Date: ____________

Directions: Answer these questions as you read the chapter. You will be able to use your answers to help you review the chapter.

1. What is customer service?

2. How can lack of competition result in poor service?

3. Why is it important for a travel salesperson to provide counseling to customers?

4. How can a travel salesperson best serve people with special needs?

5. Describe how car rental companies and hotels can increase the convenience of their products.

6. Why is it important to solicit customer feedback?

7. What should you keep in mind when resolving complaints from customers?

8. What are some ways in which a travel salesperson can stay in touch with customers?

9. What is an incentive? How can it promote return business?

10. Why is continuing education so important to improving the quality of service that a travel business offers?

11. Describe four business practices that are outlawed by the federal government.

12. Provide three examples of behavior by travel salespersons that would be considered unethical.

13. List three recent technological innovations that will positively affect the travel marketing and sales professional.

A. In the office: ______________________________

____

____

____

B. Outside the office: ______________________________

____

____

____

14. Describe three market trends that have changed the face of travel worldwide.

____

____

____

____

Satisfying the Customer

Name: ______________________ Date: ______________

CUSTOMER SERVICE COUNTS

Imagine yourself as each of the travelers described below and list specific services that you would expect or like to receive from a travel supplier or intermediary.

1. You are a teacher from the United States bringing a group of ten college freshmen to Stratford-upon-Avon, England, to explore Shakespeare's birthplace and attend the Globe Theater. What services would you want or need, and who would you expect to provide them?

2. You are a Japanese executive attending a business conference in San Francisco for one week, and your spouse has taken vacation time to accompany you on this trip. What services would you want or need, and who would you expect to provide them?

3. You are a salesperson who has been rewarded with an incentive trip to South Seas Plantation, a resort and recreation complex. What services would you want or need, and who would you expect to provide them?

4. You are a mother of one-year-old twins, taking them on their first flight, from Seattle to their grandparents' home in Sydney, Australia. What services would you want or need, and who would you expect to provide them?

5. You are the travel manager for a large corporation that uses a wide range of travel products, and you are responsible for setting travel policy, controlling costs, and choosing suppliers and intermediaries. What services would you want or need, and who would you expect to provide them?

6. You and your spouse are middle-aged visitors from Great Britain, spending a week sightseeing in New York City and then a week in Florida, including a visit to Disney World. What services would you want or need, and who would you expect to provide them?

7. You are a middle-aged woman traveling with a companion on a cruise of the Greek Islands, and you use a wheelchair. What services would you want or need, and who would you expect to provide them?

8. You are a nine-year-old boy flying alone from Dallas, where you and your mother live, to Boston, to spend the summer with your father. What services would you want or need, and who would you expect to provide them?

9. You are an account executive for a public relations firm, traveling from Minneapolis to San Diego by airplane and rental car to run a trade show exhibit, and you are responsible for transporting and setting up your firm's display. What services would you want or need, and who would you expect to provide them?

10. You and your spouse are a retired couple from Montana, taking your preteen grandchildren on a one-week vacation to Myrtle Beach, South Carolina, while their parents go on a second honeymoon. What services would you want and need, and who would you expect to provide them?

____

____

____

____

11. You and your spouse, dual income forty-year-olds with no children, want to visit New Orleans for a five-day trip that offers sightseeing, gourmet dining, jazz, and golf. What services would you want or need, and who would you expect to provide them?

____

____

____

____

12. You are a sports enthusiast who wants to scuba dive and explore the reefs of the coast of the Cayman Islands and try sailing and windsurfing—all on a reasonable budget. What services would you want or need, and who would you expect to provide them?

____

____

____

____

13. You are an American from North Dakota, whose grandparents came from Norway, and you want to visit the town where they were born as well as tour the rest of the country and sail in the fjords. What services would you want or need, and who would you expect to provide them?

____

____

____

____

Commonly Used Abbreviations

ABA	American Bus Association
ACED-I	Association of Conference and Events Directors—International
AHMA	American Hotel and Motel Association
AIMP	Association of Independent Meeting Planners
AP	American plan
ARC	Airlines Reporting Corporation
ARTA	Association of Retail Travel Agents
ASAE	American Society of Association Executives
ASTA	American Society of Travel Agents
ATA	Air Transport Association
ATM	automated ticketing machine
ATPCO	Airline Tariff Publishing Company
CCTE	certified corporate travel executive
CHA	certified hotel administrator
CHRIE	Council on Hotel, Restaurant and Institutional Education
CHSE	certified hotel sales executive
CLIA	Cruise Lines International Association
CMP	certified meeting professional
CP	continental plan
CPI	cost per inquiry
CPR	cost per reservation
CPV	cost per visitor
CRS	computer reservations system
CTC	certified travel counselor
CTM	consolidated tour manual
CTP	certified tour professional
CVB	Convention and Visitors Bureau
DIT	domestic independent tour
DMC	destination management company
DRI	Data Resources/McGraw-Hill
EP	European plan
FAA	Federal Aviation Administration
FBO	fixed-base operator
FCU	fare construction unit
FIT	foreign independent tour
GDS	global distribution system
GRT	gross registered tonnage
HTI	Hotel Travel Index
IACVB	International Association of Convention and Visitors Bureaus
IAMAT	International Association for Medical Assistance to Travelers
IATA	International Air Transport Association
IATAN	International Airline Travel Agency Network
IATM	International Association of Tour Managers
ICAO	International Civil Aviation Organization
ICC	Interstate Commerce Commission
ICTA	Institute of Certified Travel Agents
IEA	International Exhibitors Association
ISES	International Special Events Society
ISITE	International Society of Incentive Travel Executives
ISTTE	International Society of Travel and Tourism Educators
MAP	modified American plan
MPI	Meeting Professionals International
NACOA	National Association of Cruise Only Agents
NPTA	National Passenger Traffic Association
NRA	National Restaurant Association
NTA	National Tour Association
NTF	National Tourism Foundation
NTO	National Tourist Office
NTS	National Travel Survey
OAG	Official Airline Guide
OHG	Official Hotel Guide
OMCA	Ontario Motor Coach Association

PARS	programmed airline reservations system
PATA	Pacific Asia Travel Association
PC	personal computer
PNR	passenger name record
PR	public relations
RAA	Regional Airlines Association
RFP	request for proposal
ROI	return on investment
SABRE	Semi-Automated Business Research Environment
SATO	Scheduled Airline Ticket Office
SITA	Société Internationale de Télécommunications Aéronautique
STO	state tourist office
STP	satellite ticket printer
TACOS	Travel Agents Computer Society
TIA	Travel Industry Association of America
TIAC	Tourism Industry Association of Canada
TTRA	Travel and Tourism Research Association
UBOA	United Bus Owners of America
USTOA	United States Tour Operators Association
USTTA	United States Travel and Tourism Administration
VALS	values and lifestyles
VFR	visiting friends and relatives
WATA	World Association of Travel Agents
WTO	World Tourism Organization
WTTC	World Travel and Tourism Council

Travel Associations and Organizations

Please note that Internet resources are of a time sensitive nature and URL sites and addresses may often be modified or deleted.

Adventure Travel Society
6551 South Revere Parkway,
Suite 160
Englewood, CO 80111
Ph: 303-649-9016
http://www.adventuretravel.com/ats/main.html

Africa Travel Association
347 Fifth Avenue, Room 610
New York, NY 10016
Ph: 212-447-1926

Air Transport Association (ATA)
1301 Pennsylvania Avenue NW #110
Washington, DC 20004
Ph: 202-626-4000
http://www.air-transport.org

Airlines Reporting Corporation
1530 Wilson Boulevard, Suite 800
Arlington, VA 22209
Ph: 703-816-8102
http://www.arccorp.com

Airports Council International
1775 K Street NW, Suite 500
Washington, DC 20006
Ph: 202-293-1362
http://www.aci-na.org

American Automobile Association
1000 AAA Drive
Heathrow, FL 32746
Ph: 407-444-7000
http://www.aaa.com

American Bus Association
1100 New York Avenue NW #1050
Washington, DC 20005
Ph: 800-283-2877, 202-842-1645
http://www.buses.org

American Hiking Society
1422 Fenwick Lane
Silver Spring, MD 20910
P.O. Box 20160
Washington, DC 20041-2160
Ph: 301-565-6704
http://www.ahs.simplenet.com

American Hotel & Motel Association (AHMA)
1201 New York Avenue NW,
Suite 600
Washington, DC 20005
Ph: 202-289-3100
http://www.ahma.com

American Recreation Coalition
1225 New York Avenue NW, Suite 450
Washington, DC 20005
Ph: 800-257-6370, 202-682-9530
http://www.funoutdoors.com

American Sightseeing International (ASI)
490 Post Street, Suite 1701
San Francisco, CA 94102
Ph: 800-225-4432, 415-986-2082
http://www.sightseeing.com

American Society of Travel Agents (ASTA)
1101 King Street, Suite 200
Alexandria, VA 22314
Ph: 800-275-2782, 703-739-2782
http://www.astanet.com

The American Tourism Society
419 Park Avenue South, Room 505
New York, NY 10016
Ph: 212-779-4823

Association of Retail Travel Agents (ARTA)
501 Darby Creek Road, Suite 47
Lexington, KY 40509
Ph: 800-969-6069, 888-278-2669,
606-263-1194
http://www.artaonline.com

Association of Canadian Travel Agents
1729 Bank Street, Suite 201
Ottawa, Ontario K1V 7Z5
Canada
Ph: 613-521-0474

122 Wood Crescent
Mailing Address: P.O. Box 1149
Assiniboia, Saskatchewan S0H 0B0
Canada
Ph: 306-642-5500

625-25th Avenue NE
Calgary, Alberta T2E 1Y6
Canada
Ph: 403-277-9445

P.O. Box 3131
Halifax, Nova Scotia B3J 3G6
Canada
Ph: 902-422-7311

5025 Orbitor Drive
Building 6, Suite 103
Mississauga, Ontario L4W 4Y5
Canada
Ph: 905-282-9294

C.P. 8000
Montreal, Quebec H3C 3L4
Canada
Ph: 514-987-8733

#905-850 West Hastings Street
Vancouver, British Columbia V6C 1E1
Canada
Ph: 604-688-0516

17-399 Berry Street
Winnipeg, Manitoba R3J 1N6
Canada
Ph: 204-831-0831

Association of Certified Travel Agents Inc.
1209 Park Avenue, Suite B2
New York, NY 10128
Ph: 212-427-6848

Bed & Breakfast: The National Network
4224 West Red Bird Lane
Dallas, TX 75237

P.O. Box 764703
Dallas, TX 75376-4703
Ph: 800-899-4538, 888-866-4262,
972-298-8586
http://www.tnn4bnb.com

Canadian Institutes of Travel Counselors (CITC)
41 Richwood Drive
Markham, Ontario L3P 3Y7
Canada
Ph: 905-472-8533

Canadian Tourism Commission
235 Queen Street West, Floor 8
Ottawa, Ontario K1A OH6
Canada
Ph: 613-946-1000
http://www.canadatourism.com

Caribbean Hotel Association (CHA)
1000 Ponce De Leon, Floor 5
San Juan, PR 00907
Ph: 787-725-9139
http://www.chahotels.com

Caribbean Tourism Organization
80 Broad Street, Floor 32
New York, NY 10004
Ph: 212-682-0435
http://caribbeantourism.com

Cruise Lines International Association
500 Fifth Avenue, Suite 1407
New York, NY 10110
Ph: 800-372-2542,
212-921-0066
http://www.cruising.org

Earthwatch Institute
680 Mount Auburn Street
Watertown, MA 02472

P.O. Box 9104
Watertown, MA 02471-9104
Ph: 800-776-0188,
617-926-8200
http://www.earthwatch.org

Elderhostel
75 Federal Street
Boston, MA 02110
Ph: 617-426-7788,
617-877-8056

European Travel Commission (ETC)
1 Rockefeller Plaza, Room 214
New York, NY 10020
Ph: 212-218-1200
http://www.visiteurope.com

Hospitality Sales & Marketing Association International
1300 L Street NW, Suite 1020
Washington, DC 20005
Ph: 202-789-0089
http://www.hsmai.org

Hotel Association of Canada Incorporated
1016/130 Albert Street
Ottawa, Ontario K1P 5G4
Canada
Ph: 613-237-7149
http://www.hotels.ca

IATAN International Airline Travel Agent Network
300 Garden City Plaza, Suite 342
Garden City, NY 11530
Ph: 516-747-4462
http://www.iatan.org

International Air Transport Association (IATA)
800 Place Victoria
Montreal, Quebec H4Z 1M1
Canada
Ph: 514-874-0202
http://www.iata.org

International Association Convention & Visitor Bureau (IACVB)
2000 L Street NW, Suite 702
Washington, DC 20036
Ph: 202-296-7888
http://www.iacvb.org

International Association of Amusement Parks & Attractions
1448 Duke Street
Alexandria, VA 22314
Ph: 703-836-4800
http://www.iaapa.org

International Association of Conference Centers
243 North Lindbergh Boulevard
Saint Louis, MO 63141
Ph: 800-844-2327, 314-993-8575
http://www.iacconline.com

International Association of Fairs and Expos
P.O. Box 985
Springfield, MO 65801
Ph: 417-862-0156

International Council of Cruise Lines
1211 Connecticut Avenue NW, Suite 800
Washington, DC 20036
Ph: 202-296-8463

International Gay Travel Association (IGTA)
4331 North Federal Highway, Suite 304
Fort Lauderdale, FL 33308
Ph: 800-448-8550, 954-776-2626

International Federation of Women's Travel Organization
13901 North 73rd Street, Suite 210B
Scottsdale, AZ 85260
Ph: 602-596-6640
http://www.ifwto.trav.org

Meeting Professionals International
4455 LBJ Freeway, Suite 1200
Dallas, TX 75244
Ph: 972-702-3000
http://www.mpiweb.org

Metropolitan Association of Professional Travel Agents (MAPTA)
60 Sutton Place South
New York, NY 10022
Ph: 212-332-1263

National Air Carrier Association (NACA)
1730 M Street NW, Suite 806
Washington, DC 20036
Ph: 202-833-8200

National Air Transportation Association (NATA)
4226 King Street
Alexandria, VA 22302
Ph: 800-808-6282, 703-845-9000
http://www.nata-online.org

National Association Commissioned Travel Agents
P.O. Box 2398
Valley Center, CA 92082
Ph: 760-751-1197
http://www.nacta.com

National Association of Railroad Passengers
900 2nd Street NE, Suite 308
Washington, DC 20002
Ph: 202-408-8362
http://www.narprail.org

National Association of RV Parks and Campgrounds
8605 Westwood Center Drive, Suite 201
Vienna, VA 22182
Ph: 703-734-3000
http://www.gocampingamerica.com

National Business Travel Association (NBTA)
1615 King Street
Alexandria, VA 22314
Ph: 703-684-0263
http://www.nbta.org

National Council of Travel Attractions
17000 W Ih 10
Six Flags
San Antonio, TX 78257
Ph: 210-697-5457
http://www.sixflags.com

National Motorcoach Network Incorporated
10527C Braddock Road
Patriot Square
Fairfax, VA 22032
Ph: 800-822-6602, 703-250-7897
http://www.motorcoach.com

National Park Hospitality Association
P.O. Box 27
Mammoth Cave National Park
Mammoth Cave, KY 42259
Ph: 502-773-2191

National Restaurant Association
1200 17th Street NW
Washington, DC 20036
Ph: 800-424-5156, 202-331-5900

National Tour Association (NTA)
546 East Main Street
Lexington, KY 40508
Ph: 800-682-8886, 606-226-4444

Pacific Asia Travel Organization (PATO)
1 Montgomery Street, Suite 1000
Pacific Telesis Tower
San Francisco, CA 94104
Ph: 415-986-4646
http://www.pata.org

Passenger Vessel Association
1600 Wilson Boulevard, Suite 1000
Arlington, VA 22209
Ph: 703-807-0100
http://www.passengervessel.com

Recreational Vehicle Industry Association
1896 Preston White Drive
Reston, VA 20191

P.O. Box 2999
Reston, VA 20195-0999
Ph: 703-620-6003
http://www.rvia.org

Regional Airline Association (RAA)
1200 19th Street NW, Suite 300
Washington, DC 20036
Ph: 202-429-5113
http://www.raa.org

Society for the Advancement of Travel for the Handicapped
347 Fifth Avenue, Room 610
New York, NY 10016
Ph: 212-447-7284
http://www.sath.org

Society Incentive Travel Executives (SITE)
21 West 38th Street, Floor 10
New York, NY 10018
Ph: 212-575-0910
http://site-intl.org

Society of American Travel Writers
4101 Lake Boone Trail, Suite 201
Raleigh, NC 27607
Ph: 919-787-5181
http://www.satw.org

Society of Travel Agents in Government (STAG)
6935 Wisconsin Avenue, Suite 200
Chevy Chase, MD 20815
Ph: 301-654-8595
http://www.government-travel.org

Tourism Industries U.S. Department of Commerce
14th and Constitution Avenue NW, Room 1860
Washington, DC 20230
Ph: 202-482-0140
http://www.tinet.ita.doc.gov

Tourism Industry Association of Canada (TIAC)
130 Albert Street, Suite 1016
Ottawa, Ontario K1P 5G4
Canada
Ph: 613-238-3883

Trade Show Exhibitors Association (TSEA)
5501 Backlick Road, Suite 105
Springfield, VA 22151
Ph: 703-941-3725
http://www.tsea.org

Travel and Tourism Research Association (TTRA)
546 East Main Street
Lexington, KY 40508
Ph: 606-226-4344
http://www.ttra.com

Travel Center Independent Affiliates
2852 Johnson Ferry Road, Suite 100
Marietta, GA 30062
Ph: 770-640-1234

Travel Industry Association of America (TIAA)
1100 New York Avenue NW, Suite 450
Washington, DC 20005
Ph: 202-408-8422
http://www.tia.org

Travel Safe
P.O. Box 7050
Wyomissing, PA 19610
Ph: 800-523-8020, 610-678-0373
http://www.travelsafe.com

United Nations Organization
1 UN Plaza
New York, NY 10017
Ph: 212-963-5855
http://www.un.org

United States Tour Operators Association (USTOA)
342 Madison Avenue, Room 1522
New York, NY 10173
Ph: 212-599-6599
http://www.ustoa.com

World Federation of Travel Writers (FIJET)
1 Ballingswood Road
Atlantic Highlands, NJ 07716
Ph: 732-291-2840

World Tourism Organization (WTO)
Capitán Haya, 42
Madrid 28020
SPAIN
Ph: (34 91) 567 81 00

Glossary of Key Terms

A

advertising The sponsored use of space or time in order to promote a product in the mass media.

all-inclusive A term used to describe travel packages that include most needed travel products for a single, fixed price.

all-inclusive resorts Resorts that provide guests with accommodations, meals, entertainment, and other products and services for one fixed price.

allocentric A term created by Stanley Plog to describe a self-confident, outgoing person who seeks adventure, variety, and excitement, especially in travel.

arbitrary and affordable budgeting A budgeting method based solely on personal judgment and financial capability.

atmospherics Tangible aspects of a travel product's presentation meant to communicate a particular feeling or ambience.

automated ticketing machine (ATM) A self-service machine that provides customers with flight information, reservations, tickets, and boarding passes.

B

barriers to travel Reasons that people choose not to travel, including lack of time or money, fear of the unknown, reluctance to make the effort, and ignorance about the benefits of travel.

behavioristic segmenting Dividing the market into groups of people who share particular buying habits, preferences, or purposes.

benefit The value of a travel product or service to the traveler.

brand loyalty A company entices customers to keep using its product by offering various incentives, such as reduced prices, free airline tickets, and special services.

brochure A printed marketing tool created by travel destinations or companies, designed to appeal to travel customers and assist agents in making sales.

C

close the sale Secure a commitment from the customer to purchase the product or service.

code of ethics Guidelines for moral behavior.

cold call An unannounced visit to a prospect with whom a salesperson has had no previous interaction.

commission The percentage of a selling price paid to a salesperson as a fee for a sale.

communications mix A term generally referring to the three primary promotional techniques—advertising, sales promotion, and public relations.

compensation According to Marinus Kosters, the concept that travel functions as a reward for the stress and hassles of everyday life.

competitive parity budgeting A budget-setting method based on matching the marketing budgets and efforts of competing companies and their products.

complementarity The close relationship among travel products whereby some travel products are closely tied to and intertwined with other travel products.

computer reservations system (CRS) A computer system that provides information on schedules, fares and prices, and availability of various travel products; also permits travel agents to book reservations, print tickets and itineraries, and generate invoices.

consortium A group of independent firms that band together to pool their financial and company resources for an enterprise or endeavor.

consumer advertising In the travel industry, advertising aimed at prospective travelers.

contingency Allowance for unexpected expenses as a part of a budget.

conversion The marketer's goal of turning customer inquiries into actual sales.

cooperative advertising Advertising that is sponsored by and promotes the products of two or more companies.

cost per inquiry (CPI) A figure calculated by dividing the total cost of a marketing activity by the total number of inquiries it generates.

cost per reservation (CPR) A figure calculated by dividing the total cost of a marketing activity by the number of reservations produced.

cost per visitor (CPV) A figure calculated by dividing the total cost of a marketing activity by the number of visitors produced.

cultural motivators Impulses to travel in order to learn about a place and its music, art, religion, and folklore.

customer-oriented marketing A modern marketing theory that focuses on customers' wants and needs.

customer service The practice of paying special attention to the personal needs of customers.

D

database target marketing A technique for creating profiles of existing and potential target markets by combining information from multiple databases, allowing markets to be targeted more cost-effectively.

demographic segmenting Grouping people on the basis of objective criteria or measurable characteristics, such as age, income, occupation, family size/life cycle, and education.

destination management company (DMC) A larger, more comprehensive form of a receptive tour operator.

destination marketer A marketing professional who works to stimulate interest in a particular town, city, state, province, or region.

direct competition Competition between companies that offer similar travel products.

direct distribution The direct sale of travel products and services by a supplier to a customer.

direct mail Catalogs, brochures, fliers, and other information sent directly to prospective customers through the mail.

directory advertising Specific information about a company, published in Yellow Pages, maps, travel atlases, or travel business directories.

distribution system The sales system for moving travel products from suppliers to customers.

E

effectiveness ratios Statistical measurements used to evaluate an organization's marketing methods.

F

familiarization trip A sponsored trip meant to enable travel agents to evaluate travel products firsthand. Also known as a "fam trip."

feature Any fact about or characteristic of a travel product or service.

fundamental needs According to Abraham Maslow, the basic human needs of thirst, hunger, sex, and safety.

G

geographic segmenting Grouping people for marketing purposes according to the particular regions, climates, or types of environment in which they live.

guidebook A book that describes and evaluates travel products, services, and attractions, and is written with the traveler in mind.

H

host vendor An airline or other organization that owns and operates a computer reservations system.

I

image How a product or service appears to the consumer, based on the perception of its unique attributes.

incentive travel planner A travel intermediary who provides companies with tours and vacations to offer to employees as rewards for achieving goals.

indirect competition Competition between companies with dissimilar products that fill similar needs.

indirect distribution A system in which travel products are sold by suppliers to customers through one or more intermediaries.

industry reference books Standard travel reference materials that provide detailed information about a travel product.

inside sales Sales transactions in which buyers generally approach the seller; usually negotiated within the seller's office. Also called in-house sales.

intangible A term used to describe the nonphysical aspects of travel products, those that are felt or experienced rather than seen or touched, such as relaxation and romance.

interdependence The interaction between and among travel suppliers and consumers, which is created by the simultaneous production and consumption of travel products and services.

intermediary A travel seller who acts as a link between a supplier and a customer.

internal marketing A practice in which companies provide incentives for good job performance by offering employees rewards such as free trips or bonuses.

interpersonal motivator An impulse to travel for social reasons, such as making new friends, meeting different people, or getting away from everyday friends and family.

L

limited-response probe A type of question asked of customers during the selling process; intended to elicit a short response or a yes-or-no answer.

literal needs A customer's specific, tangible needs, such as schedule and budget.

M

margin of error A scientifically determined measure of confidence in the results of research.

market challenger A company that seeks to establish its product as a market leader or to expand its share of the market by attacking the current leader.

market follower A company or its product that is content with its subordinate position in the market and wishes to conserve its finances and the status quo by not challenging the market leader.

market leader The company (or its product) holding the largest share of the business of a particular market.

market niche player A company or its product with the basic marketing strategy of operating for a narrow and specialized segment of the market.

market research The gathering and analyzing of information about products and consumers.

market segment A group of potential customers who share certain characteristics.

market segmentation The concept of dividing a market into segments for specific marketing purposes.

market share The percentage relationship of a company's sales to those of its entire industry or industry segment.

marketing The promotional activities that bring buyers and sellers together.

marketing communications Forms of communication with the market—such as advertising, public relations, sales promotion, and personal selling—intended to increase the tangibility of travel products, persuade customers to purchase them, and monitor consumer expectations.

marketing director A marketing professional who directs and supervises the marketing activities for a company.

marketing mix The combination of variables used by a company as a part of its marketing program.

marketing objective A specific statement describing a market-related goal for a travel product.

marketing plan A detailed written proposal that illustrates how a company intends to reach its marketing objectives.

marketing strategy The overall plan of how a company intends to achieve its marketing goals.

marketing tactics The specific techniques used to implement marketing strategies.

meeting, convention, and event planner A travel professional who arranges transportation, facilities, accommodations, and tours for people attending meetings, conventions, trade shows, or conferences.

midcentric A term developed by Stanley Plog to describe travelers with relatively average tendencies and preferences.

motivations The internal factors at work in individuals, expressed as needs and desires.

O

objective and task budgeting A method of constructing a marketing budget by first setting objectives and then estimating the costs of the tasks needed to accomplish those objectives.

open probe A salesperson's open-ended question encouraging a customer's free response and thus eliciting more information than a limited-response probe.

out-of-home media Outdoor advertising venues such as billboards, kiosks, and transit signs on buses, streetcars, subways, and taxis.

outside sales Sales efforts that usually occur outside of the seller's office; usually initiated by the salesperson rather than the customer.

override A sales incentive: a cash payment made by a travel company, to an agency, above the standard commission rate.

P

parity The characteristic of a travel product being essentially similar to other travel products.

percentage of sales budgeting A budgeting method based on a percentage of the previous year's total sales or the current year's projected sales.

perception How a particular customer sees a particular product or service, based on its image and the customer's values.

performance standards Determinations of allowable deviations from stated marketing objectives; used when evaluating the success of a marketing plan.

perishability A characteristic of many travel products that must be used within a finite period of time; if they are not used by then, the opportunity to sell them "perishes."

personal selling Sales resulting from personal contact between the buyer and seller, either face to face or by telephone.

physical motivators Incentives for travel related to the need to reduce tension, for example, through rest, sports, or entertainment.

positioning statement A statement used within a company to differentiate its travel product from that of the competition. A positioning statement provides the basis for creating the product's image.

presentation mix The combination of five major elements—physical characteristics, location, atmospherics, price, and employee performance—used to increase the tangibility of a product and to help differentiate it from its competitors.

press conference Members of the media are invited to a presentation or announcement by a travel company, in order to promote public relations.

press release An announcement or a news article that objectively describes something newsworthy about a travel product or service.

product-oriented marketing The marketing approach of relying on a product's superior quality to attract consumers.

product positioning The marketing strategy of establishing and differentiating a product's unique characteristics and communicating them to a particular segment of the market. Also referred to simply as positioning.

product/service combination The balance of tangible and intangible elements in a travel product. The combination may be adjusted to suit the needs of the selected target market.

prospecting The process of looking for new customers by identifying the most promising possibilities.

psychocentric A term used by Stanley Plog to describe a person who chooses familiar and safe destinations because of a fear of and anxiety about traveling and new experiences.

psychographic segmenting Grouping people for marketing purposes according to their psychological makeup—their values, attitudes, lifestyles, interests, and personalities.

psychological needs In Abraham Maslow's hierarchy of needs, those placed above fundamental needs, including belonging, love, self-esteem, and the approval of others.

public relations (P.R.) A type of marketing communications involving the nonsponsored presentation of ideas, goods, or services, primarily to increase product recognition or build goodwill.

Q

qualifying the customer A travel salesperson's task of assessing a client's wants and needs before recommending a purchase.

R

recapping A verbal summary of the conversation between a customer and a sales representative, provided to give the customer an opportunity to voice any concerns or questions before closing the sale.

reception An event in a luxury location, with complimentary food and drink, designed to promote contact between travel companies and media representatives.

receptive tour operator A tour company, located in a particular destination, that has a contract with outbound tour companies who visit that destination, in order to handle the needs of its customers.

relationship marketing Marketing intended to maintain a relationship with a customer after a sale in order to encourage future business with that customer.

request for a proposal (RFP) A client's request for a formal written proposal outlining how the sales representative's products and services can meet customers' needs while providing benefits and value.

return on investment (ROI) The amount of revenue generated for every dollar spent on marketing.

S

sales The face-to-face, personal communication between seller and buyer in relation to the purchase of a product or service.

sales manager A person who trains, directs, and evaluates the sales staff of a travel company.

sales-oriented marketing The marketing theory that focuses primarily on the sales effort.

sales promotion Specialized sponsored activities other than advertising that are intended to stimulate demand for a particular product.

sales representative The person who closes the sale. Sales representatives must know their products and services extremely well and be able to explain how they meet customers' needs.

sales variance A comparison of actual sales against projected sales.

sample A group of people carefully selected to yield representative results when subjected to market research.

satellite ticket printer (STP) A machine that allows travel agents to deliver tickets electronically to a remote location, usually a client's premises.

seasonality The regular fluctuation in demand for travel at different times of the year.

segmental analysis A method for evaluating cost and profitability that looks at individual components of a marketing program.

self-actualization According to Abraham Maslow, the highest order of human needs—the fulfillment of one's full human potential.

service quality When two travel products are essentially similar, the quality of the service makes all the difference in a customer's decision to purchase one product rather than another.

simultaneous production and consumption Travel products are produced (provided by suppliers) and consumed (by customers) simultaneously, in contrast to most consumer goods, which are produced and consumed at different places and points in time.

situational analysis A statement of the current status of a company, its products, and the marketplace, including the company's strengths, weaknesses, opportunities, and threats (constraints).

slogan A phrase generated from a positioning statement that is designed to catch the attention of the target market and reinforce a travel product's image.

specialized distributor Intermediaries who focus on a particular type of travel customer or product, such as meeting and convention attendees or unsold travel products.

staged event A special event staged for members of the media, invited guests, and the general public, in order to increase a company's visibility and goodwill in the community.

status and prestige motivators According to McIntosh and Goeldner, motivations to travel in order to gain recognition from others.

status recognition According to Marinus Kosters, motivation based on a person's need to establish and demonstrate his or her status to others by selecting particular travel destinations.

supplier A travel product seller who owns or controls the travel product being sold.

T

tangible A term used to describe a product that can be seen and touched.

target market A particular segment of the total market toward which a travel company directs its marketing efforts.

target marketing A marketer's strategy of aiming its products and promotional messages toward particular types of buyers.

ticket consolidator A travel professional who buys unsold travel products and sells them to travel customers at discounted prices.

tie-in A promotional device connecting the purchase of one product with a special offer on another, often unrelated, product.

tour operator A company that contracts with hotels, transportation companies, and other suppliers to create a complete vacation package.

trade advertising Advertising within the travel industry as opposed to that directed toward consumers.

trade publication A magazine or annual guide published by a professional travel association or for commercial distribution.

trade show A meeting for travel industry personnel that features freestanding vendor displays and booths. Also known as a trade fair.

travel agent A counselor who sells the products and services of the travel businesses represented by their agencies.

travel club An organization that offers its members discount travel products.

U

unique selling proposition (USP) A positioning statement that differentiates a company's travel product or service from others on the market.

uniqueness The built-in appeal of a travel product that is impossible to duplicate, for example, the Eiffel Tower.

upgrading A sales representative's recommendation to purchase a more expensive product than the one requested by the client. Also called upselling.

V

value The quality and quantity of a travel product in relation to its price, as perceived by the travel customer.

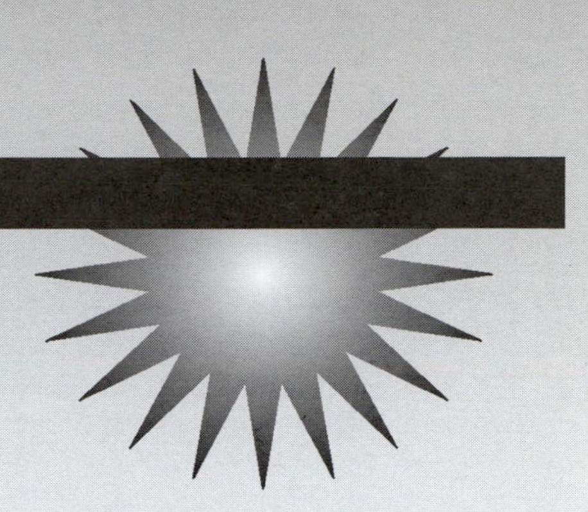

Index

A

AAdvantage, 213
Abbreviations, commonly used, 273–74
Active Adventure Tours, 233
Adventure Travel Society, 275
Advertising, 201–7
  AIDA and, 98, 99
  creating message for, 204–5
  defined, 97
  effectiveness of, 98–100
  expressiveness of, 100
  media and, 205–7
  pervasiveness of, 99
  process steps, 203–7
  purpose of, 97–98, 203
  quality of presentation and, 98–99
  selecting audience for, 203–4
Africa Travel Association, 275
Age, segmenting and, 41–42
AHMA. *See* American Hotel & Motel Association (AHMA)
AIDA, advertising and, 98, 99
Air Canada, 213
Air France, 255
Airline passenger's bill of rights, 9
Airlines
  customer service and, 252
  frequent-flier partnerships, 213
  off-season prices and, 28
  product class and, 75
Airlines Reporting Corporation, 275
Airports Council International, 275
Air Transport Association (ATA), 275
Alamo car rental, 89, 255
Alitalia, 255
All-inclusive resorts, 73
All-inclusive vacations, 94, 188
All Nippon Airways, 255
Allocentric personality, 140
American Airlines, 29, 92, 213
American Automobile Association, 275
American Bus Association, 44, 275
American Express, 14, 212
American Hiking Society, 275
American Hotel & Motel Association (AHMA), 275
American Marketing Association, 203
American Recreation Coalition, 275

American Sightseeing International (ASI), 276
American Society of Travel Agents (ASTA), 161, 184, 257, 276
The American Tourism Society, 276
Amtrak, 77, 170
Amusement parks, 3
Arbitrary and affordable budgeting, 117
Association of Retail Travel Agents (ARTA), 276
ASI. *See* American Sightseeing International
Association of Canadian Travel Agents, 276
Association of Certified Travel Agents Inc., 276
ASTA. *See* American Society of Travel Agents (ASTA)
ASTA Agency Management, 184
Atlantic City, New Jersey, 45
Atmospherics, presentation mix and, 96
ATMs. *See* automated ticketing machines (ATMs)
Attractions, customer service and, 253
Automated ticketing machines (ATMs), 32, 170
Automation, 168–70
Avis Rent-A-Car, 77, 89

B

Baby boomers, 261–62
Baedeker Guides, 184
Barriers to travel, 142
Baths of Caracalla, 10
Bed & Breakfast: The National Network, 276
Behavior classifications, 141–42
Behavioristic segmenting, 41, 46–47
Benefits, 27
  assessing travel value and, 191–92
  emphasizing, 231–32
  introducing, 229–31
  positioning and, 69, 74
  segmenting and, 47
Brand loyalty, 29
Bristow, Suzanne, CSEP, 31
British Airways, 89, 255
Brochures, 183–84
Buckingham Palace, 29
Budget, marketing. *See* marketing budget
Budget Motel, 74
Budget Rent-A-Car, 77
Business traveler, 5, 47
  differences from leisure traveler, 229
  needs of, 142, 145–46
Buyers, 4–5
Buying process, steps in, 137–38

C

Canadian Airlines, 213
Canadian Institutes of Travel Counselors (CITC), 276
Canadian Tourism Commission, 276
Caribbean Hotel Association (CHA), 276
Caribbean Tourism Organization, 277
Carnival Cruise Lines, 88–89, 93
Carpenter, Roger, 185
Car rental companies, customer service and, 252
Census Bureau, 6
Certified Tour Professional (CTP), 256
CHA. *See* Caribbean Hotel Association (CHA)
CITC. *See* Canadian Institutes of Travel Counselors (CITC)
CLIA. *See* Cruise Lines International Association (CLIA)
CLIA Cruise Manual, 183
Client files, 120
Closing the sale
  assumptive approach, 235
  direct approach, 235
  failure to, 235
  how to, 234
  types of, 234–35
  when to, 234
Club Med, 73–74, 212
Coca-Cola, 100
Code of ethics, 257
Cold calls, 236

Colleagues, as information sources, 186
Colonial Williamsburg Foundation, 11
Comfort, business traveler and, 144
Commission, 157
Communication
  expressing appreciation and, 253
  handling/resolving complaints and, 254–55
  soliciting customer feedback and, 253–54
  staying in touch and, 255
Communications mix, 201–14
Compact discs (CDs), 259
Compensation, 140
Competition, product positioning and, 75, 77
Competitive parity budgeting, 117–18
Complaints, handling and resolving, 254–55
Complementarity, 30, 156
Computer reservations system (CRS), 168–70, 180–82
  high-tech service and, 259
  how to use, 181–82
  limitations of, 182
  non-airline travel products and, 181
  types of information available from, 181
Concorde, 12
Condé Nast Traveler, 258
Consolidated Air Tour Manual, 183
Consortium, 184
Consumer advertising, 203
Consumer movement, 9
Contingency, marketing budget and, 116
Continuing education, 256
Convenience
  business traveler and, 144
  customer service and, 250–51
Conversion, 122
Cook, Thomas, 10
Cooperative advertising, 204
Corporate selling, 235–38
Corporate travel departments, 162
Cost per inquiry (CPI), 124
Cost per reservation (CPR), 124
Counseling, customer service and, 251
Couples, 90
Courier (National Tour Association), 184
CPI. *See* cost per inquiry (CPI)
CPR. *See* cost per reservation (CPR)
Creative selling, 226
Credit card companies, 144
CRS. *See* computer reservations system (CRS)
Cruise line sales representative, 15
Cruise Lines International Association (CLIA), 103, 277
CTP. *See* Certified Tour Professional (CTP)
Cultural motivators, 141
Customer-oriented marketing, 5
Customer-oriented sales promotion
  free travel products, 213
  loyalty marketing, 213
  point-of-purchase displays, 211–12
  price breaks, 212–13
  special discounts, 212–13
  sweepstakes, gifts, and prizes, 213
Customers
  as information sources, 186
  maintaining relationship with, 8–9, 27
  motivations of, 135, 136
  needs of, 191
  perception of, 65–66, 70, 191
  qualifying, 228
  satisfying, 249–62
Customer service
  actions and, 250
  appearance and, 250
  communication skills and, 250
  continuing education and, 256
  convenience and, 250–51
  counseling and, 251
  defined, 249–50
  ethical behavior and, 257
  following up on sale and, 253–56
  going the extra mile and, 251–52
  high-tech service and, 257–60
  legal responsibilities and, 256–57
  maintaining professional level of, 256–57
  marketing and, 260–62
  principles of, 249–50

Customer Service (*continued*)
- product and, 252–53
- providing superior quality of, 250–53
- sales and, 250–52
- special needs and, 251
- study guide and worksheets, 265–71

D

Database target marketing, 51
Data mining, 51
Data Resources/McGraw Hill (DRI), 143
Daugherty, Susan, 208
Davidson Peterson, 121
Deer Valley Ski Area, 75
Delta, 29
Demographic segmenting
- age and, 41–42
- defined, 41
- education and, 43
- ethnic background and, 43
- family size and, 43
- gender and, 43
- income and, 42
- life cycle and, 43
- marketers' use of, 43, 45
- nationality and, 43
- occupation and, 42–43

Denali National Park, 14
Destination management companies (DMC), 163
Destination marketer, 13–14
Destination marketing company representative, 15
Detroit Metropolitan Convention and Visitors Bureau, 204
Dickinson, Bob, 89
Direct competition, 75, 77
Direct distribution, 158–59, 161
- accuracy and, 161
- additional sales opportunities and, 159
- control and, 159, 161
- customer advantages of, 161
- increased profit and, 159
- responsiveness and, 159
- simplicity and, 159
- supplier advantages of, 158–59, 161
- time savings and, 161

Direct-fax marketing, 206–7
Direct-mail marketing, 206–7
Directory advertising, 207
Discounts, 188, 212
Disney, Walt, 3
Disneyland, 3
Disney/MGM Studios Theme Park, 3
Disney University, 94
Disney World, 3, 8, 94
Distribution
- direct, 158–59, 161
- indirect, 158, 161–66

Distribution models, 166–68
- one-stage direct distribution, 166–67
- three-stage indirect distribution, 168
- two-stage indirect distribution, 167–68

Distribution systems, 155
DMC. *See* destination management companies (DMC)
Dollar Rent-A-Car, 89
Double search process, 165
DRI. *See* Data Resources/McGraw Hill (DRI)

E

Earle Palmer Brown, 208
Earthwatch Institute, 277
Econolodge, 74
Education, segmenting and, 43
Effectiveness ratios, 124
Efficiency, need for, 142, 144
Eiffel Tower, 29
Eight *P*s, 91–94
Elderhostel, 277
Electronic information sources, 186
Employees
- behavior and attitude, 97
- monitoring performance of, 122–23

Enterprise car rental, 6
EPCOT Center, 3
ETC. *See* European Travel Commission

Ethical behavior, 257
Ethnic background, segmenting and, 43
Euro Disney, 3
European Travel Commission (ETC), 277
Evaluation, of marketing plan, 8–9, 123–27
Event management, 31
Exchange rates, 188, 189
Exclusive dealing, 257
Experimentation, in market research, 52–53

F

Facsimile machines, 259
Familiarization trip, 14, 187, 211, 214
Family size, segmenting and, 43
Fax machines. *See* facsimile machines
Features
  introducing, 229–31
  positioning and, 68–69
Fielding Guides, 184
FIJET. *See* World Federation of Travel Writers (FIJET)
Finances, monitoring, 122
Firsthand experience, as information source, 186–87
Fodor Guides, 184
Follow up, sales, 253–56
Forbes, 204
Ford, Connie, 185
Frequent traveler programs, 30, 47, 92
Frommer Guides, 184
Frontline training, 123
Fundamental needs, 139

G

GDP. *See* gross domestic product (GDP)
GDS. *See* global distribution system
Gender, segmenting and, 43
General car rental, 89
Geographic segmenting, 41, 45
Get Up and Go, 184
Gifts, 213
Global distribution system (GDS), 168
Goldblatt, Joe, CSEP, 31
Grand tour, 10
Grandtravel, 6
Gray Line tours, 101
Griffall, Keith, 233
Gross domestic product (GDP), 42
Group selling, 235–38
Guidebooks, 184

H

Hawaii, 29
Hedonism, 90
Heizer, Julie, 71
Hertz car rental, 77, 89, 255
Hidden costs, 188
High-tech service, 257–60
Hilton International, 74, 255
Holiday, influence on travel demand, 28
Holland America Line, 258
Horizon Air, 72
Hospitality Sales & Marketing Association International, 277
Host vendors, 170
Hotard Coaches, 101
Hotel and Travel Index, 183
Hotel Association of Canada Incorporated, 277
Hotels, customer service and, 252–53
Hotel sales representative, 15
Hyatt, 74, 255

I

IACVB. *See* International Association Convention & Visitors Bureau (IACVB)
IATA. *See* International Air Transport Association (IATA)
IATAN International Airline Travel Agent Network, 277
IGTA. *See* International Gay Travel Association (IGTA)

Image
positioning and, 66–68
role of, in buying decisions, 77
Incentive travel planners, 158, 164
Income, segmenting and, 42
Indirect competition, 75, 77
Indirect distribution, 158, 161–66
choice and, 165
corporate travel departments and, 162
customer advantages of, 165–66
expanded sales outlets and, 165
no-overhead sales force and, 165
price and, 165
service and, 165–66
specialized travel distributors and, 163–65
supplier advantages of, 165
tour operators and, 162–63
travel agents and, 161–62
Industry reference books, 182–83
Informal interviews, 120
Information gathering, 119–20, 122, 180–84, 186–87
Information sources
brochures, 183–84
colleagues as, 186
customers as, 186
electronic sources, 186
firsthand experience, 186–87
guidebooks, 184
industry reference books, 182–83
print sources, 182–84, 186–87
trade publications, 184
trade shows and, 184, 186
travel articles, 186
word of mouth, 186
Inquiries, 120, 122
Inside (in-house) sales, 227
Intangibility, 26, 155–56
Intangible products, marketing and selling, 26–27
Intercontinental, 74
Interdependence, between suppliers and customers, 27
Intermediary, 5, 156–57
Internal marketing, 94
International Air Transport Association (IATA), 277
International Association Convention & Visitors Bureau (IACVB), 277
International Association of Amusement Parks & Attractions, 277
International Association of Conference Centers, 277
International Association of Fairs and Expos, 277
International Council of Cruise Lines, 277
International Federation of Women's Travel Organization, 278
International Gay Travel Association (IGTA), 277
International Special Events Society (ISES), 31
International tourism, 261
Internet, 158, 166, 207, 260
Interpersonal motivators, 141
Interviews, informal, 120
ISES. *See* International Special Events Society (ISES)

J

Jarvis, Lance, 140
Jerusalem, 10

K

Kosters, Marinus, 139–40
Kosters's theory, 139–40

L

Lambsburg Visitors Center, 185
Las Vegas, Nevada, 45
Legal responsibilities, 256–57
Leisure traveler, 5, 47
differences from business traveler, 229
needs of, 138–44

Life cycle, segmenting and, 43
Lifestyle
  segmenting and, 45–46
  trends, identification of, 50
Limited-response probe, 228
Lindblad Travel, 90
Listening, 229
Literal needs, 179
Location, presentation mix and, 96
Longwoods International, 121
Los Angeles Times, 205
Loyalty marketing, 213
Lufthansa, 213

M

Magazines, 205–6
MAPTA. *See* Metropolitan Association of Professional Travel Agents (MAPTA)
Margin of error, 53
Market
  defined, 5
  nature of, 6–7
Market challenger, 89
Market cost profitability, 124
Market follower, 90
Marketing
  in ancient times, 9–10
  careers in, 12–15
  defined, 4
  in eighteenth century, 10
  factors affecting, 9
  history of, 9–10, 12
  intangible products, 26–27
  in Middle Ages, 10
  in nineteenth century, 10
  ongoing value of, 262
  sales and, 3–15
  in seventeenth century, 10
  study guide and worksheets, 17–24
  tangible products, 26
  theory of, 5–9
  in travel and tourism, 4
  in twentieth century, 10, 12
Marketing budget
  budget-setting methods, 116–19
  characteristics of, 116
  contingency and, 116
Marketing communications
  advertising and, 97–100
  forms of, 97–100, 102–3
  personal selling and, 102–3
  public relations and, 100
  sales promotion and, 100, 102
Marketing cycle, 6–9
  adjusting plan and, 8–9
  evaluating plan and, 8–9
  marketing objectives and, 7–8
  marketing strategies and, 7–8
  monitoring plan and, 8–9
  nature of market and, 6–7
  nature of product and, 6
Marketing director, 14
Marketing mix
  defined, 91
  management of, 94–103
  packaging and, 93–94
  participation and, 94
  physical environment and, 93
  place/process of delivery and, 92
  price and, 92
  product and, 91–92
  promotion and, 92–93
  purchasing process and, 93
Marketing objectives, 7–8, 70, 72, 87–88
Marketing Outlook Forum, 143
Marketing plan, 5–6
  adjusting, 8–9
  components of, 114–16
  control of, 119–20, 122–23
  defined, 113–14
  evaluating, 8–9, 123–27
  implementation of, 113–27
  importance of, 6, 114
  introduction, 114
  length of, 114
  marketing strategies and, 115
  measurement techniques for, 123–24
  monitoring, 8–9
  performance standards and, 123

Marketing Planning (*continued*)
rationale, 114
scope of, 114
situational analysis, 115
study guide and worksheets, 129–32
Marketing strategies, 8
creating, 87–104
defined, 87
examples of, 88–91
marketing objectives and, 87–88
marketing plan and, 115
in practice, 103–4
study guide and worksheets, 105–12
Marketing tactics, 88
Market leader, 88–89
Market niche player, 90–91
Market research, 6
attraction of more visitors and, 50–51
defined, 48
defining problem in, 52
developing and executing research plan for, 52–53
drawing conclusions from, 53
expanding into new geographic areas and, 48
experimentation and, 52–53
identification of lifestyle trends and, 50
making recommendations from, 53
observation and, 52
process, 52–54
producing useful results in, 53
reasons for, 48–51
recognition of growing markets and, 49–50
survey research and, 53
as a tool, 51
tools used for, 6
use of, 53–54
value of, 119
Market segment, 39–47
characteristics of, 40–41
defined, 39
one person as, 39–40
Market segmentation
behavioristic segmenting, 46–47
defined, 39
demographic segmenting, 41–43, 45
geographic segmenting, 45
methods of, 41–47
psychographic segmenting, 45–46
Market share variance, 123–24
Market trends, recognizing, 260–62
Marriott Corporation, 6, 74, 102, 255
Maslow, Abraham, 139
Maslow's theories, 139
Mastaler, Tracy, 11
Mayo, Edward, 140
Mayo and Jarvis's theory, 140
McCord Consumer Direct (MCD), 160
McCord Learning Center, 160
Measurement techniques, 123–24
Media
advertising and, 205–7
public relations and, 210
Meeting, convention, and event planners, 158, 164
Meeting Professionals International (MPI), 31, 278
Metropolitan Association of Professional Travel Agents (MAPTA), 278
Michelin Guides, 184, 187
Midcentric personality, 140
Mini Club, 73–74
Mobil Travel Guide, 187
Morgans, 90
Motels, customer service and, 252–53
Motel Six, 74
Motivations, 135, 136
Motivator classifications, 141
MPI. *See* Meeting Professionals International (MPI)
Multi-media online travel services, 260
Multiple distribution, 28
Mush Alaska, 14

N

NACA. *See* National Air Carrier Association (NACA)
NACOA. *See* National Association for Cruise Only Agents (NACOA)

NATA. *See* National Air Transportation Association (NATA)
National Air Carrier Association (NACA), 278
National Air Transportation Association (NATA), 278
National Association Commissioned Travel Agents, 278
National Association for Cruise Only Agents (NACOA), 103
National Association of Railroad Passengers, 278
National Association of RV Parks and Campgrounds, 278
National Business Travel Association (NBTA), 278
National Car Rental, 77
National Council of Travel Attractions, 278
National Demographics, Ltd., 46
Nationality, segmenting and, 43
National Motorcoach Network Incorporated, 278
National Park Hospitality Association, 278
National Restaurant Association, 278
National Tour Association (NTA), 44, 256, 257, 278
National Travel Survey (NTS), 143
NBTA. *See* National Business Travel Association (NBTA)
Needs
  to compensate, 140
  to explore, 140
  fundamental, 139
  hierarchy of, 139
  psychological, 139
  self-actualization, 139
  for status recognition, 140
  traveler's. *See* traveler's needs
New Orleans Steamboat Company, 101
Newspapers, 205–6, 210
Newsweek, 205
New York City, 13, 45
New York Convention and Visitor's Bureau, 100
New York State Division of Tourism, 141
New York Times, 205
The Night of the Iguana, 187
Non-airline travel products, 181
Northwest Airlines, 72, 255
NTA. *See* National Tour Association
NTS. *See* National Travel Survey (NTS)

O

OAG Travel Planner and Hotel and Motel Red Book, 183
Objective and task budgeting, 118–19
Observation, in market research, 52
Occupation, segmenting and, 42–43
Official Airline Guide, 183
Official Hotel Guide, 183
Official Meeting Facilities Guide, 183
Official Railway Guide, 183
Official Steamship Guide International, 183
Omni, 255
One-stage direct distribution, 166–67
Open probe, 228
Out-of-home media, 207
Outside sales, 227
Overbooking, 28
Overrides, 214

P

Pacific Asia Travel Association (PATA), 184
Pacific Asia Travel Organization (PATO), 278
Packaging, marketing mix and, 93–94
Parity, 29
Participation, marketing mix and, 94
Parties, 214
Passenger name record (PNR), 181
Passenger Vessel Association, 278
Pathfinder Vacations, 233
PATO. *See* Pacific Asia Travel Organization (PATO)
PCs. *See* personal computers (PCs)
Perceived benefits, value and, 191–92
Percentage of sales budgeting, 117
Perception, role in buying decisions, 77

Performance standards, 123
Perishability, 28, 156
Personal computers (PCs), 170
Personality classifications, 140–41
Personal observations, 122
Personal selling, 225–38
  basic steps of, 227–35
  characteristics of, 102–3
  closing the sale and, 234–35
  defined, 226–27
  disadvantage of, 102
  information gathering and, 227–29
  making recommendations and, 229–34
  qualifying the customer and, 228
  study guide and worksheets, 241–48
Peterson, Karen, 121
Phone words, 160
Physical characteristics, presentation mix and, 95–96
Physical environment, marketing mix and, 93
Physical motivators, 141
Place/Process of delivery, marketing mix and, 92
Pleasure Island, 3
Plog, Stanley, 140–41
Plog's continuum, 141
PNR. *See* passenger name record (PNR)
Point-of-purchase displays, 211–12
Polo, Marco, 10
Positioning, product. *See* product positioning
Positioning statement, 68
  compared to slogans, 72
  creation of, 72–73
  examples of, 73–75, 77
Preferences, segmenting and, 46–47
Presentation mix
  atmospherics and, 96
  elements of, 95–97
  employee behavior/attitude and, 97
  location and, 96
  physical characteristics and, 95–96
  price and, 96–97
Press conferences, 210
Press releases, 210
Price
  assessing travel value and, 188–89
  breaks, 212
  comparing, 189–91
  of fuel, 188
  marketing mix and, 92
  positioning and, 74
  presentation mix and, 96–97
Price fixing, 256
Print information sources, 182–84, 186–87
Prizes, 213
Product
  analysis of, 68–69
  class, 74
  nature of, 6
Productivity, employees and, 122
Product-oriented marketing, 5
Product positioning, 7, 65–77
  by benefits, 74
  establishment of, 68–70, 72
  identifying current position/image and, 69–70
  image and, 66–68
  marketing objective and, 70, 72
  positioning statement and, 68, 72–75, 77
  by price, 74
  principles of, 66–68
  product analysis and, 68–69
  by quality, 74
  relative to competitors, 75, 77
  relative to product class, 74–75
  relative to target market, 73–74
  steps in, 68
  study guide and worksheets, 79–86
Product/service combination, 95
Progress reports, 122
Promotion, marketing mix and, 92–93
Prospecting
  cold calls, 236
  sending letters, 237
  steps in, 236
  telephoning for appointments, 236–37
Psychocentric personality, 140
Psychographic segmenting, 41, 45–46

Psychological needs, 139
Public relations, 100, 207, 209–11
  advantages of, 207, 209
  basic principles of, 209
  disadvantage of, 209
  media contacts and, 210
  newsworthy information and, 209–10
  techniques, 210–11
Purchasing process, marketing mix and, 93

Q

Qantas, 255
Qualifying the customer, 228
Quality
  assessing travel value and, 187
  product positioning and, 74
Quantity, assessing travel value and, 187
Questionnaires, self-administered, 119–20
Questionnaires, self-administered, 119–20
Questions, 228–29

R

RAA. *See* Regional Airline Association (RAA)
Radio, 206
Radisson Hotels, 122, 255
Recapping, 232
Receptions, 211, 214
Receptive tour operators, 162
Recordkeeping, 119–20, 122
Recreational Vehicle Industry Association, 279
Red Roof Inn, 74
Regional Airline Association (RAA), 279
Registration cards, 119
Relationship marketing, 9
Religious pilgrimages, 10
Renaissance, 255
Rental car sales representative, 15
Rent a Village program, 74
Repositioning, 67
Request for proposal (RFP), 238
Research. *See* market research
Resistance, overcoming, 232
Resorts, customer service and, 252–53
Response mechanisms, 120
Return on investment (ROI), 124
RFP. *See* request for proposal (RFP)
ROI. *See* return on investment (ROI)
Rome, 10

S

Sabena, 255
SABRE (Semi-Automated Business Research Environment) Group, 170
Sales
  careers in, 12–15
  defined, 4
  following up on, 253–56
  history of, 9–10, 12
  marketing and, 3–15
  providing service with, 250–52
  setting up, 201–14
  study guide and worksheets, 217–23
  in travel and tourism, 4
Sales contests, 214
Sales incentives, 214
Sales manager, 14–15
Sales-oriented marketing, 5
Sales presentations, making, 238
Sales promotion, 100, 102, 211–14
  customer-oriented, 211–13
  objectives of, 211
  trade-oriented, 213–14
Sales proposal, writing, 237–38
Sales representative, 15
Sales variance, 123
Sample, defined, 53
Sandals, 90
Satellite ticket printers (STPs), 170
Scandinavia Air Lines, 213
Schedules, business traveler and, 144
Search engines, 207
Seasonality, 28–29
Segmental analysis, 124
Segmentation. *See* market segmentation

Self-actualization needs, 139
Self-administered questionnaires, 119–20
Sellers, 4
  identifying, 155–70
  study guide and worksheets, 173–78
  types of, 156–58
Service, customer. *See* customer service
Service quality, 32–33
Seven-Up, 74–75
Sheraton, 255
Siegel, Bill, 121
Simultaneous production and consumption, 27–28
SITE. *See* Society Incentive Travel Executives (SITE)
Situational analysis, 115
Six questions, 228
Skiing, 46
Ski resorts, 28, 75
Slogan, compared to positioning statement, 72
Society for the Advancement of Travel for the Handicapped, 279
Society Incentive Travel Executives (SITE), 279
Society of American Travel Writers, 279
Society of Travel Agents in Government (STAG), 279
Southwest Airlines, 74
Special Events: Best Practices in Modern Event Management (Goldblatt), 31
Special features, business traveler and, 144–45
Specialized distributors, 5, 158, 163–64
SRI International, 45
St. Paul (Minnesota) Winter Carnival, 29
STAG. *See* Society of Travel Agents in Government (STAG)
Staged events, 210–11
Statue of Liberty, 29
Status and prestige motivators, 141
Status recognition, 140
STPs. *See* satellite ticket printers (STPs)
Super 8, 74
Suppliers, 156
Survey research, in market research, 53
Sweepstakes, 213, 214
Swiss Air, 255

T

Tangibility, 26
Tangible products, marketing and selling, 26
Target market, 7
  positioning relative to, 73–74
  selection of, 39–54
  study guide and worksheets, 55–63
Team spirit, employees and, 122–23
Television, 206
Thomas Cook Overseas Timetable, 183
Three-stage indirect distribution, 168
Thrifty car rental, 89
TIAA. *See* Travel Industry Association of America (TIAA)
TIAC. *See* Tourism Industry Association of Canada (TIAC)
Ticket consolidators, 158, 164–65
Tie-in, 212–13
Time, 186, 205
Total dollar sales, 123
Tour and Travel News, 184
Tour company representative, 15
Tourism Canada, 93
Tourism Industries U. S. Department of Commerce, 279
Tourism Industry Association of Canada (TIAC), 279
Tourism Industry/International Trade Administration, 143
Tour operator, 5, 14, 157–58, 162–63
Trade advertising, 203
Trade-oriented sales promotion
  familiarization trips, 214
  purposes of, 213–14
  sales contests and sweepstakes, 214
  sales incentives, 214
  trade shows, parties, and receptions, 214

Trade publications, 184
Trade Show Exhibitors Association (TSEA), 279
Trade shows, 184, 186, 214
Travel
  assessing value of, 187–92
  barriers to, 142
  need to, 139–40
  where and how of, 140–42
Travel Age, 184
Travel agent, 5, 12–13, 157, 161–62
Travel Agent, 184
Travel and Leisure, 204, 205, 258
Travel and Tourism Research Association (TTRA), 279
Travel articles, 186
Travel associations and organizations, 275–79
Travel Center Independent Affiliates, 279
Travel clubs, 165
Travel Economic Impact Model, 143
Traveler's needs
  acknowledging, 229
  business travel and, 144–46
  leisure travel and, 138–44
  recognizing, 137
  special, 251
  study guide and worksheets, 149–54
  understanding, 135–46
Travel habits, segmenting and, 46–47
Travel/Holiday, 205
Travel industry, competition in, 6
Travel Industry Association of America (TIAA), 143, 279
Travel Master Seminars, 44
Travel product
  analyzing, 25–33
  appeal of, 69–70
  characteristics of, 26–30, 70, 155–56
  defined, 25–26
  evaluation of, 179–92
  free, 213
  providing service with, 252–53
  relationship with services, 32
  service quality and, 32–33
  study guide and worksheets, 35–38
  study guide and worksheets, 193–199
Travel purposes, segmenting and, 47
Travel Safe, 279
TravelScope program, 143
Travel services, 30, 32–33
Travel Trade, 184
Travel Weekly, 184
TSEA. *See* Trade Show Exhibitors Association (TSEA)
TTRA. *See* Travel and Tourism Research Association (TTRA)
Two-stage indirect distribution, 167–68
Tying, 257

U

U. S. Airways, 47
U. S. Travel Data Center, 143
Unfair methods of competition and deceptive practices, 257
Uniqueness, 29–30
Unique selling proposition (USP), 72
United Airlines, 93, 209, 213
United Nations Organization, 279
United States Tour Operators Association (USTOA), 280
Upgrading, 232
USA Today, 186, 205
USP. *See* unique selling proposition (USP)
USTOA. *See* United States Tour Operators Association (USTOA)

V

VALS. *See* values and lifestyles (VALS)
Value, assessment of, 187–92
Values and lifestyles (VALS), 45–46
Varig, 213
VCRs. *See* videocassette recorders (VCRs)
Videocassette recorders (VCRs), 259

Video kiosks, 260
Videotapes, 212
Virgin Atlantic Airways, 89
Virginia Division of Travel and Tourism, 185

W

Walt Disney World. *See* Disney World
Washington, D. C., 29, 71
Washington, D. C. Convention and Visitors Association, 71
Washington Post, 205
Web sites, 183, 186, 207, 260
Western Leisure, Inc., 233
Westin, 74, 255
Women travelers, special needs of, 145–146
Word of mouth, as information source, 186
World Federation of Travel Writers (FIJET), 280
World Tourism Organization (WTO), 280
Worldwide Cruise and Shipline Guide, 183
WTO. *See* World Tourism Organization (WTO)

Y

Yellowstone National Park, 29, 45